Journeys from the Abyss
The Holocaust and Forced Migration
from the 1880s to the Present

MIGRATIONS AND IDENTITIES

Series Editors
Kirsty Hooper, Eve Rosenhaft, Michael Sommer

This series offers a forum and aims to provide a stimulus for new research into experiences, discourses and representations of migration from across the arts and humanities. A core theme of the series is the variety of relationships between movement in space—the 'migration' of people, communities, ideas and objects—and mentalities ('identities' in the broadest sense). The series aims to address a broad scholarly audience, with critical and informed interventions into wider debates in contemporary culture as well as in the relevant disciplines. It will publish theoretical, empirical and practice-based studies by authors working within, across and between disciplines, geographical areas and time periods, in volumes that make the results of specialist research accessible to an informed but not discipline-specific audience. The series is open to proposals for both monographs and edited volumes.

Journeys from the Abyss

The Holocaust and Forced Migration from the 1880s to the Present

Tony Kushner

Liverpool University Press

First published 2017 by
Liverpool University Press
4 Cambridge Street
Liverpool
L69 7ZU

British Library Cataloguing-in-Publication data
A British Library CIP record is available

ISBN 978-1-78694-062-9 cased
ISBN 978-1-78694-063-6 limp

Typeset by Carnegie Book Production, Lancaster
Printed and bound in Poland by BooksFactory.co.uk

To the Memory of Letty Kushner (1932–2012)

Contents

Preface and Acknowledgments

The final amendments of this book were made in November 2016, a week after the election of Donald Trump as president of the United States of America. Isolationism and the attack of the 'enemy within' and the 'enemy without' in the form of the illegal/criminal 'alien' were major features of Trump's propaganda, as they were in the equally successful 'Brexit' campaign in the UK some months earlier. These happenings, alongside the rise of nationalist–racist parties to power in Hungary and Poland and the growth of far right anti-migrant groups in western Europe, make this a bleak and frightening time to write about refugees of the Nazi era and their relevance to today. The very future of liberal democracy in the west seems far less certain than at any point since 1945. Moreover, anti-migrant rhetoric has become socially and politically acceptable. And yet in 2015 there was collective shock at the death of three-year-old Alan Kurdi, who was washed up on a tourist beach in Turkey and came for a time to represent the migrant crisis. It prompted one of the most remarkable post-war responses to a refugee crisis, spearheaded by Angela Merkel, chancellor of Germany. That most other European countries failed to follow her lead and that there has been, at this point in time, a limited backlash in Germany itself does not take away from the moral stance of Merkel and millions of ordinary Germans who have offered help and support to these refugees. It is a hopeful message and example at a time when cultural and political despair among progressive forces is all too easy. Yet, however understandable, pessimism has to be resisted and all our energy placed into making the world a safer and more caring place.

The refugee crises with which each of the parts of *Journeys from the Abyss* concludes are ongoing and will no doubt intensify further. Indeed, 2016 has witnessed more migrant deaths at sea than the previous record years – a reflection of the clumsy and increasingly grotesque ways in which restrictionist measures are impacting on the ordinary people who are trying to make a better life for themselves free from persecution, oppression, and poverty. Growing global inequality, conflict, and ecological disaster will, unless fundamentally addressed and confronted, lead to even more desperate and dangerous journeys and no doubt desperate and inhumane ways of stopping them through a combination of paper and physical walls. Unless there is recognition that, ultimately, 'no one is illegal' and that the fate of Earth will not be addressed by retreating into insularity and the false security of national or racial certainty, the prospects will indeed be grim.

The hope of this study is that by taking Jewish refugee journeys in the Nazi era out of the self-contained world of Holocaust studies, continuities (and discontinuities) will be exposed. From there it will enable such journeys to become a more usable past when confronting the crises of the twenty-first century which threaten to destroy humanity and the planet which it inhabits.

Given the nature of its subject matter this has not been an easy book to research and write, and I am thus grateful to those individuals and institutions who have made my task easier. I have been lucky to have been located for 30 years now in the History Department and the Parkes Institute for the Study of Jewish/non-Jewish Relations at the University of Southampton, in which the study of migration, especially forced migration, is to the fore. In this respect, my particular thanks go to James Jordan (generous as ever with potential sources, however obscure), Shirli Gilbert, Joachim Schloer, Mark Levene, Andrea Reiter, Claire Le Foll, Neil Gregor, John McAleer, Christer Petley, Joan Tumblety, Nick Kingwell, George Bernard, Mark Stoyle, Eve Colpus, Helen Spurling, Mark Cornwall, Ian Talbot, and Kendrick Oliver. I have been privileged to have supervised very talented postgraduates, among whom I would like to mention in relation to this study Jennifer Craig-Norton, who, as a British Academy Postdoctoral Fellow, is carrying out what will be the definitive study of refugee domestics in Britain (and going beyond the memory–biographical approach adopted here).

Outside the University of Southampton – but with very close links to it – I would like thank my friends John Oldfield, Gavin Schaffer, Nick Evans (who seems now to be able to stand on his own two feet with remarkable stability since my last acknowledgements), Aimée Bunting (for help, friendship, and support throughout this book and towards working on a related project on 'Co-Presents to the Holocaust'), Bill Williams (whose energy, drive, and innovative approach continues to inspire), Barbara Rosenbaum (whose care and sense of fun is a constant source of strength), Tom Lawson, Daniel Langton, Donald Bloxham, Bryan Cheyette, Jo Reilly, Dan Stone, Brian Klug, Colin Richmond (whose parcels of his poetry and prose kept me going following emergency surgery a year ago and likewise to those among the 30-odd nationalities at Southampton General Hospital who kept me alive. God alone knows what will happen to the NHS when these professionals are banned from coming to or staying in post-Brexit Britain), Joanna Newman, Gemma Romain, and Colin Holmes. I would also like to single out Trevor Avery, who has spearheaded the remarkable 'Lake District Holocaust Project', which features in a later part of this book.

It is with deep sorrow that I also have to record the loss of my friend, former colleague, and sparring partner for over three decades, David Cesarani, in autumn 2015. While we did not agree on everything, I suspect from some of his comments on the current migrant crisis David would have had at least some sympathy with the approach I have adopted here. He was an immensely talented historian whose work was coming to its peak – his premature death will be a blow to many areas of scholarship and public debate.

This study has benefited from trips abroad, including to South Africa, where Milton Shain and Janine Blumberg illustrated the true meaning of hospitality, to Israel, to Australia, and across the continent of Europe. Most recently this has included the tiny island of Lampedusa, which was inspiring: it gave me a deep sense and appreciation of the everyday help given to migrants by ordinary people, as well as a sobering awareness of the loss of life that has so unnecessarily happened close to its shores.

I am indebted to archivists and librarians across the UK and beyond who have been generous with their time and expertise when helping me with this project. In this respect, I am deeply grateful to my colleagues Jenny Ruthven of the Parkes Library and Karen Robson at the University of Southampton Archives for their enthusiasm, and more generally their professionalism, when this is so under threat in the de-skilling climate of this disturbing and frightening century.

On a personal note, I would like to congratulate the Cavaliers Cricket team and all who sail on her, for their undefeated 2016 season. This was remarkable and unprecedented and it was only the continuing lowly status of Stockport County that made the world seem not upside down. As for Manchester City, it is remarkable how much can be achieved through so little financial backing. And finally, my family, Mag (who also provided the index), Sam, and Jack, who have, as ever, given love as well as practical support (Sam deserves special mention with regard to easing my way into the world of modern technology). It is fair to say they have also provided a sense of perspective when I get too obsessed (moi?) with my work. Brothers Ben and Mike follow my mother in also not taking my pretensions too seriously and it is in her memory that I will close.

Letitia (Letty) Kushner died just months after her eightieth birthday in 2012. Her health deteriorated rapidly at the same time as the London Olympics were being staged and the success of these games was emblematic of her life. The inclusivity and tolerance celebrated in Danny Boyle's opening ceremony (and the human solidarity represented in his portrayal of the NHS), and in the triumphs of Mo Farah, a refugee from Somalia, and Jessica Ennis, a woman of mixed heritage, showed a Britain at ease with itself and the outside world. This was my mother – a person who accepted ethnic, religious and national diversity, age, sexuality, disability, and any other form of difference without a thought. It was an essential part of her being. Even as an eight-year-old at school in north Manchester she welcomed and befriended a child refugee, Ruth Meador (née Amster). Ruth came to Britain in May 1940 on the so-called 'last Kindertransport' from Holland, having previously fled Germany. Her father, who had been in Buchenwald, managed to reach New York, whereas her sister and mother remained on the continent and were sent to Nazi concentration camps. On her own in Manchester, she wrote to me this week remembering how 'sweet and kind Letty was to me. She was the most beautiful child I had ever met. I will always remember her courage and kindness.' My mother truly was 'a woman of worth'.

Tony Kushner
Southampton, 18 November 2016

Introduction:
Migration and the Holocaust

Uniqueness, Jewish Refugees, and the Perils of Hindsight

In 1936 the political and economic status of the combined six million Jews of Germany, Poland, Romania, Latvia, Lithuania, and Austria was 'neither life nor death'. For them the world was 'divided into places where they cannot live, and places into which they cannot enter'.[1] Chaim Weizmann's pithy and politically effective contribution to the British government's Palestine Royal Commission (1936–7) has subsequently gained iconic status.[2] Much quoted, the statement of the great Zionist leader and first president of the State of Israel is presented as having foreseen the acute dilemma of European Jewry, especially with persecution and discrimination – and immigration restriction – intensifying in the last years of peace. Weizmann then appears to have predicted the devastating destruction that was to follow during the Second World War.

Referring to the 1930s, Abba Eban, Israeli minister and leading diplomat, in his *My People: The Story of the Jews* (1968), briefly mentioned those who had been turned away from places of refuge, such as the German Jews on the *St Louis*: 'No American country would admit them, and the ship finally returned to Europe.' Other boats sank, such as 'the "Capo" [*sic*]

---

1   Chaim Weizmann, *The Jewish People and Palestine: Statement Made before the Palestine Royal Commission* (Jerusalem: Zionist Organisation, 1936), pp. 5–7.
2   The pamphlet with his November 1936 evidence was produced in a second edition in 1939 with an updated Foreword highlighting the deteroriation of the Jewish refugee situation (p. 3). For Weizmann's impact on the Commission, see *Palestine: Statement of Policy by His Majesty's Government in the United Kingdom* (London: HMSO, 1937), p. 143.

with 750 Jewish refugees aboard'.[3] Indeed, there are no examples given in his simplistic narrative of successful refugee rescue except for those who reached Palestine. And it is in this context that Weizmann's Royal Commission evidence on the future of Palestine was not only reproduced but also embellished by Eban: 'There are six million people doomed to be pent up where they are not wanted and for whom the world is divided into places where they cannot live, and places where they may not enter. Six million!'[4] It is no surprise – given Eban's embellished repetition of this subsequently infamous number – that he concluded that 'In eight years' time, the problem presented by these six million Jews was to be solved. In 1945, these six million were dead.'[5] The scale of the Holocaust has led to its history being read teleologically, especially by those with a strong ideological commitment.

Frank Caestecker and Bob Moore have noted that, in spite of many other cases of forced migration in the twentieth century and beyond, 'it is the refugees from Nazi Germany in the 1930s that have received by far the greatest attention from historians, social scientists and demographers'. The reason for such imbalance is, they continue, 'not difficult to ascertain':

> the overwhelming attention given to the Holocaust within the histori-
> ography of Europe and the Second World War has created a situation
> in which the issues surrounding the movement of people from Nazi
> Germany prior to 1939 are seen as an essential pre-history.[6]

Crucially, argue Caestecker and Moore, it is one that 'implicat[es] the Western European democracies and the United States as bystanders in the impending tragedy'.[7] Abba Eban's popular history and the (mis)quoting of his hero, Chaim Weizmann, was simply an early and blatant historio-graphical example of this tendency. In such accounts, the failure of western refugee policy and the absence of a Jewish state left the victims utterly exposed to the full impact of Nazi genocide.

Weizmann argued in the Royal Commission for the continuation of unrestricted Jewish immigration into Palestine – despite growing Arab resistance, which had led to violence and boycott. In essence, the leader

---

3   Abba Eban, *My People: The Story of the Jews* (New York: Random House, 1968), p. 397. It would seem likely that Eban was referring to the *Gippo*, which sank in April 1939, not March as he suggests. See Mordechei Naor, *Hapala: Clandestine Immigration 1931–1948* (Tel Aviv: Ministry of Defence Publishing House, 1987), pp. 19–20, 109. These journeys will be discussed further later in this study.

4   Ibid.

5   Eban, *My People*, p. 397.

6   Frank Caestecker and Bob Moore, 'Introduction', in idem (eds), *Refugees from Nazi Germany and the Liberal Democracies* (New York: Berghahn, 2014 [2010]), p. 1.

7   Ibid.

of the World Zionist Organisation accepted that antisemitism was now an irresistible force on much of the continent of Europe. Furthermore, anticipation of it elsewhere in non-affected areas, such as western Europe and north America, would preclude entry. Earlier in 1936, using a metaphor coming out of his professional background as a research chemist, Weizmann had told a British Jewish conference on the refugee crisis that 'Jews have proved that they are an "insoluble" element ... the quantity which can be absorbed in each country proves to be small'. He added that 'The formula reacts quickly, and the saturation point is rapidly reached, and the Jewish communities in the respective countries are always full of anxiety lest there will be too many and that anti-Semitism may be stimulated.' Palestine was, however, different: its 'tolerability' of Jewish immigrants was 'unlimited'.[8]

But it is not only hindsight and the murder of the six million – and then the subsequent formation of an independent Israel – that has enabled Weizmann's aphorism to become part of a 'usable past', especially within a simplistic Zionist reading of modern Jewish history. Linked to it, but also with a discrete tradition of its own, has been the imperative within both the Jewish and non-Jewish spheres to see the Holocaust as unique – incomparable even within the discrete context of twentieth-century genocide. The heated (and largely sterile) debate about the uniqueness or otherwise of the Holocaust has operated largely at an emotional level relating to ownership of the Jewish tragedy.[9] Taken to the extreme, it carries the danger of mystification,[10] of taking the Holocaust *outside* history, 'a universe outside the universe', as the late Auschwitz survivor Elie Wiesel has described its horror and scale of devastation.[11]

The uniqueness debate is not only a proprietorial issue. The question of particularity/universality is also part of a genuine debate about the context in which the Holocaust should be placed. For some, such as the distinguished Holocaust historian Yehuda Bauer, the long if complex history of hostility towards the Jews provides the necessary explanatory background: 'To place the events of the Holocaust in historical perspective, we must first look backward to the history of the Jewish people and their relationship to

---

8   Anglo-Jewish Conference convened by the Council for German Jewry, 15 March 1936, Central British Fund archives, Reel 4, File 15, University of Southampton Library. On the wider context of this speech see Louise London, *Whitehall and the Jews 1933–1948: British Immigration Policy and the Holocaust* (Cambridge: Cambridge University Press, 2000), p. 275.

9   Alan Rosenbaum (ed.), *Is the Holocaust Unique? Perspectives on Comparative Genocide* (Philadelphia: Westview Press, 2009 [3rd edition]).

10 Yehuda Bauer, 'Against Mystification', in idem, *The Holocaust in Historical Perspective* (London: Sheldon Press, 1978), p. 44.

11 Elie Wiesel, 'Trivializing Memory', in idem, *From the Kingdom of Memory: Reminiscences* (New York: Schocken, 1990), pp. 165–166.

the non-Jewish world and to antisemitism in ancient, medieval, and modern times.'[12] For others, while clearly the importance of antisemitism cannot be dismissed, its significance is downplayed in relation to wider (and often inter-related) factors such as modernity,[13] nationalism,[14] or western coloni-alism.[15] The emerging field of genocide studies, in which these defining forces of the modern world have been woven together (if in a variety of patterns), has been the major site in which the place of the Holocaust has been feverishly debated.[16] Is the Holocaust a part of but still apart from twentieth-century genocide? Alternatively, as Donald Bloxham suggests with regards to the 'Final Solution', is it *a* but not *the* genocide?[17]

Within the more specific area of refugee policy during the Nazi era, there has been less concern about the wider context. If, as Caestecker and Moore argue, it is the Holocaust that has prompted most of the interest in the refugees from Nazism, a paradox still remains. In their rich cultural history of refugee Jews from 1933 to 1946, *Flight from The Reich* (2009), Deborah Dwork and Robert Jan Van Pelt have observed how 'Few histories of the Holocaust include discussion and analysis of the refugees' experience. At best on the margins, this aspect of Holocaust history typically falls literally beyond the subject bounds.' If, they continue, the Holocaust 'is the history of people murdered by the Germans and their allies', then the refugees 'play a minor role' in it.[18]

A revealing example of this tendency, and confirming their analysis, is provided by Saul Friedlander in his much-praised two-volume history of the Holocaust. The first of these, *Nazi Germany & The Jews* (1997), focused on the 1930s. Friedlander has been rightly applauded for his ambition to provide an inclusive study of his subject matter. It is one in which Nazi policies are 'the central element, but in which the surrounding world and the victims' attitudes, reactions, and fate are no less an integral part of this

12 Yehuda Bauer, *A History of the Holocaust* (New York: Franklin Watts, 1982), p. xv.
13 Zygmunt Bauman, *Modernity and the Holocaust* (Ithaca: Cornell University Press, 1989).
14 Mark Levene, *Genocide in the Age of the Nation State* (London: I.B. Tauris, 2005).
15 Hannah Arendt, *The Origins of Totalitarianism* (New York: Harcourt, 1951); A. Dirk Moses, 'Conceptual blockages and definitional dilemmas in the "racial century": genocides of indigenous peoples and the Holocaust', *Patterns of Prejudice* vol. 36 no. 4 (2002), pp. 7–36; Thomas Kuhner, 'Colonialism and the Holocaust: Continuities, Causations and Complexities', *Journal of Genocide Research* vol. 15 no. 3 (2013), pp. 339–362.
16 See, for example, *Journal of Genocide Research* vol. 12 nos 3–4 (2010) and vol. 13 nos 1–2 (2011).
17 Donald Bloxham, *The Final Solution: A Genocide* (Oxford: Oxford University Press, 2009).
18 Deborah Dwork and Robert Jan Van Pelt, *Flight from the Reich: Refugee Jews, 1933–1946* (New York: Norton, 2009), pp. xii–iii.

unfolding story'.[19] Crucially, he adds, 'Nazi attitudes and policies cannot be fully assessed without knowledge of the lives and indeed the feelings of the Jewish men, women, and children themselves.'[20] Given that more than half of the Jews of Germany, Austria, and Czechoslovakia managed to flee before the outbreak of war,[21] the almost total absence of consideration of the processes and decision-making of those that left (and those that chose not to or, more commonly, were unable to do so) in his 400-page study appears remarkable.[22] It can only be explained by Friedlander's emphasis on what he calls 'redemptive anti-Semitism' and with it the overwhelming desire of the Nazi regime, even before the outbreak of war, to destroy the Jews.

Friedlander powerfully describes the everyday impact of antisemitism on its Jewish victims, but he does not dwell on the agonising dilemmas of whether to try to leave, and if so, to where and with what family members. Instead, the emphasis is on the failure of western states and their refusal to allow in Jewish refugees. The treatment of Britain, for example, is limited to Palestine and even then only to attempts to stop 'illegal' immigration to its shores.[23] There is no acknowledgment of the 80,000 Jewish refugees who entered Britain during the timespan of Friedlander's first volume, let alone the intricate balance of forces that enabled this to take place, and, for a larger number, fail to happen.[24] Likewise, the emphasis in the treatment of Palestine is the refusal by the British to allow entry and not on the 60,000 who found refuge there between 1933 and 1940.[25] His narrative requires the Jews to be victims and the outside world to be hostile or at best passive/indifferent.

Dwork and Van Pelt argue for a different approach, referencing also the three million Jews who survived the Holocaust, including through escape. Yet '[f]leeing', they argue, 'does not write refugees out of the story; it simply takes the story elsewhere. Indeed: it takes it everywhere.' Here they highlight the methodological problem that has hindered a more inclusive

---

19 Saul Friedlander, *Nazi Germany & The Jews: The Years of Persecution 1933–39* (London: Weidenfeld & Nicolson, 1997), p. 2.
20 Ibid.
21 Herbert Strauss, 'Jewish Emigration from Germany: Nazi Policies and Jewish Responses (I)', *Leo Baeck Institute Year Book* vol. 25 (1980), p. 327 estimates that 'about three-fifths of German Jewry succeeded in leaving the country'.
22 For an overstatement of the percentages, see William Rubinstein, *The Myth of Rescue: Why the democracies could not have saved more Jews from the Nazis* (London: Routledge, 1997), p. 16.
23 Friedlander, *Nazi Germany*, p. 304.
24 London, *Whitehall and the Jews*, p. 12, which estimates that 500,000–600,000 applied to come to Britain.
25 Aviva Halamish, 'Palestine as a Destination for Jewish Immigrants and Refugees from Nazi Germany', in Caestecker and Moore (eds), *Refugees from Nazi Germany*, pp. 122–150.

approach. The Jewish refugee experience, as well as responses to them, was truly global, with all the challenges that this necessitates: 'The refugees' escape around the world defies traditional plotlines. Unlike other histories that start and end at conventionally established dates, this history has many starting points, even more end dates, and actors scattered across the globe.'[26] In contrast to the ambitious transnational centrifugal narrative attempted by Dwork and Van Pelt, the dominant historiography on the refugees from Nazism has focused on individual nation states, studied largely in isolation from one another. And even then the analytical framework has lacked sophistication, dominated by the question of whether the potential receiving societies were mean-spirited towards the persecuted Jews (and, if so, whether antisemitism was the root cause). Less common, but even more problematic, are those who seek to celebrate the saving of Jewish refugees to bolster the self-image of the receiving societies. One of the first academic studies was provided by A.J. Sherman in his *Island Refuge* (1973), which focused on the British case study, utilising newly released government documentation. Tellingly, Sherman concluded that 'When a balance sheet is ... drawn and Great Britain's refugee policy compared with that of other countries it emerges, in the context of the pre-war period, as comparatively compassionate, even generous.'[27] While the international context is essential, it is too often evoked in this field to either praise or denigrate *particular* countries as saints or sinners.

Work on the western democracies and persecuted Jewry during the 1930s and on the western Allies during the war has thus not only tended to focus on specific nation states but also alternated between the accusatory and the apologetic/defensive/apologetic. The enormity of the Holocaust – both in the devastation caused to the Jewish world and its later status as the defining point of wider issues of morality – has the inherent danger that contemporary responses to it will be taken out of history. The concept of the 'bystander' especially has become one more of wider ethical consideration than of detailed and careful historical contextualisation or basic definition. Holocaust 'moral indifference', it has been argued, has been treated as '*the* form of modern evil'.[28] Not surprisingly, the result, as Michael Marrus notes, has been 'a strong tendency in historical writing on bystanders to the Holocaust to condemn, rather than to explain'. In contrast, Marrus argues that it is crucial 'to give contemporaries a fair hearing'.[29]

26 Dwork and Van Pelt, *Flight from the Reich*, p. xiii.
27 A.J. Sherman, *Island Refuge: Britain and Refugees from the Third Reich* (Berkeley: University of California Press, 1973), p. 267.
28 Rainer Baum, 'Holocaust: Moral Indifference as the Form of Modern Evil', in Alan Rosenberg and Gerald Myers (eds), *Echoes from the Holocaust: Philosophical Reflections on a Dark Time* (Philadelphia: Temple University Press, 1988), pp. 53–79.
29 Michael Marrus, *The Holocaust in History* (London: Weidenfeld and Nicolson, 1988), p. 157.

Following Marrus, the key is to consider, analyse, and explain the intellectual, cultural, and institutional frameworks within which individuals (including the refugees themselves), as well as national and transnational states and organisations, operated, in order to avoid the benefit of hindsight and the tendency to view, for example, the failures (or successes) of refugee policy during the 1930s through the prism of Auschwitz. Equally, understanding contemporaries does not imply condoning what Marrus refers to as the 'seamy underside' of the bystander.[30]

The best work on refugee policy of particular countries during the 1930s has placed it in a longer historical context, and one that looks backwards in time and not forward. An exemplary model is Louise London's bureaucratic history of British immigration control procedures, which focuses on the Nazi era and the years immediately preceding (and following) it. London makes clear that, while the 'story proper opens in 1933, when hundreds of refugees from Nazi Germany ... arrived in the United Kingdom', her 'starting point is a little earlier'. She explains that 'This is because Whitehall policy on the new influx of aliens was made in the context of immigration restrictions from 1905.'[31] A similar approach had been utilised earlier by Richard Breitman and Alan Kraut in their study of American refugee policy from 1933 to 1945, which employs both a deeper chronology and a broader framework of entry policy. In their analysis of senior State Department official Wilbur Carr, for example, they highlight that while his 'negative view of Jewish immigrants had much to do with his support for immigration restriction during the 1920s ... Carr saw the need for immigration restriction more generally'. Breitman and Kraut add that, for Carr, 'Other groups beside Jews were objectionable, and, in any case, the country could no longer afford to absorb an unlimited number of immigrants.' They conclude that 'Well before Nazism provoked Jewish emigration from Germany ... the State Department, including Carr, was committed to administering a legislated policy of restrictionism that was anti-foreign rather than narrowly anti-Semitic'.[32]

In both British and American state refugee policy, what has been labelled in the literary–cultural sphere as 'Semitic discourse' when representing the 'Jew' was also present. It influenced the bureaucrats dealing with Jewish refugees, often with ambivalent impact in terms of their entry and exclusion. Whereas the 'right type' might be welcomed and even encouraged, the 'undesirable' was rejected based not just on level of skill but also the place of origin. In such racially imagined hierarchies, Jews from eastern Europe were deemed especially dangerous

---

30 Ibid.
31 London, *Whitehall and the Jews*, p. 16.
32 Richard Breitman and Alan Kraut, *American Refugee Policy and European Jewry, 1933–1945* (Bloomington: Indiana University Press, 1987), pp. 28–33.

and unattractive.[33] There were, however, other influences and traditions at work alongside 'Semitic discourse' in helping to shape the official mind. Such pre-history is crucial in providing contexts and in moving descriptions of policy beyond the crude binary of antisemitic/not antisemitic.

The challenge of using the longue durée as employed by London or Breitman and Kraut, rather than the self-contained and emotionally charged 'L'univers concentrationnaire',[34] is made harder, however, by the poverty of refugee historiography. Put boldly, the attention given to those that fled from Nazism reflects not a disproportionate bias (or unnecessary reworkings of an over-researched area) but a lacuna with regard to those that made up the tens of millions of other refugees in history. This is especially so of the twentieth century.

Historiography and the Refugees

As early as 1944 two pioneer scholars of the field, Arieh Tartakower and Kurt Grossman, had noted that

> in our generation the refugee movement has spread like wildfire through the continents of the Old World [including] from Soviet Russia, from Greece, from Turkey, from Bulgaria, from Armenia, from Iraq, from Italy, from Germany, from Spain, from China … . Indeed, no other period has had so many refugees as the last three decades, so that ours may truly be called the era of refugees.[35]

If anything, refugee crises have intensified since 1945: 'They have been an enduring and global issue throughout the twentieth century',[36] and their number (including and especially those refugees internally displaced) is higher in the second decade of the twenty-first century than ever before.[37] Yet, as Peter Gatrell, who has written the most inclusive account of the subject, laments, 'Refugees have been allowed only a walk-on part in most

---

33 Tony Kushner, *The Holocaust and the Liberal Imagination: A Social and Cultural History* (Oxford: Blackwell, 1994) and more generally see Bryan Cheyette, *Constructions of 'The Jew' in English Literature and Society: Racial Representations, 1875–1945* (Cambridge: Cambridge University Press, 1993).

34 David Rousset, *L'univers concentrationnaire* (Paris: Editions du Pavois, 1946).

35 Arieh Tartakower and Kurt Grossman, *The Jewish Refugee* (New York: Institute of Jewish Affairs, 1944), p. 1.

36 Claudena Skran, *Refugees in Inter-War Europe: The Emergence of a Regime* (Oxford: Clarendon Press, 1995), p. 4.

37 The UNHCR reported that the number of internally displaced people and refugees/asylum seekers had risen to 51.2 million in 2013, its highest figure since the Second World War. See *The Guardian*, 20 June 2014.

histories of the twentieth century, and even then as subjects of external intervention rather than as actors in their own right.'[38] There are still 'yawning gaps in our knowledge and understanding of the history of refugees'.[39]

The reasons why, in the words of anthropologist Liisa Malkki, the refugee 'remains curiously, indecently, outside of history', are not accidental.[40] For historians, largely rooted in the study of individual nation states, the marginal legal, cultural, and social status of refugees can be troubling. They represent the 'symbolic danger of people who do not fit, who represent "matter out of place"'.[41] The refugee, according to one of the earliest scholars in the field, Jacques Vernant, is 'the *unknown*. Every society seeks to classify foreigners, whether individuals or in groups, according to their "social coordinates", that is to say, the land they inhabited or the larger group to which they belonged.'[42] Bleakly, Vernant argued that the liminality went further than merely alien status:

> What stamps the refugee as a man apart, justifying his classification in a specific social category, is his *inferiority*; he is inferior both to the citizens of the country which gives him shelter and to all other foreigners, not refugees, living in that country.[43]

Writing a few years earlier in the heart of the Second World War, Hannah Arendt provided ammunition for Vernant's emphasis on the placelessness associated with refugees. Twice displaced herself – from Germany and then France – and now in America, Arendt stated that 'In the first place, we don't like to be called "refugees". We ourselves call each other "newcomers" or "immigrants".' She added that, before the war started, 'we were even more sensitive about being called refugees. We did our best to prove to other people that we were just ordinary immigrants.'[44]

---

38 Peter Gatrell, *The Making of the Modern Refugee* (Oxford: Oxford University Press, 2013), p. 283.

39 Peter Gatrell, *Free World? The Campaign to Save the World's Refugees, 1956–1963* (Cambridge: Cambridge University Press, 2011), p. 9.

40 Liisa Malkki, 'Speechless Emissaries: Refugees, Humanitarianism and Dehistoricization', *Cultural Anthropology* vol. 11 no. 3 (1996), p. 398.

41 Liisa Malkki, 'National Geographic: The Rooting of Peoples and the Territorization of National Identity among Scholars and Refugees', *Cultural Anthropology* vol. 7 no. 1 (1992), p. 34.

42 Jacques Vernant, *The Refugees in the Post-War World* (London: George Allen & Unwin, 1953), p. 13.

43 Ibid.

44 Hannah Arendt, 'We Refugees', in J.Kohn (ed.), *The Jewish Writings. Hannah Arendt* (New York: Schocken Books, 2007), p. 264. The article was originally published in *Menorah Journal*, January 1943.

That refugees might be both a large and a *permanent* issue was a troubling prospect. Unease at that possibility can be detected in what was the first global history of the modern refugee: John Hope Simpson's classic *The Refugee Problem* (1939).[45] Published under the auspices of the Royal Institute of International Affairs, while a work of great scholarship, this was a book written explicitly to make a meaningful contemporary contribution to what was an acute international political and humanitarian crisis. Confined largely to the European arena, his study began with the Greek, Bulgarian, and Turkish refugees and then moved on to the Armenians, Assyrians, and Russians during and after the First World War. It then moved to the 1930s, focusing largely but not exclusively on Jewish refugees from Nazism.

Yet even with this breadth of chronological and geographical coverage and the desperation of the situation in 1939, in his conclusion Hope Simpson referenced what he believed was the normal state of affairs, where refugees were a minor part of the landscape – in essence individuals or small groups who were being victimised because of their political views and activities. Hannah Arendt recognised the limitations of such an approach, which is why she distanced herself from the label: 'A refugee used to be a person driven to seek refuge because of some act committed or some political opinion held. Well, it is true we have had to seek refuge; but we committed no acts and most of us never dreamt of having any radical political opinion.'[46] Hope Simpson, buoyed by what he saw as the successful 'solving' of the refugee crisis coming out of the First World War, was confident that the current situation was temporary and removable. Now, with an 'energetic attempt to secure final absorption, and ... by anticipatory action which dealt with the root causes, the refugee problem in Europe would reduce itself to that minor feature of international life which it ought to be'. No doubt with the mid-nineteenth-century liberal model in mind, Hope Simpson conceded that there would 'always be politically active opponents of a regime, who to save life and liberty must seek sanctuary in other countries'. Currently the number of political refugees 'was abnormally great', but, with the generous granting of asylum, it could be easily solved and reduced in size; the 'refugee problem ... would not raise any of the great difficulties that now menace the whole stability of European society and impose indescribable moral suffering and hardship on groups of populations through no fault of their own'.[47] Hope Simpson was attempting such a reading no doubt to encourage a more positive response to the contemporary refugee crisis. His political and historical optimism, however, was sadly misplaced.

---

45 John Hope Simpson, *The Refugee Problem: Report of a Survey* (London: Oxford University Press, 1939).
46 Arendt, 'We Refugees', p. 264.
47 Hope Simpson, *The Refugee Problem*, p. 546.

Eight years later Malcolm Proudfoot provided a chronological update on *The Refugee Problem*, taking the story through to 1952. The confidence of his predecessor was now absent, with the trauma of the recent conflict in mind:

> so constant has been the phenomenon of refugees in flight and the problems of people displaced from their homeland, that before the Second World War it might have been assumed that nothing unique could occur in this field. Previous experience, however, provided no parallel for the magnitude and complexity of the European refugee problem of the Second World War, when some 60 million European civilians were forced to move.

This was, he added, over ten times the number displaced during the First World War.[48] The liberal nationalist solutions proposed by *The Refugee Problem* in 1939 seemed naive in the post-war era. As Hope Simpson conceded in the Foreword to Proudfoot's study, the extermination of the Jews was a 'crime unique in history in its magnitude and incredible cruelty'.[49]

Yet, even allowing for the magnitude and trauma of the recent refugee crisis, both Hope Simpson and Proudfoot linked the problem largely to global conflict. With a European focus (and thus avoiding reference to post-war refugee crises in India/Pakistan and Palestine/Israel), and written before Hungary in 1956, the *continuity* of the problem after 1945 was downplayed by Proudfoot. And, despite the quality of these pioneer studies, it would be a further 30 years *after* Proudfoot's work that a professional historian would provide an overview of the European refugee crisis from the First World War to the Cold War – Michael Marrus's *The Unwanted* (1985).[50] Neatly, there would be another three-decade gap before Peter Gatrell's *The Making of the Modern Refugee* (2013), which covered the whole of the twentieth century and was, in contrast to his antecedents, globally inclusive.[51]

That a generation had passed between these classic works emphasises how the historical study of refugees is still very much in its infancy. Moreover, within the relatively new field of refugee studies itself and humanitarian practice, the focus on the present has led to a reluctance 'to [think] about the root causes of displacement' and a temptation to treat refugees as though they had 'no history, past experience [and] culture'.

---

48 Malcolm Proudfoot, *European Refugees: 1939-52. A Study in Forced Population Movement* (London: Faber and Faber, 1957), p. 21.

49 John Hope Simpson, 'Foreword', in ibid, p. 18.

50 Michael Marrus, *The Unwanted: European Refugees in the Twentieth Century* (Oxford: Oxford University Press, 1985).

51 Gatrell, *The Making of the Modern Refugee.*

In a curious mirror image of the historical profession's amnesia, refugee studies and praxis more generally are fields 'where history dare not speak its name'.[52]

In her *Refugees in Inter-War Europe: The Emergence of a Regime* (1995), Claudena Skran insisted that 'the notion that the contemporary refugee crisis is unique lacks a historical perspective and neglects the fact: mass refugee movements are neither new nor exclusive to specific regions'.[53] Similarly, B.S. Chimni argues that a 'myth of difference' has been created in studying refugee flows from Europe and those from the 'Third World'. Chimni acknowledges that 'Of course ... every refugee differs from another in the circumstances which force her to flee.' Even so, he concludes, 'the differences which have been propagated are self-serving and refugee studies has done little to combat this'.[54]

This study follows in the direction encouraged by Skran and Chimni. It argues, therefore, that those fleeing from what would later be widely known as the Holocaust can be meaningfully set alongside refugee movements from before and after the Nazi era. In so doing, it does not suggest a simplistic homogeneity or straightforward linearity. *Journeys from the Abyss* will always insist on specific contexts of time and place, as well as scale and impact. The hope is that comparisons will shed light on all such journeys – then and now – with the ultimate aim of combatting forms of ahistorical tendency in both the specific area of Jewish refugees from Nazism and refugee studies more generally. While the focus of the three case studies forming the heart of this book is largely on Jews who fled before, during, and immediately after the Nazi regime, each one will provide a pre- and post-history of refugee/forced migration example relating to the themes selected: gender, childhood, and the desperate search for a new life through perilous sea journeys.

History and Memory

Refugees, as Peter Gatrell notes, 'have called upon history to explain their displacement and to help negotiate a way out of their predicament'. He adds that 'Refugees were created by violence and governed by regimes of intervention, but they gave meaning to their experiences through engaging with the past. History is a refugee resource.'[55] Thus the *politics* of remembering and forgetting – both within and outside the migrant groups – will be emphasised, especially in relation to contemporary and

---

52 Ibid, p. 284.

53 Skran, *Refugees in Inter-War Europe*, p. 4.

54 B.S. Chimni, 'The Geopolitics of Refugee Studies: A View from the South', *Journal of Refugee Studies* vol. 11 no. 4 (1998), pp. 357, 360, and 368.

55 Gatrell, *The Making of the Modern Refugee*, p. vii.

often controversial forced migration movements. How, for example, has the memory of Holocaust-related refugee movements of the past been used to either empathise with and support or denigrate and invalidate forced migrants today? As Gatrell also notes, 'Governments appeal to a history of "generosity" towards refugees ... but this frequently serves as a justification for maintaining tough controls on admission.'[56] And it is not only governments but also ordinary people in constructing their life stories that employ such an approach. This includes, ironically, some of migrant origin themselves. The Pakistani-origin British novelist Hanif Kureishi has written how

> The recently arrived immigrant, the last through the door, and now settling down in the new country, can himself be disgusted by the idea of [the] newer arrival or interloper, the one who could take his place, because this threatening Other does not resemble him in any way.[57]

Kureishi's insight can be enhanced by adding that the insecurity of the recent migrant and their descendants can be such that it leads them to fear being identified with the new 'threatening Other'. This is especially so if the battle for acceptance in the receiving society had been hard fought and their status in society is still marginal.

Those of migrant origin can reflect wider responses to more recent newcomers but often articulate them more acutely. More positively, they can identify with them closely and provide support and advice – refugees from Nazism, for example, have been prominent in organisations helping later victims of oppression. More ambivalently, while recognising an element of commonality, they can still distance themselves, fearing that they would be mistaken for contemporary migrants, especially so if the most recent arrivals are perceived as fundamentally alien and dangerous. And, more negatively, they can attempt to prove their sense of belonging by echoing and amplifying the xenophobia around them towards those coming now – confirming the insights of Kureishi. In an area marked by strong emotions, ambiguity, and confusion, it is not uncommon for all these tendencies to combine within the same individual.

Throughout *Journeys from the Abyss* there will be a close reading of the autobiographical practice of those of refugee origin. The first of these is the life story of a Londoner, 'Harold', who is of third-generation East European Jewish origin. His writings and rewritings show the complexity involved in juxtaposing refugeedom past and present. A retired newspaper executive born in the middle of the Second World War, 'Harold' is a long-standing

---

56 Ibid, p. 283.
57 Hanif Kureishi, 'The migrant has no face, status or story', *Guardian Review*, 31 May 2014.

contributor to the social anthropological organisation Mass-Observation. In summer 2000, responding to a moral panic about asylum-seekers 'flooding' Britain,[58] Mass-Observation asked its volunteer writers to reflect on migrants past and present in their own experiences and in those of those around them, including family history. Here 'Harold' provided a remarkable narrative of his ancestors and especially their arrival in Britain. Indeed, the migrant journey is pivotal to his story:

> Back in 1905, a young Jewish man left his village in Poland, tired of pogroms and persecution, and set sail for America. I don't know much of the details, but his ship was wrecked in the English Channel and he was able to swim ashore.[59]

It has been noted that many family memoirs relating to East European Jewish migrants to Britain first emphasise the danger from which they fled (and in the process downplaying poverty and the search for better opportunities away from the Russian Empire, which was behind so much of this mass movement). They thus want to present their ancestors, in the language of the early twentieth century, as victims of persecution and not as undesirable aliens – or, in the discourse of the early twenty-first century, as genuine refugees and not as 'bogus' asylum-seekers. Second, such accounts posit accidental arrival in this particular country of refuge, suggesting innocence/naivety and, from this, the absence of a real threat to Britain's well-being.[60] To translate again into contemporary parlance, such life story practice avoids being seen as newcomers who by nefarious means steal 'our' jobs or come here as manipulative 'benefits cheats'.[61]

The case of 'Harold' is a rich and extreme example of an imagined 'accidental arrival' and the importance of mythology in migrant storytelling. As Paul Thompson and Raphael Samuel note, 'for minorities, for the less powerful, and most of all for the excluded, collective memory and myth are … more salient [than for others]: constantly resorted to both in reinforcing a sense of self and also as a source of strategies for survival'.[62] It is thus not surprising that this narrative of survival

58 Stanley Cohen, *Folk Devils and Moral Panics* (London: Routledge, 2002 [3rd edition]), Introduction.

59 Mass-Observation Archive at The Keep Record Office (hereafter M-O A): D1602, Summer 2000 Directive 'Coming to Britain'.

60 David Cesarani, 'The Myth of Origin: ethnic memory and the experience of migration', in Aubrey Newman and Stephen Massil (eds), *Patterns of Migration 1850–1914* (London: Jewish Historical Society of England, 1996), pp. 247–254.

61 For an analysis of the British media and these widespread allegations, see Greg Philo et al., *Bad News for Refugees* (London: Pluto Press, 2013).

62 Raphael Samuel and Paul Thompson, 'Introduction', in idem (eds), *The Myths We Live By* (London: Routledge, 1990), pp. 18–19.

and personal endurance constructed by 'Harold' about his grandfather did not end after the unexpected and traumatic arrival on the English coast: 'He landed in Plymouth and, after a few days for recuperation, started the long walk to London. He had lost all his possessions, was virtually penniless and spoke very little English.'[63] The rags to respectability narrative then continued as the Observer's grandfather found his way to the East End of London. There he married a fellow Polish Jewish refugee; they had a family of four children and set up a jewellery business. Hard work and independence assured their initial success and integration. While 'Harold' never met them, he did not 'remember hearing of any special difficulties that my grandparents had in being accepted into this country, although today they would have been undoubtedly described as asylum seekers.'[64] His ambivalence towards this term will soon become apparent.

Twelve years later, in response to another Mass-Observation directive on 'Human Rights, immigration and the legal system', 'Harold' elaborated on this myth of origins and, in the process of retelling the story, provided a greater certainty than in his first, hesitant version of it. While shorter on detail, the migrant journey had moved beyond the secular realm and was now given sacred status:

> Incidentally my grandfather had left Poland to sail to the United States but his ship was wrecked in the English Channel and he was able to swim ashore saying that if this was where God wanted [him] to settle then he would follow God's will.[65]

Self-reliance also appears through his grandmother's biography. Shortly after the First World War the Mass-Observer's grandfather died in the influenza epidemic, leaving his wife to look after their four children. She faced the additional burden of speaking 'very little English'. Somehow 'she took on a tobacconist's shop in central London and managed to make enough money for the family to survive'. To the Observer, there was a wider message to be conveyed by the resilience shown by his grandfather and grandmother: 'I feel that both these stories show the grit and determination some people can have especially when they don't have the family and resources of their own country to fall back on.'[66] Here there is the potential to *identify with* and *distance from* more recent migrants which is articulated in 'Harold's' comments on would-be refugees.

---

63 M-O A: DR1602, Summer 2000 Directive.

64 Ibid.

65 M-O A: DR 1602 Autumn 2012 Directive 'Human rights, immigration & the legal system'.

66 Ibid.

Having stated in 2000 that his grandparents would now be regarded as 'asylum seekers', the Observer commented that

> Unfortunately, these two words have taken on an unwelcome signif-
> icance in recent years, largely because of the comparative few who have
> taken advantage of the system to such an extent that they seem to be
> raising two fingers to the nation that has taken them in.[67]

But, typifying many Mass-Observer responses, after the initial restraint – a critique only of the 'comparative few' – the attack gained momentum as his directive progressed:

> The trouble is that Britain seems to have become a 'honeypot' for asylum
> seekers from all over the world … . In the politically-correct times in
> which we live, the government seems determined to be lenient with
> potential immigrants, no matter how weak their case for 'asylum' or
> whatever devious and often clearly illegal means of entry they use.[68]

The contrast here with the journey of his grandfather, who, Jonah-like, is violently expelled from the immigrant ship and finds refuge in the belly of (English) safety where he can be reborn, is clear. And, whereas his grandparents contributed not only by bringing up a family but also economically, it was not surprising, 'Harold' suggested, that the 'indigenous population' was upset when contemporary asylum-seekers went to the top of the housing list and received 'massive benefits'. Reversing his earlier cautious criticism of the few who 'abused' the system, 'Harold' ended with a flourish that reversed that perspective. Indeed, his response ultimately exposed an acceptance of the dominant anti-alien discourse of early twenty-first century Britain: 'The only way to stop asylum seekers flooding in is for the government to take an extraordinarily strong hand and allow in only a few "genuine" people.'[69]

In the field of migration, and for both settled and settlers, history and memory *matters*. The ambivalence and animosity of the Mass-Observer reflect how past and present meld in the construction of his identity. His views reflect wider tendencies in society, politics, and culture, but they also relate closely to how 'Harold' perceives himself within Britain and, in spite of his economic security and success, his overwhelming sense of marginality. In 2010 Mass-Observation carried out a directive on 'Belonging', asking its writers to consider when they felt part of a wider entity such as a community of people, a place, a culture or a nation and,

---

67   M-O A: DR1602, Summer 2000 Directive.
68   Ibid.
69   Ibid.

alternatively, 'when you may have felt "not at home" or "an outsider"'. His response is revealing, again starting in one direction and ending in another, emphasising the strength of an archive that gets beyond the shallowness of opinion poll data: '[M]y immediate reaction was to write and say that yes, I like "to belong", but the more I've thought about it since … . I've decided that I do only on certain occasions, but overall perhaps I don't.'[70] Uncertain about his place within the nation, and his outsider status also within the Jewish world,[71] the possibility that his grandparents may have come to Britain in the same paperless and haphazard manner as more recent and denigrated asylum-seekers ultimately leads to an autobiographical distancing from them.

It is important to add that no ship before 1914 carrying East Europeans to America sank in the English Channel, although *The Norge* did so off Rockall in 1904 with 635 immigrant victims, including 200 Russian Jews. And it is often omitted from its mythologised history that, along with its Southampton-based crew, the vast majority of *The Titanic*'s victims were immigrants and refugees travelling steerage who found themselves at the bottom of the ship. They were physically separated and locked apart lest they endanger the health and well-being of the first- and second-class passengers. Among the steerage were, again, many East European Jews – migrants, step migrants, and transmigrants.[72]

Typifying this fluidity of movement (and the role of fortune and misfortune in the individual migrant experience) is the story of Rosalind Winton's family. She relates their traumatic relationship to this infamous ship over a century after its sinking, prompted by the opening of Southampton's SeaCity Museum in 2012, which is dominated by representation of this tragic episode:

> My paternal Great Grandfather, Harry Corn, was supposed to have travelled with his wife and two young daughters on the *Titanic*. They had sold their successful upholstery business so they could travel to America to start a new life and also, so that his wife, Rebecca, could be reunited with her sister and family [as] they were separated when the family was expelled from Russia.

---

70 M-O A: DR1602, Summer 2010 Directive 'Belonging'.

71 In response to another directive, he stated that his 'Judaism' went no further than having 'Jewish blood'. See M-O A: DR1602, Spring 2009 Directive 'Second World War'.

72 Per Kristian Sebak, *Titanic's Predecessor: The SS Norge Disaster of 1904* (Laksevag: Seaward Publishing, 2004); Tony Kushner, 'Cowards or Heroes? Jewish Journeys, Jewish Families and the *Titanic*', in James Jordan, Tony Kushner and Sarah Pearce (eds), *Jewish Journeys from Philo to Hip Hop* (London: Vallentine Mitchell, 2010), pp. 281–313.

Fate then intervened and one of their daughters was ill 'so they decided that Harry would travel alone and they would follow later'. Sadly Harry died in the disaster 'and because they had sold everything to make the trip, Rebecca then had to make a living selling lingerie in Petticoat Lane market'.[73]

This consanguineous sketch has elements of similarity to that provided by 'Harold' – expulsion rather than any element of choice in leaving the Russian Empire and the importance of family and (especially female) economic fortitude and adaptability in the place of settlement. Indeed, in the harsh reality and traditional structures of life in Eastern Europe, some Jewish migrants left to *escape* family. This was true also of step migrants of this origin – Joseph Hyman, a distant relative of the author, was aboard (and survived) *The Titanic*, it seems, to run away from an unhappy marriage and a failing business in Manchester. It took him close to a year to return from America, 'where he was having too good a time to come home!'[74] The *official* version, however, is that it was the impact of the disaster that caused the delay and that re-establishing himself successfully in the north of England (Hyman set up one of the most famous Jewish delicatessens in Britain) was somehow the result of divine intervention: 'Anyone who survived such an ordeal, the reasoning went, must have God's blessing.'[75] In similar vein, Joseph's grandson, Stanley Hyman, relates that on Joseph's return a new child was conceived. His middle name was Jonas, 'after the biblical story of the miracle of Jonah and the Whale'. Yet, even in this supernatural interpretation of Joseph's coming out of a 'watery grave', Stanley acknowledges a mundane truth: 'The family of seven thrived for a time until alas ... siblings fell out.'[76] As will be explored in Part 1 of this study, the economic and psychological fragility of family structure, especially under the strain of migration, was partly responsible for the global growth of the 'White Slave Trade', the antithesis of the Jewish self-image of domestic respectability and female purity.

For Rosalind Winton, what happened to her great-grandfather, Harry Corn, is still 'very close to my heart'.[77] It is another factor that unites her narrative with those of 'Harry' and the descendants of Joseph Hyman.

---

73 Information provided by Rosalind Winton to Maria Newbury, Curator, SeaCity Museum Southampton, 2013.

74 See the unpublished account by his great-granddaughter, Anna Bansci, 'The Life of Mr J.A. Hyman' [no date], in the author's possession and email to the author, 3 March 2009.

75 Clarissa Hyman, *The Jewish Kitchen: Recipes and Stories from Around the World* (London: Conran Octopus, 2003), p. 152. Clarissa Hyman is the granddaughter of Joseph.

76 Stanley Hyman, *Is Anything Alright? My Titanics Story* (Bowdon: Stellar Books, 2014), pp. xix–xx.

77 Rosalind Winton account to SeaCity Museum.

Anna Bansci, great-granddaughter of Joseph, was brought up with the legend of a man known locally as 'Titanic man':

> I think [he] was quite … amazing … . He survived many horrific experiences in his life ranging from pogroms and maritime disasters to untimely family deaths … . He pulled through these tragedies and brought up seven children … . The Titanic shops are still being run to this day by members of his family and the Hyman name is known throughout the Jewish community as the place to go for bagels on a Sunday morning![78]

That these later accounts contain elements which are fictitious or distorted does not invalidate their importance. Indeed, it reveals the wider significance of the journey in the memory of migration, generations later. Another Mass-Observer wrote in response to the 2012 directive: 'My parents came to this country from Poland in 1939. Being Jewish meant *their journey* [my emphasis] was for survival.' She added that for those 'fleeing from wars … we in GB are renowned for helping', but now, in contrast, migrants coming from the continent were 'dregs who are … escaping prisons – murderers, rapists etc'.[79] It is the concept and politics of the journey – real and imagined, physical and emotional – that will be the heart of this study.

Journeys

In a previous work, *The Battle of Britishness: Migrant Journeys, 1685 to the Present* (2012), I dwelt on the clash over terminology involving anthropologist James Clifford and black American cultural critic bell hooks.[80] The latter has criticised the former, who she claims 'playfully evokes a sense of *travel* [my emphasis]'.[81] In response, Clifford defends his use of the term *despite* 'its associations with gendered, racial bodies [and] class privilege'.[82] hooks insists, however, that 'travel' is not a word that can be 'easily evoked' in relation to disturbing, challenging but core aspects of American

---

78 Bansci, 'The Life of Mr J.A. Hyman'. This was a remarkably well-researched and written school project and I would like to thank Anna for sharing it with me. Sadly, Titanics has recently closed.

79 M-O A: DR F218, Summer 2012 Directive. The respondent was born in 1946 and lived in rural Suffolk.

80 Tony Kushner, *The Battle of Britishness: Migrant Journeys 1685 to the Present* (Manchester: Manchester University Press, 2012), pp. 71–72.

81 bell hooks, 'Representing Whiteness', in Lawrence Grossberg, Cary Nelson and Paula Reichler (eds), *Cultural Studies* (New York: Routledge, 1992), p. 343.

82 James Clifford, *Travel and Translation in the Late Twentieth Century* (Cambridge, MA: Harvard University Press, 1997), p. 343.

history such as slavery, destruction of the indigenous population or racist immigration control. Instead, hooks insists on the word *journey*, which can more appropriately then incorporate 'enforced migration, relocation, enslavement [and] homelessness'.[83] As with *The Battle of Britishness*, I will continue here to utilise 'journey' as opposed to 'travel' in order to emphasise, following the logic of bell hooks' intervention, the traumatic histories that are explored. Yet problems still remain with usages of 'journey' – even in relation to the Holocaust – which replicate those that hooks identifies in relation to the looser concept of 'travel'.

It has been noted with regard to the modern workplace that 'There's something peculiarly horrible about the modern bureaucratic habit of turning everything into a journey, with the ersatz thrill of adventurous tourism and its therapeutic implications of personal growth.'[84] This 'journey quest' and superficial psychology extends beyond the office and has encroached on all aspects of the everyday. We are all, it seems, on some sort of personal life journey, spiritual or otherwise. Sadly, such tendencies are also apparent in the academic sphere and can be detected in the only journal devoted to 'journeys'.

Journeys, subtitled *The International Journal of Travel and Travel Writing*, first appeared in 2000. It is significant that, in its editorial introduction, the word 'migration' is largely avoided and instead the emphasis is placed on the centrality of 'travel' in the human experience:

> people travel, and have always travelled, for vastly different reasons and in a variety of different ways – for pleasure, leisure, work; in search of spirituality or enlightenments; because they have been driven from their homes; to explore, to conquer, and to govern.

Such promising inclusivity appears to be confirmed when the editors add that, in pursuing these goals, people 'have traveled as tourists, but just as likely as pilgrims, explorers, refugees, migrant workers, pilots, guides, academics, bearers, seafarers, drivers, journalists, invaders, missionaries, as agents of governments or (of course) as travel writers'.[85]

This is certainly a diverse if somewhat curious list. But by not taking sufficient account of power relationships, its apparent comprehensiveness is illusionary. It is, for example, a prospectus that gives equal space to pilots and guides as to refugees and migrant workers. The list reveals the playfulness that hooks warns about. Yet, rather than acknowledge the inherent danger of employing loose terminology in the manner of James Clifford, the editors

83 hooks, 'Representing Whiteness', p. 343.
84 Steven Poole, 'Run this up your flagpole', *The Guardian*, 23 October 2013.
85 Robert Davis, Maria Pia Di Bella, John Eade and Garry Marvin, 'Introduction', *Journeys* vol. 1 no. 1 (2000), p. 3.

simply revel in it: 'The richness of possibility that so many aims and so many goals present is the intellectual lode in which the publication will seek to mine.' A 'broad … scope' was thus being offered to the readers.[86] In fact, all the dangers associated with the uncritical use of the word 'travel' have been subsequently made manifest in *Journeys*. Well into its second decade of twice yearly publication, not one article has been devoted *directly* to refugee journeys or to migrant workers – forced or otherwise.

As will be highlighted throughout this study and was experienced by Hannah Arendt, nomenclature and labelling matters and the loaded meaning of terminology is ignored by the editors of *Journeys*. It leads to the homogenisation and equivalency of diverse phenomena in the history of human movement: 'To say that traveling, touristing or simply wandering are among the widespread of human activities is only to claim the obvious: this has been the case since the beginnings of our species.'[87] Avoiding the term 'migration', let alone 'forced migration', is telling. It is the 'journey of the imagination', or the *idea* of the journey, that is ultimately the focus of this journal. '*Journeys* will … treat the images and practices of "travel" as metaphor for the production of the cultural experience and knowledge about "real" places.'[88]

Closing this somewhat precious introduction, the editors appropriately invited the readers 'to join us in this particular journey'.[89] As the journal has progressed there have been a couple of diversions into the area of 'dark tourism' and, within it, journeys associated with the Holocaust and also, on one occasion, transatlantic slavery.[90] Yet in none of these rare meanderings has there been consideration of the *actual* journeys associated with these catastrophic histories. Instead, they have focused solely on those who have later visited sites of destruction and perpetration or commemorative representations of them. There has been no analysis of the autobiographical practice of the victims themselves, who experienced these horrors directly. Similarly, in relation to refugee journeys, the only treatment has been on recreating that of scholar Walter Benjamin, the German Jewish exile from Nazism. Even then, the emphasis is not on Benjamin but on the author – anthropologist Michael Jackson – who has tried to emulate the last journeys of this great scholar:

> And I fell to wondering why we expend so much effort on interpreting signs – reading the sky, the sea, the faces of those we love – for insights

---

86 Ibid.

87 Ibid, p. 1.

88 Ibid, p. 4.

89 Ibid.

90 Andrew Gross, 'Holocaust Tourism in Berlin: Global Memory, Trauma and the "Negation of the Sublime"', *Journeys* vol. 7 no. 2 (2006), pp. 73–100; Cherly Finley, 'Touring the African Diaspora', *Journeys* vol. 13 no. 2 (2012), pp. 47–54.

into some inner and normally invisible state, or set such great store by trying to divine or alter the course of the future.[91]

This particular article is part of a special issue of *Journeys* devoted to 'Trauma Trails and Memory Walks' published in 2012. Ironically, Jackson's first footnote provides a clear disconnect to the elusive nature of his prose and the approach of not only this issue but the journal as a whole: 'The UN High Commissioner for Refugees estimates that between 1994 and 2004 more than five thousand asylum seekers have drowned in the Mediterranean.'[92] We thus read in *Journeys* what it feels like to be a tourist/scholar walking round Auschwitz today but *not* about those who were sent there through the most brutal and extensive form of forced migration (or the hundreds of thousands of Africans searching for refuge and better opportunities in Europe today, relegated to a minor reference by Jackson).[93]

If the study of human migration becomes associated only with 'travel', and the word 'journey' is undermined by its promiscuous and lazy usage, then it is not surprising that there is so little scholarly work on the disturbing reality of forced migration in its many forms, past and present. So, for example, while the *image* of the slave ship within the 'Middle Passage' has become ubiquitous, the actual history of such vessels have been neglected by students of transatlantic slavery.[94] Similarly, in Holocaust memory work, train journeys in sealed cattle trucks carrying hundreds of Jews crammed together to the death camps of Poland from across the continent of Europe have become 'a single, coherent and linear story'. In one of the few academic accounts devoted to the subject of Holocaust journeys, focusing especially on those relating to ghettoisation, Tim Cole has attempted to counter this powerful mythology by 'Instead [seeking] to bring difference to the fore through my focus upon particular places and people'.[95] While trains 'have entered the postwar imagination as one dominant symbol of what has been seen – perhaps rather mistakenly – as the most modern of crimes', Cole emphasises that in his particular case study 'journeys to and from Hungarian ghettos did not only involve railway stations and trains. In some [especially non-urbanised] places they involved farmsteads and horse-drawn carts.'[96]

---

91 Michael Jackson, 'In the Footsteps of Walter Benjamin', *Journeys* vol. 13 no. 2 (2012), p. 25.
92 Ibid, n. 1.
93 Nigel Rapport, 'Walking Auschwitz, Walking Without Arriving', *Journeys* vol. 9 no. 2 (2008), pp. 32–54.
94 Marcus Rediker, *The Slave Ship: A Human History* (New York: Penguin, 2007), p. 10.
95 Tim Cole, *Traces of the Holocaust: Journeying in and out of the Ghetto* (London: Continuum, 2011), p. 7.
96 Ibid, p. 28.

Cole's work highlights the importance of place and the centrality of geography in the study of migrant 'journeys' – traumatic or otherwise.[97] His intervention also makes clear the dangers when crude metaphors and vague mythologies obscure the detailed contexts required to explain the where, when, and to whom in any historical analysis. This is an even greater risk when 'the journey' is understood at a psychological, emotional, or spiritual level, losing sight of its often complex and varied pattern of actual human movement. In her study of displacement and estrangement, for example, which remarkably brings together travel writing, American immigrant autobiographies, and concentration camp memoirs (anticipating the looseness of categorisation that has typified the journal *Journeys*), Frances Bartkowski argues that all three reveal the same underlying foundation: '[T]he journey narrated and taken is a representation of earlier journeys into language and subjectivity, as we come to understand through the magical theatrics of the unconscious as we have known it and as we continue to invent it.'[98] She adds that 'The journey, a strong motif in all storytelling, is already a rewriting of the journey into culture that all of us of us must make when we learn to speak.'[99] While Bartkowski is right to highlight the importance of storytelling, her Freudian analysis risks flattening all journeys into one. She acknowledges the differences between her three case studies but even then collapses them into undifferentiated genres. The dislocation present in relation to Holocaust journeys creates what Bartkowski terms 'postmodern captivity narratives – concentration camp memoirs'.[100]

But it simply will not do to regard these accounts as 'a form of travel writing'.[101] Aside from the gulf in experience and power relationships which such narratives represent, there is also the danger that all Holocaust survivor accounts are homogenenised when in fact they vary immensely – not only in relation to literary form but also in terms of politics, gender, religious belief, nationality, age, disability, sexuality, and so on. Moreover, the point at which they were written inevitably impacts on the stories that are told (and, importantly, not told), revealing the influence of changing patterns of individual memory and the wider cultural framework in which such work is produced and received.[102] Variation in tone and content can

---

97 Anne Kelly Knowles et al. (eds), *Geographies of the Holocaust* (Bloomington: Indiana University Press, 2014).

98 Frances Bartkowski, *Travelers, Immigrants, Inmates: Essays in Estrangement* (Minneapolis: University of Minnesota Press, 1995), pp. xviii–xix.

99 Ibid, p. xix.

100 Ibid, p. 121.

101 See the critique of Bartkowski's work provided by Simone Gigliotti, *The Train Journey: Transit, Captivity, and Witnessing in the Holocaust* (New York: Berghahn Books, 2009), p. 24.

102 See the essays in the special issue of *Poetics Today* vol. 27 no. 2 (Summer 2006) devoted to 'The Humanities of Testimony' edited by Geoffrey Hartman.

thus be detected within the narratives of those individuals who wrote and rewrote their experiences after the war.

It is the exceptional, literary, voices of Holocaust testimony – especially Primo Levi, Elie Wiesel, and Charlotte Delbo – that tend to be analysed and treated as if they represented all journeys to the places of destruction. Levi's *If This Is a Man*, in which he relates the misery and horror and ultimate anonymity of the train journey to Auschwitz, is the most replicated.[103] He describes 'a human mass extended across the floor, confused and continuous, sluggish and aching, rising here and there in sudden convulsions and immediately collapsing again in exhaustion.'[104] The train journey, a preparation for what was to come, was, as Levi was to write later, 'a deliberate creation of pain which was an end in itself'.[105]

There are close to 100,000 Holocaust survivor testimonies, in written, oral, and video formats. The process of working through them critically has only just begun. And instead of the chaotic variety of voices and experiences that are present, scholarship has, with only a few exceptions, focused on Auschwitz as a menotym for the Holocaust as a whole and its most articulate and accessible survivor, Primo Levi, as *the* witness of journeys to the abyss. This leads to clichéd summaries which lose sight of any individuality:

> If the imaginative and historical renderings of the middle passage from Africa into slavery in the Americas have as a motif of learned servitude the slave ship and its arrangements of bodies deprived of light and liberty, the memoirs of deportation under the Nazi regime are focused on the death trains that took days to go from a place that was home or near home to place that was nameless and foreign, where it quickly became clear that no previous rules applied.[106]

The failure to confront the heterogeneous and dynamic nature of victim testimony relating to the experience of Holocaust journeys reflects the limitations of the historiography, ones which are exposed further with its focus on perpetrator discourse. 'In historical scholarship, the administration of deportations of Jews to death camps has been represented as the work of detached bureaucrats.' This has led to a focus on 'Timetables, quotas, euphemistic language, and numbers'. As Simone Gigliotti suggests,

---

103 For example, by Seymour Drescher, 'The Atlantic Slave Trade and the Holocaust: A Comparative Analysis', in Alan Rosenbaum (ed.), *Is the Holocaust Unique*, p. 109; Gigliotti, *The Train Journey*, p. 122; Bartkowski, *Travellers, Immigrants, Inmates*, p. 142; Hayden White, 'Figural Realism in Witness Literature', *Parallax* vol. 10 no. 1 (2004), pp. 113–124.
104 Primo Levi, *If This is a Man* (London: Abacus, 1987), p. 24.
105 Primo Levi, *The Drowned and the Saved* (London: Michael Joseph, 1988), p. 87.
106 Bartkowski, *Travelers, Immigrants, Inmates*, p. 142.

in her study *The Train Journey: Transit, Captivity, and Witnessing in the Holocaust* (2009) – tellingly, the only detailed study of the subject – 'The clinical approach of detached bureaucrats is not isolated, and has continued in historians' representations.' If such Holocaust journeys are only presented as 'train convey totals and timetables to be shipped', then 'human action, choices, and commitment' are omitted. 'Numbers', as she concludes, 'obscure the trauma of deportation as a human crime with inhumane impacts'.[107]

In this powerful critique, Gigliotti had Raul Hilberg, the political scientist who pioneered the study of functionaries in the 'Final Solution', particularly in mind. In a seminal article 'German Railroads/Jewish Souls' (1978), Hilberg's focus was on the Reich Transport Ministry (*Reichsbahn*) officials who organised the intricate bureaucratic processes to enable mass deportation by train through which 'Jews were booked as people and shipped as cattle'. The bureaucrats were, he concludes, 'solid individuals, but not mindless robots. As intelligent men they were capable of understanding the tenor of their times.'[108] Hilberg bemoans the lack of *Reichsbahn* sources available to scholars. It is telling, however, that he uses no Jewish testimony in his study. It leads to a bizarre narrative in which the impact of the pressure of resources – such as shortages of trains and busy lines – on the victims, manifested in longer journeys and doubly packed wagons, is acknowledged, but only through the eyes of co-presents: 'The sealed cars often did not have enough water for such long journeys, and nothing is so indelible in the memory of *German* [my emphasis] witnesses as crying mothers holding up parched children during stops.'[109] The idea and image of the Holocaust train journey, therefore, has become attached to a stereotypical perception of the traumatic event as a whole – one which focuses on the death camps (Auschwitz especially) and academically has given more attention to the perpetrators than the victims. It ignores the facts that several million Jewish victims were shot or clubbed to death close to their homes, that hundreds of thousands perished in ghettos large and small, that the 'where' and 'when' of such train journeys varied immensely, and, indeed, that there were other means of Holocaust transportation. Such train journeys were also experienced differently by their victims and, for those who survived, memories (and their suppression) would be shaped and reshaped in many forms after 1945.

The lacunae and distortions in our understanding of such journeys is especially unfortunate in that it could be argued that one of the exceptional features of the Holocaust within the wider history of genocide is the use

---

107 Gigliotti, *The Train Journey*, p. 54.
108 Raul Hilberg, 'German Railroads/Jewish Souls', *Society* vol. 35 no. 2 (January/ February 1998), pp. 165, 173–174.
109 Ibid, p. 170.

of transport of all sorts. It went beyond the continent of Europe and even extended tentatively into North Africa.[110] Other railway journeys, such as those associated with the partition of India in 1947, were more murderous,[111] but there are still distinctive aspects of those associated with the Holocaust. The Nazis' desire to wipe out the entire Jewish 'race' had to confront the truly diasporic nature of world Jewry. While military setbacks ensured that the 'Final Solution' remained incomplete, transport issues would have played an even greater role had the Nazis extended their geographical reach. It is thus surprising that so little attention has been given to the Holocaust journey in the literature devoted to the question of uniqueness.

In a major collection devoted to a comparison of the Atlantic Slave Trade and the Holocaust, there is only one consideration of the journey – a thoughtful, comparative analysis by Seymour Drescher, a scholar of the former. Drescher highlights similarities in the utterly dislocating *experiences* of the victims during the Middle Passage and the box cars to the death camps.[112] These journeys were 'like nothing they had experienced before'. Thirst, hunger, disease, brutality, and human dirt were common to both, though the Middle Passage could last not just days but weeks and even months.[113] Yet, as Drescher concludes, in these journeys while both 'captive Africans and Jews were designated as "pieces" … Africans were more highly differentiated goods because an African's status was derived from the exchange value of an adult male for a piece of imported textile.' By contrast, he adds, 'all Jews who were not deemed of "full" immediate labor value were immediately sent to the furnace'.[114] As Hilberg notes of the increasing delays in transporting Jews experienced in the second half of the war, 'The Jews, of course, did not have to be rushed to their destination; they were going to be killed there, not used.'[115]

In *If This Is a Man* Primo Levi recalls being part of the 'six hundred and fifty "pieces"' loaded into twelve goods wagons from the Fossili detention camp in Italy at the start of 1944: 'men, women and children pressed together without pity, *like cheap merchandise* [my emphasis], for a journey towards nothingness, a journey down there, towards the bottom'.[116] In

---

110 A small number of Jews in Libya of foreign nationality, for example, were deported to Europe, most being sent eventually to Bergen Belsen. See Maurice Roumani, *The Jews of Libya: Coexistence, Persecution, Resettlement* (Brighton: University of Sussex Press, 2009), chapter 1.

111 Gigliotti, *The Train Journey*, p. 48.

112 His overview of the Holocaust is very much Auschwitz-centred but this does not detract from his argument as a whole.

113 Drescher, 'The Atlantic Slave Trade', p. 109.

114 Ibid, p. 111.

115 Hilberg, 'German Railroads/Human Souls', p. 170.

116 Levi, *If This is a Man*, pp. 22–23.

the Nazi worldview, however, Jewish lives had *no* value – they were not even 'cheap merchandise'. Only Jewish deaths mattered. Nevertheless, it is revealing that Franz Stangl, commandant of Treblinka, who was moved from Sobibor and had earlier been involved in the T4 euthanasia programme, in his prison interviews with the journalist Gitta Sereny refers to the Jewish victims arriving at his camp as 'cargo', rather than 'pieces'. Sereny asked Stangl if he felt the Jews he was responsible for were human beings: '"Cargo", he said tonelessly. "They were cargo."' When further interrogated about how he felt about the many children who arrived at Treblinka, he responded 'You see … I rarely saw them as individuals. It was always as a huge mass.'[117]

Simone Gigliotti, analysing this testimony, suggests that Stangl attempted to rationalise his role in the killing of up to 800,000 Jews in Treblinka by arguing that he viewed them not as humans but as cattle.[118] Yet the word employed by Stangl also evokes the language of the Middle Passage utilised by slavers and, as 'human cargo' or 'cargo of slaves', that of the abolitionists.[119] Transatlantic slavery, bolstered ideologically and morally by scientific racism and religion, could be and was justified on rational grounds as good economics as well as the natural order of the world. Stangl, by using the word 'cargo', was denying the utter irrationality and inhumanity of the 'Final Solution' and thus his own intimate and crucial role within it. Ultimately, therefore, he hid from his total responsibility for mass murder.

Holocaust journeys possessed distinctive and perhaps unique features. It does not follow, however, that they stand outside 'history' and cannot be meaningfully compared with others associated with mass destruction and human misery. The case of Stangl reveals the potential for students of the Holocaust and those of slavery to find their work mutually beneficial. Likewise, the subject matter of this study, journeys *out of the abyss*, which remain in scholarship as marginal as journeys *to destruction*, will benefit greatly from wider contextualisation and comparison. At this stage I should clarify that it will prove impossible to totally separate those into and out of the Holocaust. Within the testimony of survivors, for example – the focus of chapters 3 and 4 – chronology and experiences were blurred. And even for the Jewish refugees from the 1930s, their lives would be shaped by families and friends who perished through journeys of destruction, no more so than those who came on the *Kindertransport*.

---

117 Gitta Sereny, *Into that Darkness: From Mercy Killing to Mass Murder* (London: Andre Deutsch, 1974), p. 201.

118 Gigliotti, *The Train Journey*, pp. 49–51.

119 William Smith, *A Letter to William Wilberforce* (London: Richard Taylor, 1807) and the abolitionist work of Anthony Benezet from the 1760s onwards. I am grateful to John Oldfield, director of the Wilberforce Institute for Slavery and Emancipation, for help with these references.

Liverpool Street Station, to the east of the City of London, is now home to two major memorials to Jewish (child) refugees from Nazism.[120] That there are no other major public sites remembering refugees in Britain – in spite of the long history of such (often temporary) presence – is an indication of how those who escaped Nazism have been regarded as separate and special.[121] *Now* idealised, their journeys, as noted earlier by the female Mass-Observer, are seen as ones purely of survival, to which those of other migrants, including contemporary asylum-seekers, cannot be compared without sullying memory. There is again the danger of mystification here as well as a rendering of helplessness in relation to those that escaped Nazi Europe. It perhaps explains why, in the popular imagination, more attention is given to the *Kindertransport* than to adult refugees.

As will become apparent throughout this study, however, the *agency* of these Jewish refugees – both before and after the Second World War – cannot be simply ignored because of the acute persecution they were facing or had already experienced. As with all mass migrations, these journeys were undertaken at a basic level by thousands upon thousands of individuals. And, in contrast to those *to* the abyss, those *out* of it for the victims were rarely 'choiceless choices'.[122] There were clearly patterns – geographical, temporal, and economic, among others – to Jewish refugee movements during the Nazi era and after 1945. These, however, need to be set alongside the equally complex and even more haphazard individual circumstances of each person who decided to attempt a refugee journey. In this respect, one helpful starting point in providing the context(s) for our journeys out of the abyss is the recent academic debate that has emerged between refugee studies and forced migration studies.

Methodologies

At the turn of the twenty-first century, Stephen Castles was director of what was then the Refugee Studies Centre at the University of Oxford. Internationally, he has been one of the leading scholars in global migration and it is thus appropriate to consider in depth his contribution to the field. For him, as a Marxist-influenced scholar, forced migration, which in 2003 he estimated incorporated 'somewhere between 100 and 200

---

120 They are both devoted to the *Kindertransport*. See the special issue of *Prism* vol. 5 (Spring 2013), which include two articles by Pnina Rosenberg (pp. 68–74 and pp. 91–96) on these 'rival' memorials, placing them in an international context.

121 Tony Kushner, *Remembering Refugees: Then and Now* (Manchester: Manchester University Press, 2005).

122 The phrase, now much repeated in Holocaust studies, is that of Lawrence Langer, initially in his *Versions of Survival: The Holocaust and the Human Spirit* (Albany: State University of New York Press, 1982), p. 72.

million' people – including refugees, the internally displaced, and development-induced displacement – was largely the result of unequal globalization. It was thus 'an integral part of North–South relationships'.[123] In analysing the growth in numbers Castles referred to the 'notion of the "asylum-migration nexus": many migrants and asylum seekers have multiple reasons for mobility and it is impossible to completely separate economic and human rights motivations.' This is a challenge 'to the neat categories that bureaucrats seek to impose' but also for scholarly work on migration. With regards to the latter, Castles argued that this was weak in the field of sociology and instead dominated by economists and geographers.[124] That historians may also have something distinctive to offer is not made clear.[125] In the particular definitional issue identified by Castles, for example, historians might suggest to strengthen his argument that from the early modern period through the twentieth century the division between economic migrants and refugees is hard to draw and is often perceived differently between (and within) those journeying and those receiving them. This includes such groups deemed with hindsight to be 'classic' – now undisputed refugees such as the Huguenots and Jews escaping Tsarist and then Hitlerite persecution.

There is, as Stephen Castles outlines, a fundamental difference in approach between the social sciences and the humanities in his subject area. Studying 'exile, displacement or belonging', he argues, 'seems to put too much emphasis on the subjective and cultural aspects of forced migration and to neglect its structural dimensions'. That is why, to Castles, 'the concept of a sociology of forced migration seems preferable'.[126] In the first decade of the twenty-first century there has been much agonising within the (still recent and marginal) field of *refugee* studies about how it should approach *forced migration* studies.[127] Should the two schools remain totally distinct, should they marry and meld, or, in the words of James Hathaway, 'could we agree just to "date"?'[128]

---

123 Stephen Castles, 'Towards a Sociology of Forced Migration and Social Transformation', *Sociology* vol. 37 no. 1 (2003), pp. 13, 15.

124 Ibid, p. 17.

125 Ibid, p. 22. Here Castles does, however, call for an interdisciplinary approach and sees a role for 'history, anthropology, geography, demography, political economy and economics in explaining the causes of forced migration and the dynamics of movement'.

126 Ibid, p. 21.

127 See Roger Zetter, 'More Labels, Fewer Refugees: Remaking the Refugee Label in an Era of Globalization', *Journal of Refugee Studies* vol. 20 no. 2 (2007), pp. 172–192, and B.S. Chimni, 'The Birth of a "Discipline": From Refugee to Forced Migration Studies', *Journal of Refugee Studies* vol. 22 no. 1 (2009), pp. 11–29.

128 James Hathaway, 'Forced Migration Studies: Could We Agree Just to "Date"?, *Journal of Refugee Studies* vol. 20 no. 3 (2007), pp. 349–369.

Hathaway, a scholar of international refugee law, argues that 'Put simply, refugees are different: not only are they by definition both seriously at risk and fundamentally disfranchised, but they are within the unconditional protective competence of the international community.' He sees a real danger in 'the collapsing of refugee studies into forced migration studies' (and between the study of migration more generally and forced migration). Revealing a key difference to Castles' approach, Hathaway highlights 'that the centrepiece of refugee studies should be the persons and not just the phenomenon, and that the specificity of the refugee's circumstances does and should matter.'[129] To do justice to Castles, in his plea for an interdisciplinary approach, he did allow among his methodological principles 'A *historical understanding* of both the sending and receiving societies [which] is vital in understanding any specific forced migration situation'. He also acknowledged that it is 'vital to investigate the *human agency* of the forced migrants and of the sending and receiving communities'.[130]

In practice, however, the individual is almost inevitably lost sight of in the wider structural vision of mass migration, forced or voluntary. Castles has provided the most detailed account of the 'methodological principles' in which forced migration studies should be based. It is telling that the study of *identity* does not feature in them and that, for example, literary and cultural studies are either ignored or marginalised in the approach he promotes, presumably because they over-emphasise the 'subjective'.[131] At an institutional level, the Castles model appears to be dominant. It is significant that the Refugee Studies Centre at Oxford, one of the largest and best-funded at a global level, has since 2006 been renamed the International Migration Institute.

A balance is needed between the two approaches, and here that of Hathaway will be followed when he suggests that

> a more flexible understanding of forced migration studies has most merit: rather than replacing either refugee studies or migrant/migration studies, the umbrella of forced migration studies might be best conceived as a loose structure within which to subject our work to a final level of scrutiny.

As he concludes, 'there is still enough overlap among our scholarly worlds to ensure that we will often have something meaningful to say to each other'.[132] It is the aim of this study to create (as well as problematise) such dialogue, one that will bring in Holocaust studies as well and, methodologically, a multi- and inter-disciplinary historical approach.

---

129 Ibid, p. 365.
130 Castles, 'Towards a Sociology of Forced Migration', pp. 29–30.
131 Ibid, pp. 22, 27–30.
132 Hathaway, 'Forced Migration Studies', p. 366.

In balancing what is particular and what is generic, *Journeys from the Abyss* will juxtapose and problematise a variety of critical themes. The first is that between the national and the transnational. Writing in 2003, Castles suggested that 'Some years ago one might have stated the task of the sociology of forced migration as the study of people forced to flee from one society and becoming part of another.' He added that 'Globalization and transnationalism make this conceptualization anachronistic, since the boundaries of national societies are becoming increasingly blurred.'[133] Again, from a historical perspective, Castles' division between 'then' and 'now' can be queried – migration in the past, whether forced or voluntary, was rarely a straightforward process. Transmigration, step migration, and return migration have always been present in such journeys. Moreover, since the introduction of immigration controls, especially in the twentieth century, many migrant journeys have been haphazard. They have ended up in unexpected places or have simply failed to happen.

Inevitably, *Journeys from the Abyss* will have a transnational focus. Those undertaking such journeys, or attempting them, came from many places and passed through, or settled, in many more. There will, however, be a focus in its central narratives on those that had a connection to Britain and its colonies. This partly reflects geo-politics and the importance of the British empire, leading to a numerical reality – if Britain and Palestine are taken together, for example, they were by far the largest place of refuge for Jews escaping Nazism before the start of the Second World War. Moreover, Britain from the nineteenth century onwards was a key player in the important business of transmigrancy and this role continued in a different guise through the 1930s and beyond. And lastly, any study of journeys – migrant or otherwise – has to consider the importance of place and space and the 'meanings assigned to [them]'. It has been noted that 'At its most fundamental, a geographical approach to the Holocaust starts with a question of *where.*'[134] To comprehend the transnational and the 'global' requires also a parallel understanding of the national and the 'local'. Indeed, such compartmentalisation, as Doreen Massey has argued, is never watertight:

> The attempt to align 'us' and 'them' with the general concepts of 'local' and 'global' is always deeply problematical. For in the historical and geographical constructions of places, the 'other' in general terms is already within. The global is everywhere and already, in one way or another, implicated in the local.[135]

---

133 Castles, 'Towards a Sociology of Forced Migration', p. 23.
134 Knowles et al., *Geographies of the Holocaust*, pp. 2, 4.
135 Doreen Massey, 'Double Articulation: A Place in the World', in A. Bammer (ed.), *Displacements: Cultural Identities in Question* (Bloomington: Indiana University Press, 1994), p. 10.

And nowhere are these observations more appropriate than with regard to the place of refugees in the world. Ultimately, *Journeys from the Abyss* will, because of refugee realities, cover all parts of the planet.

Second, it will consider the importance of individual initiatives *and* migrant networks. The spectre of the Holocaust clouds not only the historiography relating to Jewish refugees from Nazism but also many subsequent life stories of such journeys. The emotionally overpowering background has, understandably, overshadowed consideration of the tactics of those undertaking refugee journeys and how decisions were made regarding whether to undertake them or not. Family considerations (including members who were not able to leave or others who were already in places of safety), were important, as were those of other networks, informal (for example, friends and associates) and formal (including national and international refugee organisations). What was known about the possibilities of refuge, what were the sources of such intelligence, and how were they communicated inside and outside the place of persecution? Rather than undermine the 'refugee' status of those who left, the rationality of such decision-making highlights the importance of detail in a world where transportation, at least in peacetime, was often cheaper and easier but 'paper walls' increasingly complicated and restrictive. Even when studying the specific refugee, and how they constructed their narratives, the importance of networks will become apparent. Equally, as Hathaway reminds us, in refugee studies, the individual and her/his specificity and agency always matters and should never be marginalised in significance.

Third, the approach will be further enhanced by juxtaposing history and memory, which enables a richer understanding of refugeedom and migration more generally. As Julia Creet argues: 'Between times, place, generations, and media, from individuals to communities and vive versa, movement is what produces memory – and our anxieties about pinning it to place ... Movement always attends memory, yet we tend to take statis as its measure.'[136] Each 'historic' case study will start with a pre-history and close with a contemporary case study, providing an apparently straightforwardly linear chronology of 'then' and 'now'. The range of geographical examples chosen allows for 'the importance of comparison as a way of going beyond national categories'.[137] Such temporal progression will be further complicated, however, by exploring how the refugee movements which form the heart of each section have been subsequently remembered

---

136 Julia Creet, 'Introduction', in idem and Andreas Kitzmann (eds), *Memory and Migration: Multidisciplinary Approaches to Memory Studies* (Toronto: University of Toronto Press, 2011), p. 9.

137 Nancy Green, 'The Comparative Method and Poststructural Structuralism – New Perspectives for Migration Studies', *Journal of American Ethnic History* vol. 13 (1994), p. 3.

(and often equally, if not more, importantly, forgotten), both by those who undertook journeys and by those who received them. A complex matrix will thus be employed, which considers the relationship of the past to the present incorporating both popular (including museums, films, literature, art, and memorials), political (national and international), and historiographical confrontation with refugeedom in a wider context of forced migration studies.

Directions and Contents

Devorah Dwork and Robert Van Pelt, in their *Flight from the Reich*, having realised 'that the so-called grand narrative could not encompass the story [they] sought to tell', instead 'devised a grid to capture pivotal moments and core issues'. These were 'people, places, papers and problems', which they believed would provide both 'a grand story and a tale of details'. They add that 'If our new narrative form is fractured, so too were the lives of those we study.'[138] The four organising themes of Dwork and Van Pelt's study will feature throughout *Journeys from the Abyss* – each one is core to the modern refugee experience. But this study will incorporate others, including life story, memory, gender, class, age, place and space, legality, performativity, and the politics of naming. Uniting them all will be the nature of the journey which is essential in understanding how refugee *and* non-refugee identities are constructed and reconstructed.[139] Lastly, in this introduction, it is necessary to explain why the case studies that make up the two substantive Parts have been chosen.

Until recently, within refugee studies and migration studies more generally, gender has been neglected.[140] This is true also of the specific area of Holocaust studies. In the last field, the introduction of gender themes has been met by unease and resistance, with the suggestion made that it will lead to a hierarchy of victimhood, most blatantly in the claim that Jewish women suffered doubly under Nazi persecution.[141] The work that has been done tends to be on women's experiences and to focus on the concentration

---

138 Dwork and Van Pelt, *Flight from the Reich*, p. xiii.
139 Gadi Benezer and Roger Zetter, 'Searching for Directions: Conceptual and Methodological Challenges in Researching Refugee Journeys', *Journal of Refugee Studies* vol. 28 no. 3 (2015), pp. 297–317.
140 Castles, 'Towards a Sociology of Forced Migration', p. 28, acknowledges that neglect and lists gender alongside 'the political economy of forced migration' and 'an organizational sociology of humanitarian and refugee agencies' as 'overarching issues' still to be confronted.
141 Dalia Offer and Lenore Weizmann (eds), *Women and the Holocaust* (New Haven: Yale University Press, 1998); Judith Tydor Baumel, *Double Jeopardy: Gender and the Holocaust* (London: Vallentine Mitchell, 1998).

camp experience, marginalising earlier periods of persecution and attempts at finding refuge.[142]

With regards to migration studies, in their 'Feminist Interventions' Ingrid Palmary and her colleagues state that their aim is not to '"add" gender'. Instead, they aim to explore the 'absences, silences and exclusions of understandings of gender that have become part of the production of knowledge about migration while offering new analytic starting points for thinking through the connections'.[143] The purpose of Part 1 of this book will be similar: it will study what was an almost exclusively female movement out of the Third Reich – the possibilities of becoming a domestic servant in places of refugee entry, principally in the United Kingdom. Yet, rather than simply recovering a lost or marginalised aspect of women's history, the approach here is broader. Race, gender, and class interweaved in state and popular responses to the entry and treatment of refugee domestic servants and this neglected movement (which took place largely during the 1930s, though it continued into the post-war era) thus provides an acute insight into the workings of these receiving societies. The core of Part 1, however, is on the agency and experiences of these refugee domestics.

There is a tendency to treat migrant women, especially those subject to forced migration, 'exclusively as victims (of racism, sexism, neo-imperialism, patriarchy, slave-trade)' which 'fixes them in a subject position of fatalistic subjection'.[144] By analysing in depth the testimony of these domestic servants from their earliest days as refugees through to the twenty-first century, and by placing them in the context of earlier and forced migrants linked to (sexual) exploitation, Part 1 will explore how far they could control their own destiny. Did, for example, working and living in 'other people's houses'[145] preclude or encourage the finding of a new place called 'home'? It will conclude by considering the issue of migrant domestics and sex workers in the modern world, again exploring the question of agency and whether it is possible or not to find the voice of these women, past and present.

From gender, Part 2 moves to analysis of age and especially concepts of childhood, both legal and socio-cultural. The specific points of reference are the orphans who survived the Holocaust. As with women, the experiences of the young have been largely overlooked in general studies of migration. One such lacuna is the history of young Serbian refugees during the First World War, which Part 2 will recover and explore as a precursor to those that came fleeing from Nazism.

---

142 Elizabeth Baer and Myrna Goldenberg (eds), *Experience and Expression: Women, the Nazis, and the Holocaust* (Detroit: Wayne State University Press, 2003).

143 Ingrid Palmary et al., 'Gender and migration: feminist interventions', in idem (eds), *Gender and Migration: Feminist Interventions* (London: Zed Books, 2010), p. 1.

144 Alexandra Zavos, 'Gender, migration and anti-racist politics in the continued project of the nation', in Palmary et al (eds), *Gender and Migration*, p. 22.

145 Lore Segal, *Other People's Houses* (London: Gollancz, 1965).

In relation to specific studies of Jewish refugee movements, the journeys of the child survivors *after* the war have been marginalised, especially in comparison to the increasing attention given to the *Kindertransport*, which brought close to 10,000 children to Britain before September 1939.[146] Mainly of eastern European origin, some of these orphans were brought to the United Kingdom in 1945 and 1946 initially to recuperate. Explicitly and implicitly, it was decided by those looking after these children (the youngest of whom came without even a name) that they would be 'remade' in Britain before being retrained to move on elsewhere.

The meanings associated with *place* will be the overarching theme of this chapter: how did the children remember (or forget) their place of birth and then of persecution? What meanings were associated (by themselves and those receiving them) with the places which they first came to in Britain and with those that they then moved on to? The number of unaccompanied forced migrant children has grown in the last decades of the twentieth century and into the new millennium, in 2016 totalling roughly 80,000 in Europe alone. It will consider those that have come through more random, individual journeys, as well as the mass movements of children that have become such a politicised issue in twenty-first century America and elsewhere. This chapter will explore whether changing concepts of childhood have allowed a greater understanding of their situation, and, as with the refugee domestic servants, how issues of agency and the willingness to hear the migrant voice have been addressed.

In both the above case studies the concept and reality of the refugee journey are integrated into the analysis. The third and final case study, in chapter 4, goes further and places the journey – as noted, the quintessential organising theme of this study – at centre stage. The specific reference point is post-1945 and those who attempted to reach Palestine by boat in the last stages of the British Mandate. With their origins in the pre-war period, these journeys became infamous in the wider world, climaxing with that of the *President Warfield* (renamed *Exodus 1947*) in summer 1947. The emphasis here will be on performativity and the storytelling associated with these ships, and how competing narratives were constructed utilising both a deep and a recent past, especially the motif of slavery – Biblical *and* Transatlantic. Place, placelessness, and the disputed space of the sea will feature throughout this case study, with the attempt to control and demonise the migrant as 'illegal' to the fore.

As with refugee children, the number of those trying to find freedom and opportunities through extraordinarily hazardous sea journeys has escalated in the past half century. The Italian island of Lampadusa has

---

146 For most recent work, see Andrea Hammel and Bea Lewkowicz (eds), 'The Kindertransport to Britain 1938/39', *The Yearbook of the Research Centre for German and Austrian Exile Studies* vol. 13 (2012).

infamously become the first point of destination for many African and other migrants, whose desperation is highlighted by the fact that up to half of those who begin their journey die en route if their pre-maritime journeys are included. This case study will conclude by comparing these and other maritime asylum seekers to the Jewish refugees who attempted to reach Palestine before 1948. Were their motives the same and does the colonial/ postcolonial prism separate or unify these hazardous Mediterranean journeys?

Journeys from the Abyss is thus a study which dissects the complexity of both migrant identities and the identities of those receiving them (or refusing to receive them). As the above outline indicates, it explores how the idea of 'the refugee' has been constructed and reconstructed in relation to power in the form of gender, class/occupation, age, place/space, and the territorialization of 'home'. Attention is given to the politics of nomenclature (including what is regarded as legal/legitimate or illegal/ illegimate, and by whom); the relationship between autobiographical praxis and collective story telling; and conflicts with regard to performativity in both the everyday and in more formal cultural production and representation. The aim, therefore, is to produce an intricate and multi-layered narrative from which to understand, contextualise, and demythologise Jewish refugee journeys away from Nazism. And, as with all pioneer comparative, interdisciplinary, and multidisciplinary work, *Journeys from the Abyss* will be challenging. It is thus in keeping with the importance of its wider subject matter of forced migration, which remains a defining issue of the modern era and one that is certain to be even more pressing in the twenty-first century.

Part 1

Gender, Forced Migration, and Testimony:
From 'White Slavery' to 'Trafficking' via Refugee Domestic Servants

Chapter 1

From the 1880s to 1945

Contexts, Historiographies, the Personal

Personal testimony runs throughout *Journeys from the Abyss*. In the following two chapters, however, it is at the forefront, utilising numerous accounts from a variety of genres. It has been suggested by Daniel Bertaux and Isabelle Bertaux-Wiame in their study of bakers that 'one life story is only one life story. Thirty life stories of thirty men or women scattered in the whole social structure are only thirty life stories.' Yet, they continue that

> thirty life stories of thirty men who have lived their lives in one and the same sector of production ... represent more than thirty isolated life stories; taken together, they tell a different story, at a different level: the history of this sector of production, at the level of its pattern of sociostructural relationships.[1]

The heart of these first two chapters is devoted to refugees who came to Britain as domestic servants during and immediately after the Nazi era. The number of accounts explored exceeds those suggested by Bertaux and Bertaux-Wiame, yet it will query whether their positivist approach to creating a 'strong body of evidence' is sufficient to understand this particular refugee experience. Instead, how this testimony was created in relation to context, lifecycle, and individual agency will be the focal points. The approach follows that of literary scholar James Young. As he notes in *Writing and Rewriting the Holocaust* (1988),

---

1 Daniel Bertaux and Isabelle Bertaux-Wiame, 'Life Stories in the Bakers' Trade', in Daniel Bertaux (ed.), *Biography and Society: The Life History Approach in the Social Sciences* (Beverly Hills: Sage, 1981), p. 187.

without understanding the constructed nature of evidence ... and then separating the need for evidence from its actual rhetorical function as that which both naturalizes and is naturalized by a writer's governing mythos, we forfeit a deeper understanding of the interpretation between events, narrative and historical interpretation.[2]

Through such a critical approach to testimony, the fluid and contested nature of identity (individual and collective) will be made manifest. Ultimately it asks how far testimony enables an understanding of migrant identity within the constraints not only of language but also of power – most specifically in this case relating to gender, class, race, and nationality.

Yet, before moving to the particular and the 'personal', a more generic question has to be raised with regard to our subject matter: how do we remember and historicize refugees who, by circumstances beyond their control, are transient and placeless? Which groups become part of local or even global memory and why, when the majority of refugee history remains obscure and forgotten? In 1963 the British Home Office commissioned an internal history of its Immigration and Nationality Department. A mere paragraph was devoted to the Belgian refugees who fled to Britain in 1914 following the German invasion of their country. Half a century on, only a vague, confused but essentially negative official memory remained of this fleeting Belgian presence. This was despite its size: at up to quarter of a million people, it was and remains the largest concentrated refugee movement to Britain. In reality, the Belgians contributed significantly to the war economy and many returned to the continent as Allied soldiers before the end of the conflict. According to the official history, however, the Belgians were

> a persistent cause of concern to the authorities because of their largely indigent state. At this distance, it is difficult to realise what perturbations they must have occasioned since, as it appears that they all with very few exceptions returned to Belgium after the Armistice.

Its final, damning, comment on the Belgians is telling: 'their former presence has left no mark'.[3]

A century on from the start of the First World War attempts have been made to rediscover this lost history, but are hampered by the rarity of memorialisation or other physical reminders of the Belgian refugees'

---

2   James Young, *Writing and Rewriting the Holocaust: Narrative and the Consequence of Interpretation* (Bloomington: Indiana University Press, 1988), p. 37.

3   National Archives, HO 367/3: R.M. Morris, 'Supplementary notes to Mr Eagleston's memorandum "History of Immigration & Nationality Department"', 25 October 1963.

temporary asylum.[4] As early as 1917 a 'Repatriation Committee' had been set up by the Home Office to ensure the prompt return of the Belgians. This was speedily achieved at the end of the conflict, with the British governmment providing the 'carrot' of free passage home and the 'stick' of the removal of any state assistance for those that lingered in their place of temporary exile.[5] Compulsion was generally avoided but in an atmosphere of intensifying and increasingly indiscriminate anti-alienism, the remaining Belgians were not immune from state intolerance. In March 1919, for example, Edward Cosmon, aged 24, was deported to Antwerp simply as 'an undesirable Belgian refugee'.[6] With this swift and often unceremonious ending to their brief stay in Britain, it is not surprising that there are few traces of their presence today. Such erasure is all the more surprising because the refugees had initially been viewed as typifying 'Brave Little Belgium' – victims of the 'evil Hun' who deserved nothing but sympathy. The thousands of committees created to welcome and look after them were testiment to widespread grassroots support.[7] Indeed, recollections of the Belgian presence have lived on for many generations in local but, revealingly, far less so in national or official commemoration.[8]

Contrast this with the intense memory work carried out in relation to the *Kindertransport*. In the Introduction, mention was made of the two rival memorials to this now famous movement of refugee children to Britain before the Second World War. Sharing the same location in one of London's busiest railway hubs, the more prominent of the two, Frank Meisler's *Kindertransport – The Arrival* (2006), has a wider space devoted to it – 'Hope Square'. This is 'dedicated to the children of the Kindertransport who found hope and safety in Britain through the gateway of Liverpool

---

4   See, for example, Denise Winterman, 'World War One: How 250,000 Belgian Refugees didn't leave a trace', *BBC News Magazine*, 15 September 2014, http://www.bbc.co.uk/news/magazine-28857769, accessed 15 September 2014. Rare examples include a marble plaque at Copgrove Church, north Yorkshire, erected by Julius Vissers, a Belgian refugee and stonemason, 'In Gratitude to God and in Memory of the Kindness of the Parishioners'. I am grateful to Margaret Stacey, who alerted me to this memorial.

5   See National Archives, HO 45/10882/344019.

6   National Archives, HO 372/20, deportation order 377272.

7   There were over 2,500 local committees. See *First Report of the Departmental Committee Appointed by the President of the Local Government Board to Consider and Report on Questions Arising in Connection with the Reception and Employment of the Belgian Refugees in this Country* (London: HMSO, 1914 Cmd 7750), p. 36.

8   See, for example, the plaque referred to in note 4 and the sculptures by Jules Tuerlinckx in the building of the Spalding Gentlemen's Society, Glasgow. I am grateful to Michael Honeybone for the latter reference. More generally, see the special issue of *Immigrants & Minorities* vol. 34 no. 2 (2016) devoted to the Belgian refugees in Britain.

Street Station'. Alongside it is an abbreviated version of the wording on a plaque unveiled in the House of Commons in 1999: 'In gratitude to the people of Britain for saving the lives of 10,000 unaccompanied mainly Jewish children who fled from Nazi persecution in 1938 and 1939.'[9]

When these children first arrived in Britain they were subject to much media interest, both nationally and internationally. But for many decades after, their history – like that of the Belgians – became obscure. Unlike the Belgians, however, the *Kindertransport* was rediscovered and, from the late twentieth century, it has become the most remembered and celebrated refugee movement in British history. Indeed, it has become a usable past for those campaigning for and against the entry of unaccompanied migrant children from the continent, especially from the 'Jungle' in Calais since 2015.[10] The increasing focus on the Holocaust as the key point in discussions of morality and modernity might superficially explain why so much attention is now devoted to the *Kindertransport*, not only in Britain but also in North America and elsewhere. For the receiving society especially, as the plaques in the House of Commons and Liverpool Street station illustrate, it has been reconstructed as a fairy story with a happy ending of righteous rescue, in contrast to the fate of the one and a half million Jewish children who perished in the Holocaust. Making the point less than subtly, the version of Meisler's sculpture in Berlin's Friedrichstrasse is entitled 'Trains to Life – Trains to Death'. The children are crudely portrayed and separated, back to back, some going to safety in the West, the others to face certain murder in the East. 'The difference between those groups is accentuated by the vivid, vigorous march forward of the rescued children, cast in brownish hues, in contrast to the almost-black group of desperate and anxious children clinging to each other as they seek comfort.'[11]

The memory of *Kindertransport* has thus now been instrumentalised to present a universal message of what was and, of equal importance, what was not done to help the Jews in their hour of desperate need. Meisler's Manichaean colour coding does not do justice to what was a more complex reality. On the one hand, as will be explored in Part 2 of this study, over 10 per cent of Jewish children survived the Holocaust on the continent. While clearly a horrendous and obscene statistic and a far higher percentage than Jewish adults murdered, it has suited some narratives, as we will see, to suggest that these children who came out alive could be numbered in the hundreds, rather than between 100,000 and 200,000. On the other hand, the

---

9   Author site visit, Liverpool Street Station, 15 September 2007.

10   See Tony Kushner, *Remembering Refugees: Then and Now* (Manchester: Manchester University Press, 2006), chapter 4; and the special issues of *Shofar* vol. 23 no. 1 (2004); *The Yearbook of the Research Centre for German and Austrian Exile Studies* vol. 13 (2012) and *Prism* vol. 5 (Spring 2013).

11   Prinza Rosenberg, 'Foosteps of Memory: Frank Meisler's *Kindertransport* Memorials', *Prism* vol. 5 (Spring 2013), pp. 93–94.

Kindertransportees were often scarred by their experiences of loss (especially of parents and other close relatives) and spacial dislocation and, for some, the adjustments and trauma were too hard to bear. *Kindertransport* memory has become increasingly celebratory, homogenised, and sanitised. It has, in short, become part of a morality tale featuring Britain as 'fairy godmother' helping the children to be 're-born' with all traces of ambiguity removed.[12]

Intriguingly, there were larger movements of Jewish refugees under different schemes during the 1930s which remain largely unrecognised: it is not simply the fact that Britain offered (temporary) rescue to 10,000 young people that has enabled the memory of the *Kindertransport* to be revived and sustained. At the time, officials and refugee organisations were concerned that only the 'right type' of individuals should be allowed entry to Britain and its Empire. More than anything, policy was highly selective.[13] This is true also of the memory of its refugee procedures and forms of entry. A total of 20,000 Jews – the vast majority, bar several hundred, women – came to Britain from Germany, Austria, and Czechoslovakia from 1933 to the outbreak of war to work as domestic servants. In contrast to the *Kindertransport*, there are no statues to their presence or any other form of physical memorial – even though, ironically, many of the refugee children were often treated as domestics or were trained to be such.[14]

There were indeed some who came as (very) young *au pairs* who totally blurred the two categories. These included Elli Adler, who was aged 13 when she came after the *Anschluss* and *Kristallnacht* to Britain from Austria on the Children's Transports. She worked in Bath as a carer for a disabled girl. Elli's treatment in what was a chaotic and primitive nursing home was exploitative and there was 'a point when I was going to run away because it was so horrible'. Dependent on the goodwill of her sponsors, the Society of Friends, and her aunt, who was in England, she did not feel 'entitled to complain. [The sense was] I was lucky to be in England at all.'[15]

In November 1938 the Ministry of Labour began to confront the problem that *au pairs* were being used 'to obtain cheap foreign domestic labour' – one that has revived, as will be explored, since the late twentieth

---

12 Kay Andrews, 'The British Government and the *Kindertransport*: Moving Away from the Redemptive Story', *Prism* vol. 5 (Spring 2013), pp. 54–60.

13 Louise London, *Whitehall and the Jews 1933–1948: British Immigration Policy and the Holocaust* (Cambridge: Cambridge University Press, 2000).

14 For the best-researched and most critically aware study see Jennifer Craig-Norton, 'Contesting Memory: New Perspectives on the Kindertransport' (unpublished PhD thesis, University of Southampton, 2014). In the home for refugee children in Southport, five of the 15 girls were being trained for domestic service. See the 'Harris House Diary', Manchester Jewish Museum.

15 Her written testimony is reproduced in Jewish Women in London Group, *Generations of Memories: Voices of Jewish Women* (London: Women's Press, 1989), pp. 133–154, here pp. 141–142.

century.[16] Its attempt to tighten regulations clearly did not help Elli Adler, nor a 14-year-old refugee who was visited just after the start of the war by Nina Massel, a paid worker for Mass-Observation. Massel recorded in her diary that the young girl was working as a nursemaid and was 'extremely unhappy'. Although mature for her years both physically and mentally, the girl told Massel that she was unable to receive a normal work permit because of her youth. Massel noted that the refugee schoolgirl/nursemaid felt she was 'wasting her time. Then, like all refugees, she [was] intensely worried about her parents.' The teenage refugee's mental state was clearly fragile. Massel said 'She spoke about dying and insanity.' The Mass-Observer, although only a few years older and from the poverty of the Jewish East End, was aware of the experiential gulf between them. She later reflected in her diary that 'I did my best to comfort her, which was not much.'[17] The sad circumstances of this refugee girl are a world away from the confident and carefree *Kinder* represented so clumsily in Meisler's memorial at Liverpool Street station.

It will be argued that a complex combination of gender/sex, race, age, class, and occupation in the case of the refugee domestics has encouraged various levels of forgetting which, in contrast to the experience of the (now sanitised) *Kindertransport*, has been persistent. It was not until 2008, for example, that *AJR Information* (the journal of the Association of Jewish Refugees) acknowledged, following yet another feature on the *Kindertransport*, that

> Far less attention has been focused on another group of refugees, who were admitted to Britain for menial purposes and whose image does not tug at the public heartstrings as does that of the rescued children: the thousands of Jews ... who [came] as domestic servants.[18]

This lacuna has encompassed the receiving society as well as the refugees themselves and their descendants. And it will become apparent that such amnesia has made it very difficult to make comparisons with earlier and later gendered migrant movements to Britain.

In 1941 a retired senior civil servant, Mr A.J. Eagleston, formerly Assistant Secretary of State for the Home Office, was commissioned to write a 'History of the Aliens Branch'[19] which came to be regarded as the 'urtext' for British bureaucrats in the field of immigration control and was a precursor of the

---

16 Memorandum, November 1938 in National Archives, LAB 8/871.

17 Nina Massel, diary entry, 14 September 1939 in M-O A. Massel was an East Ender of East European Jewish origin.

18 Anthony Grenville, 'Underpaid, underfed and overworked', *AJR Information* vol. 8 no. 12 (December 2008), pp. 1–2.

19 Eagleston had slowly worked his way up through the Home Office since 1894 and retired in early 1932. See *The British Imperial Calendar and Civil Service List 1932*

1963 history of the Home Office Immigration and Nationality Department mentioned above. It was a 'classic memorandum',[20] or simply 'the magnum opus!'.[21] As Eagleston's *Times'* obituarist commented, 'He was a repository of much administrative precedent and learning' whose minutes 'had a permanent value to his department'.[22] Within his 'History', Eagleston provided an account of the procedures enabling refugees to come to Britain as domestic servants. It was written at a key point – very close to the refugee influx and before Nazi atrocities against Jews and others had been fully implemented and exposed. Eagleston himself recognised that it was not a heroic narrative, but for this he was unapologetic and unembarrassed. Indeed, his early history gives a strong indication of the reasons why silence on the particular refugee journeys of the domestics was to be so persistent.

Covering the 'alien' influx for the 1930s from a statistical perspective, Eagleston noted the marked increase in aliens admitted for work to Britain from 1936 onwards – 16,390 for that year, rising to 22,347 in 1938. Much of this was due to Ministry of Labour permits for domestics (8,449 in 1936 and 13,792 in 1938).[23] It was for this reason that Eagleston devoted some attention to this singular movement. It is significant that the word 'refugee' is totally absent from his account:

> 'Domestics' … means for practical purposes women who undertake domestic service or work of a similar kind in a private family. They are admitted in large numbers and are treated as a special case *for the simple reason* [my emphasis] that there has long been a shortage of British servants and aliens therefore [are] welcome in this occupation.

In a context in which entry to Britain was severely restricted following legislation immediately after the First World War,[24] Eagleston added that 'With regard to aliens seeking employment as female domestic servants the settled policy [was] to admit them freely provided the wage offered [was] not below £36'. Reversing normal policy, in which aliens had to prove that they had specific and locally unmatched skills (or major capital) to gain entry, the only reason to reject those coming for domestic work was if 'they made untrue statements on landing or there [was] some other special objection'.[25]

(London: HMSO, 1932), p. 192 for his last entry and *The Times*, 26 January 1944 for a brief obituary. A full copy of 'The History' is in National Archives, HO 213/1772.

20 National Archives, HO 352/53: Minute, J.B. Paice, 14 January 1963.

21 National Archives, HO 367/2: Penn to Morris, 6 December 1963.

22 *The Times*, 26 January 1944.

23 National Archives, HO 213/1772: Eagleston, 'History of the Aliens Branch' section on 'Numbers and classification of aliens allowed to take employment'.

24 The 1919 Aliens Restriction (Amendment) Act.

25 National Archives, HO 213/1772: Eagleston, 'History of the Aliens Branch'.

By July 1938, however, Eagleston noted that both the Home Office and the refugee organisations were concerned about 'the abuse of domestic service permits'. While differentiated from what he labelled the 'other evils' of refugee entry because 'there was a real demand for domestic servants in considerable numbers in this country', it was still necessary 'to keep out the undesirable persons who were exploiting the Ministry of Labour permits'. In response, the Coordinating Committee, which consisted of all the large refugee organisations and government representatives, set up the Domestic Bureau. In addition, an attempt was made to insist upon a more robust visa policy on the continent to be implemented by British consular officials when granting alien domestic permits.[26]

In *The Refugee Problem* (1939), published, as noted, at an acute moment of the pre-war crisis, John Hope Simpson stated that

> Great Britain's record in the admission of refugees is not distinguished if it be compared with that of France, Czechoslovakia, or the United States of America. The strictly enforced and selective policy of immigration … has kept the number of admissions to figures that have little significance in the total number of post-war refugees.

Hope Simpson concluded, with more than a hint of heavy-heartedness, that 'Owing to the excessively cautious post-war immigration policy Great Britain has ceased to be a country of asylum on a large scale.'[27]

Writing only two years later, Eagleston reacted with a 'certain shock' to this statement, incredulous that Hope Simpson 'should single out his own country for attack in this way when … he makes no attempt to distribute praise and blame all round'. Yet, rather than go on the offensive by highlighting what Britain did (if restrictionism dominated in the 1920s, it was modified in the following decade and the country, as noted, played a major role for refugees escaping Nazism before the Second World War, especially in the last 18 months of peace), Eagleston merely defended the stringent control of entry:

> The unfairness of [Hope Simpson's] attack upon British immigration policy becomes apparent when it is noted that the author does not mention, and shows no sign of appreciating, the grave reasons (unemployment, density of population etc) which made it necessary to restrict immigration after 1918.[28]

---

26 Ibid. See National Archives, HO 213/107 for Home Office analysis of the visas granted by Consuls.

27 John Hope Simpson, *The Refugee Problem: Report of a Survey* (London: Oxford University Press, 1939), p. 344.

28 National Archives, HO 213/1772: Eagleston, 'History of the Aliens Branch'.

There was a consistency in Eagleston's logic and he was determined to maintain the analysis that all the western liberal democracies during the interwar period followed, in reality, immigration rather than refugee policies – or rather that benevolence in the latter was totally dependent on the self-interest of the former. When Hope Simpson, for example, 'pointedly contrast[ed] the liberality of France to refugees with the restrictive immigration policy of Great Britain', he failed in Eagleston's view to connect this directly to the French need for foreign labour in 'mines, factories and agriculture'. Eagleston wanted credit where credit was due, and this did not apply to interwar France, or, for that matter, to the more open aspects of British immigration procedures during the 1930s:

> There is no particular generosity [Eagleston had initially chosen 'virtue'] in accepting refugees for whom there is both room and crying need in the country's industries, and France is no more entitled to praise on this account than Great Britain is for welcoming capitalists and domestic servants: from this point of view the fact that the numbers are larger in one case than the other is irrelevant.[29]

A case can and will be made that the policy towards the entry of foreign domestic servants during the second half of the 1930s contained both elements of immigration and refugee policy – of pursuing utilitarian procedures and bending the rules to allow entry to those desperate for a place of safety. Indeed, the so-called abuses and 'evils' identified by Eagleston in the bountiful granting of domestic permit visas were a disguised and forgotten part of British consular work by figures such as Frank Foley in Berlin and Robert Smallbones in Frankfurt which have only recently been rediscovered and celebrated. Both these figures were generous in giving out such visas to distressed Jews in these cities of German Jewish concentration.[30] The statement, made in relation to the *Kindertransport*, that 'The motive for the admission of domestic servants was not humanitarian, though it undoubtedly saved lives', thus requires modification.[31] And this is not simply a battle over memory 'now', some three-quarters of a century on: it was something that divided senior civil servants 'then'.

---

29 Ibid.
30 A ceremony and the unveiling of a plaque to Robert Smallbones and his deputy, Arthur Dowden, took place at Golders Green crematoria on 17 October 2013. An earlier plaque in the same location was devoted to Frank Foley, 'who saved over 10,000 Jews while serving as Passport Control Officer at the British Embassy in Berlin'. Author site visit, Golders Green crematoria, 17 October 2013.
31 John Grenville, 'The Kindertransports: An Introduction', in Andrea Hammel and Bea Lewkowicz (eds), *The Kindertransports to Britain 1938/39: New Perspectives* (Amsterdam: Rodolphi, 2012), p. 7. This is vol. 13 of *The Yearbook of the Research Centre for German and Austrian Exile Studies*.

The opening up of domestic permits for refugees, often led by significant figures such as Foley and Smallbones, infuriated Captain Jeffes of Foreign Office Passport Control, who visited the British consular offices in summer 1939. At Vienna he was 'appalled to see the bad type of refugee presenting [refugee committee] cards and Ministry of Labour permits to enter the UK'. Jeffes continued that he

> interviewed several women who produced Ministry of Labour permits for domestic service in England, and who were so filthily dirty both in their person and their clothing, that they were utterly unfit to go inside a decent British home. I think it imperative that something be done to prevent this indiscriminate distribution of permits.[32]

His colleague in Passport Control, R.T. Parkin, objected on more general grounds. Immigration procedures led in practice to 'the better type of refugees, eg professional people, [being] absolutely ruled out at the start, whilst the only ones allowed to come are those who profess that they are willing [to be employed] here for private domestic service'. Parkin added that he believed many had 'no intention of seriously undertaking such work'.[33]

The response of the Home Office was more sanguine. While agreeing that greater control should be exercised in the issuing of permits, and encouraging the refugee organisations to be more discriminating in this respect, greater empathy and realism was present. Sir Ernest Holderness, who was in charge of the Home Office Aliens Department throughout the pre-war Nazi era, patiently outlined the situation to his less sympathetic colleagues. First, Holderness recognised that the Home Office knew 'that many of the women who are coming here on Ministry of Labour permits for domestic service are of Jewish origin and once admitted will have to be allowed to stay here'. Second, and reflecting a sensitivity lacking in many other officials and then employers of these potential refugees (but also an inherent belief in the normality of social stratification) he acknowledged that 'Many of the women are not of the domestic class and we anticipate that they will not be content to remain in domestic service and will probably wish to take up some other occupation.' Indeed, Holderness had a clear sense of what would be a fair compromise. There was in Britain a 'large unsatisfied demand for domestic servants'. With the help of the refugee organisations, the intention was to 'keep the [refugee women] to domestic service for at any rate two or three years'.[34]

---

32 National Archives, HO 213/107: Jeffes to E.N. Cooper of the Home Office, 5 June 1939.
33 National Archives, FO 371/24100 W7740: R.T. Parkin memorandum, 8 May 1939.
34 National Archives, HO 213/281: Holderness to Major General Martelli, Governor's Office Jersey, 4 July 1938.

Ultimately, it was the Home Office and not the Foreign Office that controlled the permits and Jeffes and Parkin remained largely frustrated in their attempts to keep out refugee domestics they deemed 'undesirable'. Even so, their interventions led to the creation of even more intricate paperwork in granting permits. Furthermore, reflecting the underlying prejudice against the *ostjuden* (Jews of East European origin) at the heart of Passport Control's irritation, the refugee organisations, which selected those allowed to come to Britain as domestics, decided definitively in 1939 that they were 'not at present dealing with Polish Jews at all'.[35]

As will emerge, the actual procedures – partly because of Jeffes' and Parkin's intervention – were far from unproblematic from the refugee domestics' perspectives, especially at a time when conditions for the Jews in 'Greater Germany' were deteriorating by the day. Even so, the overall policy contained a greater degree of humanity than Holderness's former colleague, Mr Eagleston, was willing to concede. In 1952 another internal Home Office history on 'The Alien Problem', which was more critical of interwar policy, was produced by a Mr Conlan. Conlan was clearly uneasy at draconian Home Office control of the alien population in the past and how it was 'aimed at eliminating the undesirable, sometimes somewhat ruthlessly. Aliens were deported for no greater offence than failure to notify a change of address within the UK.'[36]

The deportation of Belgian Edward Cosmon certainly falls within that remit. Conlan was also aware that interwar policy was not static and that from 1938 'Humanitarian considerations caused us to relax the Aliens Order in many respects to meet the needs of [the] refugees' from Germany, Austria, and Czechoslovakia.[37] But, much to Conlan's irritation, his document was unread and it is significant that it was the Eagleston 'History' that remained the official point of reference. More widely, the overriding ethos of Eagleston's narrative dominated. It helps explain the general silence over refugees that came to Britain as domestics. It is relevant, for example, that in his more nuanced and balanced account Conlan did not cover the granting of refugee domestic permits, instead mentioning the rescue of children as evidence of greater British openness. Even then, it was only in passing: during the 1950s the *Kindertransport* had largely entered obscurity, but not to the degree of the refugee domestic scheme.[38]

The tendency to sideline or ignore the refugee domestics has continued into the twenty-first century. Even in recent popular memory work celebrating Britain's 'heroes of the Holocaust', with the refugee assistance

---

35 M. Stephany, letter to the Domestic Bureau Executive, 8 March 1939, CBF archives, reel 7.

36 National Archives, HO 352/51: Mr Conlan, 'The Alien Problem', October 1952.

37 Ibid.

38 Ibid.

provided by Frank Foley and Robert Smallbones to desperate Jews, little or no mention is made of them providing domestic permits.[39] As will be illustrated later with regard to the representation/non-representation of these domestics, there is something tarnished and inglorious about this aspect of refugee policy which makes it unsuitable as a usable past in the public domain. It is not, superficially at least, a glorious and valiant story. Indeed, the relegation of these women to a footnote is also to be found more particularly within the specific historiography on refugees from Nazism.

Slow to develop in the post-war era, the literature devoted to this subject has tended to focus on the (male) elite's achievements, followed by the subsequent recognition in their adopted home. Titles such as *Hitler's Gift: Scientists Who Fled Nazi Germany* (2000)[40] or *The Hitler Emigres: The Cultural Impact on Britain of Refugees from Nazism* (2002)[41] illustrate this 'ethnic cheerleader' approach. Tellingly, both volumes feature exclusively male figures on their covers. While these works are aimed at a popular market, the same discourse has also been present in scholarly publications. Thus the first academic books in this area, both published in 1984, bemoaned the 'lack of interest' in the subject, which was 'amazing in view of the economic, cultural and academic impact which the German-Jewish refugees have had on British society'.[42] Many of the refugees from Nazism were indeed highly literate and articulate, and they themselves produced their own foundational history as early as 1951. Just a decade after Eagleston's account, but in the public domain, it provided an overview with a totally different perspective.

Britain's New Citizens, subtitled 'The Story of the Refugees from Germany and Austria', was published to mark the tenth anniversary of the Association of Jewish Refugees in Great Britain.[43] A slim volume,

39 Lyn Smith, *Heroes of the Holocaust: Ordinary Britons Who Risked Their Lives to Make a Difference* (London: Ebury Press, 2013) does not mention domestic servants but instead highlights those involved with the *Kindertransport*. More specifically, there is no reference in Michael Smith, *Foley: The Spy Who Saved 10,000 Jews* (London: Hodder & Stoughton, 1999).

40 Jean Medawar and David Pyke, *Hitler's Gift: Scientists Who Fled Nazi Germany* (London: Richard Cohen Books, 2000).

41 Daniel Snowman, *The Hitler Emigres: The Cultural Impact on Britain of Refugees from Nazism* (London: Pimlico, 2003 [2002]).

42 Marion Berghahn, *Continental Britons: German–Jewish Refugees from Nazi Germany* (Oxford: Berg, 1988 [1984]), p. 1. There are similar sentiments in Gerhard Hirschfeld, 'Introduction', in idem (ed.), *Exile in Great Britain: Refugees from Hitler's Germany* (Leamington: Berg, 1984), p. 5.

43 Anon, *Britain's New Citizens: The Story of the Refugees from Germany and Austria* (London: AJR, 1951). For the history of the AJR through its journal, see Anthony Grenville, *Jewish Refugees from Germany and Austria in Britain, 1933–1970: Their*

sections were devoted to trade and industry, science, and the arts. In this respect, it was a forerunner of more recent works that celebrate the remarkable contribution of refugees from Nazism which have been utilised to bolster self-pride within the group and among their descendants – as well as being a narrative employed by advocates of more recent arrivals fleeing persecution. With regard to the last mentioned, in order to counter xenophobic and racist attacks on asylum-seekers, there has been a desire to show that those granted sanctuary past and present can be a 'credit to the nation': in 'erecting barriers to deny entrance to the country we are in danger of denying future generations the benefits that refugees bring with them'.[44]

Britain's New Citizens was, however, a complex and multi-layered document and it acknowledged different realities – gratitude for lives saved and resulting loyalty to Britain, but also acknowledgment that becoming a refugee was never an easy process. While emphasising that it was not aimed at producing a 'Who is Who in Refugeedom', by listing the many achievements of this movement in the country of their adoption it hoped to 'give some self-assurance to our fellow-refugees'.[45] Yet there was still recognition that the 'success stories' should, in the words of leading Association of Jewish Refugees (AJR) figure Werner Rosenstock, be 'seen in proper perspective'. He emphasised that 'against the few who were successful as scientists or business men stand the many others who have to struggle hard for their living as employees'. Rosenstock thus wanted to pay

> Special tribute ... to the vast army of 'common refugees' who have bravely adjusted themselves to the new circumstances of life, especially to the old ones who, had things remained 'normal', would now have spent the rest of their days in leisure and comfort.[46]

It is revealing that even here Rosenstock had a very gendered interpretation of the 'common refugee'. This 'army' consisted not only of 'former merchants, but also former lawyers and other professionals who could not work any longer in their old field'.[47] It was left to the only female contributor to the volume, Gabriele Tergit, to mention women refugees other than in passing. Ironically, her page devoted to the 'woman as breadwinner' perversely focuses on its impact on the male and how the loss of his prestige

---

Image in the Association of Jewish Refugees Information (London: Vallentine Mitchell, 2010).

44 Katharine Knox, *Credit to the Nation: A Study of Refugees in the United Kingdom* (London: Refugee Council, 1997), p. 4.

45 'Introduction', in Anon, *Britain's New Citizens*, p. 3.

46 Werner Rosenstock, 'The Jewish Refugees: Some Facts', in ibid., p. 19.

47 Ibid.

and status made 'married life very difficult'.[48] Moreover, Tergit made hardly any mention of domestic service – only the vague and oversimplified statement that 'It was much easier for the women to find work', followed immediately by the gendered qualification that 'The highly specialised men seemed suddenly to be worthless.'[49]

The refugee women themselves did not necessarily dwell on what was for many a brief and often uncomfortable period of their lives in Britain. Typifying many, Marion Smith wrote to *AJR Information* some 50 years after her arrival as a refugee stating bluntly that she could not 'think with any affection of the time I spent as a domestic'.[50] Similarly, Edith Argy, reflecting in her nineties of the time when, aged 18, she arrived in Britain from Germany, could only regard it as a 'miserable chapter' in her life. Working in as many as nine different homes in 16 months, she 'found it very hard to adjust. I had never done any housework before. In fact, I was so unhappy and so lonely in my first job that I no longer wanted to live.'[51] Argy's extended testimony will be explored in the following chapter.

In the mid-1960s the AJR launched a 'Thank-You Britain' Fund – a form of memorial to express gratitude to the receiving society. It was not without criticism at the time and subsequently. Rejecting this initiative, a former refugee domestic pursued the logic of Eagleston's private memorandum and, simultaneously, providing a devastating critique of it and government policy during the 1930s:

> I feel England and I are even ... . I have given so much. I do not feel they have done me such a fantastic service, that they have let me in at the last minute ... . Strictly speaking, a refugee should be accepted anywhere. And they have allowed the people in so that they would become domestic servants and do miserable chores. One should not forget that either.

She concluded that 'They have opened the doors for me, but I have enriched them.'[52]

In her anthropological study of these 'continental Britons', Marion Berghahn highlighted generational conflict for those that came as families. She quotes an elderly refugee in *AJR Information* who had observed that 'A girl may have felt resentful that her mother had ceased to be "a lady" and

48 Gabriele Tergit, 'How They Resettled', in ibid., p. 62.

49 Ibid.

50 In *AJR Information* vol. 43 no. 4 (April 1988), p. 13.

51 Quoted in Jennifer Lipman, 'Refugees who escaped to "Downton"', *Jewish Chronicle*, 3 May 2013. See also Edith Argy, *The Childhood and Teens of a Jewish Girl in Inter-War Austria and Subsequent Adventures* (Charleston: BookSurge, 2005).

52 *AJR Information* vol. 20 no. 1 (April 1965), p. 1; Berghahn, *Continental Britons*, pp. 142–143, using interviews carried out in the early 1980s.

was [now] a domestic servant'.[53] Elsewhere, Berghahn reported interviews in which former refugee domestics had worked for Anglo-Jewish families of eastern European background. In one case, Mrs H, the 'mistress' of the house, 'went on and on about how badly Polish Jews had been treated by German Jews'. Berghahn adds that 'Since Mrs H was still young, she did not know what it was all about. "I did not know what to say, so I cried."'.[54]

There were thus many reasons, and others that will be covered below, which explain why there has been silence from these women on their lives as refugee domestic servants. Even so, they have produced a remarkable amount of testimony (totalling at least 200 accounts). Furthermore, it comes in a fascinating variety of genres, crossing many, and was produced at different moments from the 1930s through to the early twenty-first century – in spite (or perhaps even because) of the challenging memories they relate to. But, as will emerge, these narratives have to be dealt with critically – even if in some cases their format is superficially straight-forward, as 'reports' of everyday life or, as one extended and multi-layered autobiography rather misleadingly suggested, 'a simple story recounting the actual experiences of one of the girls whose life was spared'.[55] They are, like all forms of auto/biographical writings, complicated and defy 'rigid forms of classification'.[56] As Mary Chamberlain and Paul Thompson highlight: 'Any life story, whether a written autobiography or an oral testimony, is shaped not only by the reworkings of experience through memory and re-evaluation but always at least to some extent by art.'[57]

Famously, in respect of Indian women and *sati* or widow sacrifice in the eighteenth century, Gayatri Chakravorty Spivak has asked of the archive and wider scholarship, 'Can the subaltern speak?' Spivak is pessimistic: 'As one goes down the grotesquely mistranscribed names of these women, the sacrificed widows, in the police reports included in the records of the East India Company, one cannot put together a "voice".'[58] She concludes that 'The subaltern cannot speak. There is no virtue in global laundry lists with "woman" as a pious item. Representation has not withered away. The female intellectual as intellectual has a circumscribed task which she must not disown with a flourish.' Or, as she put it more basically, 'Clearly, if you are poor, black, and female you get it in three ways.'[59]

53 Berghahn, *Continental Britons*, p. 136; *AJR Information* vol. 14 no. 10 (October 1959), p. 10 letter from Dr Hildegard Forres.

54 Berghahn, *Continental Britons*, p. 232.

55 Myra Baram, *The Girl With Two Suitcases* (Lewes: The Book Guild, 1988), p. 7.

56 Mary Chamberlain and Paul Thompson, 'Genre and Narrative in Life Stories', in idem (eds), *Narrative and Genre* (London: Routledge, 1998), p. 4.

57 Ibid., p. 1.

58 Gayatri Chakravorty Spivak, 'Can the subaltern speak?', in G. Nelson (ed.), *Marxism and the Interpretation of Culture* (Basingstoke: Macmillan, 1988), pp. 294, 297.

59 Ibid., pp. 294, 308.

On the surface, the refugee domestics were also subjugated through class, race, and gender.[60] While not imperial subjects, they came to the metropole of what was still the world's largest empire. If their origins were often (but not always) bourgeois, they were quickly redefined as coming from 'below stairs'. Their Jewishness had forced them to leave Nazi Europe, yet it was something that could still be regarded as problematic in Britain. There was, as upper-class actress Joyce Grenfell put it, when explaining why she did not want to employ a refugee servant, 'something a bit un-cosy about a non-Aryan in one's kitchen; I'm a bit insular, I'm afraid!' This was despite her desperation for a servant and being 'open to almost any one'.[61] With excruciating irony, their 'Germanic' origin could also lead these women to become racialized and discriminated against, especially in the early period of the war, when they were subject to draconian alien restriction. There were also those whose xenophobia was less specific. In 1938, when an MP had suggested to the Home Secretary that refugees should be treated with more sympathy than other foreign nationals applying for domestic work permits, a right-winger responded bluntly that neither category of women should be allowed in: 'down Evesham way we believe in British girls for British homes'.[62]

Gender was also an issue, most blatantly in the form of sexual harassment and economic exploitation. The three categories of race, class, and gender combined intricately yet often in surprising directions. In London a journalist and Mass-Observer analysed the response of her mother, who had employed a refugee maid because it was 'her contribution. We must do what we can at a time like this.' The daughter was amused that her mother's 'class feelings' were with the refugee domestic because of her former status, whereas 'her *English* feelings ... oppose her to the foreigner'. The mother was snobbish towards the other maid under her employ but united in shared national origins. It was a 'kind of triangular balance of forces, with the mistress of the house at the apex'. The Mass-Observer herself was somewhat less torn: 'Our German refugee maid [a widow] is inclined to make her chief virtue her claim on our sympathies: in fact she is damned inefficient.'[63]

What complicates the attempt to categorise further was the possibility of mutability in this singular migration. Hortense Gordon, for example, was the daughter of a German Jewish doctor from Breslau and thus 'used to having servants, not being one'. Despite her background, when she came

60 Gayatri Chakravorty Spivak, 'The Rani of Sirmur: An Essay in Reading the Archives', *History and Theory* vol. 24 no. 3 ((!985), pp. 247–272.

61 Letter of 28 September 1941 in James Roose-Evans, (ed.), *Joyce Grenfell. Darling Ma. Letters to Her Mother 1932–1944* (London: Hodder & Stoughton, 1988), pp. 231–232.

62 Brigadier-General Spears and Mr De la Bere in *Hansard* vol. 335 col. 1419, 10 May 1938.

63 M-O A D5349, 27 October 1939, The Keep.

to Britain she found her place was 'very much in the kitchen'. Hortense left domestic service in 1941 to train to be a nurse and 'Once I changed my status, the whole attitude changed'. Revisiting the house in which she had worked, she was introduced as 'Hortense, who used to be our lady-cook'.[64] If there are resemblances to the subaltern subjects of Spivak, where acts of 'resistance are always already filtered through dominant systems of political representation',[65] critical differences in relation to power and permeability of status have also to be recognised here. They were, as Lucy Delap has outlined, part of the general dynamics of domestic service in interwar Britain.[66] Here, further layers of complexity were added by the refugee presence to what was, as will be illustrated, an occupation already in flux.

Indeed, it is the unstable and fluid nature of refugee domestics' identity and the difficulty of 'placing' them that makes these women such an engaging and revealing case study of external and self-representation. What will follow is especially a study of agency in determining their situation and how this was reflected in the domestics' testimony. But to place this in a deeper and comparative historical context, consideration will be given to an earlier movement of Jewish migrant women whose status was even more marginal and whose voices are far harder to locate: those associated with prostitution and what was perceived as its sinister, global organisation in the form of 'white slavery'. This case study has been chosen carefully: through the nineteenth century and since the last decades of the twentieth century onwards there has been major slippage between those working in domestic service and prostitution. It has been estimated that in the late Victorian period up to 50 per cent of prostitutes had formerly been in service.[67]

Can the Jewish Prostitute Speak?

In December 1908 Jane Cohen, a young Jewish woman born in the Russian empire, was found guilty in London of 'disorderly prostitution' and served with a deportation order to Warsaw. She reappeared eight months later in the port of Southampton, where she was found guilty of being in contravention of the order and given a month's imprisonment before being deported again.[68] These terse and legalistic details are gleaned from the Home Office deportations ledgers, created after the 1905 Aliens Act, which empowered the Home Secretary to remove foreigners he deemed

---

64 Hortense Gordon, quoted in Lipman, 'Refugees who escaped to "Downton"'.
65 Stephen Morton, *Gayatri Chakravorty Spivak* (London: Routledge, 2003), pp. 66–67.
66 Lucy Delap, *Knowing Their Place: Domestic Service in Twentieth-Century Britain* (Oxford: Oxford University Press, 2011).
67 Ibid., p. 183.
68 National Archives, HO 372/3: Home Office deportation ledgers.

'undesirable'.[69] It was this arbitrary power which Mr Conlan of the Home Office later drew attention towards, correctly predicting – as he grumpily left the Civil Service in 1955 – that it might take some time and a different perspective for this unsavoury aspect of British immigration procedure to be recognised and reflected upon critically.[70]

Beyond the bureaucratic archive, slightly fuller indications of Jane Cohen's circumstances are provided by an account of her Southampton court appearance in August 1909. The local paper reported that she was 'a young married woman, who appeared in the dock with a baby in her arms'. Liable to three months in prison owing to the contravention of the expulsion order, Jane Cohen was sentenced 'only' to one month's hard labour. Here the agency of the alien herself came into play, but only in terms of the desire to mitigate her sentence within a legal and moral discourse that underlay the state's efforts to deport. Jane Cohen explained to the court that 'her husband [had] brought her back to the country', hinting at a degree of coercion on the part of her spouse and thereby aiming (and partially succeeding) to gain sympathy from the magistrate.[71]

A much more dramatic scene had occurred in the same port nine years earlier. In June 1898 the *Ionic* left Southampton for Cape Town. On board were notorious white slave traffickers, including the infamous Joseph Silver, and a group of Jewish prostitutes who were under their charge. A police officer from Scotland Yard and the secretary of the Jewish Association for the Protection of Women and Children (hereafter the Jewish Association), were chasing this party and boarded the *Ionic*, but they failed to get the women to leave the ship. Charles Van Onselen, Silver's biographer, comments that 'Scorned, [the two men] disembarked to raucous cheering, hooting and taunts from the pimps lining the upper decks.'[72] The detective later reported to the Home Office that 'it was found that the whole of the girls, some twenty in number, were prostitutes, known to us, who, in company of their bullies had taken passage to Cape Town for the purpose

---

69 *Aliens Act, 1905* (5 EDW.7); Jill Pellew, 'The Home Office and the Aliens Act, 1905', *Historical Journal* vol. 32 no. 2 (1989), pp. 369–381.

70 National Archives, HO 352/51: Conlan, minute of 16 November 1955. Mr P. Conlan was initially a Staff Officer in the Ministry of Home Security before moving to the Immigration Branch of the Aliens Department as a Higher Executive Officer in 1949, a level which he remained at until his departure. See *The British Imperial Calendar and Civil Service List*, p. 239 and from 1945 to 1955 for his career as a whole.

71 *Southampton Times*, 28 August 1909.

72 Charles Van Onselen, *The Fox and the Flies: The World of Joseph Silver, Racketeer and Psychopath* (London: Jonathan Cape, 2007), p. 6. See also the *Annual Report* of the Jewish Association for the Protection of Girls and Women, 1898, p. 20 in Claude Montefiore pamphlet collection, London Library, M124 and Edward Bristow, *Prostitution and Prejudice: The Jewish Fight Against White Slavery 1870–1939* (Oxford: Oxford University Press, 1982), p. 204.

of continuing their mode of life there.' As the women were not forced, there was no action the police could take.[73]

Van Onselen has constructed a remarkable life story of Joseph Silver that incorporates his many careers, here listed largely alphabetically:

> arsonist, bank robber, barber, bigamist, brothel-owner, burglar, confidence trickster, detective's agent, gangster, horse trader, hotelier, informer, jewel thief, merchant, pickpocket, pimp, policeman, rapist, restauranteur, safe-cracker, smuggler, sodomist, special agent, spy, storekeeper, trader, thief, widower, wig-maker and white slave trafficker.[74]

It is the last on which Van Onselen focuses, and he provides an astonishing account not just of Silver's brutality but also of his entrepreneurial flair, exploiting the Atlantic world of trade, migration, and the latest forms of communications. 'Using telegraphic codes known to merchants in the white slave trade they imported prostitutes from Europe at a rate that struggled to keep pace with the demand of local brothels.' This was big business and those gaining from it could be found at a local, national, and global level: 'The Union and Castle shipping lines, whose ships plied the Southampton-Cape Town route, were indirect beneficiaries as pimps and *madams* escorted 'fresh goods' and 'remounts' on the journey south.'[75]

Van Onselen's historical detective work is breathtaking, yet it is notable that in his 600-plus-page account, we hear little of the Jewish prostitutes themselves. In contrast, Silver has had an afterlife not only through Van Onselen but also in historical exhibitions, as well as through popular media. The biographer's account of the *Ionic* in 1898 tells us of the triumph of Silver and his fellow procurers, and the archive record makes clear the frustrations of those trying to suppress the traffic in 'White Slaves', whether the Metropolitan Police or Jewish organisations. We do not know, however, what the 'fallen' women themselves were thinking as the ship left the port. Much like Spivak's female colonial subjects, the voice of the Jewish prostitute is only occasionally heard and then largely through legal records and more rarely, and equally problematically, through the organisations aimed at suppressing their activities.

As the migration of Jews from Eastern Europe and especially the Tsarist empire intensified in the 1880s, middle- and upper-class Jews in the West were confronted with the reality that some of the immigrants were engaged in prostitution – including attempts to organise the movement of women. For the well-established Jews in countries such as Britain and Germany, a dilemma was presented: should the problem be confronted, helping to

73 National Archives, MEPO 2/558: CID Special Report, 'Traffic in girls', 2 May 1901.
74 Van Onselen, *The Fox & the Flies*, p. 11.
75 Ibid., pp. 155–6.

mimimise its extent, or, alternatively, ignored, as it might draw more attention to the issue, which, with luck, might disappear? The decision was made in Britain to take the former path and in 1885 the Jewish Ladies' Society for Preventive and Rescue Work (later the Jewish Association) was formed. It was the first in the world to devote itself to combatting Jewish prostitution and it played a major role thereafter in campaigning against what was a truly international trade encompassing Europe, the Americas, Asia, and South Africa.[76]

For the settled and well-respected Jews it was a risky strategy, but one that they thought on balance had to be pursued. It was justified in 1902 by one of the leading members of the Jewish Association, the aristocrat Claude Montefiore. At this point the 'problem' was escalating on a global level, but his organisation already had a strong reputation for countering its 'evils'. Montefiore noted that while

> the knowledge ... that the traffickers in girls and women were to a very large extent Jews and Jewesses became public property [t]he fact ... that Jews and Jewesses were doing their utmost to combat this horrible trade would be in his opinion be the best antidote for Antisemitism and against the charges levelled by the enemies of the Jews against the whole of Jewry.[77]

As with the Home Office deportation ledgers, however, in the minutes and (public) annual reports of the Jewish Association the women to be rescued from prostitution were rarely given room to speak for themselves. Indeed, the response of the organisation was often similar to that of the British state – that such women should be removed back to Eastern Europe.[78] Significantly, if they were not to be repatriated, the next stage of the Jewish Association's strategy was to retrain the 'girls' as domestic servants. In some cases these two options were combined: in 1904 the Council of the Jewish Association reported that 'One girl, Flora Levy, who has a bad home, has been emigrated and sent to a home in Canada whence she will be placed in service.'[79]

---

76 Bristow's *Prostitution and Prejudice* remains the most thorough overview. More specifically, see Lloyd Gartner, 'Anglo-Jewry and the Jewish international traffic in prostitution 1885–1914', *American Jewish Studies Review* vols 7–8 (1982–3), pp. 129–178 and Paul Knepper, '"Jewish Trafficking" and London Jews in the Age of Migration', *Journal of Modern Jewish Studies* vol. 6 no. 3 (2007), pp. 231–256.

77 University of Southampton archive (hereafter SUA), MS 173/2/3/1: Claude Montefiore, Secretary, in Council Minutes of the Jewish Association, 11 February 1902.

78 Jewish Association, Council meeting, 12 December 1904 where it was agreed to repatriate 'girls' in conjunction with the Jewish Board of Guardians. SUA, MS 173/2/3/1.

79 SUA, MS 173/2/3/1: Council Meeting of the Jewish Association, 11 February 1902.

In the 1890s the 'Objectives' of the Jewish Association made explicit the moral progression required in its rescue work. First, the girls and women at risk would be identified. Second, they would be 'protected' from the 'vice' of prostitution by being befriended and provided with temporary accommodation. The third stage was clear – it was to 'train them for domestic service'. No other employment alternatives whatsover were offered to these 'girls'. This would lead to the fourth and ultimate aim: 'To reform and help them to lead *respectable* [my emphasis] lives'.[80] Domestic service would teach discipline and hard work. It would reverse the disreputable and highly visible occupation that they were previously engaged in with one that was, by its nature, away from the public eye and (largely) acceptable in 'decent' society. Domestic work was thus seen by 'the established Jewish community ... as an effective form of socialization and exposure to middle-class habits'.[81]

A house was set up by the Jewish Association for retraining the 'girls' to work as servants, the success of which was in reality very uneven. Many of the organisation's leaders failed to see why prostitution might be, relatively, a more attractive proposition in terms of remuneration and independence. It was not until 1911 that it was hesitantly acknowledged by its 'Gentlemen's Committee', following several repeated failures to reform their charges, 'that it would be for the welfare of some of the girls to be taught a trade, instead of being placed in service where many of them were liable to be overworked and underpaid'.[82] This message was not one that the senior women in the Jewish Association necessarily wanted to hear. In the Jewish International Conference devoted to 'The Suppression of the Traffic in Girls and Women' held in London in 1910, Mrs L.S.M. Pyke found herself 'constantly asking why the advantage of service' was not more frequently pressed by poor immigrant mothers for their daughters to consider.[83]

While there were exceptions (the 1901 census in Dublin revealed 66 domestic servants out of a population of just over 2000 Jews),[84] East European immigrant Jewish women tended to avoid service – it did not provide enough independence and its very nature made it incompatible with the practice of Jewish orthodoxy because of the long hours, family separation, and absence of kosher food. A more basic objection was cultural. As one female British Jewish philanthropist conceded: 'It is sad to have to

---

80 SUA, MS 173/2/1/3: Jewish Association, General Committee, 22 February 1899.

81 Susan Tananbaum, *Jewish Immigrants in London, 1880–1939* (London: Pickering & Chatto, 2014), p. 154.

82 SUA, MS 173/2/3/1: Mr Cohen of the Gentlemen's Committee reporting to the Council, 22 November 1911.

83 *Official Report of the Jewish International Conference* (London: Jewish Association, 1910), p. 169.

84 Statistics in Harold Pollins, *Economic History of the Jews in England* (East Brunwick: Associated University Presses, 1982), p. 178.

state that among Russian Jews domestic service is undoubtedly considered a degregation.'[85] Thus less than 1 per cent of 14- to 20-year-old Jewish women in a 1913 survey of Jewish Friendly Societies were entered under the category of domestic work – even though it included the additional occupation of waitressing.[86] It remained simply beyond the imagination of most members of the Jewish Association that, for better or worse, these women had *chosen* to enter the sex industry, not necessarily permanently, but because it offered opportunities and independence that service did not. In contrast, the narrative provided by the Jewish Association presented the 'girls' under their control as choiceless victims.

In 1899, for example, its 'Gentlemen's Committee' boasted of the work that had already helped some 655 'girls' keep off the streets. Their fate without the Jewish Association's support was then outlined in melodramatic terms:

> these girls were travelling alone; they were ignorant of the language and customs of this country and, what was still worse, were ignorant of the dangers awaiting them at the Port. The river-side landing stairs, the docks, the railway stations, [were] frequented by men and women who are looking out for these girls.

There was worse to come. These evil procurers

> speak their language and, by misrepresentation, often gain their confidence. On the pretence of safe escort to their destination, or to the ocean steamers by which the girls would continue their journey to other countries, they take them to houses of ill-fame.

The girls were by then beyond rescue: 'Once entrapped, escape is almost impossible.'[87]

Such reports were aimed at a wider public in order to gain financial and moral support for rescue work. Yet, the same analysis was provided in private discourse as well. When the 'girls' were allowed to speak within this archive, it was purely to confirm their status as rescued victims who showed the necessary degree of gratitude for being 'saved'. In the same *Annual Report* in which the fate of the unlucky ones was outlined, a letter from one of the 'foreign girls' to her mother was reproduced with approval. 'You need not be unhappy about me … for I am in a good home, with good

---

85 Miss Adler reported by *Jewish Chronicle*, 1 August 1902.

86 Ibid., p. 249.

87 London Library, Montefiore Pamphlet collection, M131: *Report of the Jewish Association for the Protection of Girls and Women 1899* (London: Jewish Association, 1899), p. 18.

Jewish ladies. Friday night and Shabbos are the same as at home, every Shabbos the lady reads the Bible to us'.[88] The home, whether as place of employment or for the celebration of the Sabbath, could restore the girls' sense of moral fortitude. The religiously purified domestic sphere would help provide safety and then rebirth.

Another rare occasion in which the Jewish prostitute's voice was heard in Jewish Association records was as late as 1927, when an international Jewish conference was held to suppress 'the traffic in girls and women'. At it, a Jewish Association representative related how a young girl had been tricked into white slavery in Buenos Aires. She had sent a letter 'in a trembling hand' to the Jewish Association's agent in this notorious city which stated starkly: 'I am a prisoner, in great danger. Help me.' But to give the story the necessary redemptive ending, the girl was rescued and her abductors were arrested by the police.[89]

It is revealing that in an earlier international conference on the same theme, also held in London but some 17 years earlier, Lady Battersea reported a brief encounter with a group of Jewish prostitutes in the East End. Battersea, one of the founders of the Jewish Association and a member of the Rothschild family,[90] was told by these women to speak to a young, vulnerable girl – Lizzie. Battersea talked to her but did not manage to persuade the girl to leave the streets. Lizzie's reasons were not repeated by Battersea, who instead provided the conference with her own sanguine perspective: 'I hope and trust that she did so ultimately.'[91] Here, in the 1910 conference, the experiential and social divide between these women and the reformers was clearly articulated. It was not, in contrast to Nina Massel's refugee au pair some two decades on, recognised by the earlier observer. The overpowering narrative of the upper-class Battersea in effect rendered the Jewish prostitute mute.

If, in the case of Lizzie, pathos dominated, elsewhere the case files of the Jewish Association reveal irritation and frustration that its support and advice was so easily dismissed. Thus Rachel Pokarerw, who ran away from Warsaw with a man and was found in the streets of London, 'persists in leading a life of immorality'. Similarly, Meral Birkowitch arrived in London from Lodz in the company of a man and 'insisted on going to Mrs Lazarus, known as a trafficker'.[92] Another Warsaw Jew, Fanny Epstein, also ran away

88 Ibid., p. 32.
89 *Official Report of the Jewish International Conference on the Suppression of the Traffic in Girls and Women* (London: Jewish Association, 1927), p. 11, M131, Montefiore pamphlet collection, London Library.
90 Lady Battersea, *Reminiscences* (London: Macmillan, 1922).
91 London Library, Montefiore pamphlets, M528: *Official Report of the Jewish International Conference on the Suppression of the Traffic in Girls and Women, April 5–7 1910* (London: Jewish Association, 1910), p. 22.
92 SUA, MS 173/2/2/5: Minutes of the Case Committee, 15 July 1900.

with a man and ended up running a brothel in Bombay. Her father was convinced that she had been abducted by white slave agents but, typically of many such Jewish female migrant journeys, the subsequent legal enquiry in India found that she had 'come to Bombay of her own accord'. Indeed, the colonial Police Commissioner investigator concluded that 'she gave me the impression of being a somewhat determined young woman and well able to look after herself'.[93]

The dominant discourse in the Jewish establishment presented a far more conspiratorial and monstrous picture than the remarkable – but everyday – stories of global migrant journeys as represented by Fanny Epstein. In 1908 the *Jewish Chronicle* devoted an editorial to the 'Burning Shame of a Terrible Scandal'. The men involved in 'white slavery' were presented as 'human vampires' engaged in 'nefarious practices'.[94] In reality, while there were exceptions, such as Joseph Silver, most of those involved – men and women – were less pathologically damaged or morally corrupt. It took a maverick outsider, the Jewish novelist and commentator Israel Zangwill, to provide a different perspective. In what was an unwelcome and roundly dismissed intervention, Zangwill told the international conference in 1910 that the work of the Jewish Association and other such bodies was pointless unless the wider 'emigration question' was addressed.[95] In other words, this was an issue tied up with the complexity and trauma of mass migration across continents and cultures rather than a story of evil on the loose. Moreover, Zangwill's sympathy with feminism and the East European Jewish migrant more generally enabled an understanding of the Jewish women's agency lacking in other elite responses.

On 11 March 1910 the local ledger of the Southampton Jewish Association reported the arrival in the port of Rosa Witrowski on board the *Aragon*. The details are sparse. 'She was rescued by the Association co-worker in B[uenos] A[ires]. She was taken out there by her intended.'[96] What are we to make of this compressed summary of a distressed life story? In 1987 Lara Marks produced a revisionist article on Jewish prostitution, part of a new, self-confident approach to Jewish heritage and historiography which focused on the world made by East European Jewish migrants from within. Marks, following the more general feminist scholarship of Judith Walkowitz on commercial sex in Victorian society, emphasized that it was 'very difficult for middle-class reformers to fully understand why women took up prostitution and were willing to sell their own bodies'. While

93 Case details in Kenneth Ballhatchet, *Race, Sex and Class under the Raj* (London: Weidenfeld and Nicolson, 1980), p. 127.
94 *Jewish Chronicle*, 30 October 1908.
95 *Official Report of the Jewish International Conference*, p. 68.
96 Hull History Centre, Jewish Association for the Protection of Girls and Women, Southampton branch, 1910.

not dismissing the possibility of the 'entrapment of innocent women', Marks concluded that this was relatively rare and that the 'image of the prostitute purely as victim ignores the social and economic conditions many women faced, and the fact that, for some women, prostitution may have been a matter of choice'.[97] Marks insisted on giving agency to these Jewish women and representing them beyond the actions of the well-meaning philanthropists. In the case of Rosa Witrowski, however, the archive simply does not allow us to know of her circumstances and the role played by force and trickery when she ended up in Buenos Aires. But the record is much fuller in our final case study, that of Raquel Liberman, who also migrated from Eastern Europe to this Argentinian colonial port city. Does, at last, a much fuller and richer archive allow the Jewish prostitute to speak?

Raquel Liberman (or Rachel Lieberman) was born in Berdichev, Kiev, in 1900 and emigrated as a child from Russia to Poland. Married in 1919, she had two sons. In 1921 her husband emigrated in advance to Argentina, settling in a small village in the province of Buenos Aires. She followed a year later. In a tragic story that was not unfamiliar in such migrant journeys, Raquel's husband died in 1923 and she became, in the words of her biographer, Nora Glickman, 'the sole support of her family'. Her situation was more than challenging: 'As a widow, aged 23, with two small children, and with poor knowledge of Spanish, Raquel found little chance to earn a living in a provincial village.'[98]

Glickman, who has also produced a play about her subject, divides her narrative into two parts: 'Raquel Liberman: The Historical Version' and 'The Unknown Raquel'. The former is from the public domain and relates to the life story Raquel constructed for the successful legal proceedings against the 'white slavers' which she helped instigate herself in the late 1920s. In this version Raquel is tricked into prostitution on arrival in Argentina, removing from the picture her husband and children. After four years she buys her freedom from the traffickers but is deceived and blackmailed into returning into prostitution before successfully giving evidence against the *Zwi Migdal*, the society of Buenos Aires' pimps.[99]

---

97 Lara Marks, 'Jewish women and prostitution in the East End of London', *Jewish Quarterly* vol. 34 no. 2 (1987), pp. 6–10; Judith Walkowitz, *Prostitution and Victorian Society: Women, class and the state* (Cambridge: Cambridge University Press, 1980). Marks' work provides a very different reading than that provided by Gartner, 'Anglo-Jewry and the International Traffic in Prostitution'. This article provided an important, pioneer study but presents the women largely as victims through the eyes of the Jewish elite.

98 Nora Glickman, *The Jewish White Slave Trade and the Untold Story of Raquel Liberman* (New York: Garland, 2000), pp. 54–55.

99 Ibid., pp. 53–54. This is briefly told, for example, in Bristow, *Prostitution and Prejudice*, p. 317.

The latter – 'The Unknown' – comes from correspondence between Raquel and her husband before her arrival in Argentina and also from interviews carried out as part of Glickman's research with her grandchildren. Here, the decision to become a prostitute, while a hard one, is taken by Raquel to provide for her children. After four years she was able to save enough to abandon the profession and open her own thriving antiques business. She remarries, but unknowingly (according to Raquel) to a leading member of *Zwi Migdal*, who takes her money and forces Raquel to become a prostitute again.[100] At this point Raquel resists and provides evidence against the organisation, which had previously carried out its extensive business without police interference (in 1929 there were roughly 500 *Zwi Migdal* members who controlled 1000 brothels, employing 3000 women).[101]

The surviving letters between Raquel Liberman and her husband, Yaacov, are remarkable. This is especially true of Raquel's, which as Glickman suggests, 'rescues a lost genre and reveals ... her eloquent voice, her vibrant, clear style ..., her careful calligraphy'. Glickman adds that they show Raquel's 'mastery of the Yiddish language and of Jewish history' and, one might add, non-Jewish literary classics. When begging her husband to hurry up and send her the tickets and money so she can join him in Argentina, Raquel writes of the misery she and her children had experienced living in poverty-stricken post-war Warsaw with her sister's family. By April 1922, Raquel is excited that their separation will soon be over. She writes to Yaacov:

> now, seeing we are leaving, [her inlaws] show respect for me once again. Like the Jews, who were ill-treated and enslaved by the Egyptians, but thought of with respect after they left ... . We'll talk about it later on. Nu, as they say, *sof tov, hakal tov*: All's well that ends well.[102]

Glickman concludes that, through the letters, and the deep concern and love they show between Raquel and Yaacov and also the mutual concern for the welfare of their children, any 'conjecture regarding the reasons that drove her to prostitution is related [only] to her circumstances'.[103] Yet elsewhere the biographer concedes that, while the personal archive she has discovered 'refutes all previous claims that she was forced to work as a prostitute', it remains that 'We do not know the precise circumstances that led Raquel Liberman to seek employment in prostitution.'[104] Raquel

---

100 Glickman, *The Jewish White Slave Trade*, pp. 54–59.
101 Bristow, *Prostitution and Prejudice*, p. 139. Glickman, *The Jewish White Slave Trade*, p. 7 gives the distorted figure of 30,000.
102 Raquel, letter to Yaacov, 20 April 1922 reproduced and translated in Glickman, *The Jewish White Slave Trade*, p. 143.
103 Ibid., p. 94.
104 Ibid., pp. xii, 55.

created a suitable narrative for the legal proceedings which necessitated hiding her 'other' life as mother and widow. It led to a silence that continued within the family until the third generation. The private correspondence enables Raquel to speak, but it is from her life before the migration to Argentina. Her experiences as a prostitute are thus confined purely within legal discourse. In much more dramatic fashion than Jane Cohen some 20 years earlier, Raquel managed to turn the court to her own advantage and to the wider suppression of *Zwi Migdal*. In so doing, she disguised her own agency in how she became involved with organised prostitution. 'The person she showed the public was that of a woman who arrived alone to Buenos Aires, and who was forced into prostitution.'[105]

The *Zwi Migdal* court case of 1929/30 was sensational and was followed locally and internationally and in both Jewish and non-Jewish circles. More mundanely, Edward Bristow notes that it was the 'habit of many prostitutes to practice the oldest profession for three or four years and then give it up'. He adds that 'Rachel Lieberman was such a woman; but for reasons that remain obscure the Zwi Migdal Society tried to retain her.'[106] Nor was prostitution confined to the Jewish sphere. The sex industry thrived in rapidly expanding colonial settings such as Argentina and South Africa, where migrants, as would be the case in other places and in other times, would play a leading role within it as both workers and clients. Thus in Buenos Aires at most one-quarter of prostitutes were Jewish and they worked alongside French, Italian, and other migrant women who were also heavily involved in the trade.[107] There were specific elements which explain Jewish involvement, including clandestine marriages with no legal status or the problem of abandoned wives unable to obtain a divorce. But more important, as Israel Zangwill had perceptively recognised, were the generic factors within migrant journeys of poverty, misfortune, and dislocation, alongside the desire to get on. East European Jews, as one of the largest groups within the mass movement of peoples from the 1870s to the 1920s, were bound to be caught up in its less savoury aspects. And, as with Raquel Liberman, their work as prostitutes tended to be an important but relatively temporary part of their lives and one in which the women themselves had agency. The shame associated with this involvement, however, has led to the suppression of its memory in the Jewish sphere and, more recently, beyond, so as to avoid offence.

Nora Glickman notes that in the court case against *Zwi Migdal* Raquel 'kept secret her legal marriage in Poland, and the birth of her children in order to protect their future'. It is apparent that she partly failed in this ambition: her sons 'did not succeed in freeing themselves of their mother's shady past. The suffering of so many years had shamed them to the point

---

105 Ibid., p. 57.
106 Bristow, *Prostitution and Prejudice*, pp. 321–322.
107 Ibid., p. 313.

of silence.' This was true initially of Raquel's grandchildren, who 'Although they knew none of the details of their grandmother's life ... lived in fear of disclosure'.[108] It is such anxiety which is explored by American–Jewish author Nathan Englander in his novel *The Ministry of Special Cases* (2007). Set in Buenos Aires during the 1970s, it is the era of the 'disappeared', among whom the Jews are prominent, and Argentina's 'Dirty War'.[109] The main character, Kaddish Poznan, is the son of a Jewish prostitute who is employed by the now successful and respectable Jews of the city to literally erase the memory of their parents' involvement in the 'Benevolent Self' – a fictionalised version of *Zwi Migdal*. 'In quieter times it had been enough to ignore and deny.' But these were not quiet times and 'being accepted one day doesn't mean one will be welcome the next'.[110] Banned from the synagogue and even Jewish burial rights, the pimps and prostitutes created their own spaces. Kaddish and his son earn their money from the separate Jewish cemetery, chipping away from the tombstones the names of those both in the past and present regarded as 'unclean'. Out of financial necessity Kaddish continues his work, but it is not labour that he welcomes. He seeks reassurance from a friend of the same heritage, who tells him: 'In every people's history there are times best forgotten. This is ours, Poznan, let it go.'[111] Kaddish, however, is not ashamed of his family's involvement in prostitution and will not deny it. Ultimately, *The Ministry of Special Cases* proves that such surface erasure cannot remove the past.

In her afterword, Raquel Liberman's biographer ends on a note of cautious optimism. After discovering the archive of letters, photographs, and documents Raquel's grandchildren 'came to realize that [she] deserved to be vindicated in the history of immigrant women, and understood as a wife and mother who provided for the sustenance of her family'. They are now the 'faithful voices of their grandmother's plight, and they are now beginning to talk with clarity'. Writing in 2000, Glickman concluded that 'One should hope that soon the literature written on this subject will be radically modified.'[112]

Englander's well-received and well-researched novel also suggests that progress has been made in 'normalising' the wider story of Jewish involvement in 'white slavery', including that of the prostitutes and the pimps. It still remains the case that heritage sites in port cities which have an intimate connection to the narrative presented here, which include the London Jewish Museum (reopened after major government and private funding in 2010), Southampton's SeaCity Museum (2012), and the Buenos Aires Immigration Museum (2013), are *all* silent on Jewish prostitution. The

---

108 Glickman, *The Jewish White Slave Trade*, pp. 57, 59.
109 Nathan Englander, *The Ministry of Special Cases* (London: Faber and Faber, 2007).
110 Ibid., p. 4.
111 Ibid., p. 7.
112 Glickman, *The Jewish White Slave Trade*, p. 59.

exception is the Bremerhaven Emigration Centre and its 2012/2013 exhibition, 'The Yellow Ticket: Traffic in Girls 1860 to 1930'. While still largely reliant on archives which tend to silence the Jewish prostitute, 'The Yellow Ticket' put the issue of agency at centre stage: 'Were they forcibly abducted, tempted by fantastic promises or did they go voluntarily?' The overarching aim was to give 'a closer view of the lives of the unaccompanied emigrant girls'.[113]

It is telling that the Bremerhaven Emigration Centre provides a challenging history of its subject matter that gives an alternative, inclusive perspective rather than disguising the colourful underside of the town's vibrant past as the major port for European transmigrancy until the mid-twentieth century.[114] Prostitution was equally important and notorious in Southampton,[115] but instead the SeaCity Museum has focused on the tragic story of the *Titanic* and the local impact on the working-class dock community. While a neglected aspect of this maritime disaster, it is now comparatively safe territory and one that does not expose the lawlessness and diversity of a classic sailortown port.

Other than in Bremerhaven, the lingering unrespectability of the Jewish involvement in prostitution and white slavery has ensured that it is a past that dare not explicitly speak its name. Thus in the successful BBC television Victorian heritage detective programme *Ripper Street*, a figure closely modelled on Joseph Silver who drugs innocent young women before crating them to Argentina is presented initially as Victor Trumper. It emerges that he is in fact Victor Silver, but it is the surname alone that he has in common with the notorious 'white slaver'. The fictional character is an English, non-Jewish, aristocrat.[116] While the Cape Town Jewish Museum, in its pathbreaking exhibition 'The Jews of District 6' (2012), has provided brief space for Silver and the 'seamier side of life',[117] it remains that this, *The Ministry of Special Cases*, and 'The Yellow Ticket' are still rare incursions into a difficult past. Indeed, it is one not totally free from danger. While the evocative museal recreation of Jewish life in the cosmopolitan world of District 6 is subtitled 'Another Time Another Place', websites still exist in the twenty-first century aiming to prove, by instrumentalising the history of white slavery, that Jews are an innate sexual danger to society.[118]

---

113 Irene Stratenwerth, *Der Gelbe Schen: Madchenhandel 1860 bis 1930* (Bremerhaven: DAB, 2012) for catalogue and related essays.

114 Author visit, Deutsches Auswanderer Haus, Bremerhaven, 15 December 2014.

115 See Walkowitz, *Prostitution and Victorian Society*, chapter 10, which compares Southampton and Plymouth.

116 'What Use Our Work?', *Ripper Street*, BBC 1, 24 February 2013.

117 'The Jews of District 6: Another Time Another Place', Cape Town Jewish Museum, November 2012 to April 2013.

118 For example, the websites 'Four Winds 10' and 'Jewish Tribal Review'. See http://www.forwinds10.net/sirrun_data/health/abuse/slavery/news.php?q=13618946 and http://www.rense.com/general132jewsandwhiteslavery.htm, both accessed 6 March 2014.

The Nature of Domestic Service

The purpose of revisiting the pre-history of refugee domestic service through Jewish involvement in prostitution is not to muckrake an embarrassing past for scurrilous purposes. Instead, the intention is to provide a foundation from which to study another marginalised history of Jewish female migration in which questions of agency and voice are equally crucial. Moreover, chronologically it followed closely from the international demise of 'white slavery' from the early 1930s, in which the successful legal proceedings against *Zwi Migal* provided a symbolic turning point. When represented either through elite interventions or in subsequent culture, the dominant image of the Jewish prostitute has been as choiceless and hapless. Thus, in terms of representation, rather than Nora Glickman's multi-layered and reflexive study of Raquel Liberman, Isabel Vincent's popular account of her and two other women controls the market place. *Bodies and Souls: The Tragic Plight of Three Jewish Women Forced into Prostitution in the Americas* (2006) is a study solely of pathos and victimhood.[119] The same has been true with regard to the domestic servant in Britain, even though the reality has often been far more complex. Carolyn Steedman, for example, has argued that a model from the Victorian age emphasising marginality, poor conditions, and sexual exploitation is not applicable for domestic service in the Georgian era.[120] As Lucy Delap notes, a 'similar comment might be made for the twentieth century, in which the melodramatic account of nineteenth-century service as a site of victimhood has persisted'.[121] But, before turning to the refugee domestics' testimony, a brief summary is necessary to explain the dynamics of an occupation that 'has served as a foundational narrative amongst the stories British people tell about the twentieth century and its changes'.[122]

Domestic service remained the largest occupation for women in Britain before the First World War, its continuing importance emphasising the limited alternative work available. After 1918 working-class women, having experienced a wide range of employment and higher wages during the First World War, were generally reluctant to return to service. Yet, although it was often remarked that, before the conflict, the problem for the employing classes was the quality of servants and after, the quantity, in reality the situation was somewhat different.[123] The reinstatement of male workers

119 Isabel Vincent, *Bodies and Souls: The Tragic Plight of Three Jewish Women Forced into Prostitution in the Americas* (New York: Harper Perennial, 2006).
120 Carolyn Steedman, *Labours Lost, Domestic Service and the Making of Modern England* (Cambridge: Cambridge University Press, 2009).
121 Delap, *Knowing Their Place*, p. 4.
122 Ibid., p. 2.
123 Violet Firth, *The Psychology of the Servant Problem* (London: C.W. Daniel, 1925), pp. 11–13.

and widespread poverty pushed women back 'below stairs'. The 'feminisation' of domestic service that had developed in the nineteenth century was thus ongoing and reflected lack of choice. Typical was Edith Edwards in Cheshire, who 'stressed that she only entered domestic service in 1929 because "we were very, very poor"'.[124] She was not alone: from 1921 to 1931 the number of domestic servants in Britain increased from 1.1 to 1.3 million. The number was still rising at the start of the Second World War, and this occupation remained almost totally female,[125] representing nearly a quarter of employed women in the interwar period.[126] Even so, that this fraction had gone down from one-third, as measured in 1901, reflects the wider range of work now available to women. The quantitative growth of service in the interwar period, however, reveals the gender limitations of the job market. While the women made the most of the situation, domestic work was rarely one of choice, explaining the volatility of employment patterns.[127]

Demand still went beyond supply and it was this gap, the so-called 'servant problem', that enabled the space for alien workers to operate. By 1931, for example, 10 per cent of the 111,000 foreigners employed in Britain were German and Austrian servants.[128] As with prostitution, it reflected a wider international, racialised and gendered pattern of labour migration, forced and voluntary. Immediately before the First World War one-eighth of all immigrants coming to America were domestic servants. After 1918 and the introduction of stringent controls, the possibility of escaping poverty in Europe via this route disappeared and 'live in' domestics were largely replaced by black female 'day workers'.[129] Within the continent of Europe, there was a small internal market for domestics which was undermined by the dismal economic climate.

As Steedman and Delap emphasise, domestic service in Britain was notable for its dynamic nature. While it is the aristocratic stately home that has become the site of remembrance of domestic service (including, as we will see, that of refugee involvement), after 1918 the large majority of servants were located in small middle-class households with only one or two employees. This reflected a new demand within fast-expanding suburbia and exurbia in which status and status anxieties played a leading role. Within such homes, it has been suggested, 'the really intense antagonism

124 Quoted in Selina Todd, 'Domestic Service and Class Relations in Britain 1900–1950', *Past and Present* no. 203 (2009), p. 185.

125 A. Chapman and R. Knight, *Wages and Salaries in the United Kingdom 1920–1938* (Cambridge: Cambridge University Press, 1953), pp. 215–217.

126 Leonore Davidoff, 'Mastered for Life: Servant and Wife in Victorian and Edwardian England', *Journal of Social History* vol. 7 (Summer 1974), p. 410.

127 Todd, 'Domestic Service', pp. 181–204.

128 1931 statistics in National Archives, LAB 8/871.

129 David Katzman, *Seven Days a Week: Women and Domestic Service in Industrializing America* (New York: Oxford University Press, 1978), pp. 272–273.

seems to have been felt between mistress and servant'.[130] It was also here that the demand for servants was most acute.

Although the internal labour market continued to grow, there were still opportunities for foreign workers, as the 1931 statistics indicate. From 1933 Jewish and other victims of Nazism would join other 'aliens' seeking opportunities as domestics in Britain. In the early years of the Third Reich there was as much continuity as change in those granted Ministry of Labour permits. Only slowly and incompletely did it emerge as a distinct scheme of entry with particular emphasis on and procedures for refugees rather than 'foreign nationals' as a whole. The change was formalised in summer 1938 by the creation of the Domestic Bureau in Britain – as noted, a partnership between the Home Office and the refugee organisations – and concomitant training schemes in Greater Germany. Announcing this subtle shift, Sir Samuel Hoare, the Home Secretary, told the House of Commons in May 1938 regarding foreign domestics, 'In the case of refugees admitted to this country, sympathetic consideration is given to the question of allowing them to take employment.' Even then, it had to be proved that the employer was 'unable to obtain the services of a person in this country for the post in question'.[131] But, taking the figures for the year from April 1937 to March 1938, it is notable that while close to half those granted permits came from Austria the second largest nationality was Swiss, representing almost twice those from Germany. Women from the Scandinavian countries – 1159 – totalled just under the German number and, as with those from Switzerland, they were not refugees. Furthermore, a good number of those coming from Germany and Austria at this point were not Jewish or from other persecuted groups.[132] Only by the end of 1938, when the Jewish position was becoming desperate *and* the Nazi government encouraged 'Aryan' domestics to return home, was the balance fundamentally altered in favour of refugees.[133]

In February 1939 a new magazine was launched dedicated 'to the housewife that's thrifty'. Its first issue included a breezy and cheerful article 'Your opportunity! The Case for the Foreign Maid'. Accompanied by a photograph of two smiling, dirndl-wearing young frauleins skipping with mountains in the background (uncannily predicting the iconic poster for *The Sound of Music*), its advocacy seemed irrestible. On the one side was the problem of unsatisfied demand:

130 Delap, *Knowing Their Place*, pp. 5–6.

131 *Hansard* (HC) vol. 335 col. 1419, 10 May 1938.

132 Written answer from the Minister of Labour, Mr Brown, in *Hansard* vol. 335 cols 1250–1251, 9 May 1938.

133 See Traude Bollauf, *Dienstmaden-Emigration Die Flucht judischer Frauen aus Osterreich und Deutschland nach England 1938/39* (Vienna: Lit Verlag, 2011), pp. 100, 106 and National Archives, FO 371/22541 W17162: letter from Nevil Bland to Viscount Halifax, 20 December 1938.

Maids have become so difficult to find and keep nowadays, especially if you happen to live in the sort of place that can't boast more than one good cinema, that it is no wonder that the servant problem is discussed round nearly every afternoon tea table.

Sooner or later, someone is bound to say to you, 'But why don't you get a German refugee?' Or an Austrian, or a Czechoslovakian, as the case may be.

On the other side were the merits of this form of supply: strong, hard-working girls who could cook, be happy in remote locations as they came from small towns or the country, would look attractive in their national dress, and, as an additional bonus, could help children to learn a foreign language.[134]

As with the entry of refugees as a whole during the 1930s and specifically the entry of foreign domestics, there was confusion within this article relating to the identity of these prospective workers. The title, illustration, and description of what to expect reflected a stereotyped image of a young (non-Jewish) Austrian – 'a stalwart young alien who insists on throwing all the bedding out of the window to air on the front lawn'. It was a picture of the 'foreign maid' who had been a growing presence in the British household since the 1920s. Yet there was also an acknowledgment, if not a fully convincing one, that these 'girls' now being promoted were somehow different – they were refugees in distress. Trying to put self-interest aside, altruism was suggested as another (if less convincing) incentive to employ:

> you can have the satisfaction of knowing that, while you are helping yourself to a good maid, it is in your power to do a wonderful work of kindness by rescuing a young Jewish girl from unhappiness and persecution in her own country.

Immediately, however, the labelling switched back and the article concluded by returning to the question of supply: 'How exactly do you set about getting a foreign maid?'[135] The reader was told that 'You won't find it difficult' and given details provided by the Domestic Bureau that suggested that within less than a fortnight a Home Office permit could be obtained and, not long after, 'the girl herself'.[136] Perhaps the curious expectations articulated in *Housewife* are best summarised through the memories of a former refugee domestic. Marion Smith recalls her mistress requesting that 'she would like me to wear *dirndls* with matching aprons when assisting the butler at table'.

---

134 *Housewife* mo. 1 (February 1939), p. 28.

135 Ibid., pp. 28–30.

136 Ibid., p. 30. It suggests that the Domestic Bureau had encouraged the article but there is no direct evidence of a link in the minutes of the Domestic Bureau in CBF archive, Reel 6 File 38 for early 1939.

As Marion drily noted, 'In 1938 Berlin *dirndls* were not easy to find but my mother patiently scoured several large stores and eventually managed to find two'. She felt 'rather stupid' wearing them, but 'Obviously, my mistress had considered this the correct uniform for a German maid.'[137]

The perspective from those trying to obtain a domestic visa was far less certain and sanguine. Edith Argy eloquently outlines her tense situation in post-*Anschluss* Vienna. With Europe and America closing its borders, 'what was a family like us, with no money and no connections abroad, to do?' Her father and step-mother were anxious that she should leave 'and it became known that England needed domestic servants'.[138] Jewish organisations in Greater Germany with resources from abroad, and aware of tightening regulations, provided training in domestic work for prospective refugees. Edith remembers attending 'a course that was to prepare me for my new career: a bit of cooking, a bit of waiting at table, a bit of ironing, some tips on cleaning a house efficiently.' Perhaps with the hindsight provided by her time as a servant, in which she changed positions with remarkable frequency ('I had more jobs in those 16 months than in my entire subsequent working life'), Edith concluded that 'Alas, it was all wasted on me. Only that you always needed to serve from the left stuck in my mind.'[139]

It was as well that Edith left Vienna in September 1938. From May 1939, under pressure from trade unionists and uneasy civil servants such as Captain Jeffes, the Domestic Bureau insisted that permits would be granted only if applicants had passed a test in approved German and Austrian Jewish training schools.[140] This followed the Home Office and Ministry of Labour in effect delegating 'the adequate selection and inspection of candidates' to the Domestic Bureau earlier that year.[141] It remains that the large majority of these refugees who came to Britain were unprepared for their new careers.[142] Having had expectations raised so high, the *Housewife*'s readership may well have been disappointed had they had subsequently employed a refugee domestic. In what was an already tense arena, the refugees' lack of relevant experience added another area of potential conflict on both sides of the 'servant problem'.

Nor was Edith's bureaucratic path out of Austria anything like as simple as suggested by 'The Case for the Foreign Maid'. Through an advert placed in an English national newspaper Edith obtained an offer from a family in

---

137 *AJR Information* vol. 43 no. 4 (April 1988), p. 13.
138 Argy, *The Childhood and Teens*, pp. 127–128.
139 Ibid., pp. 128, 131.
140 University of Warwick Archives, TUC archive, 456: Domestic Bureau minutes, 1 May 1939.
141 Domestic Bureau minutes, 24 February 1939 in CBF archive, Reel 6 File 38.
142 The leader of the Cambridge Refugee Committee, Margaret Burkill, claimed that only 2 out of 500 women were suitably prepared as servants. Imperial War Museum refugee tapes, no. 4588.

Southsea. A permit was granted by the Home Office which then allowed her to apply for a visa from the British Consulate in Vienna. This was when

> the queueing began. The Nazis made it as difficult and as humiliating for Jews to leave as they could. They insisted on this certificate and that, purely out of chicanery. Everywhere, there were endless queues. I spent days gathering all the paperwork needed and, of course, my British visa, and the French transit visa.[143]

Early in December 1938, weeks after the scheme that would become known as the *Kindertransport* was announced in the House of Commons, the first arrivals came to Britain. The children were greeted at the ports and especially Liverpool Street Station by journalists from the newspapers, newsreels, and radio. While the story was then obscure for half a century, striking material in print, image, and sound was created for subsequent memory work.[144] While the Domestic Bureau had at exactly the same point 400 block permits to issue each week,[145] this was a scheme that promoted *individual* refugee journeys and ones that received no media attention at the point of arrival. Even so, the *collective* element within the refugee domestic story must not be downplayed.

Within Greater Germany word of mouth within networks of kith and kin, information provided by Jewish organisations and publications, and retraining courses created general awareness of the possibility of domestic work in Britain. So too did the past tradition (especially in Austria) of such female employment migration, which made it seem less alien as a way out of Nazism. Indeed, British domestic employment agencies had thrived in Germany and Austria from the 1920s.[146] International refugee bodies, especially Jewish and Quaker ones, helped locate positions and from 1939 the Domestic Bureau vetted those applying for permits. This provided structure and support. In essence, however, the process of getting a post was a matter between prospective employee and employer. In the place of refuge itself, the refugee domestics took comfort in each other's company where this proved possible. As will be explored shortly, a minority became organised within the trade union movement and worked to further their body as a whole. It remains that domestic service was, by nature, noted for its isolation. This was even more the case than prostitution: testimony from former East End Jews suggests the integration of Jewish prostitutes in everyday life during and after the period of mass immigration. One of

---

143 Argy, *The Childhood and Teens*, p. 128.
144 See, for example, 'Their First Day in England', *Picture Post*, 17 December 1938.
145 Domestic Bureau memorandum of 26 January 1939 in 195/910/454, TUC archive, University of Warwick.
146 National Archives, LAB 8/92.

them recalls how her mother told her that she 'mustn't do that yourself but if that's what you are [you should not] ostracise them'. Indeed, she remembers how a prostitute friend of her sister was invited in for tea by her mother.[147] For the refugee domestics, however, as with their journey to Britain, working life was experienced alone. It is why the focus here will be on how individuals have constructed and reconstructed this neglected movement through their testimony both contemporary and beyond their years in service.

Lucy Delap has emphasised how 'Twentieth century servants were not a silent class, but were articulate, vocal, and active participants in the presentation of service.'[148] She qualifies this statement by adding that there have been few contemporary accounts produced by domestics: the bulk of autobiographical material that is now available was inspired by the social history movement from the 1970s onwards and was articulated through local publishing projects and oral history initiatives.[149] In the case of the refugee domestics, it is also the case that the bulk of their testimony has come from the last decades of the twentieth century in either written or audio form, and was prompted by similar historiographical impulses. There is, however, a surprising amount of earlier writing, including from the time of their attempts to reach Britain. The analysis which follows breaks this testimony into four broad chronologies – the 1930s, the 1950s/60s, the 1980s and the 2000s – to chart continuity and change in narrating the refugee domestic experience.

Early Refugee Narratives

The first and most desperate form of autobiographical writing from the refugees, or would-be refugees, came in the form of newspaper and other adverts in British papers and in applications for posts. By necessity brief, typical were those in the *Manchester Guardian*, the newspaper most sympathetic to the Jewish cause during the Nazi era. Indeed, with regard to domestic service, in July 1938 it had carried an anonymous article entitled 'The Refugee Housekeeper: First Year' by 'J'. Not disguising that there had been 'some difficulties', the educated background of the 'German Jew' – a former economist – was seen as a good thing, as she had 'something of our own interests'. While the refugee domestic was unable to understand the logic behind the appropriateness or otherwise of certain cutlery for the table or for the kitchen, and other such pressing issues of bourgeois propriety,

---

147 See Lara Marks' interview with 'FS1', 28 September 1987, London Jewish Museum, no. 431.
148 Delap, *Knowing Their Place*, p. 8.
149 Ibid., pp. 22–23.

overall she had proved hard-working (a way to 'drown her worries') and reliable. And, differentiating itself from the article that appeared later in *Housewife*, 'J's' article concluded that there was only one disadvantage of taking on a refugee housekeeper: 'thence forward one is inescapably aware of the misfortunes of Europe's persecuted minorities'. This, however, was ultimately a good thing: as a result it was now impossible 'to cultivate wilful blindness'.[150]

Yet the title 'Refugee Housekeeper' indicated the tension inherent in the scheme. Even the most sympathetic treatment of the Jewish maids had still to take account of employer/employee realities. The pleas for posts in the *Manchester Guardian* were to be found in a section labelled 'Refugee Advertisements', contrasting with those in *The Times* and *The Telegraph*, which were within generic 'Situations Wanted'. Even so, the juxtaposition of 'Refugee' and 'Advertisements' reveals the two-ness inherent within this particular international migration market. One, from a Viennese woman able to provide 'best references', read 'Good cook, confectioner as well, experienced in all household duties, needlewoman, well mannered, Seeks post: able to act as housekeeper'.[151] Carefully constructed, her advertised skills conformed to the virtues highlighted by *Housewife* magazine. Another was written by a refugee already in Britain working as a domestic: 'Wanted, Position for my Sister, still in Vienna, perfect in house and needlework'.[152] Both of these were published in April 1939, when the search for a place of refuge, six months after *Kristallnacht*, was particularly acute.

Anonymous, these advertisements were tailored, like those for refugee children – 'Guarantee and Hospitality in Good Family sought for pretty, well-educated, healthy 8-year-old Girl' – to those who it was hoped would open their home, whether as foster parents or employers.[153] These notices provided truncated curriculum vitae to portray the ideal child or the perfect domestic. By being framed within the border of 'Refugee Advertisements' self-interest could be melded with philanthropy and altruism for the employer: 'J', for example, with the birth of her daughter, needed a live-in domestic if she 'was to go on working'.[154] These three- or four-line and typographically dense self-descriptions highlight the ambivalence fitting for a memorial to the refugee housekeepers who were caught between seeking asylum and the restraints of domestic service. Each one reflected the unique anxieties of each person trying to get out. Yet, grouped together in their own section of the national and Jewish newspapers, they meld with little variation in form or content.

---

150 'J', 'The Refugee Housekeeper: First Year', *Manchester Guardian*, 13 July 1938.
151 *Manchester Guardian*, 4 April 1939.
152 *Manchester Guardian*, 22 April 1939.
153 Ibid.
154 'J', 'The Refugee Housekeeper'.

These lists do not have the potential for sentimentality that has now overtaken the representation of the *Kindertransport*. They convey, however, the dire nature of the Jewish plight on the eve of conflict *and* the ambiguity of British responses to it. And a foundation for such alternative memory work has been laid. In 1988 Zoe Joseph's self-published history of Jewish refugees in Birmingham – a superb example of 'people's history' of that decade – featured the 'Refugee Advertisements' on its front cover. At a more commercial level, Lucy Lethbridge's *Servants* (2013) utilised this grassroots intervention for a general audience, integrating the refugees into a 'downstairs view of twentieth-century Britain' and understanding the poignancy and desperation of these requests for posts.[155]

The pathos inherent in such notices was even more intense within the records of the Jewish refugee organisations. Few of these survive or are available to the public, but those from the Manchester Jewish Refugee Committee include a file with many hundreds of examples. Details such as age, gender, and skills mirror those of the newspaper advertisements, except that the English is less polished – 'firm in all household duties, cooking and baking very good references'.[156] What further distinguishes these applications is that they were accompanied by a name and, occasionally, personal details ('42 years of age, divorced 2 children').[157] Most evocative is the attachment of photographs to the forms. These were also used with prospective child refugees, providing a visual equivalent of the 'pretty' eight-year-old in the *Manchester Guardian* advertisement. Indeed, the 'selection' of the *Kinder* was highly gendered, and 'less attractive' boys often found themselves at a serious disadvantage.[158] Similarly, photographs in the individual files of domestic applicants cannot be regarded as being without a wider, disturbing significance. These were not simply neutral passport-style images. One applicant, for example, Rosa G, aged 20, was photographed from the side to emphasise her attractive figure.[159] In an occupation firmly associated with sexuality – suppressed or otherwise – some applicants could use their looks and age to obtain a post.[160]

Sadly only a minority of these case files within the Manchester Jewish Refugee Committee records were matched up with employers. Many women

---

155 Zoe Josephs, *Survivors: Jewish Refugees in Birmingham: 1933–1945* (Oldbury: Meridian Books, 1988), front cover and p. 138; Lucy Lethbridge, *Servants* (London: Bloomsbury, 2013), p. 240 and more generally chapter 20, 'Of Alien Origin'.

156 Johanna W, case no. 820 in Barash papers, Manchester Central Reference Library, M533, Box 9.

157 Ibid., Else F, no. 23.

158 Leslie Brent, *Sunday's Child* (New Romney: Bank House Books, 2009), p. 40.

159 Rosa G, no. 822, Barash papers, M533, Box 9.

160 Delap, *Knowing Their Place*, chapter 5 on sexuality; Todd, 'Domestic Service', pp. 200–201 on the male of the household still making major decisions about servants, hence the possibility of utilising sex appeal.

were rejected because of the age restrictions – the lower limit was 18 and the upper 45. Others, disastrously, because of the regulations and paperwork required, did not manage to come to Britain before the outbreak of war. One such tragic case was that of Marianne Hellman from Prague. She applied for a domestic permit in July 1939 and while a permit was granted by the Domestic Bureau, along with one for her two sons, a technicality delayed the accompanying visa. Her husband, Fritz, simultaneously applied for and was given a transit visa but did not want to leave without his wife and children. Once war was declared the Home Office refused to allow the family permission to enter Britain – in spite of support from the Central Office for Refugees within the Domestic Bureau. Marianne and her two sons, Peter and Robert, were subsequently murdered in Auschwitz, having earlier been incarcerated in Terezin concentration camp. Fritz survived but was refused entry after the war. As a Home Office civil servant minuted in August 1945 with cold legal precision: 'There is no British interest in this case.'[161]

Some, with family responsibilities – especially elderly/infirm relatives – or hoping to find more attractive possibilities of refuge, did not take up the permits. All in all, as few as half of those given 'green cards' to come to Britain as domestics had actually arrived by the summer of 1939, declining to around 15 per cent at the outbreak of war.[162] Others were simply rejected. In the end, roughly 7000 came on Ministry of Labour permits and between 12,000 and 13,000 under the Home Office scheme.

In the advertisements and refugee files, if the subaltern speaks, it is for a distinct audience appealed to on grounds of pity ('Tragic couple in Prague, must leave, urgently desire Posts')[163] – or ability ('German–Jewish couple, 34, 28, seek position in domestic service; excellent appearance; healthy; trustworthy; well-educated, both expert photographers; wife perfect all housework, cooking, good needlewoman; husband reliable Chauffeur – Manservant, bookeeping').[164] With regard to the last notice, it is far from certain that employers would necessarily have regarded academic achievements and photography as desirable assets. One young refugee recalls that she was shouted at by her 'mistress': 'You are no use to us playing the piano or speaking a few languages.'[165] 'J' enjoyed the flute playing of her

---

161 National Archives, HO 382/25: J. Hughes minute, 21 August 1945.
162 See National Archives, FO 371/24100 W7740: R. Parkin memorandum, 8 May 1939, for general figures of permits and arrivals. Covering the period from 31 December 1938 to 16 May 1939, the Domestic Bureau stated that of 6330 green card permits, 3226 had arrived. See Domestic Bureau minutes, 19 May 1939. By the outbreak of war, however, of the 14,000 who came as either 'list cases' (11,000) and 'special cases' (3,000) only 15 percent had not come. Domestic Bureau minutes, 22 September 1939 in CBF archive, Reel 6, File 38.
163 *Manchester Guardian*, 22 April 1939.
164 *The Times*, 3 January 1939.
165 Frances Goldberg, 'Memoirs', p. 8, Manchester Jewish Museum.

refugee housekeeper, but many other employers would have resented any reminders that their servants were better educated or more cultured than themselves.[166] It is equally unlikely that in reality the photographer couple and many of those advertising in this way possessed all the domestic skills they professed. There are hints in the advertisements of previous professions cruelly destroyed – such as the refugee economist employed by 'J' – but in general the would-be domestics created a persona that was required of them and one that did not reflect their past lives or current reality.

Self-advertisements were one important way of obtaining a post. Contacts in Britain – however obscure – were another. The personal archive of Gertrud Landshoff, a widow in Berlin who was born in 1896 (and was thus close to the upper age limit for refugee domestics) provides a unique insight into how these contacts were exploited. In addition, it reveals how she shaped her life story to fit the expectations of her potential employers in Britain and generally maximised her chances of a post. Gertrud not only preserved copies of the letters she sent in late 1938 applying for various posts but also kept drafts of them (translated from her own German), improved by those helping her to master the English language. Each phrase and detail was carefully considered to present a picture of herself as having the right skills *and* the right attitude to become a good domestic. With regards to the latter, they include a balance of gratitude and awareness of what would be expected of her.[167]

Her widowed and childless status gave Gertrud greater freedom to consider the domestic service option, as she did not have close relatives to worry about. But being on her own left her vulnerable and the energy she put into applying simultaneously for several positions is clear: coming to Britain on a domestic visa was her only viable option. Her agency in crafting these applications comes to the fore. While she mentioned her career as an administrator in her husband's law business following training in a commercial school, Gertrud put greater emphasis on how she looked after her ailing father for many years and did 'all the cooking'. Aware that she might be seen as unlikely domestic material because of her bourgeois background, Gertrud stressed that she understood 'all household work and am ready to undertake anything in that line'.[168] To further enhance her suitability, her letters were accompanied by an endorsement from the rabbi of the Reform Jewish community of Berlin.[169] Gertrud, in fact, received several offers of posts, choosing in the end one in which all the necessary paperwork had been obtained by her future employer – a vicar and his wife in Cambridgeshire. She was lucky that they had been persistent in

---

166 'J', 'The Refugee Housekeeper'.
167 See London Jewish Museum, Landshoff papers, 1995/20.
168 London Jewish Museum, 1995/20/45: Draft application letter to Mrs Canon Raven, 20 November 1938.
169 London Jewish Museum, 1995/20/48: Dr B. Gottschalk.

chasing the permit from the Home Office when it was 'so much pressed with similar requests from so many people'.[170]

The notices, letters of application, and self-portraits within the refugee files were necessary but not sufficient to gain entrance to Britain. Taken on their own, they reveal only a distorted fragment of the life stories of these women. Fortunately there is other contemporary material that allows more space for the refugee servants to 'speak' for themselves. The nature of domestic service meant that, once in Britain, there was little time for anything but work. Family back home, however, was the issue that occupied much of their anxieties. And it is through letters to relatives – especially parents – and others that another form of refugee literacy practice or everyday writing was made manifest.

The genre of immigrant letter writing is a largely neglected but important one.[171] From the second half of the nineteenth century improvements in transport meant that correspondence could be carried out on a regular and generally reliable basis even if loved ones were thousands of miles away. For those such as Raquel and Yaacov Liberman it meant that intimate relationships could be maintained across continents. More practically, such letters provided details about the emigration process. Although Raquel's are particularly eloquent, they are a reminder that proper consideration needs to be given to the complexity of such autobiographical expression. Here, two examples of those who were or wanted to be refugee domestics will be analysed to show how these letters conform to the pattern of other migrant correspondence. Nevertheless, they possess unique characteristics relating to the particular circumstances of Nazi persecution in the last months of peace which define them through time and space.

The first was from Hronov, Czechoslovakia, from Karl and Lenka Bermann, the mother and father of a five-year-old Jewish child, Tommy, who went to Scotland on the *Kindertransport*. Sent in June 1939 to Tommy's foster parents and in reply to their letter telling them that he had settled in well, it expressed gratitude as well as subtle advice on the parenting of their child. The loss that is part of any migration is powerfully evoked: 'We are extremely longing for the child, the house is as quiet as the grave and we are very lonely.' Immediately, however, the specific circumstances are made clear: 'we bring the great sacrifice of parting with the child to save him perhaps from great suffering'.[172]

Details are then provided 'about us for we may well imagine even you would like to know whose child you have in your house'. Written by Lenka,

170 London Jewish Museum, 1995/20/54: Mrs Raven to Gertrud Landshoff, 4 December 1938.

171 See, for example, Gur Alroey, *Bread to Eat & Clothes to Wear: Letters from Jewish Migrants in the Early Twentieth Century* (Detroit: Wayne State University Press, 2011).

172 Letter reproduced in Bertha Leverton and Shmuel Lowensohn (eds), *I Came Alone: The Stories of the Kindertransports* (Lewes: The Book Guild, 2000 [1990]), pp. 34–36.

the letter explains the Bermann's background and how she was the daughter of a doctor and her husband a successful factory manager. The purpose was two-fold: first, it was intended to highlight the Bermann's respectability and how Tommy had come from a good home; second, it was an opportunity to extol their virtues as potential migrants. The latter part of the letter was in many ways a longer version of the refugee advertisements that appeared in the national broadsheets and Jewish press. Both had permits to go to America, but they knew that it would be years before their quota number came up: 'Therefore we should like to go to England if it were possible.'[173]

Lenka knew that it was 'very difficult to get a permit there', but had been told in a letter from an Austrian cousin in London that the only way of entry was through a 'position in domesticity'. This she would

> gladly take as I can lead the most pretensious [sic] domesticity, perfectly cook and bake ... I have secretarial training, but I was very much engaged in the domesticity and now I have attended many special courses such as cold meat, English cookery and I have learned to make Carlsbad wafers. Next time I shall send you a sample as Tommy likes them as well.

If this was a thinly disguised request for a position, there was also awareness that it would be much harder for Karl to get a permit to enter Britain. Although he was an expert in his field of textile manufacture, 'Alas! We do not know in which way he will be able to make use of his qualifications.' She added that 'I cannot leave him here until he would get a permit.' They did not succeed in getting out and were subsequently murdered in the Holocaust. Tommy became a professor in aquatic science and settled in Israel.[174] Part love letter to her son, part a deeply felt thank you letter, part family memoir and part a plea for a post, it is a testament to the acute dilemmas facing those attempting to flee Nazism whose families had already been dispersed. Showing the Bermanns' reliance on the goodwill of their son's foster parents, it provides a dimension lacking in the refugee advertisements. Nevertheless, barriers to free expression are still evident – partly through writing in a second language but also through the conventions of good manners which restrained Lenka from asking directly for a domestic position.

A different form of constraint operated in the second letter to be explored, written by two refugee domestics, Inge Ader (20) and Marta Hertz (25), to their families in May 1939. Working in a wealthy Jewish home in north Manchester, they outline the damp conditions and cold house

---

173 Ibid., p. 35.
174 Ibid., pp. 35–37. Tommy Berman (he removed the second 'n') died in an accident in the Galapagos Islands, aged 79. See the obituary in *Haaretz*, 18 April 2013.

in which they wore multiple layers of clothing to keep warm: 'a woollen
vest, 3 woollen underpants, 2 jumpers and a dress'. The house 'for our
German taste is furnished in quite a horrible fashion, lots of nick-nacks,
artificial flowers ... awful red carpet on the floor'. Full of clutter – 'because
nothing must be thrown away' – the work was 'tiring because dishes, silver
etc are kept in different places and rooms'. The Faust family consisted of
five members, the mother being of nervous disposition and the father
moody and with 'a liking for Marta from the first day'. One son was in
an institution and the other, although 17, had the mental age of a three-
year-old and 'would come out of his room, stark naked, jump at us [and]
start spitting into our faces'. The daughter was spoilt and stole from the
young refugees.[175]

Having outlined this early Jewish Mancunian version of the 'Addams
Family', what followed was a detailed summary of their daily routine:

> at seven two alarm clocks go off ... Marta dashes to start the fires,
> clean the shoes, dust, sweep. Inge cleans the dining room, prepares
> 3 breakfast trays, lays the table for the house guest. Thereafter, the
> cleaning, cooking – towards half past ten Mr Faust has his breakfast. 1
> o'clock lunch – then the big clearing; at half past one we go to our rooms,
> write or sleep a bit. Half past three we make sandwiches – teatime is
> approaching. After tea we work for the family: darn stockings, iron or
> bake a cake. At seven supper has to be ready: after half past eight we
> are free. If we ask whether we can have a bath – Madam reminds us
> not to be wasteful with the water.

Not surprisingly, the two domestics looked for other posts. The letter ended
by stating that Inge had obtained one in London and that Marta was hoping
to follow. Ominously, Inge's place was being taken by another refugee. No
doubt the dysfunctional Fausts found it hard to get local servants to work
for them.[176] In later testimony Inge stated that she complained about the
Fausts to the local Jewish refugee committee, who said that they 'knew
everything about the family, they *are* awful'. Yet overriding that reality was
the Committee's desire to 'give more permits to Jewish girls, why should
they die in Germany?'[177]

Given the grotesque nature of this description, it seems remarkable that
Inge remembers that self-censorship had taken place. 'As not to worry our

---

175 Marta Herz, Inge Nord, letter to their mothers, 22 May 1939. I am grateful to Inge
    Ader (nee Nord) for sending me a copy of this letter and to Andrea Reiter for its
    translation.

176 Ibid.

177 Inge Ader, interviewed by Bea Lewkowicz, 4 June 2003, AJR 'Refugee Voices
    Audio-Visual Teaching Archive'.

mothers too much we did not mention in this letter the unfair treatment we received; we never had enough food, Mr Faust often appeared in our rooms without knocking (the door keys had been removed), the working hours were even longer than stated.' Looking back half a century later, Inge concluded that she 'was of course very grateful to be in England, but it was "Servitude"'.[178] Inge was not alone in masking the truth for close relatives back in Germany. Charles Hannam came to Britain on the *Kindertransport*. His sister came earlier on a domestic permit and 'It seemed that Margot was not nearly as happy in her place as a maid servant as her letter home had suggested. She told Charles 'I just didn't want to worry Father ... it must be bad enough for him to have to go on living in Essen, so I just tell him everything is lovely.'[179]

Returning to Inge and Marta, it is hard to believe that their mothers would have been reassured by this disturbing communication, beyond relief that their daughters were leaving this deeply unpleasant home. The letter combined various functions, including gothic horror to entertain wider family and an outlet for their misery and anger to the figure who traditionally provides support and reassurance – the mother. It provides a remarkably graphic account of the hardship of their situation with an immediacy lacking in many later accounts. While we learn nothing about their past and how they got to Manchester, the letter is a rare example showing the relentless and exploitative nature – sexual and menial – of domestic service, whether refugee or not. It also shows the importance of solidarity for those refugees who were lucky enough not to be alone in this occupation. If taken together, the letters of Lenka, Inge, and Marta (and Margot's experience as referred to by Charles Hannam) show the competing forces facing these Jewish women: agency/resistance and dependency/hopelessness; gratitude and frustration; and relief at coming to Britain but fears for those left behind. They show the relative freedom of the young women to take up domestic service as against the older woman's marital commitments. These binaries not only restrained their life chances but also impacted on their ability to write about them without inhibition.

For Inge and Marta, the ultimate form of revolt was (beyond in this case parodying their employers), as for many domestics in interwar Britain, to seek new posts. In contrast to British servants, if they were not free before the war to take up other occupations, they could at least attempt to find less exploitative positions. Other refugees went further, however, and were part of the organised struggle to improve conditions in domestic service. In July 1938 the Trades Union Congress sponsored the formation of the National Union of Domestic Workers. Its leader, Beatrice Bezzant, was initially hostile to the arrival of foreign workers. They were, she

178 Inge Ader, letter to the author, 11 February 1988.
179 Charles Hannam, *A Boy in Your Situation* (London: Andre Deutsch, 1977), p. 164.

argued, through cutting wages and working longer hours, 'making the bad conditions in domestic employment even worse'.[180] Although there was no evidence this was happening, it was still widely believed within the world of service.[181] But, through the campaigning of refugee activists, some of whom had been trade unionists in Austria, Bezzant slowly came round to providing some support and allowed them to be members on an individual basis.[182]

While many refugee domestics found themselves physically isolated, those in the big cities were able to combine either through clubs or, in the case of London, the creation of their own hostel. It was especially women linked to the left-wing Austrian Centre and Austrian Self-Aid who linked up to the union and created a wider dialogue.[183] Through the hostel in London and the Hampstead Club of the Austrian Domestic Workers the refugees constructed their first collective writing. These were clumsily typed and copied leaflets entitled 'Our English colleagues and us' and 'The first breakfast', as well as a short-lived journal 'Our Paper'.[184]

All these publications, written in relatively strong English, were aimed equally at refugee and British domestic servants. They explained the rights of servants regarding pay and conditions of work, highlighting the importance of solidarity and explaining to the British worker that, alongside the same problems,

> most of us are still worse off. Why [is] that? Because we are expelled from our homeland, because our families are scattered all over the world, because we lost our friends, because for some time we lost our home, our mountains, our forests, our lakes ...

Even then, an attempt was made to connect all domestics through a crude Marxist analysis of their plight: 'the reason for all [this] is Hitler and the ten thousand upper class people, the masters of the mines and the big industries, the landlords and the big bankers'.[185]

Promoting refugee agency was key to these papers: 'As England has given us asylum we are most grateful. But it is on us to do as much

---

180 University of Warwick Archives, TUC archives 54/76 (4): Bezzant to Franklyn of the Domestic Bureau, 20 December 1938.

181 National Archives, LAB 8/92 for the absence of evidence concerning a negative impact.

182 University of Warwick Archives, TUC archives, 54/76 (7): Minutes of National Union, 8 July and 9 December 1941.

183 Marietta Bearman et al, *Out of Austria: The Austrian Centre in London in World War II* (London: Tauris, 2008).

184 These are all located in University of Warwick Archives, TUC archives, 54/76 (4) and are dated early in the war.

185 'Our Paper' in ibid.

self-aid as possible.' The authors of 'Our Paper' were aware that it was written by 'only a few of us' and they urged that its second issue 'must be a collective work', as 'Everything we can gather of the Austrian people's resistance against the brown barbarism gives us more strength to overcome this difficult time.'[186] The Austrian Centre and related organisations were an important part of the cultural and political life of those who regarded themselves more as 'exiles' than 'refugees'. For them, and their German equivalents, the long-term future was in a new Austria and Germany.[187] It is doubtful, however, whether the majority of refugee domestics subscribed to their Communist worldview. Nevertheless, as with Inge and Marta's letter, these contemporaneous documents provide rare insights into the everyday nature of being a servant for those used neither to the occupation nor the peculiarities of British household management.

In 'The first breakfast' the tone is more comic than class warfare in describing two refugee domestics struggling in the kitchen and failing to cook bacon. Producing burnt toast and other shrivelled offerings, its author tells her 'lady' that this 'is the way they do the bacon in Vienna'. English politeness comes to the rescue: 'Oh, it looks lovely', said the lady'. As with Inge and Marta's description of their daily routines, while much is revealed of the 'foreignness' of their work, there is careful editing in this contemporary account when presenting the refugee domestic. In 'The first breakfast' there is not only a desire to entertain through the farce of two strangers left alone to cope with an antiquated British kitchen but also the impulse to render the newcomers less threatening by their incompetence. Against this a counter-narrative opens the description. While not annotated by the author, it hints at a different reading, thereby questioning the inherent kindness of the mistress:

> 'You have to get up at 7 o'clock in the in the morning. I'll wait for you in the kitchen.' These were our lady's last words. Very tired from the long journey we went to bed. Half asleep I got up once more to get our alarum clock out of one of the suitcases … . At 7 o'clock sharp we were in the kitchen.[188]

The emphases and silences and, most critically, the ambiguity and conflicted feelings expressed in the contemporary autobiographical writings examined so far reveal the articulacy of the refugee domestic servant. If there is not full freedom to give testimony because of the restraints of audience – whether prospective employers, family, or co-workers – beyond the refugee advertisements there is a depth that is absent and irrecoverable in the case

---

186 Ibid.
187 Bearman et al., *Out of Austria*, chapter 9.
188 'The first breakfast', TUC archives, 54/76 (4).

of the earlier Jewish prostitutes. Indeed, for some refugee domestics, as with 'Our Paper', the issue of agency and resistance was self-consciously raised. The last two examples in this sub-section will allow further exploration of these issues in extended forms of autobiographical writing: the first memoir and the second diary.

It has been shown how self-censorship was at work with Inge and Marta's joint letter in order not to upset relatives still at 'home'. A different form can be detected in Theodora Bernstein's 'Warning to My Beloved England'. A journalist in Vienna, she lost her job following the *Anschluss* and came to Britain as a domestic. Her account of 'Hitler's reign of terror' in Austria and its impact on the Jews was accepted by the London publisher Harraps. Following the invasion of Holland in spring 1940, however, it was 'shelved indefinitely' – perhaps an early victim of the anti-alien panic that gripped Britain and which climaxed with mass internment. Typewritten in English, its power comes from the unresolved tension within the manuscript between her personal struggle to come to terms with the past and the desire to communicate a wider, more redemptive message to a British audience. It expressed both gratitude to the country of asylum and a warning about its lingering complacency concerning the danger of Nazism.[189]

While Theodora started by stating that 'Slowly I am beginning to feel that I can look back and think calmly' about the past two traumatic years, the events were still too close for this to be achieved.[190] Britain, or more often England, as she would have it, is presented as the antidote to Nazism, but one that for all its virtues cannot quite come to terms with the poisonous impact of Hitlerism. The initial setting is one of quintessential Englishness, the fireside of a historic stately home and the location of domestic service in wider memory. But while it was 'true that I am sheltered by the roof of a unique 400-year-old Tudor house', Theodora cannot be at ease because her heart was 'so full of the horrors of the past'.[191] The fact that she is not a guest but a servant in this ancient pile is not yet revealed to the reader.

'Warning to My Beloved England' reveals her journalistic talent in her description of the atmosphere of panic among Austrian Jewry following the *Anschluss*: 'We were always active, always on the desperate search for an entrance permit to some country.' As the situation worsened and borders closed, all options were considered, belongings were abandoned, and, with the chances of escape diminishing, 'We had long given up the idea of trying to keep together.'[192] The desire to help family is a strong feature of later refugee domestic memoirs. Theodora's account highlights the near

---

189 Imperial War Museum, 96/55/1: Theodora Bernstein, 'Warning to My Beloved England'.
190 Ibid., p. 1.
191 Ibid.
192 Ibid., pp. 89–95.

impossibility of doing so, leading to the global dispersal necessitated to escape:

> how in heaven's name should we be able to help each other when we were scattered to the four corners of the earth? How could we help when one of us would be starving in America, another slaving as a domestic in England, and a third pining away in China ... ?[193]

Theodera's hope was to go to America. Her friend, Eva, however, had come to Britain as a domestic and Theodora began to realise that this was the only realistic way she too could get out. Her account shows the problems of paperwork even when granted a permit, but this is blamed on the Nazis and not on the receiving society: 'They commanded me, on the one hand, sternly and threateningly, to leave the country as quickly as possible, while, on the other hand, they did all in their power to prevent me from doing so.'[194] Dealings with the police in Austria 'were too frightful'. In contrast, 'that the English policeman smiled was in itself a miracle for me'.[195] The nightmare of gathering documentation in Austria and being told endlessly 'Come again tomorrow' is juxtaposed with the official 'resembl[ing] a quiet dreamy scholar' who 'registered my arrival in England'. Some form is missing from her file, but she is told 'Perhaps we can manage without it'. Theodora thanks the Englishman for his understanding and is told 'that is what we are here for – to help'.[196]

It is in this context of idealised Englishness that the author describes or, more accurately, fails to describe her experiences as a domestic servant. The decision to take this way out of Austria was partly prompted by Eva. As a gregarious person, Eva had found the isolation of English domestic service alienating. Theodora comments 'What an ironical trick of Fate, that she, who was so full of life, and loved to have people around her, should be transplanted to some desert.' Yet Eva had written to Theodora: 'all in all this 'new profession', the accounts of which had so frightened us, is quite bearable. People are understanding, and treat us well. They don't demand the impossible.' The letter ended with stern advice to Theodora: 'be sensible. Drop your Parisian plans. You will never get there.'[197]

The closeness to the events and literary talent evident in 'Warning to My Beloved England' reveals acutely the dilemmas of a woman in Theodora's position: 'Drop your plans ... Drop your plans ... Become homeless ... Become a maid-servant. Thus hammered my brain; thus the

193 Ibid., pp. 121–122.
194 Ibid., p. 198.
195 Ibid., p. 5.
196 Ibid., pp. 36, 124.
197 Ibid., pp. 151–152.

winter rain whipped against the window-panes; thus ticked the clock.' She remained nervous, however, of domestic service, which was utterly foreign to her: 'my body, unaccustomed to such work, how would it re-act? How should I recover my passport? How should I overcome all the countless difficulties?'[198] Still uncertain of whether it would be 'a good thing for me to go to England as a domestic', her boyfriend also urged her to go. He tells her 'anything is better than staying on here' and reassures her that it will be only temporary and that he will find a way for them both to get to America.[199]

The moment of departure is powerfully evoked by Theodora, highlighting the loss but also the pitiful nature of the refugees. The author was probably aware that her British audience was still unsure of the genuineness of those they were offering (temporary) asylum to:

> The scene of the last painful duty of the emigrant in his homeland was the luggage hall of the big Viennese Railway station. It was overcrowded. The few earthly possessions which the emigrants hoped to take with them were examined carefully piece by piece.[200]

Yet, in contrast to the detailed and moving description of persecution and resistance in Vienna, Theodora's treatment of her 'new life' in England is relegated to two sentences. Being a domestic was 'less dark and less difficult than I had feared and expected'. This she put down to the inherent decency of her hosts and, following the same pattern of the Austrian Domestic Workers, the importance of self-agency: 'I have not only to thank the fine, hospitable British, but also my determination to pull through.' She then ends with a universal warning about the danger of nationalism, which, at the moment at which the mythology of 'Britain alone' was born, may further explain Harraps' decision not to publish the memoir.[201]

Theodora Bernstein's account is thus notable for what it does and does not reveal about her feelings and experiences of being a refugee domestic. It is significant that in her narrative she unburdens herself only to a 'magnificent English dog' who spends 'many hours in my room [where] I tell him … about my life'. It is through her communication with this hound that Theodora tries to convey the dislocation she has experienced: 'He knows that my present work is somewhat different from my real profession, and understands that I am sometimes very tired, and often sad, when I think of my friends who are scattered far and wide'.[202] Subtly,

---

198 Ibid., p. 152.
199 Ibid., p. 177.
200 Ibid., p. 172.
201 Ibid., p. 199; Angus Calder, *Myth of the Blitz* (London: Jonathan Cape, 1991).
202 'Warning to My Beloved England', p. 26.

the intended British reader is being asked whether they fully comprehend why the Jewish refugees left and what this entailed. While her memoir has frequent references to this 'fine and hospitable land',[203] there is an underlying impetus to confront British naivety about Nazism. Anything that smacked of overt criticism or ingratitude is excluded – hence Theodora's less positive experiences of being a domestic are brief and relegated to a canine conversation. Criticisms can be found, but the reader has to read between the lines to find them. And, even then, they were speedily followed by a description of Nazi persecution and wider Austrian collaboration. Theodora writes of observing the humiliation inflicted on a Jewish woman being forced to scrub the Viennese streets while freezing water was thrown at her by a supportive crowd.[204] English domestic work, for all its drudgery and exhaustion, is a world apart. Britain remains the epitomy of civilisation, fairness, and, through the granting of refugee permits, generosity.

Theodora Bernstein's autobiographical writings were intended for wider consumption but ended locked away from the public eye. She retrained as a chiropodist and committed suicide in retirement during the 1970s: perhaps the loss of her homeland and vocational calling finally caught up with her. The manuscript was deposited in the Imperial War Museum in the 1990s, reflecting a new willingness to move beyond a narrow, Anglocentric approach to the Second World War and its run-up. Belatedly, a limited audience had been found for her memoir.[205]

The final contemporary document was, in contrast, written for the private sphere, suppressed by the author for 60 years and then published in 2002. It provides the most intense and sustained contemporary 'voice' of the refugee domestic and one largely free from the more blatant constraints of audience operating on her fellow writer, Theodora Bernstein. Both were in their early 20s when they came to Britain as refugee domestics, but in substance, style, and outlook their autobiographical writings are markedly different. Hanna Spencer (nee Fischl), a teacher of assimilated Jewish background and academic training (she had a doctorate from Prague University), was born in the German-speaking part of Czechoslovakia. She came to Britain as a domestic in March 1939 aged 22. Her boyfriend Hans Feiertag, a composer, was non-Jewish and in 1938 he went to Germany, forcing them to live apart and, for his safety, to keep correspondence between them indirect and innocuous. Hanna then started writing her diary at Hans' suggestion in the hope that they would be reunited 'so that he might catch up with me'.[206] The possibility that there would be a joint 'later on' became to Hanna 'almost …

203 Ibid., p. 9.
204 Ibid., pp. 28–29.
205 See notes by K.A. Binney, March 1995, in ibid.
206 Introduction to Hanna Spencer, *Hanna's Diary, 1938–1941. Czechoslavakia to Canada* (Montreal: McGill-Queen's University Press, 2002), p. xvi.

an existential necessity ... . Without Hans, my life seemed empty, without purpose.' Hanna, later a professor in the German Department, University of Western Ontario, reflected in 2000 that 'Unlike most diaries, this is not a monologue; it is a one-sided dialogue.'[207]

Six notebooks were filled with Hanna's diary, written in German, one of which was devoted to the two years she spent in Britain as a domestic servant. Yet it is necessary to query in this specific example, in the quest for the unadulterated voice of the female refugee, whether any diary is free from the constraints of readership – even one intended to be purely private. Indeed, the diary is a varied and complex genre only recently taken seriously by literary and cultural scholars. Margaret Kertesz has argued with regard to the Mass-Observation Second World War diaries (arguably the largest collection from one time and place) that they cannot simplistically 'speak for themselves'. On the contrary, they must be seen 'as a form of autobiographical writing, which means that the reader is not presented with the "truth" or with "sincerity", but with the image which the diarist wishes to communicate'.[208] In conceptualizing the genre more generally, Felicity Nussbaum adds that 'Diary is the thing itself, not a failed version of autobiography ... . The diary delivers narrative and frustrates it; it simultaneously displays and withholds.'[209] And, by its very nature, diary writing varies intensely in form and style. As Steven Kagle emphasises, 'It is for ... insights into the experiences and emotions of individuals that readers should carefully examine the literary characteristics of diaries, characteristics which make the best diaries works of literature'.[210] This is certainly true of Hanna Spencer's.

Hanna's diary starts in August 1938 and before she returned to teaching in the small town of Olmutz. It covers her last months in Czechoslovakia through its dismemberment and Nazi invasion, her three months as a domestic in England and then her first 18 months in what turned out to be her final place of settlement, Canada. The diary has its own dynamics over these three years as the chances of reuniting with Hans dissipate. At first, the 'Dear Diary' is her boyfriend and then, gradually, as with the Holocaust's most famous chronicler, it becomes the forum through which she tries to make sense of the fast-changing world around her. The diary ends abruptly at the point when Hanna finds a new love, and one who will be her life partner thereafter. This is not simply the end of Hans in her everyday world but also, it must be suggested, when she decided that the traumas of the

---

207 Ibid.

208 Margaret Kertesz, 'To Speak for Themselves? Mass-Observation's Women's Wartime Diaries', *Feminist Praxis* nos 37–38 (1993), pp. 77–78.

209 Felicity Nussbaum, 'Towards Conceptualizing the Diary', in James Olney (ed.), *Studies in Autobiography* (New York: Oxford University Press, 1988), p. 137.

210 Steven Kagle, 'The Diary as Art: A New Assessment', *Genre* vol. 6 (1973), p. 425.

past, her refugeedom, were attempted to be put aside: 'I had pulled down my own "iron curtain", shutting out the memories preserved in these pages.'[211]

Hanna, like many female refugees, especially those who had a professional career, did not see domestic service in Britain as her preferred route of escape. The first mention was in December 1938, when she got information from a friend in London, writing dismissively that 'The only jobs available are for domestics who can cook.'[212] The Czechoslovakian part of her diary outlines not only the slow exclusion she experienced from the school in which she taught, but also the places that she became aware of as places of entry. In January 1939 another friend told her of possibilities in Uruguay.[213] Hanna also explored a teaching post in Australia, but she was realistic and knew that it was unlikely to materialise.[214] Despite the hardships she knew it would entail, Hanna thus took domestic courses designed for those going to Britain.

Hanna's description of this instruction reveals her sense of humour – one that she later records having been temporarily removed by the reality of her first domestic position. She is a star pupil preparing for an 'exam' for WIZO (the Women's International Zionist Organization) in Prague: 'To this end I am studying *Herrenhemdenbugeln* – the art of ironing men's shirts.' Recalling her past life with Hans, she adds 'Remember the mountain that is awaiting my attention?'[215] Hanna's friend in England places an advertisement for her in the *Daily Telegraph*. By March 1939 she had an offer of a post looking after twins in Sheffield and received the paperwork to leave her homeland. In what she described as a 'red-letter day' she announced to her diary that the domestic 'permit has arrived', allowing Hanna entry into the United Kingdom 'on condition that she does not enter any employment other than as a resident in service in a private household'.[216]

Hanna's first post in England was not as unremittingly miserable as that of Inge and Marta, but it had elements in common. The position looking after the twins did not materialise but another in Sheffield was found with the Andersons. This household had undoubtedly struggled to obtain non-refugee labour because of its demands and abusive mistress. And, as with the two young women in Manchester, Hanna was put straight to work and issued lengthy instructions which, even with her good command of English, she failed to understand. Hanna's description of these first moments reflect her wider ambitions as a writer – she was working on a play with Hans – and her intellectual breadth and education:

211 Spencer, *Hanna's Diary*, 'Preface', p. xi.
212 Ibid., diary entry 5 December 1939, p. 60.
213 Ibid., 8 January 1939, p. 67.
214 Ibid., 2 December 1939, p. 60.
215 Ibid., 27 January 1939, p. 77.
216 Ibid., 20 February 1939, p. 79.

I felt like Parsifal, 'the dumb knight' on the Mount of the Grail, who was speechless when faced with the sick Kurneval. The entire atmosphere was eerie. It was almost as if there were a veil between me and the world.

It was the loss of agency that Hanna found most dislocating within this post. In the few weeks before leaving she had been 'more active and more energetically in charge than I had ever been in my life'. She had been 'running around, organizing, disposing, preparing, training, doing'. In contrast, 'now all I could do was try and guess what was being decided about me and wonder what would happen to me next'.[217] Hanna struggled with the conflicting emotions of feeling grateful (and the expectation that she was meant to feel indebted to her hosts) and the reality of being redefined as a domestic by her employers, 'who don't want to see a long sad face'. Her uneasy solution was to 'try to look cheerful while I work, from 7 AM to 9 PM. This morning I cleaned eight rooms: made beds, dusted, wiped floors, all without a mop or broom, as usual.'[218]

Constantly worried about her parents and sister still in Czechoslovakia as the situation there for the Jews deteriorated by the day, for Hanna, as for so many refugee domestics, it was the isolation and powerlessness that was hardest to bear: 'I feel terribly lonesome – surrounded by strangers and imprisoned in a foreign language.'[219] In the first weeks in Sheffield her resistance was low and Hanna found herself bullied by Jean, the Andersons' young daughter. She wrote to Hans/herself of the reversal of control in her everyday life: 'Would you believe that this seven year old has me scared? Is this the experienced teacher who was able to turn those ruffians in Olmutz into loyal friends?'[220]

At this stage, literacy practice as a way of connecting to Hans and her old self became Hanna's one point of refuge:

Dear diary, I have come to you for comfort. They treat me like a slave. From 6.45 in the morning until 9 or 10 at night I feel so harried with work that I have barely time to get to the bathroom.[221]

Hanna was demoralised by her still faltering English and the inability of her employers to understand her situation, alongside the energy-sapping nature of the work. The diary/longed-for partner provided a confessional space within which she articulated the acute distress felt in her first weeks

217 Ibid., 6 March 1939, pp. 84–85.
218 Ibid., 16 March 1939, p. 89.
219 Ibid., 13 March 1939, p. 88.
220 Ibid., 13 March 1939, pp. 88–89.
221 Ibid., 20 March 1939, pp. 90–91.

in England: 'Never before have things seemed so hopeless, so joyless, and so bleak.'[222] It is significant that Hanna was precise in dating this particular entry to 'Sunday afternoon': that is, beyond her normal habit of placing it in the day of the week. Indeed, the diary format allowed her to express the immediacy of her alienation in an emotional intensity rarely found in later testimony of these former domestics.

This clearly was the low point and slowly thereafter Hanna began to assert her authority over the situation. First it came through helping her sister to come to Britain as a domestic and then in challenging the abusive behaviour of Mrs Anderson. Subject to emotional blackmail in being made to feel obliged to stay, Hanna decided to confront her mistress over the behaviour of her daughter. Mrs Anderson responded by admonishing 'This must never happen again', to which Hanna replied firmly: 'Quite, Madam, I don't believe this can go on.' Stunned at this challenge, her mistress realised she had met her match.[223] Shortly after, Hanna left and was fortunate to find another position in which she was treated with great respect and understanding as an intellectual and cultural equal. Indeed, her new employers, the Cunninghams, became lifelong friends.

Hanna's experiences of both a 'bad' home and a 'good' home typified those of domestic service as a whole in interwar Britain.[224] It is probable that these Jewish women experienced, as did Hanna, more of the extremes – either those households who struggled to find 'local' labour that would tolerate exploitative conditions or bizarre employer behaviour, or those who saw their domestics as equal human beings with rights and feelings and were sensitive to the rupture of being a refugee. Unlike other servants, these refugee women were not, until the outbreak of war, free to leave service. As Hanna later reflected on her passport permit to come to Britain: it came with 'strings attached'.[225] In this respect, she was lucky – her aunt and uncle had transferred a business to Canada and eventually Hanna, her sister Mimi, and their parents joined them in rural Ontario. It was not a smooth process – Mimi was almost rejected by the Canadian immigration authorities because of a minor eye condition – but in early June 1939, Hanna set sail for Canada.[226]

'Heterotopia' – Michel Foucault's concept of the ship as a 'piece of floating space'[227] – is made manifest in Hanna's description of her journey

---

222 Ibid., 26 March 1939, p. 95.

223 Ibid., 31 March 1939, pp. 98–99.

224 Celia Fremlin, *The Seven Chars of Chelsea* (London: Methuen, 1940), chapters 3 and 4 uses and problematises these categories.

225 Editorial addition, 3 March 1939 in Spencer, *Hanna's Diary*, p. 82.

226 Ibid., 3 June 1939, p. 108.

227 Michel Foucault, 'Different Spaces', in James Foubion (ed.), *Essential Works of Michel Foucault* vol. 2 *Aesthetics, Method, and Epistomology* (London: Allen Lane, 1998), pp. 184–185.

from Southampton to Montreal via Quebec: 'Sea, sea, sea. A miraculous, breathtaking experience. We are a happy group of passengers, a very mixed bunch. No one knows anything about anyone else. All that matters is whether a person is pleasant, friendly, and a good sailor.'[228] As they sailed up the St. Lawrence Hanna was struck by the vibrancy of its river banks in what, at first sight, she decided was her new home: 'Never before have I seen grass of such a vibrant green. Is it simply the contrast between the grey days behind us and the lush green of early June – or symbolic of greener pastures ahead?'[229]

In a farm colony, named by her family (somewhat overstating their gratitude) as 'New Haven', Hanna as an attractive and articulate young woman became a minor local media personality. She performed their collective status as ideal refugees – hard-working, assimilating (including adopting Christianity), and proud to become Canadians. It is significant, however, that in radio and newspaper interviews, as well as in many talks in her first year in Ontario, Hanna focused on Czechoslovakia and Canada, largely bypassing her brief spell in Britain.[230] It reflected a wider silence about refugee domestic service, one aided at the start of the war when many (8000 within the first week) were sacked from their posts owing to a mixture of economic necessity, government restrictive measures, anti-Germanism, and antisemitism.[231]

Suppression from within and without, following (if in a different pattern) that of Theodora Bernstein's memoir, led to an abrupt closure on this subject and one that Hanna did not return to until later life. She was not alone. Refugee writing in the Second World War focused on the alien internment episode, gently re-establishing for a British audience that those that had fled from Nazi persecution could be trusted again. Internment was presented as an understandable, sometimes humorous but ultimately unnecessary action which had temporarily stopped the refugees from contributing to the war effort.[232] The refugee domestics themselves were more likely to be regarded as a threat to national security than other 'enemy aliens', reflecting a mixture of xenophobia, class, and gender prejudices at work.[233] As the *Daily Mail*, ever to the forefront of anti-refugee sentiment, warned in April 1940, 'the paltriest kitchen maid with German connections' was a 'menace to

---

228 Spencer, *Hanna's Diary*, 6 June 1939, p. 109.

229 Ibid., 14 June 1939, p. 111.

230 Ibid., section 4.

231 University of Warwick Archives, TUC archives, 456: Domestic Bureau minutes, 14 September 1939.

232 Alfred Lom, 'Never Mind Mr Lom' (London: Macmillan, 1941); Livia Laurent, *A Tale of Internment* (London: George Allen & Unwin, 1942) and Alfred Perles, *Alien Corn* (London: George Allen & Unwin, 1944).

233 Francois Lafitte, *The Internment of Aliens* (Harmondsworth: Penguin, 1940), pp. 36–39, 62–63.

the safety of the country'.[234] There was, for the most part, neither a desire to speak about the domestic service interlude or to find an audience for it.

Celia Fremlin, a middle-class writer, became a servant in London at the same time as the 20,000 refugee domestics. She did so partly because she needed a job but largely through a desire to view the British class structure. Fremlin was, as someone prominent in Mass-Observation, aware of the barriers to communication across different social groups in Britain and that with domestic service especially there were difficulties in understanding its nature. First, servants 'don't write books'. Second, attempts to interview them would face an insurmountable problem: 'The trouble is that the two of you speak different languages; you think different thoughts; you live in different worlds.'[235]

With the refugee domestics, they did write – and, as we have seen, in many different genres and for purposes that ranged from the desperate (the search for a post) to the reflective. They also took up service out of necessity rather than to observe. Their contemporary writings provide a unique anthropological insight not only into their own experiences but also of the occupation as a whole at a key moment in its evolution. Compared with the migrant Jewish prostitutes who preceded them, there is a wealth of testimony written during the Nazi era: more than anything its variety and richness allows the agency of these women to be recognised.

Yet, even in its most 'private' form, as with Hanna's diary, the issue of readership has to be kept in mind. The refugee domestic could speak and she did so with eloquence and power, revealing everyday resistance as well as the intense pressures they faced and the unhappiness they experienced. That voice, however, in its contemporaneous form, was expressed to a lesser or greater extent through the prism of gratitude. It was undoubtedly provided by the author voluntarily and sincerely but it also met the expectations of the receiving society. Refugees from Nazism, including those that came as domestics, were constantly reminded to whom they were in debt.

In an atmosphere in which they were regarded ambivalently, with a mixture of sympathy and suspicion, there was a defensive nature to the writing of refugee domestics as they tried to explain their 'out of placeness' to an often non-comprehending British audience. As with all the refugees from Nazism, there was the necessity of establishing that they were *genuine* victims. This was complicated, however, by the rigidly stratified nature of British domestic service in which the (mainly) formerly middle-class women were inserted. And lastly, in letters home, as with many migrants, there was a desire to reassure family and friends, compounded in this case by an acute awareness of the precarious status of those left behind. Considering all these factors, as well as the refugee domestics' marginality and the relentless

234 Quoted by Lethbridge, *Servants*, p. 247.
235 Fremlin, *The Seven Chars*, pp. 1–2.

nature of their work, it is astonishing that so much autobiographical writing was created (perhaps more than by the million plus other servants at the time combined) and that its quality was so intricate and multi-layered.

The next chapter will explore how, in the post-war era, narratives of the refugee domestics were reconstructed. Were the restraints outlined for the contemporary period removed and were there others that then emerged to replace them? Context, again, will be crucial: how, for example, did advancing through the life cycle of the individual, the knowledge and impact of the Holocaust, ongoing refugee crises, and changes in British society shape the testimony and cultural representations of these female refugees? Was anything approximating to a collective memory produced? And when was the silence that had started to emerge about the experiences of refugee domestics during the Second World War broken and why? Finally, it will ask whether acknowledgment of this challenging Jewish past, including within the world of heritage, has enabled links to be made to later forms of female migration, especially domestic work, or the reverse? What, then, were the *politics* of remembering and representation of these former refugee servants?

Chapter 2

1945 to the Present

Memory and Representation of Refugee Domestics, 1945 to the 1960s

Faced with thousands of unemployed refugee domestics at the start of the war, and requiring female labour for the war economy, the Home Office relaxed the work restrictions that had been an absolute condition of entry. While the government and the refugee organisations had always assumed that these women would not remain in service long-term, the conflict precipitated their exit. Even so, many remained in service throughout the war – perhaps a larger percentage than their British equivalents. After 1945 a small number of Holocaust survivors joined their ranks. Entry through the Home Office's Distressed Relatives scheme was highly restrictive, but, informally, some women turned down were given a second chance of entry by being granted Ministry of Labour foreign domestic permits.[1]

Ironically, while such procedures had deliberately eased the entry of Jewish female refugees in the late 1930s, they were in danger now of discriminating against them. At a point when schemes to recruit alien workers were rapidly expanding, the government was wary of letting too many Jews into Britain. A sympathetic official noted in July 1946 that excluding Jewish 'near relatives whilst admitting other foreigners' could be subject to public disapproval as being 'unfair'.[2] This was the route into Britain for Elizabeth Weisz, sister of the famous Hungarian Jewish refugee cartoonist 'Vicky'. His biographers sardonically note that 'She entered – such were the requirements of a concentration camp victim – on a "Domestic Service Permit" which allowed her to be somebody's maid.'[3]

---

1   National Archives, HO 213/1360.
2   National Archives, LAB 8/92: Dennys minute, 5 July 1946.
3   Russell Davis and Liz Ottoway, *Vicky* (London: Secker & Warburg, 1987), p. 79.

Yet, if domestic service was becoming a minority rather than the dominant occupation of Jewish refugees by the early years of the Second World War, its memory and representation had a longer life. In fact, fictional portrayals of refugee servants went back further, starting with Ruth Feiner's *Fires in May* (1935). One of the most remarkable features of the refugees from the 1930s was their almost instant articulacy in a foreign culture – whether in film, art, or literature. Feiner was a young Jewish refugee from a distinguished German artistic family and this was already her second book. The title page of *Fires in May* stated that 'the distance from the Continent to England is greater by thousands of miles than the distance from one end of the world to the other'.[4] Yet Feiner and others, such as Alexander Korda and George Mikes, used that space to their own advantage. It enabled anthropological insights that allowed these newcomers to audaciously explain the nature of Englishness.

Feiner's work was translated and, no doubt to appeal to a wider audience, she made her chief protagonist, Vera, non-Jewish and a political rather than a racial victim of Nazism. As Louise London notes, this decision was 'misguided and her characterisations are generally weak'.[5] It might be added that, not being a domestic herself, Feiner did not have a deep insight into either its dynamics or the permit system that underpinned entry to Britain: Vera is told that 'the work will be light, and you will get some pocket-money'.[6] Yet the insecurity of her status and of those around her was presented astutely by Feiner: it was a feature of refugee life as early as the mid-1930s, when the novel was published. To stay in Britain Vera has a marriage of convenience and, as London adds, 'the novel accurately portrays the pressures on lone refugee women'.[7]

The next major literary foray into refugee domestic service was then not until the Second World War – that is, at the point at which it was in rapid decline. Like *Fires in May*, Helen Ashton's *Tadpole Hall* (1941) was unrepresentative of the experience as a whole. It was set in a decaying English manor house owned by a retired military gentleman (Colonel Heron) and his sister. In this setting a highly unlikely refugee couple become cook and butler. Herr Kahn was a former lawyer in Austria and is of Jewish origin. His wife is of aristocratic non-Jewish background. Ashton, a popular novelist, highlighted the impact of the Nazi persecution that Kahn had faced, but his cringing, cowardly nature appears both inherent in his character and to pre-date the *Anschluss*. And, while the author gently mocks the xenophobic panic of 1940 that transforms the

---

4   Ruth Feiner, *Fires in May* (London: Harrap, 1935).
5   Louise London, *Whitehall and the Jews 1933–1948: British Immigration Policy and the Holocaust* (Cambridge: Cambridge University Press, 2000), pp. 52–53.
6   Feiner, *Fires in May*, p. 33.
7   London, *Whitehall and the Jews*, p. 53.

refugee domestics into enemy aliens (and does so with less restraint than the refugee authors referred to in the previous chapter), Kahn is presented as a wreck of a human, physically repulsive, and of dubious loyalty. He literally stumbles into semi-accidental suicide (not having the courage to do it properly) – leaving the 'real man', Colonel Heron, to marry Kahn's 'Aryan' and fellow upper-class widow.[8]

The difference from Feiner's novel is remarkable. Kahn is presented as grotesque and effeminate. Most significantly, he is portrayed as lacking any agency – an enduring feature within representations of refugee (and other migrant) domestics. In marked contrast, despite its clumsiness, Feiner's novel reflects a wider tendency present in the contemporary testimony and writing of the refugee women themselves. Within the legal and economic restraints imposed on them, they took control of their lives through acts of resistance as reflected in their autobiographical writing. Instead, Ashton, as an outsider to the inner world, presented the Jewish domestic as at best a victim and at worst a damaged, passive, and ultimately undesirable creature. It would take another two generations for Ashton's narrative to be overturned in the form of Natasha Solomons' *The Novel in the Viola* (2011) in which the female Jewish refugee domestic, Elise, wins over the hearts of the son and then the lord of the English manor house, asserting her agency from the moment she placed a newspaper advertisement. Parodying this desperate form of self-advertisement, Elise boasts that she spoke 'fluid English' and promises that she 'will cook your goose'.[9] Solomons, a popular novelist, is, significantly, the daughter of refugees from Nazism. Her confidence in exposing the class and gender prejudices faced by her parents reveals the ease with which many from a second generation of this forced migration have advanced in British culture and society.

It remains that such positive portrayals and gentle satire had to wait until the late twentieth and early twenty-first centuries. In the immediate period after 1945 – remarkably so, considering the wealth of earlier testimony – self-representation almost totally disappeared. Former refugee domestics were perhaps too busy rebuilding lives and did not want to dwell on their difficult first experiences in Britain. But it was perhaps the incongruity of these former professionals in service within bourgeois homes that made others utilise their tragicomic potential in the post-war era. The first to do so was the playwright Wynyard Browne, in *Dark Summer*. First performed in a minor London theatre in 1947, it had an afterlife as a BBC radio play (1948) and later in a television production.[10]

One of its main characters was Gisela Waldstein, a former research

---

8   Helen Ashton, *Tadpole Hall* (London: Collins, 1941).

9   Natasha Solomons, *The Novel in the Viola* (London: AudioGO, 2012 [2011]), p. 5.

10   The full script is in the BBC Written Archive. My thanks to James Jordan for providing me with a copy.

chemist in Vienna and now, in early post-war Britain, a servant to Mrs Hadow in a genteel English provincial town. Stephen Hadow, the son, is a former RAF pilot blinded in action, who relies on Gisela for moral and practical support. Miss Loder, a local spinster who has lost her house in the blitz, is also kept by Mrs Hadow as a companion/home help. She bitterly resents the presence of Gisela on the grounds of her race but also because of her jealousy of the foreigner's former professional status. The plot is thin and melodramatic: when Stephen regains his sight he rejects the prematurely aged and unattractive Gisela for his beautiful, young (but flighty) English former girlfriend.

The reviewer for *AJR Information* argued that it was 'clear where the sympathies of the author [were]' before adding that 'he did not seem to have always carried away the audience'.[11] Gisela is presented as a generous, self-sacrificing, and caring person who has suffered greatly as a Jew in pre-war Vienna. The author also makes clear the humiliating positions many refugees had to endure when coming to Britain as domestics. In the end, Wynyard Browne allows Gisela to leave service and to return to her work as a chemist.[12] Yet there is a clear sense that she will remain alone and that she is too damaged to be a true partner to Stephen. Gisela is not Mr Kahn of *Tadpole Hall* – indeed, she talks Stephen out of suicide, having witnessed it herself among her friends in Vienna – but she fits into the wider literary trope of the beautiful 'Jewess' who ages badly. As 'Narrator', the *AJR Information* reviewer, concluded:

> If the heroine had been a negress who had feared ever to be seen by the blind lover, I am sure the play would have been destined to be a great success in the West End. But here was a story only of a Jewess and, at that, one from Vienna.[13]

The play makes passing reference to events in Palestine, and it was perhaps for this reason that the audience was even less sympathetic to Gisela Waldstein. When Miss Loder, whose antisemitism in the play is undisguised, objects to Gisela that 'You refugees always think no one else has suffered. But they have, you know', she was expressing a wider irritation that many Jews and other victims of persecution had encountered when trying to communicate the particularity of their experience.[14] For all its use of stereotypes, *Dark Summer* was aimed at increasing understanding of the refugee plight, even if it did not fully succeed. In the hands of Agatha Christie, there was far less attempt at empathy.

---

11 *AJR Information*, December 1947, p. 94.
12 BBC Written Archives.
13 *AJR Information*, December 1947, p. 94.
14 BBC Written Record Archives.

A Murder is Announced (1950) was one of her most successful 'Miss Marple' crime novels and one subject to endless television and film versions. Whether borrowing from *Dark Summer* or simply reflecting the recent presence of refugee domestics in the English home, the central character of Mitzi has many features in common with Gisela. Described as a refugee from Nazism and as 'Mittel European', Christie stops short of labelling her Jewish – something that she did not hesitate in doing with her criminal characters in pre-1939 writing. Mitzi is too comic to be tragic and even witnessing the murder of her relatives in the concentration camps is treated largely as a joke and part of her tendency to exaggerate. Mitzi, as befitting a foreigner, is utterly hysterical, but she is also innocent of the murders carried out and ultimately a minor hero. Christie teases the reader with their xenophobic prejudices but does not fundamentally query them. Mitzi would have met the approval of the *Housewife* in that her puddings were delicious (though she protests 'I am not really a cook. In my country I do intellectual work').[15] It is Mitzi's culinary wizardry which explains the mistress tolerating her eccentricity. Unlike in the case of Gisela Waldstein, however, the class system represented by Christie has to remain in force. Mitzi is allowed to escape the murderous household but only by remaining as a cook – she will remain in the English kitchen. But Christie's lack of imagination is made manifest when one of her characters at the end proclaims that all was for the best. Her former mistress has committed two murders and had nearly killed her as well but the outcome had 'made a wonderful difference to Mitzi. She told me yesterday that she was taking a post near Southampton.'[16] The domestic servant had long been the butt of British popular humour.[17] Christie makes no effort to treat Mitzi – a survivor of the concentration camps – any differently.

Returning to *Dark Summer*, as 'Narrator' in *AJR Information* noted, 'There were many Gisela Waldsteins in England in the first years of the war.'[18] With their difficult memories to contend with, alongside negative representations of their experiences such as *Tadpole Hall* and *A Murder is Announced*, it is not surprising that for the first decade and a half after 1945 hardly any of the former refugee domestics would confront their years as domestics in any form of writing. Indeed, the three examples of autobiography produced during the 1960s that will now be examined were exceptional – in one case through its literary quality and in the other two because they represent ordinary, everyday, stories when there was no immediate audience for them.

---

15 Agatha Christie, *A Murder is Announced* (London: HarperCollins, 2002 [1950]), p. 237.

16 Ibid., p. 373.

17 Lucy Lethbridge, *Servants* (London: Bloomsbury, 2013), passim.

18 *AJR Information*, December 1947, p. 94.

Very different in style and authorship, they have one factor in common: all three relate to domestic servants who came as married couples. As these represented only 2 per cent of those allowed entry, it seems beyond coincidence that they were the first to be constructed in the post-war era. Indeed, it would seem that there is something about this experience that prompted earlier, extensive, autobiographical reflection. Two inter-related factors might be put forward – those coming together tended to be older and they were more likely to re-establish family networks in the place(s) of settlement sooner than those women who left alone. From the 1980s a far greater number of former refugee domestics either wrote or gave their testimony. It was at the point of the end of their careers and when their children had left home, allowing greater time for reflection. This self-reflexivity happened much earlier in the following cases of post-war writing, explored in chronological order.

The Other Side of the Fence was a short memoir allegedly written by Joseph and Bronka Schneider but in fact authored solely by the latter. It was written in 1960 and rejected by the American popular journal the *Ladies' Home Journal*. The manuscript remained unread until after the death of its author and was then published as *Exile: A Memoir of 1939* by Ohio State University Press in 1998. It was edited by Erika Bourguignon, an anthropologist and niece of Bronka, and Barbara Hill Rigney, an English professor.[19] Both ponder what led Bronka to write down the experiences she shared with her husband some 20 years earlier, as refugee cook and butler to an ex-colonial English couple, the Harringtons, in a remote Scottish castle. They give mundane reasons – Bronka, a former accountant in Vienna, now living in semi-rural Illinois, was not employed and 'seems to have been rather isolated and bored with her life in Peoria'.[20] More immediately, Bronka begins her account by reporting that they had heard the news that the castle had just burnt down. Her niece ponders whether Bronka had read Daphne Du Maurier's *Rebecca*, which also 'begins with the narrator's memory of a country house destroyed by fire'. To Bourguignon, the opening of the memoir 'conjures up movie images' of such ancient and remote buildings 'set in great parks in the countryside'.[21] Indeed, as will emerge, concepts of 'heritage' and British domestic service are important when considering the specific representation of the refugees in this occupation.

Beyond the specific, Rigney suggest that, more deeply, 'Bronka wrote because she felt herself a part of history, and that to record that history, no matter how selectively or with fictionalized elements, was a kind of

---

19   Erika Bourguignon and Barbara Hill Rigney (eds), *Exile: A Memoir. Bronka Schneider* (Columbus: Ohio University Press, 1998).

20   Ibid., Bourguinnon, 'Foreword', p. xi.

21   Ibid., Bourguignon, 'Commentary', p. 121.

trust.'[22] Yet, even if Bourguignon and Rigney's assumptions are correct, it is significant that the connection to either an unchanging and clichéd British past or what was, by the early 1960s, beginning to be known as the Holocaust, was not enough to ensure the memoir's publication. As we will see, more recent fixation with the latter has enabled space to be given to those who escaped Nazi annihilation. Moreover, refugees have been represented in popular heritage relating to domestic service – but only since the 1990s. There was, in short, no niche market for Bronka's account in 1960, just as Theodora Bernstein's memoir (also set in an ancient historic house) remained unpublished in 1940.

Most crucially, as Rigney states, 'Bronka is not a victim and never sees herself as such.'[23] Her account has moments of humour as Bronka and Joseph struggle in their new roles and deal with their eccentric employers in this most unlikely of settings. Yet neither of them, whatever their failings to deliver what is expected of them, are presented as the comic figure of Agatha Christie's making. Bronka's resistance begins in Vienna, where she is determined, against the odds created by British immigration procedures, that they will leave together. Through persistence and good fortune, they manage to obtain their post through a Scottish domestic agency.[24] Bronka also recorded everyday acts of defiance, typical of servants as a whole, which maintained their self-worth. Joseph, to relieve the monotony, in one of the castle's major halls, swept dust under a rug. Unfortunately caught in the act by his employer, he related the incident to his wife later in the day: 'Mrs Harrington came into the room, lifted the rug, took the sweeper out of my hand, swept the dust back into the middle of the room, gave the sweeper back to me, smiled and left the room.'[25] Not a word was said: the social distance between mistress and domestic, regardless of their refugee status, had to be maintained.

While the long hours, hard work, and lack of freedom echo contemporary accounts such as Hanna Spencer's diary (much time is spent on how long it took for Bronka to visit a dentist to fix a broken tooth), the fact that the memoir was written two decades after they left the castle enabled a different perspective. The internal tension between expressing a sense of humiliation and gratitude, so prominent in accounts written at the time, is less pronounced, and the emphasis is placed on the latter. At the outbreak of war Bronka and Joseph are transformed into 'enemy aliens' and it is clear that their employers' attitude changes accordingly. Doors previously open were now locked by the mistress of the house.[26] Later, although this

---

22 Ibid., Rigney, 'Foreword', pp. xvi–xvii.
23 Ibid., p. xvii.
24 Ibid., 'The Other Side of the Fence', p. 6.
25 Ibid., pp. 58–59.
26 Ibid., p. 95.

is not included in her memoir, Joseph was interned on the Isle of Man. Yet, rather than dwell on Mrs Harrington's coldness, suspicion, and final relief when they left for another post, Bronka is generous in describing their departure: 'We understood that she felt some responsibility towards us and wanted to part in the friendliest way possible as we would always be thankful for the permit we received when we needed it so badly.'[27] Erika Bourguignon suggests that 'Bronka tells a simple story, and tells it simply.'[28] Her fellow editor, however, from a literary perspective argues for the text's complexity. Both agree that Bronka was a 'talented observer of a too-real world', but Rigney adds that 'her characters share with fictional ones many elements of the fantastic'. The Tandies, the gardener and his wife who befriend the Schneiders, 'might have emerged from the pages of a Dickens novel, so cozy and quaint is their existence', and the Harringtons 'are fictionalized but never idealized versions of the British gentry with their financial roots in the Colonial project'. Rigney adds that 'These characters and others in Bronka's text are literary stereotypes, all of which would be more comfortable in a novel than in a memoir.'[29]

Bronka's memoir ends abruptly, stating that 'seven years later, exactly to the day we arrived in Britain, we left for the USA to be reunited with our family and to start a new life again in a country that was so different from the one we left behind.'[30] Developing Rigney's analysis further, the memoir, with its focus on a version of Britishness rooted in a very outdated, semi-feudal past and a redemptive ending in Illinois, appears to have been constructed with a specifically American audience in mind. The refugee domestic clearly has space 'to speak' in this neat autobiographical reflection. As ever, however, such writing has to be situated in time and place.

The editors also locate the memoir firmly within the context of the Holocaust and are surprised that there is silence on this subject within the text, in spite of the murder of the Schneiders' relatives who were unable to get out.[31] It would be better, however, to view the text more openly as exploration of refugeedom. In spite of their isolation in rural Scotland, Bronka and Joseph bonded with other continental Jews. In precious meetings which, because of the work routine and lack of spare time, had to be organised well in advance, these refugees gained solidarity and shared information on how to improve their situation. *The Other Side of the Fence* also shows the concern for friends and relatives left behind, and attempts before the war to get them out to safety. The memoir's ending, in contrast to the other two written in the 1960s, presents the Schneiders as simply

---

27 Ibid., p. 98.
28 Ibid., Bourguignon, 'Commentary', p. 101.
29 Ibid., Rigney, 'Foreword', p. xv–xvi.
30 Ibid., 'The Other Side of the Fence', p. 99.
31 Ibid. See both their 'Forewords'.

being happily reborn in America, ending their refugee status. That this linear journey was not, in reality, so straightforward is indicated in the epilogue provided by Bronka's niece. Shortly after the death of her husband in 1976, Bronka attempted suicide. As with Theodora Bernstein, the trauma of becoming a refugee was long-lasting and intense.[32]

Rigney, following Roland Barth's dictum that biography is 'a novel that dare not speak its name', highlights how genres rarely exist in watertight compartments. Her critical engagement with Bronka's memoir also emphasises the need to take the literacy practice of ordinary people seriously.[33] In the second post-war example, the uncertainty of identifying 'fact' and 'fiction' through the complex processes of memory is self-consciously at the heart of the work. Lore Segal's *Other People's Houses* is thus cautiously subtitled in a later edition, some 30 years after its original publication, 'A Novel' by its author – by then a teacher of creative writing at Ohio State University.[34] Indeed, Segal (née Groszmann) alerts the reader to any certainty of categorisation in the preliminaries to *Other People's Houses*: 'The "Carter Bayoux" of my book once told me a story out of his childhood. When he had finished, I said, "I know just where your autobiography stopped and fiction began." He said, "Then you knew more than I."'[35] *Other People's Houses* is one of the most powerful testimony-related pieces of prose to emerge from those who managed to get out of Greater Germany before the war: 'there is no doubt that she spoke as a witness for many thousands who, though lucky enough to have escaped, nevertheless suffered social and family upheavals which would mark them forever'.[36] Indeed, it is a classic of refugee writing for all periods. In introducing a revised version of the book to a 'young adult' audience, the children's author Naomi Lewis helped contextualise Segal by suggesting that 'she belongs to history's vast procession of wanderers: exiles in search of new roots'.[37]

Other People's Houses is a multilayered text not simply because of the blurring of autobiography, family memoir, and fiction, and its deliberate melding of history and memory, but also through the complexity of its literary evolution. Although published (largely) whole in 1964, its origins can be traced as early as the author's arrival in Britain at the start of 1939.

---

32 Ibid., Bourguignon, 'Commentary', p. 129.

33 Ibid., Rigney, 'Foreword', p. xvi.

34 Lore Segal, *Other People's Houses: A Novel* (New York: New Press, 1994). All quotes from the book are taken from this edition, the text of which is the same as in the original.

35 Ibid., p. xii.

36 Philip Cavanaugh, 'The Present is a Foreign Country: Lore Segal's Fiction', *Contemporary Literature* vol. 3 no. 3 (1993), p. 487.

37 Naomi Lewis, 'Introduction', in Lore Segal, *Other People's Houses: A Refugee in England 1938–48* (London: Bodley Head, 1974), p. v.

Only ten years old, Segal began informally committing her thoughts and experiences to paper and was empowered by recognising that there was an audience for them. Segal had decided from an early age that she was destined to be a writer and even before leaving Austria she was self-consciously working towards this career. From the early 1950s she returned more formally to the subject matter of her family's forced migration. It was a slow process: 'It took me six years to write *Other People's Houses*. I was at pains to draw no facile conclusions – and all conclusions seemed, and seem, facile', she reflected in 1989.[38] The commitment to the project grew in intensity at the end of the 1950s, leading to extended pieces in the *New Yorker* from March 1961 which in turn (and modified) formed the basis of the book's chapters.[39] And, if *Other People's Houses* is marked by constant reflexivity, the author has continued that process beyond, returning to its origins and the writing and rewriting process. Segal, like the great chronicler of Auschwitz, Primo Levi, has been concerned about the nature of remembering and misremembering, or what she calls the 'problems of imagining the past':

> Recollection is a double experience like a double exposure, the time frame in which we remember superimposes itself on the remembered time and the two images fail to match perfectly at any point. The remembrer has changed, and so, in all probability, has the thing or the place remembered.[40]

Other People's Houses provides perhaps the most devastatingly penetrative and perceptive account of refugee domestic service during the Nazi era. Its treatment, however, as a form of autobiographical writing, is further complicated by the fact that Segal came on the *Kindertransport* from Austria and it was her parents who came shortly after on domestic permits. It is included in this chapter not simply because of its potency and energy, but because of the success of Segal in conveying the experiences of her father (and especially her mother) as domestics. This is not only carried out through the author's imagination; as Segal noted in one of the chapters devoted to her mother and father as cook, butler, maid, and gardener inside a series of English homes, 'From the letters my mother [Franzi] wrote to me in Liverpool [where Segal was originally placed as a *Kindertransportee*], and the stories she has told me since, I have an idea of my parents' life those first months in England.'[41]

---

38 Lore Segal, 'The Bough Breaks', in David Rosenberg (ed.), *Testimony: Contemporary Writers Make the Holocaust Personal* (New York: Times Books, 1989), p. 245.
39 Lore Segal's articles were published in the *New Yorker* from 4 March 1961 to 25 July 1964.
40 Lore Segal, 'Memory: The Problems of Imagining the Past', in Berel Lang (ed.), *Writing and the Holocaust* (New York: Holmes & Meier, 1988), p. 65.
41 Segal, *Other People's Houses*, p. 76.

Segal is especially powerful in evoking the tensions created by the class change of the refugees from servant-owning to a life below stairs. Her mother tried to impress on their first employers, the Willoughbys, that her husband, Ignatz, was a distinguished chief accountant in Vienna and she herself a trained musician. When first entering the household, Franzi looked enviously at the piano. She is told that she can play it – but only 'when everyone is out'.[42] Franzi, struggling with inner emotions of 'silent outrage' while expressing outwardly the necessary gratitude to Mrs Willougby,[43] survives by developing what her daughter labels 'a small pocket of resistance'. Sometimes she was successful, such as when she refused to wear a cap and apron when serving dinner. As Franzi later recalled: 'They treated me like an English maid. But I wasn't an English maid – I couldn't behave like that. I made my own rules in the kitchen to be able to work.'[44] Similarly, Hilda Schindler, who came from Berlin, 'flatly refused' to wear a cap because of the humiliation it reflected. Interviewed in 1988, she noted how its impact still lingered: 'to this day I can't bear wearing a hat or any head covering.'[45] Hilda and Franzi were not alone: by the 1930s uniform, and especially the cap, was 'the hated symbol of service'.[46] Franzi failed, however, when asking for her husband to be addressed as *Mr* Groszmann. Gardeners, she was told, were not entitled to this prefix.[47]

Matters of status came to a head when Franzi, in effect doing two or three jobs, fell down the stairs in exhaustion. Mr Willoughby looked accusingly at Ignatz: 'And so the Willoughbys had put my parents in their place; the refugees belonged to the class of people who eat in the kitchen, sleep on cheap mattresses, and throw their wives down the stairs in an argument … .' With the sardonic wit that typifies *Other People's Houses*, Segal adds 'which goes to show that people have, after all, an innate sense of justice and cannot with equanimity be served by their fellows when these too closely resemble themselves'.[48]

It is for this reason that Mrs Willoughby cannot confront what the Groszmanns have experienced in Austria. Segal relates this wilful incomprehension through the prism of the refugee journey. Mrs Willoughy

42 Ibid., p. 78.

43 Ibid., p. 85.

44 Franzi Groszman, testimony in Mark Harris and Deborah Oppenheimer (eds), *Into the Arms of Strangers: Stories of the Kindertransport* (London: Bloomsbury, 2000), p. 176.

45 London Jewish Museum, tape 121: Hilda Schindler, interviewed by Mark Burman, 23 March 1988.

46 *Servants*, BBC 2, Episode 3, 21 November 2012 presented by Pamela Cox. See also Margaret Powell, *Below Stairs* (London: Peter Davies, 1975 [1968]), p. 38 on the reflections of a former servant and the wearing of uniform.

47 Segal, *Other People's Houses*, pp. 81–2.

48 Ibid., pp. 84–85.

expresses only irritation about the 11-week delay in Franzi and Ignatz's arrival, which was the inevitable result of the endless paperwork required and the necessarily complex route out of Vienna. Frustrated, Franzi told the mistress of the house what was happening to the Jews under Nazi control, but found that 'her eyes began to wander. Mrs Willoughby would rather not know.' Instead, Mrs Willoughby places them as if they were simply the foreign domestics who had come to Britain previously: 'Why didn't you embark in Austria and come direct? Why did you come such an awkward way around?'[49]

Other People's Houses is not a text that should be treated simplistically: its remarkable vignettes of life as a *Kindertransportee* or refugee domestic cannot be treated as pure reportage: Segal is not relating just her own experience or that of her family or, for that matter, the wider refugee experience of Jews escaping persecution. Her aim is more universal – to explore the human condition. As poet Karen Gershon, a fellow *Kinder* and an equally astute chronicler, noted, Segal succeeded in presenting 'events related briefly, without comment, complete in themselves, which remain in the mind as symbols or touchstones as if they belonged to one's own experience'.[50] Dealing with the question of anxiety, Segal later noted that this 'is not the prerogative of the refugee ... . The novelist does not claim peculiarity or singularity of experience ... .'[51] Segal adds, 'As a writer ... my business is to imagine you and to make you know me.'[52] The American critic Cynthia Ozick was quick to grasp that, beneath 'the plain surface of her narrative', Segal was saying 'in our time, in the face of everything that happened to those Others, we must question the legitimacy of our very lives'.[53]

If, as these two chapters have highlighted, the complexity of autobio-graphical praxis has to be recognised even for 'ordinary' writers, this is even more the case for Lore Segal's *Other People's Houses* – a text that so blatantly defies easy categorisation. It was, as its reviewer in the progressive American journal *New Republic* recognised, an 'unclassifiable book'.[54] Here, attention will focus on one particular moment related by Lore Segal concerning her father. In the previous chapter the gendering of the refugee experience and the apparent greater ease of women in adjusting to their new situation has been noted. It was presented problematically and through a negative Semitic discourse in Helen Ashton's *Tadpole Hall*. More subtly and ambivalently, Bronka Schneider's memoir presents her husband as less quick to adapt on

49 Ibid., p. 83.
50 Karen Gershon, 'Perturbed Adolescence', *AJR Information* vol. 29 no. 10 (October 1974), p. 5.
51 Segal, 'The Bough Breaks', p. 245.
52 Ibid., p. 248.
53 Cynthia Ozick, 'A Contraband Life', *Commentary* vol. 39 (March 1965), p. 89.
54 Richard Gilman, 'One Refugee Child's Story', *New Republic* vol. 151 no. 24 (12 December 1964), p. 15.

a practical level but more able to deal with the psychological challenges they faced in Britain. When Joseph says that they will need to learn more about Britain and British people (including differentiating Scottishness and Englishness), Bronka sees this as unfair and one-sided, replying 'They know nothing about us.' Joseph, however, has understood their new position in society: '"Don't you see", he said, "they don't have to; they didn't have to come to our country, but we had to come to theirs".'[55]

On the surface, Lore Segal presents her father as a man who simply cannot adjust to his new life as a butler and whose uselessness has to be compensated for by his wife, who takes on his chores and wider responsibilities. As one commentator noted, 'When Lore's parents turned into servants, the mother bent to the wind and found a new vocation; the rigid father broke.'[56] Yet this is to miss the self-excoriating theme that runs through *Other People's Houses* – at the time Lore cannot feel pity for her father, whose health was in a perilous state *before* they left Austria, and was exacerbated by Nazi persecution and the strain of finding a way out for his family from persecution. He is simply not physically strong enough to withstand the hardships of domestic service (and, briefly, internment in the Isle of Man), and he dies after a series of strokes just before VE Day. Yet emphasising his declining health is not an attack on her father's failings but a mechanism through which Segal critiques an earlier self and her absence of compassion for this figure who had loomed so large in her earlier life in Vienna.

In their desperate attempt to keep together as a family and to find less exploitative positions, alongside restrictions on where they, as 'enemy aliens', were allowed to live, Lore and her parents moved regularly in the early years of the war. They found themselves in a historic market town, 'Allchester' (Guildford), in Surrey, which Lore finds epitomises an Englishness she is desperate to become part of. But it is in this town that a traumatic moment occurs, one which her mother blames for the premature death of her husband. It is because of the tension between the writer's deliberate amnesia and the active memory of her mother that Segal painfully returns to the incident's wider significance:

> My mother tells me a story that I seem to have chosen to forget, for I want nothing to spoil my infatuation with that formal, gentle town. Its Georgian and Victorian houses stand amidst lawns, bird-baths, rock gardens, flower beds, all enclosed by high rose- and ivy-covered walls.

Lore's father was working as a gardener for a Mrs Lambston, who kept a donkey 'to amuse her children in the school holidays'. In term-time, the

---

55 Bourguignon and Rigney, *Exile: A Memoir*, 'The Other Side of the Fence', pp. 41–42.
56 Lewis, 'Introduction', p. viii.

donkey was used to transport manure and garden waste. Lore adds that her mother had said 'that one day Mrs Lambston thought the donkey was looking tired and told my father to unharness the poor dear and pull the cart himself. My mother swears that this is what brought on a new hemorrhage that laid him up in the Allchester County Hospital.'[57]

Reviewing the work of Lore Segal, the poet Carolyn Kizer wondered 'if any of the families anatomized in "Other People's Houses" ever read the book and felt any pangs other than the nip of the serpent's tooth'. Kizer commented 'One meanly hopes so.'[58] The inclusion of this story of heartless treatment leave the reader and critic dismayed and angered, and understandably so. Whether such incidents directly led to the premature death of Lore's father or not, it reveals how only the physically and mentally robust could cope with the reality of being a refugee domestic. Yet Lore Segal's main objective is not to dismiss as simply uncaring and indifferent those she and her parents came into contact with in these English homes. Indeed, she later commented with regard to her own reception in Liverpool and beyond: 'I think the people who took that feisty little uncomfortable alien child, Lore, into their inmost homes did something extraordinary and good.'[59]

The story of her father replacing the donkey literally as 'workhorse' can be read at different levels. To quote Gershon again, 'She knows how to tell such events so that far more is revealed than what actually happened.'[60] First, it is to express guilt at the indifference and shame she felt towards her father, leading to an inability to mourn him properly for many years. He is humiliated, yet she can only feel embarrassment about him. Second, audience has to be kept in mind, and Segal wrote essentially for an American market. When, for example, *Other People's Houses* was published in Britain a year later, it was largely ignored or misread.[61] To Ozick, the households in which Segal's parents found themselves, including that of Miss Douglas and Mrs Dillon, 'who with their great house and tea-with-the-vicar and their quiet garden, emerge not-quite-intact, and rather savagely, out of all the genteel English novels of all our childhoods'.[62] This, then, is the heritage world of Agatha Christie but seen

---

57 Segal, *Other People's Houses*, pp. 120–121.

58 Carolyn Kizer, 'The Education of Ilka Weissnix: *Her First American*', *New York Times*, 19 May 1985; Julia Baker, 'From *Other People's Houses* into *Shakespeare's Kitchen*', *The Yearbook of the Research Centre for German and Austrian Exile Studies* vol. 13 (2012), p. 199 note 5.

59 Mary Tabor, 'A Conversation with Lore Segal', *Missouri Review* vol. 30 no. 4 (2007), p. 60.

60 Karen Gershon, 'Uprooted', *Jewish Chronicle*, 2 April 1965.

61 See, for example, the short and unpleasant review in *Times Literary Review*, 5 August 1965.

62 Ozick, 'A Contraband Life', p. 90.

from below stairs and through the eyes of an astonishingly astute and
acerbic alien observer. As Segal later noted: 'I am dazzled, from the point
of view of the writer, by having had the experience of the English class
system from the inside … . Seems to me it was a gift.' But, revealing her
refusal to use hindsight to sanitise the past, she adds starkly: 'It didn't
seem so at the time.'[63]

Third, and most importantly, if Segal writes about Mrs Willoughby, Miss
Douglas, Mrs Dillon, and Mrs Lambston and their failure of imagination
and unthinking moments of cruelty, it is to universalise their limited vision
and not to distance herself from them. Reflecting on Ecclesiastes and his
warnings about evil, Segal states that 'it is my business to imagine the
oppressions that are done under the sun, *particularly those which I am in a
position to perpetrate* [my emphasis]'.[64] And in this respect the Groszmann
family before and after the war were themselves, ironically, the employers
of servants. Franzi recalls how when they were given their first room as
domestics she said to her husband: '"Can you remember the room our
maid had in Vienna?" … We had it a little bit worse in England, and I
thought, it serves us right.'[65] Later, when the wider Groszmann family was
united in the Dominican Republic, they employ a 'native' who is treated
badly and accused of stealing.[66] While the connection to her parents' lives
as domestics is not made explicit, Segal (and her mother) reveal how tables
can quickly be turned and power abused.

When evoking his Victorian childhood, Robert Graves recalled in
Goodbye to All That that servants 'seemed a foreign body in the house'.[67]
Such attitudes did not disappear in the twentieth century. Warning about
the possible treatment of aliens coming to work as domestics after the
Second World War (some of them, as mentioned, Holocaust survivors), a
Ministry of Labour official cautioned that there were still 'certain employers
[who] regarded domestic servants as of an inferior race and treated them
accordingly'.[68] If, as Graves continued, the physical separation of the
servants added to his sense that they were 'not quite human', the double
'alien' nature of refugee domestics rendered them as 'the beast within'.[69]
In Mrs Lambton's perspective, Ignatz Groszmann was a lesser species
within the animal hierarchy than her much loved donkey. This was a man,

---

63 Lore Segal testimony in Harris and Oppenheimer, *Into the Arms of Strangers*,
    pp. 254–255.
64 Segal, 'The Bough Breaks', p. 248.
65 Franzi Groszman, testimony in Harris and Oppenheimer, *Into the Arms of Strangers*,
    p. 176.
66 Segal, *Other People's Houses*, pp. 235, 237.
67 Robert Graves, *Goodbye to All That* (London: Penguin, 1960 [1929]), p. 20.
68 National Archives, LAB 8/92: W. Crookenden memorandum, 28 November 1945.
69 Kay Anderson, '"The beast within": race, humanity, and animality', *Environment
    and Planning D* vol. 18 no. 13 (2000), pp. 301–320.

Lore Segal explained to her *New Yorker* readers, who was the 'originator of an accounting system for one of [Vienna's] largest banks'.[70]

One final question needs to be raised with regard to *Other People's Houses*: is it to be placed under the heading of Holocaust literature? In the introduction to this study the approach of Robert Van Pelt and Deborah Dwork was applauded: rather than treating refugees as being on the periphery of the Holocaust, they argue that they are very much part of it: 'All European Jews ... were targeted for death. Some six million were killed. The remaining three million survived camps, endured life in hiding, 'passed' as a gentile [or] fled to safety.' They continue 'All were victims of the Holocaust. Had Jews not hidden or passed, they too would have been deported. Had they not sought asylum elsewhere, they too would have been caught in the machinery of death.'[71]

In contrast, Philip Cavanaugh's study of Lore Segal's fiction regards Auschwitz as being the heart of the Holocaust: 'The center remains a witness in a gas chamber.' From there, he argues *Other People's Houses* 'is spun out with the Holocaust as backdrop'.[72] Yet, rather than suggest that Segal 'experienced the Holocaust from the outside',[73] it is better to understand her writing as that of a refugee who is part of a Jewish and wider global human catastrophe in which homelessness and displacement was both normal and ongoing. To return to Dwork and Van Pelt, 'The history of refugee Jews during and after the Nazi era is literally, from the Latin *centrifugal*, to flee the center.' Dwork and Van Pelt have authored a definitive study of Auschwitz, but to them this infamous camp complex is not the only hub of the Holocaust. 'That center comprised Germany; then Greater Germany ... and finally all of German-ruled Europe. The sites of flight grew ever more distant from the countries adjacent to Germany to all the peopled continents.'[74] This was certainly true of the Groszmann family. In her first article for the *New Yorker*, Segal described each close relative and their quirks of character. All, she could assure her readers, were to 'come away safely' but 'we travelled by outlandish routes'. It meant the dispersal of the wide Groszmann family, reflected in the sites of their death: 'My father is buried in the East End of London, my grandfather in Santiago. My grandmother lies in a big cemetery in New Jersey.'[75]

Lore and her mother left Britain after the war, when they were united with Franzi's parents and brother in the Dominican Republic. After

---

70 Lore Segal, 'Other People's Houses: A Liberal Education', *New Yorker*, 4 March 1961, p. 37.

71 Deborah Dwork and Robert Van Pelt, *Flight from the Reich: Refugee Jews, 1933–1946* (New York: Norton, 2009), p. xiii.

72 Cavanaugh, 'The Present is a Foreign Country', pp. 476–477.

73 Ibid., p. 476.

74 Dwork and Van Pelt, *Flight from the Reich*, p. xiii.

75 Segal, 'Other People's Houses: A Liberal Education', p. 37.

several years there they were able to get into America, the country to which they had sought entry since the *Anschluss*. Yet, even in the land of immigrants, experiencing the ethnic diversity of New York, and married to an American, Segal remains the refugee. While her husband 'accepts without alarm this normal season of our lives', Segal cannot. She ends *Other People's Houses* powerfully on a note of troubling uncertainty: 'I, now that I have children and am about the age my mother was when Hitler came, walk gingerly and in astonishment upon this island of my comforts, knowing that it is surrounded on all sides by calamity.'[76] It is perhaps fitting that this conclusion elicited a prejudiced response (objecting to both its particularity and its universalism) from the reviewer in the London-based *Times Literary Supplement*: 'She is too much a Jew, too good an actress, ever to be quite satisfied ... she sees the world and herself from too many points of view'. Not surprisingly, he/she had earlier objected to the repeating of the violent antisemitism faced by Austrian Jewry following the *Anschluss*. It had 'been told so often that the heart puts up a barrier against it'.[77] The Mrs Willougbys of *Other People's Houses* were still alive and well in Britain during the 1960s. It explains why, in contrast to America, its initial publication made so small an impact in the country in which Lore and her parents had initially found refuge. Only Karen Gershon could explain its wider significance to a British audience: 'her knowledge of refugee life extends far beyond a child's world. Her interest in people and in her surroundings, combined with her great talent, enables her to show not only her impressions but the reality behind them'.[78]

The third and final memoir from the 1960s provides a bridge between that period and the rediscovery of the refugee domestic experience in the last two decades of the twentieth century. As noted, pure chance prevented the loss to posterity of Bronka Schneider's memoir. Its later publication reflected the strong interest in the Holocaust since the 1980s that had developed in North America. This was also the case with Hanna Spencer's diary and the revisiting and republishing of *Other People's Houses*. In contrast to the other two memoirs in this section, however, little is known of the origins of Hilde Gerrard's 'We Were Lucky'. It is the story of her and her husband's life in Britain as domestics and that of their twin children. It was probably written during the 1960s and then deposited by its author at the newly founded Museum of the Jewish East End in 1984. The author simply left a note saying that the manuscript, which ends abruptly, had been 'lying for many, many years in a drawer'.[79]

---

76 Segal, *Other People's Houses*, p. 312.
77 *Times Literary Supplement*, 5 August 1965.
78 Gershon, 'Uprooted'.
79 Jewish Museum, 34/84, additional note on deposit: Hilde Gerrard, 'We Were Lucky'.

That there was interest in it by the 1980s reflected the growth of 'history from below' and writing back the story of ordinary people into the past. The Museum of the Jewish East End was formed initially to explore the inner lives of immigrants from Eastern Europe, but it soon expanded its scope to cover other Jewish refugees, including those from Nazism. The focus was on 'ordinary' people and this was to include refugee domestic servants and the *Kindertransport*.[80] It remains that Hilde Gerrard's memoir lay gathering dust for decades, reflecting the general silence and lack of interest from 1945 (either as social history or as part of Holocaust narratives with an intimate connection to Britain) in the refugee domestic experience.

The literary qualities of 'We Were Lucky' are variable, even in comparison with Bronka Schneider's memoir and certainly in relation to the 'minor masterpiece' of *Other People's Houses*.[81] It still provides, however, an important account of the fluidity and messiness of refugee journeys from the Third Reich and one that is unique in the timing of its compilation. If Bronka's account was prompted by a lull in employment and news that their former castle home/place of work had burnt down, it seems that Hilde wrote following retirement during the 1960s. She was then reflecting on three decades of dislocation and the slow battle to re-establish a place called home.

'We Were Lucky' is not an ironic title, although the trials and heartbreak relayed by Hilde Gerrard leaves the reader querying whether it was meant as such. Yet, if compared with another account of refugeedom from the Nazi era, it begins to make sense. In 2004 Milena Roth, a former Czech *Kinder*, published *Lifesaving Letters* – ones that her mother, Anka, had sent to an English friend, Mrs Campbell, throughout the 1930s and into the Second World War. Like the Gerrards, Anka had hoped to bring her daughter to Britain on the *Kindertransport*, aiming to come later with her husband on a married domestic servant permit. With the first she succeeded and several times it seemed that she had also obtained posts for them to join her. The difficulty of getting offers of work followed by the necessary permits and visas is a recurring theme in the refugee domestic story. The problem of coordination was far more acute for a married couple. Devastatingly, this proved to be the case for Milena's parents. The paperwork did not arrive in time and they were both subsequently murdered in Auschwitz, having survived Terezin.[82]

---

80 The Museum of the Jewish East End became the London Museum of Jewish Life which merged with the Jewish Museum. It was reopened after Heritage Lottery funding in 2010 and a refugee domestic apron has been on permanent display since then.

81 Gershon, 'Perturbed Adolescence'.

82 Milena Roth, *Lifesaving Letters: A Child's Flight from the Holocaust* (Seattle: University of Washington Press, 2004).

These letters were thus only partially effective as 'lifesavers', but it is in the context of the agonising bureaucratic delay which ultimately doomed the Roths and others that the epithet 'Lucky' is employed by Hilde Gerrard. The point is amplified as Hilde and her husband, Gerhard, arrived in Britain without the necessary paperwork for their twin daughter and son. Hoping to 'arouse very little notice' at the port of arrival, their plans were scuppered when the twins began to cry. It did, however, block out all attempts at communication with the officials: 'I cannot say whether that helped but the tense moment came and our immigration papers were stamped and we were allowed to land [and] board the train at Dover'.[83]

Booksellers, the Gerrards left Berlin in 1934 as their livelihood was threatened, and moved to Italy. Like the Frank family of Frankfurt, such early movement was made easier by their international business connections, if on a more modest scale. The Gerrards also wanted to be close to Germany, especially as their parents were unable or unwilling to emigrate at this stage. The life Hilde and Gerhard made there, both socially and economically, was very much refugee-orientated, but one that was also integrated within wider Italian society. Revealing their remarkable entrepreneurship away from home, they created a private library and weekend tour business for the German Jews around the Milan area, quickly assimilating the surrounding topography and local heritage.[84] Acculturation was further exemplified in the naming of their twins, Renato and Gabriella, who were born several years after their arrival in Milan.[85]

The lives of the Gerrards and other German Jewish refugees were relatively settled, even if not fully secure in fascist Italy. Such temporary stability was abruptly ended in September 1938. The new antisemitic laws were particularly aimed at 'alien' Jews who were now subject to deportation. Another search for asylum was urgently required for people who were now refugees twice over. As with the Groszmanns, America was the Gerrard's preferred choice, but they faced a similar long wait if their quota numbers were to come up. It is here, again, where 'luck' in the form of personal contacts played a key role. Through their knowledge of the world of books the Gerrards had contacts with PEN (the international writers' body) and its members in Britain. One of these, the writer and broadcaster Gerald Bullett, arranged domestic posts for them both. Being at the heart of the refugee community in Italy, the Gerrards soon learnt the rules of the game:

We heard that the consul was very critical of friends of ours who had clean and very unspoiled hands, questioning their ability to do

---

83   Jewish Museum, 34/84, additional note on deposit: Hilde Gerrard, 'We Were Lucky', p. 13.
84   Ibid., passim.
85   Ibid., p. 7.

housework. After that tip-off we scraped carrots and peeled potatoes and after a few days our hands were ingrained with dirt and we had no difficulty on that score.

Gerhard learnt cooking and Hilde, as with Hanna Spencer in Czechoslovakia, the art of applying the 'finishing touches to ironing shirts'.[86]

Once in Britain, as with so many refugee domestics, the problem of unsuitable homes with dysfunctional employers (and then alien restrictions when war was declared) necessitated constant moving between posts. This, plus the separation from her twins and the increasing desperation of their parents' pleas to get them out of Germany, led to Hilde suffering acute anxiety. From September 1939 letters from their parents arrived via America describing their perilous state: 'I was not able to help and nearing a nervous breakdown.'[87]

In contrast to many domestic memoirs, the fate of those left behind looms large in Hilde's testimony. When Gerhard was released from internment the Gerrards succeeded in reuniting as a family and moved to the small town of Colne, Lancashire. Living together as one unit was something the Groszmanns, for example, were never able to achieve in England. In Colne, Hilde initially worked as a day servant and her husband in a factory. Yet, rather than reflecting on this moment of domestic stability in the north of England, 'We Were Lucky' focuses on the continent:

> We were completely separated from our parents and our only contact were Red Cross messages which we got once a month – at most consisting of twenty five words. These messages told us that our parents have had to leave their home [and move to a room] ... . They could not stay long even there and after a few messages the address changed to Graupenstrasse, which was already the Sammellager, the place from which the deportation started.[88]

In her stark prose Hilde portrays her feeling of utter, excruciating powerlessness: 'What could I do? I approached every organisation I knew ... . I approached people. I was so helpless.'[89] Physical exhaustion as a result of her domestic job, looking after her children, and the emotional strain of the news that her parents had been deported led Hilde to collapse. It took her many years to recover. The Holocaust thus permeates 'We Were Lucky', and not only through implication in its title. As a result, although the years as a domestic are not regarded nostalgically, there is the absence

---

86 Ibid., p. 12.
87 Ibid., p. 16.
88 Ibid., p. 27.
89 Ibid.

of resentment that typified contemporary accounts and later ones such as Bronka Schneider's and that related by Lore Segal. Instead, expressions of gratitude are to the fore.

Perhaps with the benefit of hindsight that she and Gerhard had created a successful book business after the war, Hilde was willing to present some of their domestic employment more positively than did other, earlier narratives. In one of the happier households, for example, the mistress 'paid me a compliment, which cheered me up ... "Hilde, we never had such clean toilets as we have at present".' Hilde added 'How else can one show one's gratitude if one is employed to clean than by doing it as well as possible. She thought that everything sparkled.' In what was a rare attempt to inject some lightness into her account, Hilde remembered that it 'gave me hope that if things got worse I could always make my way as a lavatory cleaner with such a recommendation'.[90] Further distant, there is none of the anguish here that those such as Franzi Groszmann had expressed at the loss of status and humiliation with their new lives as domestic servants.

The memory of losing parents through journeys to the abyss underpins 'We Were Lucky'. Their murder emphasises Hilde's sense of marginality in the wider world alongside her apparent rootedness in England. What emerges strongly from her brief memoir is a two-ness that so typifies the wider refugee experience. There is pride in their local integration, alongside loyalty and gratitude to Britain, but no denial of their complex migrant journey that led them there. All these elements of identity and experience were expressed in Hilde's recollection of VE Day in Colne and her culinary response to it: 'The town was illuminated and everybody was in the streets. I had only rice in the house, made a large bowl of risotto and the neighbours came in for supper – we were accepted.'[91] Yet immediately in her text this seemingly redemptive ending is qualified: 'Our nearest and dearest were amongst the heaviest casualties. Six million Jews were killed.'[92]

Ironically, a year after opening their bookshop in Colne, a letter from the American Consulate arrived: the Gerrards could now enter the United States. Coming to the end of her account, and summing up her years of constant flux, Hilde pondered 'How much heartache, distress, homelessness would have been avoided if that permission would have come earlier. Heaven would have opened in our eyes.' But having 'lived through the battle, the hardship [and] the same chances of life or death', and with their children now at secondary school, they decided to stay in Britain. They had at least created something of a new life and livelihood for themselves.[93]

---

90   Ibid., p. 20.
91   Ibid., p. 31.
92   Ibid., p. 32.
93   Ibid., p,35.

The last page of her memoir is the only one that Hilde appeared to struggle with. It was typed out twice and amended. At first, 'We Were Lucky' ends on an upbeat note, relating their love of the local countryside and praising Lancashire hospitality, which was 'very warm … we were asked to tea and also invited by our neighbours and friends'. There is also pride expressed in the success of their business. All of this was then crossed out as Hilde reflects on the decision not to go to America, leading to a somewhat resigned, ambivalent final assessment of their situation: 'We live isolated in a small town. We have accepted our surroundings. We have made some good friends and have nice neighbours. We go to Synagogue in Manchester at least twice a year.' Hilde was still clearly far from convinced by this ending and she edited it to close on a questioning note – one which closely mirrored that of *Other People's Houses* in articulating the refugee dilemma: 'We were uprooted in 1933. Are we really at "home" – are we cosmopolitans and able to live anywhere? Or are we strangers everywhere?'[94] It is perhaps not surprising that the Gerrards later moved to north-west London, closer to a larger community of refugees from Nazism, in a further attempt to rediscover 'home'.[95]

More precisely, these three forms of autobiographical writing from the 1960s revealed different approaches to refugeedom during the Holocaust which in turn influenced how the experience as domestics was remembered and constructed. In Bronka Schneider's account domestic service is at the heart of the narrative, but of the three she downplays the possibility of permanent refugee status and ends by asserting a new, American identity. In relation to Britain, there is gratitude expressed, but also criticism of the conditional acceptance, lack of empathy, and temporary asylum offered. But if America is presented as the happy endpoint, her later attempted suicide suggests a more troubled reality. With Hilde Gerrard, the ambiguity of belonging and not belonging is expressed explicitly. Nevertheless, the permanent settlement in Britain and sense of gratitude, alongside the greater chronological distance of her memoir, act as a barrier to more critical perspectives on what Hilde and her husband had experienced 'below stairs'.

Lastly, the insights of Lore Segal, the only professional writer to confront this history, allows for a self-reflexive anthropological gaze through the prisms of time, place and generation on the incongruities and tragi-comedy of refugee domestic service. Even then, the process of writing and rewriting took her several decades and autobiographical praxis utilising a unique blending of genres. It is that which makes *Other People's Houses* one of the

---

94   Ibid., p. 36 (and retyped p. 30).

95   I am grateful to Esther Saraga, who has found correspondence between her mother and Hilde which reveal that the Gerrards had moved to Harrow by the later 1970s and were part of a wider refugee circle. Email to the author, Esther Saraga, 26 July 2013.

classic refugee memoirs and much more. As its reviewer in *New Republic* perceptively noted, it was on the surface 'an account of flight from the Nazis of displacement and transplantation'. But 'beneath that it contains an extraordinary rendering of the self' which gave it universal significance: 'a displaced person before having had time to become a person'.[96] Indeed, it provides a bridge to later narratives of female forced migration which will conclude this chapter.

For all the richness of these texts, it remains that only Segal's was published during the 1960s and its positive reception was limited largely to America. Furthermore, while there were other former refugee domestic voices articulated from the 1950s through to the 1970s, these were few in number. This sparseness reflected not only an unwillingness to share this past but also, and perhaps more importantly, an absence of audience for such memories. The refugees from Nazism whose experiences were published tended to be already in the public eye, such as the actress Lili Palmer.[97] The exception was Karen Gershon's anthology *We Came as Children*, published in 1966 and the first account of the *Kindertransport*.[98] While it matched Segal's work for evoking outsiderdom and the question of belonging, even it failed to stimulate further reflection for another generation. Nevertheless, it attracted far greater attention in Britain than *Other People's Houses*. It was an early indication that, when the refugees from Nazism were to be rediscovered, the domestics would be the poor relations compared to the favoured *Kinder*. While, for example, there are now a handful of *Kindertransport* anthologies and collective biographical documentaries, there is no equivalent for those who came as servants.

From the 1980s to the 1990s:
Social History, the Holocaust, and Refugee Domestics

For four decades after the war finding the voices of former refugee domestics is a difficult task, requiring both historical detective work and a careful reading of the small amount of material that was produced, or survived, alongside a querying of why the large majority of these women remained silent. Since the 1980s the problem for the scholar of this migration is the reverse – there are literally scores of testimonies and in a variety of forms – published memoirs as well as oral and video testimony. While no particular extended scheme has been devoted to interviewing refugee

---

96 Gilman, 'One Refugee Child's Story', p. 15.

97 Lilli Palmer, *Change Lobsters – and Dance: An Autobiography* (London: W.H. Allen, 1976).

98 Karen Gershon (ed.), *We Came as Children: A Collective Autobiography* (London: Gollancz, 1966).

domestics,[99] the fact that so many of those that escaped to Britain during the 1930s through this route, along with the longer life expectancy of women, has ensured that they are present in the many projects set up to record the experiences of refugees and survivors from the Holocaust. These are local (such as the Manchester Jewish Museum and London Jewish Museum, 1980s/90s), national (the Imperial War Museum 1978–81 and the Association of Jewish Refugees' 'Refugee Voices', 2009), and international (the Fortunoff Video Archive 1979–81 and the Spielberg Visual History Foundation, 1994 onwards).

Two factors have been at work in this 'rediscovery'. First was the social history revolution in which the lives of ordinary people were valued and attempts made to create a 'history from below'. Within this, the experiences of migrants and minorities, the working class and women were especially valued. Grassroots projects emerged aimed at empowering those suffering contemporary injustice through recovering past presence and the resistance of earlier oppressed groups and individuals.[100] Such approaches evolved rapidly during in the 1970s. The second development was a fraction later – a popular engagement with the Holocaust which took off in America during the 1980s. Britain followed with major developments such as the incorporation of the Holocaust in the school curriculum, retrospective war crimes legislation, the Imperial War Museum's permanent Holocaust exhibition, and Holocaust Memorial Day, all in the 1990s and early 2000s. If the history and memory of refugees in Britain remained neglected, there was now another, specific, context in which to place those who escaped Nazi persecution.

It is not possible to separate these two new impulses when dissecting the testimony of refugee domestics in this late period. Both, however, have to be kept in mind when exploring, for the last time in this chapter, how their voices were articulated/silenced and how their experiences were represented by others. Indeed, to make sense of this material, juxtaposing what might be contrasted as British versus continental perspectives – sometimes in separate spheres, sometimes in conflict and sometimes in productive tension – provides a helpful template.

For all the testimony that has emerged from the very late 1970s, it remains that almost none relating specifically to refugee domestics has been produced in what might be deemed the mainstream. Memoirs, for example, have tended to be self-published or in local projects. And the larger refugee oral/video history projects have not sought out former servants per se. Indeed, the focus of the sponsoring bodies has tended to limit the space

---

99 The Museum of London Jewish Life in the late 1980s/early 1990s was a particular exception.

100 Paul Thompson, *Oral History: The Voice of the Past* (Oxford: Oxford University Press, 1988), chapter 3.

given to this occupation or distorted the direction of the refugee voice when remembering these first experiences in Britain. In short, the greater volume of autobiographical material has not necessarily enabled the refugee domestic experience to be articulated extensively or freely.

The first testimony to be analysed is from the Imperial War Museum's 'Britain and the Refugee Crisis' oral history project, the first to be undertaken. Its initial title was 'Civilian Internment in Britain 1939–1945' and it reflected the limitations of a museum which, until recently, marginalised the history of the Holocaust. The recordings in this project thus focused primarily on how refugee experiences related to a domestic military-related matter – alien internment – and therefore fell within the narrow remit of the Museum's objectives to record twentieth-century conflict. A handful of former domestics were interviewed, but they are tantalising in respect of the individual's brief experiences as such. All the issues outlined previously, including the awareness of such posts, gathering paperwork, the refugee journey, and the experiences of such work, are condensed by the interviewers into fleeting responses. They constantly steer the interviewees back to the measures taken against the aliens and life in the internment camps.

Typical in this respect is the testimony of Margot Pottlitzer, a journalist in Germany before she came to Britain on a domestic permit following *Kristallnacht*. Pottlitzer is happy to talk about that aspect of her refugee life, proudly proclaiming at the start of her interview that 'I came over like all the best people on a domestic permit.'[101] Margot provides snippets about her life as a servant. She had clearly reflected on the nature of the scheme and how 'we were given refuge but no security at all'. The confusion caused to those around her by her being a professional woman now working below stairs was also hastily narrated. On the one hand, Margot remembered that she was accepted because 'whilst they were all very class-conscious, I was classless'. On the other, she recalled how she struggled to adjust to her new status in the rigid hierachy of domestic service, where one's place had to be clearly delineated: 'I wasn't even allowed into the kitchen if I wanted to make a cup of tea or something.'[102] Yet, rather than pursue these tensions, the interviewer insists on internment being the dominant theme – Margot was sent first to Holloway Prison and then the Isle of Man. In the transcript of 46 pages, only a few paragraphs mention domestic service, even though she was in such work for far longer than she was interned. Margot at least had the last word: she wrote in some 'Additional Remarks', criticising the focus on her life as an 'enemy alien' and whether the refugees were really a threat to national security: 'You asked and I answered a few questions which I thought should be obsolete by now.'[103]

---

101 Imperial War Museum, Sound archive, 003816/05.
102 Ibid.
103 Ibid.

In a very different way, the refugee domestic experience was also largely silenced in what was the first published life story by a former refugee who came to Britain through this route. As with so many of the testimonies, the title revealed much about the context(s) in which the life story was to be presented: Martha Lang's *The Austrian Cockney* (1980), accompanied on its cover with a street map of north-east London and a topographical overview of Vienna's surrounds.[104] Martha, like so many former refugee domestics, was brought up in the Austrian capital and she came to Britain following the *Anschluss*. Eventually settling in Hackney, her brief memoir was published by Centerprise, a classic social history project set up in 1971 'to provide for working class people in the area the opportunity to create their own books'.[105]

Two forms of universalisation are present in the publication of *The Austrian Cockney*, which both allow and limit the refugee domestic's freedom to speak. First, Martha's work as a domestic is put alongside her other experiences in factories and offices. No special attention is thus given to her life serving several different houses: there is no acknowledgment that such employment had special significance for refugee women coming to Britain during the 1930s. Instead, her career is presented as being part of a normal female proletarian work pattern: 'In Martha Lang's case, as for many women, [it was] one job after another, many for firms which no longer exist in Hackney.'[106] Second, she is identified as a typical newcomer to Britain: 'The difficulties she faced are those which confront many immigrants: a new language, strange customs and the problems of finding work.'[107] Here linkages to more recent migrant stories are made, but it ignores both the specific experiences of refugees from Nazism and those who came after to work as domestics.

Refugeedom is thus downplayed in *The Austrian Cockney*. Neither the procedures to get to Britain nor her refugee journey are mentioned – Martha presents herself as having been simply transplanted from one place to another: 'I managed to escape to England, and one late evening in May 1938 I found myself at Victoria Station'.[108] Similarly, the Holocaust is summarised tersely and obliquely so as to save herself and her readers from contemplating the horrors of journeys into the abyss: 'I feel we all have read, seen and heard enough of the tragic happenings of this epoch, one way or another. All I will tell you is, that, like millions of others, my mother and brother lost their lives.'[109] This lacuna was even more pronounced in our

---

104 Martha Long, *The Austrian Cockney* (London: Centerprise, 1980).
105 Ibid., p. 71.
106 Ibid., back cover blurb.
107 Ibid.
108 Ibid., p. 17.
109 Ibid.

previous example. So narrow was the focus of the Imperial War Museum's refugee project that Margot Pottlitzer and others were not even asked what happened to the families and friends left behind on the continent. With Martha Long and this migrant form of 'History from below', the refugee domestic is allowed to speak but the emphasis on class is at the expense of ethnicity/refugeedom.

Much greater freedom is evident in Myra Baram's *The Girl With Two Suitcases* (1988), the second such account in the public realm.[110] Self-published, the title reveals her life after leaving Berlin in 1939. It reflects what she calls her endless 'wanderings' in Britain before, during, and after the war. In total contrast to *The Austrian Cockney*, the fate of relatives in Germany and then Denmark is a constant feature of her early chapters. She also dwells on the isolation of being a refugee, especially as a domestic. Running through all refugee domestic autobiographical writing, thanks are given to the place of asylum. In this case, as with much later testimony, it is expressed with full knowledge of what happened to those left behind:

> This book has been written as a token of gratitude to England ... and its many wonderful people who tried to assist a young and lonely refugee. It is a simple story recounting the actual experiences of one of the girls whose life was spared.[111]

Again, it is far from a straightforward 'simple' account – despite claims to the contrary. Its style ranges from the novelistic, with a focus on her tragic war romances, to the more sociological, exploring the nature of being an alien in a foreign country. The domestic experiences Myra relates are equally complex for the refugee identity they reveal.

In contrast to Martha Lang's testimony, the anxiety of leaving (in Myra's case, by ship from Hamburg) and the possibility of her papers and belongings not being in order are highlighted. Set alongside the world of persecution and uncertainty she has fled, England is presented as benign and relaxed. In Southampton the immigration officer 'looked slightly amused when I replied to the usual question on how long I wished to stay in England, with a fervent "for ever"'.[112] Myra came from a wealthy family, but she presents positively her new life as a servant in the early stages of her narrative. If there were not enough British people wanting to be domestics, 'all the better for refugees like myself. Without working permits, we could not have entered the country. Dear God, would I find a job for my parents so that they, too, would be saved from the clutches of the Nazis'.[113]

110 Myra Baram, *The Girl With Two Suitcases* (Lewes: The Book Guild, 1988).
111 Ibid., p. 7.
112 Ibid., p. 10.
113 Ibid., pp. 16–17.

The family that she was working for, the Stuarts, were kinder than most, but, alongside praise, Myra presents a more critical perspective that at least begins to question her earlier tolerant image of Britain. Myra relates this initially through the Stuarts' inability to understand her background and why she had to leave. Their different worlds were exposed when Mr Stuart 'cross-examined me about my family, my education and the situation in Germany, of which he was very ignorant. I was quite offended when he doubted my statement that my brother had been in a concentration camp because he was Jewish.'[114]

The Stuarts also took on a husband and wife refugee cook/gardener, the former of whom found it hard to adjust to his new lowly status. Myra was not sympathetic: 'We had to thank our lucky stars to be alive and have food and shelter. I was intelligent enough to realize that the English people were not interested in our glorious past, but rather took us at face value.'[115] There is, however, further ambiguity in her text in this respect. With the outbreak of war, and with greater work freedom, Myra became a nurse, albeit relegated to what was regarded as its least desirable form – mental health. With the alien panic of spring 1940, she lost her new job and returned to being a domestic. She now wanted to pursue nursing as a profession and was successful in this quest. But, finding a new post, Myra was treated badly by the matron and resigned. For this she was told off by her former employer, Mrs Stuart. In turn, Myra 'felt quite offended. I was indeed a trained kindergarten teacher.'[116]

The sense of working beneath her normal station was made explicit later in the war, when Myra was again between posts and had to register with the local Labour Exchange. The official criticised her, reflecting both class and gender prejudice melded with xenophobia: '*You* girls are always changing your jobs … . I am putting you down as a "domestic".' Myra remembered that 'it was like a slap in the face. This stamped me into the lowest category of employment. I protested, "I am a trained kindergarten teacher. I am not a domestic servant", but to no avail.'[117] This repetition in her memoir of her former status, in spite of the earlier criticism of her fellow employee, the refugee gardener, is revealing. Even for a positive-minded young refugee, the prospect of remaining in domestic service beyond an initial and necessary period was anathema. Her status, but also her individual agency, was being undermined. Myra remains the refugee, the girl with two suitcases in England.

It is not surprising that, unable to fully root herself in the country which she had at first proclaimed was now hers forever, she became active in the

---

114 Ibid., p. 17.
115 Ibid., p. 25.
116 Ibid., p. 56.
117 Ibid., pp. 69–70.

Zionist movement and then emigrated permanently to Israel. Having left Britain, and ceasing formally to be a refugee, there is no connection made, in contrast to that made crudely in *The Austrian Cockney*, to the life of later migrants. There is acceptance of the need to come to Britain through the route of domestic service, but equally, and against the dominant grain of gratitude, increasing irritation expressed that in practice and on paper she was still, after several years in Britain, expected to remain in her place below stairs.

The recovery of the refugee domestic experience from the very late 1970s thus stimulated and created fresh testimony. If nothing else, the scale of the various projects, alongside individual memoirs such as those by Lang and Baram, revealed the variations in experiences *and* the differing memories of it that were constructed in post-war identities. Oral history projects at the Manchester Jewish Museum and then the London Museum of Jewish Life rescued and rediscovered a neglected migration that had become marginalised even within the study of the refugees from Nazism. There was, as yet, no bureaucratic history to explain the procedures that allowed these women to come to Britain and, in this respect, when some of the testimony collected was distorted through memory, it remained unchallenged by the interviewer. This included Hilda Dahl, who claimed that she was told that she had to be a domestic only on arrival in England, to what she relates as her immense disappointment.[118] The interviews for the London-focused museum tended not to focus on the time spent as a domestic, in one case representing less than 2 per cent of the testimony even though the individual was in service for several years.[119] Even so, common and challenging aspects emerged, including the often tense relationships between the refugees and their co-religionist employers in these two major cities of British Jewish settlement.[120]

Inevitably, the lens through which these life stories were viewed impacted on the testimony collected and published. The Imperial War Museum and the Centerprise projects severely limited the freedom of the former domestics to speak beyond narrow confines. In contrast, *The Girl With Two Suitcases*, which was privately published, articulated the ambiguities of being a refugee servant from a professional background. Even then, the desire to express gratitude acts as a self-imposed restraint on exploring these tensions further. Although uneven, because of the weak sociology of knowledge regarding domestic servant entry (and the Holocaust more generally), the oral history projects in Britain's two Jewish museums were the first to take seriously in their own right the experiences

---

118 Manchester Jewish Museum: Hilda Dahl, interview J282.

119 London Jewish Museum, oral history no. 121, Hilda Schindler.

120 Including households which were either too unobservant or too Orthodox for the refugee domestics. See Manchester Jewish Museum: J281, J314.

of such ordinary women. They reflected the success – but also the still early stages – of the 'history from below' movement and its impact on museology and wider heritage in Britain as articulated within a specifically Jewish sphere.

The social history revolution of the 1970s/1980s also helped produce a classic of autobiographical writing: Ronald Fraser's *In Search of a Past* (1984).[121] As with Lore Segal's *Other People's Houses*, it is an astonishing examination of 'self' and, as with this earlier work, *In Search of a Past* covers the refugee domestic service experience by incorporating testimony from an older generation. Fellow oral historian Paul Thompson has described Fraser's book as 'rare, original, and fascinating'. For the soul-searching project, which took decades to complete, Fraser interviewed the servants who worked for his upper-class parents at the Manor, a large estate in the Home Counties village of Amnersfield. He also talked to his elderly, increasingly fragile father, with whom his relationship had been strained. With its mixture of social history and psychoanalysis, the 'result is a completely new form of autobiography, confronting the great issues of time and class, yet intensely intimate'. Thompson adds that 'It is also a fugue on the nature of memory. The apparently straightforward life story evidence of the servant is shown, by juxtaposition, to have its own silences and evasions.'[122]

While Thompson does not explicitly mention the material relating to the refugee servants (and the earlier Austrian nanny and, in effect, his substitute mother, who was sacked at the start of the conflict), his comments have equal validity. Twenty years after *Other People's Houses*, a second acutely reflexive account was thus published, its different chronological and national context adding to its significance when confronting this remarkable movement. A narrative of many voices, and resembling in this respect Gershon's *We Came Alone* in its fluidity and sharply contrasting testimonies, Nelly Wintermann and her daughter Lisel appear over halfway through the text. It is spring 1940 when many of the pre-war staff had departed. The Wintermanns had left Vienna together – Nelly's husband had earlier managed to reach safety in India, where he joined his brother's business.[123] After working in the East End for an exploitative Jewish family, Nelly heard about a vacancy at the Manor to work as a cook. Revealing the flexibility necessitated by war-time servant shortages, Nelly was allowed to move there with her daughter.

Ronald Fraser interviewed Nelly and she also wrote down her experiences for him. Lisel, later Lizzie or Elizabeth, provided oral testimony, as did many of the English servants from the war years. Fraser's approach allows for a

121 Ronald Fraser, *In Search of a Past* (London: Verso, 2010 [1984]).
122 Thompson, *Oral History*, pp. 150–151.
123 Fraser, *In Search of a Past*, pp. 133–134.

kaleidoscope of memories and one in which the centrality of Nelly to the dynamics of the Manor is made clear. 'The Manor's centre of gravity, the kitchen, remained empty until small, plump Nelly came to fill it for the rest of the war ... .'[124] Taken on its own, Nelly's testimony appears straight-forward. Yet, read alongside that of other servants from the Manor, it is problematised, revealing in a unique way the multilayered identities of a refugee domestic and her place/placelessness in the world above and below stairs. It starts with Nelly's description of her introduction to this new life. It is a reflection in two distinct parts, which intricately reveal acceptance and its limitations:

> At the Manor Madam [Fraser's mother] was ever so sweet. She spoke German, her behaviour was wonderful, she understood everything. She say to me one day. It doesn't agree with me to call you Cornelia or Nelly. Can I call you Cookie?[125]

Whereas the status politics of such renaming had caused Lore Segal's mother distress and anger, Nelly presents it in a matter-of-fact way: 'that's the way it happened'. The refusal to probe further illustrates how silences in autobiographical praxis have to be considered alongside what is said or written.[126] Most of Nelly's testimony relates to the abundance of food and drink in the war-time Manor and her worshipping of 'Madam': 'I would do anything for her.' Her daughter, however, provides a different perspective on the mistress–maid relationship: 'Lisel says, Mummy, you worked so hard there, don't you remember? ... I say, No, I don't, I don't remember because I loved her ... .'[127] And against Nelly's sanguine account the xenophobia and jealousy aimed at her and Lisel comes out strongly in the testimonies of the former servants. Some were able to reflect with hindsight at their own prejudices ('the sort of things I wouldn't dream of saying today') while others still harboured resentments: 'She seemed to work an awful lot, but really she fiddled about and didn't get on with it.'[128] In larger houses, servant hierarchies and tensions were the norm.

There is only the vaguest hint in Nelly's testimony of the world left behind and the dispersal of her family. Explaining her professed lack of interest in servant gossip, Nelly recalled 'I wasn't very interested, my thoughts were far away.' On its own, and in the context of her wider memories, too much could be read into this sentence. But Mary, then a young servant, recalled:

---

124 Ibid., p. 133.
125 Ibid., p. 134.
126 Ibid., p. 134.
127 Ibid., p. 136.
128 Ibid., pp. 144–145.

Poor old Cookie, she used to go round deep in thought, thinking of her husband or the relatives she's had to leave behind. Maria, she used to call me, Maria, I'm so sad … . She told me that some of her relatives had been killed, told me about the Jews and how awful it was. Her face would be drawn, you could see how she had suffered. She lived for the war to end.

While Mary's memories (themselves distorted, perhaps, through later knowledge of the Holocaust) act as a counter to the overly rose-tinted ones of 'Cookie' herself, the former English servant consciously stops short of defining Nelly solely as 'victim'. Mary added that Nelly 'was happy to be in England with Elizabeth and know that they were safe. It wasn't often she spoke about her sadness, most of the time she'd laugh and joke with us.'[129] Indeed, the last sentence questions the isolation from the other servants that Nelly remembered, the querying of which took away from her special relationship with Fraser's mother and placed her firmly 'downstairs'.

Nelly's testimony within *In Search of a Past* is brief and fragmentary, but the holistic and meditative nature of the book is far more revealing than other accounts from the late 1970s/1980s (Myra Baram's partially excepted). It is rooted in English social history and the psychology of the individual, yet, reflecting the diversity of the Manor's inhabitants, one steeped in migrant and, specifically, Holocaust-related journeys. For Ronald Fraser, brought up by a much-loved Austrian nanny forced to leave because of the anti-Nazi war, who had his first sexual relations with Lisel, it was at the heart of his childhood and adolescence. Through Fraser's painfully open family archaeology, Nelly/'Cookie' is a part of, but far from constrained by, the Manor. Her place identity was between Amersfield, the continent of Europe, and India – with all the complexities of security and uncertainty that entailed.

If the subtlety and multilayered nature of refugee domestic identity is outlined and contextualised by *In Search of a Past*, mainstream cultural representations of it during the 1980s and early 1990s are more notable for their crudeness. While important exceptions will be explored, the two that dominated have a feature in common – the lack of agency they bestow on their Jewish refugee characters. These individuals have no depth and in the first example, *Change*, a novel by Maureen Duffy, published three years after Fraser's book, the refugee domestic is instrumentalised to illustrate wider issues.[130]

Duffy is a well-respected, popular, and prolific writer, and *Change* has a surface resemblance to *In Search of a Past*. It is a story of Britain at war told from a variety of different perspectives and in fragmentary style. One

---

129 Ibid., p. 145.
130 Maureen Duffy, *Change* (London: Methuen, 1987).

of the lives explored is Tilde, a refugee domestic working for a London Jewish family, the Fentimans. Tilde's purpose in the novel is both to observe the blitz and wartime life as an outsider and more basically to narrate a simplistic (and chronologically misleading) account of the Holocaust. Duffy's attempt to show that a different type of war was happening on the continent was no doubt well-meaning. The mistakes she makes in outlining the evolution of the 'Final Solution' reflect the lack of detailed knowledge on this subject in Britain as late as the 1980s.

Tilde is defined by the Holocaust. She is unable and unwilling to forget those she has left behind and damaged in her self-worth by the persecution she has endured and witnessed. She survives and no more: 'Her shell must be kept intact while it grew inwards, calcifying the still soft interior until the shell met the stone heart at its core.'[131] Her part in the narrative ends when Dr Fentiman shows her pictures from Belsen; thereafter, it is hard to imagine her enjoying any future happiness.[132] Following the example of Gisela Waldstein in *Dark Summer*, some 40 years earlier, Tilde will, thereafter, merely exist.

In *Change* Tilde was at least given a voice but even this was absent in what was a far larger cultural production. The film *The Remains of the Day* was released by Columbia Pictures in 1993 and was a Merchant Ivory Production with an all-star cast, based on the novel of the same title by Kazuo Ishiguro which won the 1989 Booker Prize.[133] In both book and film the action, focused on life in Lord Darlington's stately home, shifts from pre-war to post-war Britain. There are, however, subtle differences between the two versions. Stevens, the butler, had remained in the house after Lord Darlington's death, but Miss Kenton, the housekeeper, has long since left. In a tale of unconsummated love and the confines of Englishness, they meet up many years later and relive the momentous events that had taken place during the 1930s. Then Lord Darlington had become an apologist for Hitler and used his house as a centre for anti-war appeasers. As part of his naive belief that all was well with Nazi Germany, the aristocrat becomes antisemitic, linking to Mosley and the British 'blackshirts'. Once converted to racism, the aristocrat orders Stevens, through Miss Kenton, to sack his two Jewish maids, named in Ishiguro's novel as Ruth and Sarah. Miss Kenton is dismayed: 'Mr Stevens, I cannot quite believe my ears. Ruth and Sarah have been members of my staff for over six years now. I trust them absolutely and indeed they trust me. They have served in this house excellently.'[134] Threatening to resign, Miss Kenton still carries out the order and the two maids tearfully come to see him. 'As I recall, neither of them

131 Ibid., p. 99.
132 Ibid., p. 212.
133 Kazuo Ishiguro, *The Remains of the Day* (London: Faber and Faber, 1989).
134 Ibid., p. 148.

said anything of note throughout the whole interview, which lasted perhaps three or four minutes, and they left sobbing just as they had arrived.'[135] These literally speechless servants are there to illustrate the moral turpitude of the upper classes in the 1930s, of which the naive but highly political antisemitism of Lord Darlington is an example. The Jewish maids are silent because they are not important in themselves. Their presence in the novel is purely to illustrate the potential of prejudice, even in tolerant England.

While it is not explicit, the length of time the Jewish girls have been in service and their names suggest that they were not of refugee origin. As noted, few Jews of East European origin went into service, and those that did tended to work for middle-class Jewish families and rarely at all after 1914. The idea that 'there were many Jewish persons on the staff at Darlington Hall' is thus ahistorical,[136] but this is not the point of Ruth and Sarah's brief and mute appearance in the novel: they are victims of prejudice and no more.

In the film version, some four years later, with a screenplay by Ruth Prawer Jhabvala (who herself had escaped from Nazism), the Jewish maids were explicitly refugees. Ruth and Sarah become Elsa and Irma and are initially brought into Darlington Hall as a humanitarian gesture. They are briefly allowed a collective voice to express gratitude to Lord Darlington, which they do with appropriate deference. The pathos of Elsa and Irma, as well as their terror and misery, is amplified by their age in the film. Rather than adults, they are young teenagers. Elsa and Irma are thus too young to have been eligible for domestic service and appear more as *Kindertransportees*, the wider experience of whom was being recovered from the late 1980s. The full implications of their expulsion from Darlington Hall is articulated in the film by Miss Kenton, who warns Stevens that they would be sent back to Germany. Inseparable and desperate, Elsa and Irma are at the mercy of others: they are defenceless creatures who are turned into unwanted pets.[137] If Duffy's Tilde is there to illustrate the basic historical truth of how the Home Front was contemporaneous to the Holocaust, then the treatment of Jewish domestics (refugee or otherwise) in *The Remains of the Day* reveals the malign potential of antisemitism within England itself. In both cases the Jewish servants are constrained, even voiceless, ultimately unable to shape their self-destiny.

It was left to the alternative world of culture to challenge the representation of the Jewish refugee domestic as powerless. This was most powerfully

135 Ibid., pp. 149–150.

136 Ishiguro relates the research he carried out for the book, which included 'books by and about British servants'. At this point they would not have included material on Jewish refugees. Kazuo Ishiguro, 'On writing *The Remains of the Day*', *Guardian*, 6 December 2014.

137 *The Remains of the Day*, Columbia Films, Merchant Ivory Production, 1993.

articulated in Philip Osment's *This Island's Mine*, a play produced by the Gay Sweatshop theatre company. It was first performed on 24 February 1988 in the Drill Hall Arts Centre, London, and then toured inside and outside the UK.[138] Loosely based on *The Tempest*, it was written in the context of the Conservative government's introduction of Section 28. This clause forbade local councils and schools from 'promoting' homosexuality or regarding it as anything other than subnormal and harmful to the 'family'. The contents of the play were also a response to the related AIDS hysteria, which added new layers of prejudice to British homophobia. More generally, the Gay Sweatshop company was founded in the 1970s to present gay men and lesbians positively and counteract the dominant image of them either as a danger or as irredeemably damaged.[139]

By the 1980s, partly through collective action during the 1984 Miners' Strike, wider alliances were forged within gay politics. Issues of sexuality were now linked to race, class, and gender. *This Island's Mine* was part of this movement. Osment wanted to write a play that connected those who came to Britain as exiles and

> people who feel like exiles in their own country … . I wanted to include a wide range of characters who did not, at first glance, have anything in common such as a young [gay] West Indian actor and an elderly Jewish refugee.[140]

Miss Rosenblum is a central character in *This Island's Mine*: a former refugee domestic who now provides a refuge for those escaping different forms of persecution in contemporary Britain. She tells her lodger, Martin, who has just been sacked for his sexuality:

> 'Beware!
> It can happen again.
> I can see the signs, Mr Martin,
> They want someone to blame.'

Martin is not convinced, but she persists in highlighting the fragility of British tolerance: 'Pinching his arm in a bony grip: "Do not think it cannot happen here!"'.[141] A year earlier than *The Remains of the Day*, it differs in presenting prejudice as an ongoing problem and not one confined to a 'heritage' past.

---

138 Philip Osment (ed.), *Gay Sweatshop: Four Plays and a Company* (London: Methuen, 1989), pp. 83–120 for the script and notes.
139 See Philip Osment, 'Finding Room on the Agenda for Love', in Ibid., pp. vii–lxviii.
140 Ibid., p. lxi.
141 Ibid., script of *This Island's Mine*, pp. 87–88.

Osment's work is notable for the complexity of his characters, who are allowed freedom to move beyond stereotypes or idealised figures against the pathological portrayal in the media: *This Island's Mine* was thus far more than a political intervention. Miss Rosenblum is there to provide a historical bond between 'then' and 'now'; she resists any temptation to regard her own experiences as special and beyond comparison. Having left her initial job in Britain before the war as an exploited domestic, Miss Rosenblum became the companion for Irina, a White Russian aristocrat who had escaped to Britain from Bolshevism. While close, Miss Rosenblum could not share the prejudices of her employer and her

> Complaining right until the end
> About this country,
> About the riff-raff they were letting in.

Miss Rosenblum adds in posthumous conversation with her friend that 'You never seemed to realize that we were part of the riff-raff.'[142]

Miss Rosenblum's critique of the late Irina goes further, reflecting on the latter's wasted life 'waiting for the day when you would return to your land of dreams'.[143] Indeed, for the first time in the representation of a former refugee domestic, a character is created who moves beyond victim (whether deserving or not), a figure of fun, or purely a signifier of something else. Miss Rosenblum has a vivid past – a love affair with an American serviceman in the war which *she* ends, wanting to make a full life for herself in Britain. She also has a rich present, not only helping those around her from diverse, contemporary Britain but as part of a circle of fellow refugees who maintain their past culture, whether through music, food, or literature.[144]

The general approach of Philip Osment is to allow for the creation of '"ordinary people" who are given the right to be complex and contradictory, whose human variability can elicit our sympathy, dislike and amusement all in the same breath'.[145] This is true more of the gay figures in the play than Miss Rosenblum, who is a source of comfort and wisdom to those drawn to her house of safety. She is a less eccentric version of Armistead Maupin's Anna Madrigal in his *Tales of the City*. Yet, if somewhat idealised, Miss Rosenblum is still a three-dimensional figure who was drawn from real people: first, from Philip Osment's own experiences living in a decrepid

---

142 Ibid., p. 119.

143 Ibid.

144 For a less positive reading of the play and its attempt to connect 'then and now', see Nicholas de Jongh's review in *The Guardian*, 27 February 1988.

145 Mike Alfreds quoted in Introduction to *This Island's Mine* in Daniel Fischin and Mark Fortier (eds), *Adaptations of Shakespeare* (London: Routledge, 2000), p. 255.

council property in West Hampstead, in the form of fellow tenant, Mrs Reichstaler, who shares the past of his fictional character; and, second, from *The Housetrample*, a 1994 play by a drama student, Sue Frumin, that he had directed. Frumin's mother, Vera, was a Jewish refugee who came to work as a domestic in Liverpool and this earlier work was based on her experiences.[146]

Frumin, a leading lesbian drama writer, wanted to write a play which featured 'the experiences of refugees from Europe and particularly ... the experiences of women'. Vera had come from Czechoslovakia in 1939 and 'it had often struck me that the she (and women like her) had stories to tell about coming to England, but that such stories were not documented nor assumed to be a relevant part of women's history'. Tellingly, Sue Frumin notes that her mother had rarely talked about her experiences of being a refugee and therefore the author spent an intense period of interviewing her and carrying out related research to rediscover this past.[147] As with *The Remains of the Day*, a lack of wider historical knowledge in the 1980s/ early 1990s is reflected in the distorted chronology and inaccurate details in *The Housetrample* – in this case, Vera arrived in England as a domestic after the war had started.

Although there is a strong female friendship at the heart of her work, Frumin was anxious not to make it explicitly lesbian because she 'felt it [was] important not to make it too overt in case this distracted from other elements in the play'. Instead, she wrote a story 'of an immigrant survivor, a story which not only had resonances for Jewish women, but for all women from immigrant backgrounds; a story of differences and of surviving in an alien culture'.[148] The tension caused by juxtaposing 'now' and 'then', there (Czechoslovakia) and here (England) in *The Housetrample* has mixed results. Positively, Frumin allows for the specificity and ambiguity of the refugee domestic experience. On the one hand, she relates the hard work, loneliness, frustration, and anxiety for those left behind. On the other, she highlights the humour, resilience, and determination of Vera as she moves from being a servant in pre-war Liverpool (Frumin translates 'housetrample' as 'to scrub and clean and look after children') to a clippie and then a factory worker in war-time Manchester.[149]

---

146 Osment, 'Finding Room', in *Gay Sweatshop: Four Plays and a Company* (London: Methuen, 1989), p. lxi and Philip Osment, email to the author, 30 November 2014; Sue Frumin, 'The Housetrample' in Jill Davis (ed.), *Lesbian Plays: Two* (London: Methuen, 1989), pp. 93–108.
147 Frumin, 'The Housetrample', p. 107.
148 Ibid.
149 Ibid., p. 103. Phyliss Lassner, *Anglo-Jewish Women Writing the Holocaust: Displaced Witnesses* (Basingstoke: Palgrave Macmillan, 2008), pp. 179–185 provides the only academic treatment of this work, mistakenly but tellingly noting (pp. 180–181) that Vera 'escaped on the Kindertransport'.

The author is also determined to make connections to the world of immigration controls during the 1980s and here the historical details are contrived. Vera arrives direct from Czechoslovakia in Liverpool (in reality a port of transmigrancy), and she is subjected to procedures that had not been invented in the 1930s. In the play Vera is in a queue in the customs hall with a woman and her small child, who have been there for four days: 'They say my visa isn't in order – they send people back you know, even if they have tiny children, and sometimes they take the children and send the adults back.'[150] While some refugees during the 1930s *were* deported and others refused entry, families were not divided in this way at the port of entry. In this respect there is a contrast to late twentieth-century asylum policy: the desire to link the experiences of migrant women past and present leads to melding what were still evolving bureaucracies of control. As with *The Austrian Cockney*, instrumentalising history too blatantly comes at a price of losing historic specificity.

Even allowing for these limitations, it remains that with the important interventions of Frumin, followed by Osment, the new politics of the 1980s had enabled vibrant representations of former refugee domestics, crucially restoring agency to these women. Frumin notes that she wanted to write a piece 'which created a sympathetic and non-stereotypical picture of a Jewish woman' and this was true also of Osment's Miss Rosenblum.[151] If past and present were sometimes linked clumsily, a challenging dialogue was created. Moreover, the Manchester Jewish Museum and the Museum of the Jewish East End recorded interviews and collected artefacts that enabled the experiences and material culture of the refugee domestics to become part of heritage and history. There was recognition that it was not only those coming from Eastern Europe a generation earlier who had entered menial jobs.

Linked to that archive recovery, in 1988, a small travelling exhibition for schools and other groups, 'Refugee from Nazism', was created by the London Museum of Jewish Life (which had just changed its name from the Museum of the Jewish East End so that other ordinary Jewish migrant stories could be incorporated). This was the first (and so far, last) time that heritage work focused solely on a refugee domestic. It was based on the life story of Hilda Schindler (whose testimony featured earlier in relation to servant headware), which conveyed 'the tragedy, sorrows and fears that travelled with all those refugees, the problems of assimilation and of creating a new life in Britain', including her post-war career as a school teacher.[152] Its successor, the London Jewish Museum, has items on permanent display from these initiatives. These include a Viennese

---

150 Frumin, 'The Housetrample', p. 102.

151 Ibid., p. 107.

152 See *Newsletter of the London Museum of Jewish Life* no. 6 (September 1988).

cookbook for prospective refugees explaining the intricacies of making Yorkshire pudding, the apron of Lisbeth Sokal given to her by her parents in Germany when she came to Britain as a domestic, and a photograph of Hansi Finkler at work in this role. The exhibition also includes items reflecting the bureaucratic trail of these refugee journeys: a letter from the German Jewish Aid Committee to Gertrude Landshoff in 1938 warning of the long waiting list for domestic positions and her later naturalization certificate in 1947 (as noted in Chapter 1, she managed in 1939 to get a post in Cambridge). There are also reproductions of the refugee domestic advertisements in the *Jewish Chronicle*.[153]

It remains that the material relating to refugee domestics is not prominent, and is secondary in importance to the attention given to the *Kindertransport*. Nevertheless, taken together it is still the most extensive treatment of the refugee domestic experience in a permanent museum display. Moreover, since its reopening in 2010, the London Jewish Museum has an explicit commitment to anti-racism and multiculturalism. The items relating to domestic service illustrate one aspect of London's diverse populations and diverse histories, thereby complementing the earlier memoir of Martha Lang and the theatrical work of Frumin and Osment.

From the 1980s onwards social and socialist history, women's history, gay rights, and anti-racism, alongside new approaches to Jewish history (including increasing engagement with the Holocaust), had thus given space for the refugee domestic experience to be rediscovered and confronted. And, for some, this provided an opportunity to use that knowledge to make broadly defined political connections between 'then' and 'now'. Yet the dominant trend was to continue amnesia of this movement or to continue the tendency to relegate it firmly to the past and for the Jewish refugees to be viewed as agent-less victims. As late as the 1990s this was still a largely forgotten story. What were the politics of memory in the new millennium, when the last testimony of the refugee domestics was recorded and the issue of forced female migration again became an issue of contemporary concern? Was the period of (partial) rediscovery from the 1980s onwards sustained and has the voice of the refugee domestic become more prominent and open?

---

153 Author, visit to London Jewish Museum, 4 December 2014.

The Twenty-First Century:
The Politics of Memory and Experience

In 2005 Edith Argy wrote *The Childhood and Teens of a Jewish Girl in Inter-War Austria and Subsequent Adventures*.[154] That it was self-published through an obscure American company, despite its writerly quality, is yet further indication of the ongoing marginality of the refugee domestic experience. Moreover, its curious title (with its last word suggesting something light-hearted) reflects that there was still no clear place for such experiences within Holocaust studies, migration studies, or British social history. Yet, for all its surface marginality, this is the most important autobiographical writing of a former refugee domestic. The self-reflexivity which runs through the text enables an understanding of the author's identity 'then' and some 70 years later. It also provides a link to the politics of 'now', but one drawn with perhaps greater authority than those attempted in the 1980s and 1990s because of its first hand status.

Already in her nineties, Edith began her account in 2003. Sitting at her computer, she tells her readers that she is 'impatient, I feel time is running out, and I want to tell my story'.[155] As shortly emerges, the chronology of her literacy practice was far more complicated than simply writing down her experiences before it was too late. Part of the story, concerning Edith's deep emotional attachment to a teacher during the early 1930s, had been executed many times: 'I have been writing and re-writing this chapter for most of my life.'[156] Indeed, one of the many remarkable aspects of *The Childhood and Teens* is the deliberate blurring of time frames. Starting her autobiography, Edith notes that it was 65 years and three days since the *Anschluss*, when she was 18 years old: 'Somehow, I am still that young girl, and the child before that, and the young and middle-aged woman after that.'[157] Initially, this was to be 'the story of my life between 1919 and 1938'. How she ended up in Britain was 'an accident' and her life as a refugee was not to be part of the narrative.[158] In fact, as with Edith's relationship with her teacher, she writes and rewrites her life as a domestic, devoting two overlapping chapters in her account to this troubled period of her life.

Little detail is provided of how she got her domestic post in Britain – initially with a Jewish family in Portsmouth. Having outlined briefly the closing of the world to refugees, Edith, as noted in the previous chapter, was aware of domestic service permits, 'so England it was going to be for

---

154 Edith Argy, *The Childhood and Teens of a Jewish Girl in Inter-War Austria and Subsequent Adventures* (Charleston: BookSurge, 2005).
155 Ibid., p. 13.
156 Ibid., p. 25.
157 Ibid.
158 Ibid., p. 13.

me and a great many other Jewish girls and women'.[159] Her 'Uncle Arthur' had already come to Britain and he placed an advertisement for her in the national press. She remembers the endless queues for paperwork but blames only the Nazis and not British bureaucracy for this: the former 'made it as difficult and as humiliating for Jews to leave as they could'.[160]

Edith's failure to learn from her training in Vienna has been narrated earlier. Indeed, there is no hiding in her autobiography that she was not suited to being a domestic servant.[161] Edith left Vienna on 6 September 1938. Of the leave-taking at the station with her step-mother, father, and brother, 'my mind has chosen to blot out ... . I remember nothing'. The journey is remembered as a harrowing one, fearing being taken off the train but then arriving safely in France: 'There is freedom.'[162]

The Childhood and Teens provides a brief 'postscript' which includes a concentrated account of 'My career as a maid'. This was 'colourful but mercifully short – mercifully both for me and many hapless employers'. Edith relates how 'A friend asked me the other day exactly how many [domestic] jobs I had had. I honestly don't know; dozens, certainly. I remember only a few of them.'[163] This treatment in her autobiography, revelling in her incompetency, is at one with her title in suggesting a humorous episode in the author's life. There is, however, a gentle initial querying of it when Edith recalls being a 'tweeny' – a position in the household where 'You can't get any lower.' All the staff were refugees from various parts of Greater Germany. Edith recalls a silent, dysfunctional couple whose 'servants were invisible'. When, however, 'the mistress accused the Czech [parlour-maid, a former medical student from Prague] of theft, we all left in a show of solidarity'.[164] Here, refugee agency and resistance is inserted into the historical record, understated but clearly articulated.

The postscript then moves to outlining the fate of Edith's family and friends, including how her father and brother managed to get into France without papers, both surviving the war. It ends on a political statement which is both strident and then qualified, reflecting a conflicting sense of belonging/alienation and loyalty/criticism: 'There is much disparaging talk these days about asylum seekers and illegal immigrants. I shall never forget that I was once an asylum seeker, and my father and brother were illegal immigrants.' If this devastating attack on historical amnesia was not enough, Edith then critiqued the dominant portrayal of her fellow refugees, who have become, as we have seen, the idealised migrant group:

159 Ibid., pp. 127–128.
160 Ibid., p. 123.
161 Ibid.
162 Ibid., pp. 128–129.
163 Ibid., p. 131.
164 Ibid., p. 132.

'It is fashionable now to talk approvingly of the wave of Continental Jewish refugees in the thirties, and quite a few of them have been made knights and even peers of the realm ... .' She adds insightfully 'but it was not always so. Britain, like every other country, was nervous of being "swamped" by Jewish foreigners at the time.'[165] And, rather than simply reflecting the findings of a new, censorious writing on British refugee policy, her understanding was based partly on personal experience. Earlier in her testimony Edith recalls how, when applying for posts in Britain, she got a number of replies. One stated bluntly 'Stay where you are. We already have too many Jews in England. We don't want any more.'[166]

Edith counters such comments with a final and unambiguous love letter to her place of asylum: 'But Britain gave me life, and I, personally, have never encountered anything but civility, tolerance and friendship in my dealings with the British.' Echoing the AJR appeal of the 1960s, she exclaims her gratitude: 'Thank you, Britain!'[167] *The Childhood and Teens* is, however, a complex and multilayered text and, having finished her life story, Edith then begins it again, re-remembering her journey to England and her days as a domestic servant.

In the first chapter of the second half of Edith's autobiography her life as a maid is still represented as 'my inglorious career'. But, alongside her incompetence, she also recalls the cold, the loneliness of being forced to eat alone. The comic tone is now utterly out of tune with the misery Edith remembers: 'I was desperately homesick. I wanted to die ... . My employers found me with my head in the oven.'[168] Edith presents the Jewish couple with generosity. She was useless as a maid and suicidal and is therefore understanding of why they wanted rid of her (which they did within a week).

The tension between expressing gratitude and relating the misery of being a refugee and a maid is a recurring theme throughout the many testimonies examined. It is neatly and self-consciously presented by Edith, acting as the last spokesperson for this movement (she features in the final programme of Pamela Cox's excellent three-part 2012 BBC2 documentary, *Servants: The true story of life below stairs*).[169] In Golders Green she recalls her Jewish mistress, 'who treated me like a servant'. Edith adds, 'Of course, I *was* a servant but couldn't come to terms with the fact.' She also is aware that her amnesia about the number and type of jobs she had was not accidental: 'What the brain does not wish to remember it chooses to forget.' She was so desperate that in 1939 she attempted to return to Austria.[170]

165 Ibid., p. 140.
166 Ibid., p. 128.
167 Ibid., p. 140.
168 Ibid., p. 145.
169 *Servants*, BBC 2, 21 November 2012.
170 Ibid., p. 146.

Edith describes domestic service as a 'condition that was not so very much better than slavery'. As with so much of her text, she immediately qualifies herself by stating 'I exaggerate, of course. I was not owned or beaten; I was free to leave my post ... at any time, provided I kept the police informed of my movements.' But Edith is not fully satisfied with this caveat and adds that servants in Britain were 'considered to be some sub-species of the human race', devoid of the freedom to 'speak freely'.[171] A question remains: have the subsequent seven decades allowed Edith to regain her voice?

What is evident within *The Childhood and Teens* is the author wrestling with what she can, and cannot, say with the sensitivities of her (largely British) readers in mind, these being for the most part people she was closely associated with. The pattern of criticism, qualification, and then further criticism is maintained through the second chapter on her life as a domestic: 'I had been dehumanised by Hitler, and I felt, rightly or wrongly, I was being dehumanised all over again.'[172] The 'rightly or wrongly' provides an escape clause for those not wishing to accept the degregation she experienced in her early years in Britain. Yet Edith is anxious still not to leave too much uncertainty in her account, stating 'what I do remember, throughout my life as a domestic servant, is permanent exhaustion; the longing to have just one day completely to myself'. She concludes this description by the clear statement that it was the 'most unpleasant part of my life'.[173]

The counter-narrative provided by Edith Argy, even with its ambiguities, has caused a memory war within the circles of refugees from Nazism, in spite of its amateurish form of publication. In late 2008 and early 2009 the journal of the Association of Jewish Refugees entered into its first thorough treatment of 'refugees in domestic service'. It was started by an article by its editor, Anthony Grenville, the tone of which was highly critical of this mode of escape. Grenville relied heavily on Edith's memoirs, which he had reviewed earlier and favourably. He emphasised the harsh conditions endured by these refugees and how difficult it was for middle-class refugees to adjust to a life below stairs.[174] The article was followed by heated discussion within the letter columns of the journal which was still going strong three months later.

The letters selected were equally divided between those supporting Grenville's analysis, providing similar stories of the misery experienced by Edith Argy, and those appalled by what he had written. With regards to the latter, there were some who queried the negative portrayal, pointing out

---

171 Ibid., p. 147.
172 Ibid., p. 147.
173 Ibid., p. 148.
174 Anthony Grenville, 'Underpaid, underfed and overworked: Refugees in domestic service', *AJR Journal* vol. 8 no. 12 (December 2008), pp. 1–2.

that in their case they were treated with sympathy and understanding as if they had been relatives or friends. More dominant, however, was outrage at the raising of any form of criticism. Margot Allan (née Brauer), who was a domestic with her sister, stated bluntly 'We did the work we were given and we were grateful for it. Without which, we would have been condemned to slave labour along with our elder sister or to the gas chambers along with many more from our family.' She added that it was a 'dreadful thing to accuse the country which saved me, and so many, by taking us in during our desperate time of need'.[175]

Similar sentiments were voiced by another former domestic, Ruth Lansley, who was equally 'disappointed' by the article:

> Let us please remember that those left behind ... were starved, tortured and eventually murdered. We were allowed to enter this amazing country – now our England – and spared the horror of the death camps, which made the complaints in your article not worthy of the *AJR Journal*.

And yet, in reverse order from the narrative constructed by Edith Argy, Ruth's protestation of gratitude is followed by an acknowledgment that she was not 'the happiest domestic'. Fearful of what was happening to her parents left behind, she felt isolated and lonely: we 'were completely ignored by the English Jewish residents of Bournemouth ... . I think we were an embarrassment to them.'[176]

Gratitude was the dominant tone of these letters, even if tempered by an acknowledgment of some ill-treatment. It led to a stark representation of choices: 'I cannot help thinking "Better a living abused domestic servant in England than a dead one in Auschwitz"'.[177] But one former domestic engaged with the longue durée of the Jewish experience more critically, enabling connections between the deeper past and 'now'. In what was the conclusion of the AJR debate, Marion Smith noted how none of the contributors had drawn 'parallels with the arrival of mainly Polish Jews after the First World War who had been hoping to find a better life in Germany'. Provocatively, and looking beyond the Holocaust, she concluded:

> We, of all people, should be free of all prejudices in view of our history constantly repeating itself. But have we learned this important lesson? Are our brothers in Israel not making the same mistake again by treating the Arabs not as their equals?[178]

---

175 Letter to the editor, *AJR Journal* vol. 9 no. 2 (February 2009), p. 5.
176 Ibid.
177 Bronia Snow, letter *AJR Journal* vol. 9 no. 2 (February 2009), p. 5.
178 *AJR Journal* vol. 9 no. 4 (April 2009), pp. 4–5.

Twenty years earlier, Marion had contributed to a less intensive debate about her life as a domestic service in *AJR Information*. As noted in the previous chapter, it was not an occupation she remembered positively, even if acknowledging that 'some of the things I learnt during that period came in quite handy afterwards when I had a household of my own.' More vitally, through her employer's connection to the central refugee organisation, Marion managed to get her parents entry as domestics.[179]

In contrast, Edith Argy was not successful in securing such a permit for her (step)-mother, Claire, who refused to leave Austria illegally, despite her husband urging her to do so. 'The age limit was 55 – Claire was 57. All my entreaties at [the Domestic Bureau] ... fell on deaf ears. There was nothing they could do: the Home Office would not bend the rules.'[180] Edith continued to correspond with Claire, who was deported to Poland in July 1942. Like most narratives of former refugee domestics, the journeys into the Holocaust of friends and relatives are not fully confronted in her testimony: 'I try not to imagine that last stage of her life. I am simply not brave enough.'[181] In later testimony Edith comments on her 'failure' to help Claire: 'I lived with that guilt for the rest of my life.'[182]

Edith, as Marion, linked her experiences as an 'alien' to other migrants past and present. For many former refugee domestics, the enormity of the Holocaust which engulfed so many of their close relatives, though rarely confronted directly, still framed their memories. In turn, as with much *Kindertransport* testimony, it has encouraged a cult of gratitude towards Britain and an unwillingness among some to criticise its refugee policy either past or present. In the case of Edith Argy's autobiography, the Holocaust is not absent: 'I might ... have ended up in Auschwitz, one of the six million. But I didn't.' Yet she also acknowledges 'That I am here is an accident' and she is insistent on *not* distinguishing herself from contemporary asylum-seekers.[183] In this case, journeys in and out of the Holocaust come together to enable a connection to the wider world of modern forced migration. A similar pattern can be located within Lore Segal's writing.

In her *New Yorker* articles, which formed the basis for *Other People's Houses*, Lore Segal constructs different versions of her family's collective journeys. The first, published in March 1961, provided a relatively reassuring narrative: 'As it happens, everyone in my story came away safely.' Yet, to entice interest, she adds that 'We travelled by outlandish routes', outlined by the burials en route – London, Santiago, and New Jersey. Her neutral/benign description of these resting places for the dead has already been

---

179 *AJR Information* vol. 43 no. 4 (April 1988), p. 13.
180 Argy, *The Childhood and Teens*, p. 131.
181 Ibid.
182 Argy in *Servants*, BBC Two.
183 Argy, *The Childhood and Teens*, p. 13.

quoted earlier in this chapter. Further comfort is provided to the reader by the knowledge that almost all her surviving relatives had successfully remade lives for themselves in New York.[184] Segal initially appears to put forward America as the redemptive 'promised land' following Mary Antin's classic fin de siècle immigrant text.[185] But in her penultimate piece for the *New Yorker*, some three years later, Segal returns to this collective migrant journey, changing both its narrative voice and its tone:

> 'We follow one another across the world, and we leave our dead behind', my mother said. 'My Igo in a huge graveyard in a Jewish slum in London, Paul's Ilse on a hill in Sosua, and my father in a Catholic graveyard in Santiago.'

Lore's grandmother then intervenes to darken the mood further: 'And Ibolya in Auschwitz ... And Sari God knows where in Hungary ... And Feri and Kari taken away in Poland.' Lore adds that her grandmother 'went down the gallery of her ten dead brothers and sisters, naming the places where they had been murdered'. The old lady continued 'of the three of us alive, Wetterl is in Paraguay, and Hilde in Canada, and I will go to the ground in New York'.[186] The reader is then prepared for the final instalment and the closing statement that even in New York she walks 'gingerly ... surrounded on all sides by calamity'.[187]

Segal is referring not only to her particular vulnerability as a Jew in the twentieth century but more universally to all those marginalised in the modern era. And, as ever with Lore Segal, it leads to a position of cold self-criticism. Giving testimony to the Warner Brothers film on the Kindertransport, *Into the Arms of Strangers* (2000), she notes

> I am now impressed that [her British foster parents] took in this alien child with a foreign language. I have noticed with interest that I have not done the same in the many political situations where there were children who needed taking in.[188]

In the testimony explored in this Part of the book, the increasingly dominant trend has been to place the refugee domestic experience within a self-contained context of the Holocaust. From there, it has been removed from comparison with other experiences, especially past and present female migration. There are important exceptions – in representation through the

---

184 Segal, 'Other People's Houses: A Liberal Education', p. 37.
185 Mary Antin, *The Promised Land* (Princeton: Princeton University Press, 1969 [1912]).
186 Lore Segal, 'Other People's Houses: Santiago', *New Yorker*, 13 June 1964, p. 88.
187 Lore Segal, 'Other People's Houses: New York', *New Yorker*, 25 July 1964, p. 55.
188 Harris and Oppenheimer, *Into the Arms of Strangers*, p. 212.

work of Sue Frumin and Philip Osment and in testimony particularly that of Edith Argy and more blatantly Martha Lang. A parallel (and reinforcing) process can be detected with regards to the treatment of servants within the world of popular representation. As Lucy Delap suggests, 'The heritage performances of domestic service seem predominantly backward-looking, and locate the social institutions of the past as distant or foreign.'[189] In this respect, the popular BBC television costume drama series *Upstairs, Downstairs*, when revived in the twenty-first century, is revealing in its portrayal of Jewish refugees. The Jewish maid Rachel Permutter, a former lecturer from Frankfurt, is a doomed character who dies of an asthma attack, whereas her daughter who comes on the *Kindertransport* has a future in and as part of Britain.[190] But, as Delap adds, placing domestic service in a long-lost past is curious, as 'Twenty-first century estimates of the amount spent annually on domestic workers range from £4 to 9 billion.'[191] This figure is for Britain alone and is mirrored in other western nations. Moreover, it continues to grow – the figure for Britain in 1987 was 'just' £1 billion.[192] At the turn of the twenty-first century it has been estimated that there are 'two million domestic workers in Britain ... – more than there were in Victorian times – and 2.7 million British households ... employ some kind of domestic help'.[193]

What is also clear is that the labour supply is truly global, not only continuing but intensifying a trend notable through the industrial age: most domestic work is now carried out by migrants, especially from the Far East, South America, Africa, and Eastern Europe.[194] For example, in the early 1990s it was estimated that there were roughly one million Filipino women working as domestics in over 120 countries.[195] Is there a parallel here with the earlier refugee servants who came to Britain during the 1930s, or was it such a peculiar movement and the contemporary situation so different that comparisons are either ethically illegitimate or historically unhelpful?

---

189 Lucy Delap, *Knowing Their Place: Domestic Service in Twentieth-Century Britain* (Oxford: Oxford University Press, 2011).
190 The series originally ran through the 1970s. Rachel Permitter appears in the 2010 series on the BBC.
191 Delap, *Knowing Their Place*, p. 234.
192 Bridget Anderson and Annie Phizacklea, 'Migrant Domestic Workers: A European Perspective' (Report to the Equal Opportunities Unit, Commissioner of the European Communities, 1997), p. 1.
193 Rosie Cox, *The Servant Problem: Domestic Employment in a Global Economy* (London: I.B. Tauris, 2006), p. 3.
194 Bridget Anderson, *Doing the Dirty Work? The Global Politics of Domestic Labour* (London: Zed Books, 2000).
195 Bridget Anderson, *Britain's Secret Slaves: An Investigation into the Plight of Overseas Domestic Workers* (London: Anti-Slavery International/Kalayaan, 1993), p. 34.

Contemporary Migrations

Alongside the demand for foreign domestic workers in the modern world is the international market in prostitution, sometimes in the form of organised trafficking.[196] This is not new. Migrant women have been prominent in the often overlapping fields of domestic and sex work from the nineteenth century onwards. But from the last quarter of the twentieth century onwards they have been the dominant source of domestic labour in the western world. It reflects growing global inequality, ease of transport and communications, and the pressure of modern living in advanced economies for the professional classes and the higher status that the employment of servants confirms.

In Britain and other western nations the greater use of appliances cut the reliance on 'live in' servants in the decades following 1945. It went alongside a diminishing supply of local labour as young women had the possibilities of better paid and less exhausting jobs. The reluctance to enter or return to domestic work was so great that there was a revival in government-led recruitment of foreign labour, especially for cleaners linked to hospitals and health care. In 1960, for example, nearly 21,000 Ministry of Labour domestic work permits were granted, almost all to European women.[197] More recently, however, the availability of cheap 'live in' domestic labour has enabled double income household to function. It has also allowed care to be provided for the young, sick, disabled, and elderly as the welfare state comes under increasing pressure.[198]

It would be wrong, however, to draw too clear a line between 'then' and 'now' in terms of the *necessity* of domestic labour. Today tasks are carried out by domestics which are 'pointless work', often imposed to humiliate those forced to carry them out rather than being essential activities in household management.[199] In a report for the Commission of the European Communities, Bridget Anderson and Annie Phizacklea provide examples of 'invented work', including one revealingly humiliating example 'where it would cost the employer less effort to flush the toilet, than the maid to fish paper out of the bowl, dispose of the paper and then flush'.[200] In a South African study, only roughly one-quarter of the married women employing domestics were working themselves. The intersection of class, race, and gender continue to make it acceptable for some women to be

---

196 Janice Raymond et al., 'A Comparative Study of Women Trafficked in the Migration Process' (Unpublished report, Coalition Against Trafficking in Women, 2002). This is available as a pdf through www.catwinternational.org.

197 Pamela Horn, *Life Below Stairs in the 20th Century* (Stroud: Sutton, 2001), p. 222.

198 Delap, *Knowing Their Place*, pp. 16–17, 234.

199 Anderson, *Doing the Dirty Work?* p. 16.

200 Anderson and Phizacklea, 'Migrant Domestic Workers', p. 42.

seen as 'natural' servants who can only expect to be treated as slaves or near slaves.

The comparisons that follow between the experiences of 'then' and 'now' will avoid presenting a hierarchy of victimhood. Instead, and to maintain the overall thrust of this Part, the emphasis will be on the agency and testimony of these women workers, including individual and collective acts of resistance. It will return to its overarching theme: the freedom, or otherwise, of these migrant women to speak. In what is a rare deep historical study on the globalisation of domestic service from the 1500s onwards, Raffaella Sarti has noted that 'even two or three centuries ago several thousand migrants found jobs as domestics abroad each year. The "new" domestic service is thus less new than one might imagine.' She adds, however, that 'in relation to the past there are important discontinuities, too'.[201] What follows confirms her analysis.

One fundamental commonality relating to the refugee servants of the 1930s and contemporary domestic workers is the variation in experience. In a global study researched in the late twentieth century it was concluded that 'while some workers are happy in their work and are well treated by their employers, many feel exploited and demeaned by employers' demands'.[202] This could easily be a description of refugee domestics in the Nazi era. Similarly, the processes by which migrant women have obtained jobs as domestics follows the paths of their predecessors 70 years earlier – through individual initiatives, advertisements, informal networks, and employment agencies.[203] Nevertheless, there are significant differences and the comparisons that follow will not ignore those in circumstance, context, and severity of treatment. This includes, of course, the issue of choice in the migratory process. The refugees from the 1930s had experienced the trauma of persecution. Domestic service in Britain was, for many, the only realistic option available as a form of escape. Recent domestic workers have, in theory, more options. Their decision to migrate, however, often reflects the poor wages (in spite, often, of their professional status at home) and inability to look after family that push them to leave. The differences in background between forced and voluntary migrants in terms of individual identity should not be minimised. This does not imply that experiences of exploitation and marginality abroad cannot be meaningfully compared.

Bridget Anderson's *Britain's Secret Slaves* (1993) is a study of overseas domestic workers in Britain, sponsored and published by Anti-Slavery International (the successor to the Anti-Slavery Society, formed in 1839)

---

201 Raffaella Sarti, 'The Globalisation of Domestic Service – An Historical Perspective', in Helma Lutz (ed.), *Migration and Domestic Work: A European Perspective on a Global Theme* (Abingdon: Oxford, 2008), p. 77.

202 Anderson, *Doing the Dirty Work?* p. 48.

203 Ibid., chapter 3.

and Kalayaan, which promotes 'Justice for Overseas Domestic Workers' (Kalayaan is the Filipino word for 'freedom').[204] Based on a 1992 survey of 247 domestics from 17 nationalities, Anderson provided a table listing 'the percentage of those workers interviewed who had experienced nine different forms of abuse commonly encountered'. These consisted of 'Psychological Abuse' (89%); 'Physical Abuse' (31%); 'Sexual Abuse' (9%); 'Regular Denial of Food' (61%); 'Not Having a Bedroom' (51%)' 'Not Having a Bed' (52%); 'Imprisonment' (26%); 'Confiscation of Passport' (83%); and 'Not Paid Regularly, As Promised, or At All' (74%).[205] For those especially who were brought to Britain as domestics with their employers, 'their entire livelihood and immigration status' was dependent on those who they came in with. It was 'how slavery returned to these shores'.[206] While the immigration procedures by which such workers came to Britain changed positively with the Labour government that came into power in 1997, abuses continued. A later study by Kalayaan in 2006 found that 26% were still suffering physical abuse, 72% psychological abuse, and 10% sexual abuse, while 61% did not have their own bed, 70% had no time off and 62% were not allowed out of the house.[207]

Both in their contemporaneous and later testimony, some Jewish refugees have described their time in domestic service as 'slavery' – the last to do so being Edith Argy. Unlike the female migrants analysed by Anderson, it would be hard to make a case for those from the 1930s fitting legally within the term, even with new, flexible definitions. It is still significant, however, that for them it is the category of 'unfree' labour that described their emotional reaction to their lowly status and demeaning treatment when entering Britain. The use of the term 'slavery' was not simply a rhetorical device but reflected a state of mind, whether recalled instantly or many decades later. Likewise, while recognising the differences, it is still illuminating to go briefly through the nine (often overlapping) categories outlined in the 1992 Kalayaan survey to explore continuity and change in the migrant domestic experience.

Under 'psychological abuse', the survey included 'threats, name calling, constant shouting and insults'. While its intensity may have been less, it is a category under which many refugee domestics in the 1930s suffered. As they had to be 'remade' as servants, for the majority their treatment was the same as for non-refugees in this occupation (if experienced differently because of their sudden loss of status). There were, however, employers

---

204 Ibid., pp. 121, 125.

205 Ibid., p. 67. Whilst those who were unhappy in their positions were more likely to take part in this survey, Anderson adds that those who had fled their employers because of abuse were not represented at all (p. 97).

206 Ibid., p. 11.

207 Vanina Wittenberg, *The New Bonded Labour?* (London: Oxfam and Kalayaan, 2008), p. 13.

who exploited the vulnerability of these foreign women. The testimony scrutinised has shown the tendency to employ refugees in households which struggled – because of their physical isolation, their marginal economic status, or their dysfunctional nature – to find 'local' labour. Moreover, some used the uncertain legal status of the refugees to their own advantage.

In December 1938 the secretary of the Domestic Bureau wrote to the leader of the National Union of Domestic Workers stating her concern about 'undesirable employers who exploit these terrified [refugee] girls and threaten deportation'.[208] An example is provided in the testimony of Frances Goldberg. Frances came from Austria to become a domestic in Liverpool and managed to get her sister Rose a post in the same city. Rose was treated badly and Frances intervened with her mistress: '"Well", the lady told me, "I sent her the work permit and that means she can either work here or, I shall send her back to Nazi Germany"'. Frances' employer was, however, very different. She treated her with kindness and respect, helping to bring Frances' parents to Britain and getting a better position for Rose.[209] Refugees *were* deported from Britain during the 1930s.[210] Whether any were on domestic permits is unclear. While actual deportation was rare, the fear of this happening through employer threats was a real one. Yet there is nothing in refugee testimony that matches the following account relating to a contemporary migrant domestic worker.

Bridget Anderson notes how 'Running away ... is often the only solution that many abused domestics have'. It is a desperate option that employers recognise and attempt to counter. One woman recalls being threatened:

> I will cut your face ... . You are my slave. You will do exactly what I say ... . Remember, I hold your passport. If the police find you, you will be deported to where you came from. And, if you are, you will be killed – if I do not manage to kill you first. Don't forget – there are plenty more where you came from.[211]

But rather than regard the experiences from the 1930s and from the late twentieth century as incomparable, it is more profitable to view them in this particular aspect as reflecting the marginal status of all such migrant women whose legal status is unclear. Modern immigration procedures have built on a long bureaucratic foundation, a theme that runs throughout this study.

---

208 University of Warwick Archives, TUC archive 54/76 (4): Franklin to Bezzant, 19 December 1938.
209 Manchester Jewish Museum: Frances Goldberg, unpublished memoirs, pp. 12–13.
210 See National Archives, HO 372/26.
211 Anderson, *Britain's Secret Slaves*, p. 50.

Returning to the varying experiences of the sisters Frances and Rose, these reflect a wider trend for these domestics during the 1930s. That they were refugees led some to make allowances and to provide the support they needed alongside the work they had to do. For others, their refugeedom perversely enabled the exploitation of their vulnerability. Indeed, it could be suggested that the fact that they were refugees perhaps allowed employers to think they were doing nothing but good, even when abusing these women. The blunt content of a well-meaning advertisement from the 'Anglo-Jewish Domestic Agency' in the *Jewish Chronicle* provides an insight into how this process might have happened: 'Mistresses will obtain efficient maids and at the same time assist in the humanitarian task of rescuing helpless victims of persecution': if the former was carried out then the latter might be regarded as happening automatically, regardless of the actual treatment meted out.[212] Reflecting on the 'private' nature of domestic work, Bridget Anderson, interviewing British employers, has noted how in their testimony 'the beastliness of power is clothed in the language of obligation, support and responsibility, rather than power and exploitation'. It provides 'a particularly convenient model for employers when the worker is very vulnerable as a result of immigration status'.[213] Indeed, the systematic mistreatment of the marginal in the modern era within a variety of 'care' situations suggests that the ability of those in positions of power to convince themselves they are doing no harm has universal applicability.

The employment of domestic servants from the 1930s to 1945 was as much about status as need. The refugees, for the most part, had to be put in their place, which involved some level of humiliation. They were not equals and, as with Lore Segal's father, could be treated as lower than animals. And, while contemporary domestic labour is more 'essential' to the modern household, the treatment of foreign workers has maintained and greatly extended its abusive element with the intention to dehumanise: 'In the presence of my employers I had to remove my shoes. If they passed me I had to bow ... . They did not use my name, only bad words like "You Dog", or "Donkey".'[214] Renaming was a common feature of pre-1945 domestic service in Britain and refugees' resistance to it has been mentioned. Again, it was not so severe as the racist designation above, but it was part of the same tendency to make domestics 'not like us' and fundamentally inferior, altogether an 'alien species'. Refugee servants were often shouted at and told off for getting things wrong. Their status as both domestics and foreign often countered any sympathy to treat them as refugees. There is a parallel, therefore, if rarely as extreme, in the

---

212 *Jewish Chronicle*, 6 January 1939.

213 Bridget Anderson, 'A very private business: migration and domestic work', Working Paper no. 28 (2006), Centre on Migration, Policy and Society, p. 18.

214 Anderson, *Britain's Secret Slaves*, p. 13.

psychological abuse that some suffered in comparison to contemporary migrant domestic workers.

In marked contrast, reference to physical abuse is rare or non-existent in Jewish refugee testimony. There is some evidence of male employers trying to take sexual advantage of younger female refugees, but nothing to compare with the frequent rape that has occurred among contemporary domestics. Again, this reflects different levels of vulnerability. The brief testimony of Lucy Long, written in 1979, recalls her arrival from Vienna and being greeted by 'Mr Smith', her employer. Arriving at Harwich and staying over in a hotel there, he made two clumsy attempts to share her bed. In post, Mr Smith objected to Lucy leaving the house, demanding to know where she had been. Lucy found a new job, much to the annoyance of her employer, who attempted to stop her moving. This he did by bringing in a policeman to question Lucy's legal status, denouncing her as a spy. The allegation was dismissed and the policeman told Lucy that she had 'nothing to fear'.[215]

Lucy Long's account begins by stating boldly: 'Refugees make headlines again. I was once a refugee.'[216] In terms of power and agency, there is clearly a gulf between the ease with which she avoided, in the policeman's words, how her 'employer tried to make love to you',[217] and the rape of maids not yet in their teens who have come to Britain as domestics on other people's passports. Yet from the photographs that had to be provided and in their everyday working lives, there was an element of sexualisation relating to the refugee domestics that was part of a wider abuse in the treatment of servants as a whole. While far less extensive than in the nineteenth century, economic and sexual exploitation sometimes came together. The rape of migrant domestic workers from the late twentieth century onwards reflects a longer trend, if one that has been frighteningly intensified.

In terms of denial of food, some Jewish refugees reported their hunger and the inferiority of the meals they were given compared to those of their employers. None, however, were systematically starved, as has happened more recently. Likewise, while their accommodation was often very poor and sometimes shared, no refugees were denied the basic facility of a bed. And, while Lucy Long's employer would no doubt have liked to have kept her under lock and key, no refugees were imprisoned in British homes. Payment was at the lowest acceptable rate agreed with the government, at 15 shillings a week, but, again, while it was meagre, there is no reference to it being refused. This leaves two remaining categories which reveal similarities but also critical differences between the refugees of the 1930s and migrant domestics today – hours of work and their alien status.

---

215 Lucy Long, 'unpublished memoirs', 18 August 1979, in author's possession.
216 Ibid.
217 Ibid.

For most refugee domestics, the working day was the same as for other servants. This was roughly 12 hours, with half a day off a week. Alongside the poor pay, it was the lack of freedom and exhaustion this created that made service so demoralising. The refugee women, most unaccustomed to such work, found it particularly difficult from both physical and psychological perspectives. The 1992 survey and later research has found that the average is now 18–19 hours a day, and that 'days off almost never existed'. With payment rare (some employers demand the 'paying off' of air fare), it is why the label 'slavery', especially for 'live in' domestics, has such validity. Tiredness and demoralisation are common to both the historic and contemporary migrant domestic experience, but, as with so many of the abuses suffered, they are simply more extreme in the modern example.

Finally, in relation to abuse, the question of legal status and freedom has to be addressed. Much to the frustration of many employers, the refugee domestics, while initially restricted to this occupation, were free to move between jobs. Like 'local' labour, they did so regularly (Edith Argy being on the extreme side in this respect) and thereby at least partially avoided abusive households. Until they gained naturalisation in the post-war period, their nationality status was insecure and the internment of many refugee domestics in 1940 illustrated such vulnerability. Their freedom was thus relative, but it was far greater than that of those who are not simply tied to an occupation but also to an employer – as was the case with many 'live in' domestics in Britain until the late 1990s. More recent immigration procedures threaten to undermine the limited progress that was made in the first decade of the twentieth century in giving migrant domestics greater status and independence.[218]

Abuse is clearly very much part of the contemporary migrant domestic labour experience, as it was to a lesser extent with those who came during the 1930s. This chapter will close, however, by returning to the agency of these women through their resistance and sense of solidarity. Even in remote locations, such as that of the Schneiders in Scotland, refugee domestics found ways of coming together to provide mutual support. In the larger settlements more formal associations were created, such as the domestic club in Liverpool that was supported by the local refugee committee. Frances Goldberg recalled how 'Our once a week meetings were very important to us as refugees. At first we arranged to meet in the railway station's waiting-room. There we came together and discussed our problems, failures and shared our worries.' Initially numbering around 50 domestics, 'week by week new girls arrived and everybody made sure to inform every newcomer about our meetings, to avoid people feeling lonely

---

218 Wittenburg, *The New Bonded Labour*; Bridget Anderson, 'Mobilizing migrants, making citizens: migrant domestic workers as political agents', *Ethnic and Racial Studies* vol. 33 no. 1 (2010), pp. 60–74.

and lost as we felt at the beginning'.[219] On a practical level, information was provided about moving from exploitative posts and in helping relatives still in Greater Germany.

Self-help is also evident within the world of recent overseas domestic workers and Britain has been at the forefront of such developments. In 1984 'Waling Waling' was formed by a group of Filipino domestics in London so that they could share experiences and confront common work and immigration problems.[220] This was empowering to those joining, who had previously internalised their experiences:

> Before, when I was alone, I didn't trust anyone. My experience with my employers meant that I couldn't speak up. It makes you silent and not open. When I began to talk to people in similar situations, and I saw that I was not alone, I realised that the problem was not just to do with me, that it was the Philippines and Britain and the government in those countries.[221]

Numbers (initially 17) grew to hundreds, bringing in domestics from other nations. The scope of activities also expanded: 'As time went by and they grew in confidence, workers began to organize events and trips, concerned that members should be leading as "normal" a life as possible, whatever their immigration status.'[222] Three years later Kalayaan was created, which was a support group initially for Waling Waling. It drew 'its members from migrant and immigrant support organisations, trade unions, law centres and concerned individuals'. Through legal representation, political and media campaigns, and training, it has campaigned at a national level as well as concerning 'itself with the practical needs of the workers'.[223] The importance of maintaining migrant agency was reflected in the relationship between the two bodies. As Anderson comments, working together closely, 'Waling Waling members were on the management committee of Kalayaan (and not vice versa) in order to facilitate accountability to migrant domestic workers'.[224] The contrast here to the *absence* of prostitute voices in bodies such as the Jewish Association for the Protection of Children and Women is marked. And, even with refugee domestic groups in the 1930s, the national and local organisations that encouraged them still had the ultimate aim of keeping the women in service and out of the public gaze.

---

219 Manchester Jewish Museum: Goldberg, 'Memoirs', pp. 8–9.
220 Anderson, 'Mobilizing migrants', pp. 60–61.
221 Anderson, *Britain's Secret Slaves*, p. 59.
222 Ibid., p. 62.
223 Ibid., p. 121.
224 Anderson, 'Mobilizing migrants', p. 62.

A more recent self-help group is 'Justice for Domestic Workers' (J4DW), which continues to fight against the tied visas that are responsible for ongoing exploitation. Artist Ciara Phillips worked in conjunction with J4DW to produce a series of posters, including 'No 2 Slavery', some of which appeared in her Turner Prize finalist exhibition at the Tate Modern (2014).[225] These were regarded by critics as 'pointless', 'entirely vacuous',[226] and 'supposedly thought-provoking',[227] and such dismissals raise the question returned to throughout these first two chapters: can the refugee or foreign domestic be allowed to 'speak'?

From the 1930s through to the twenty-first century the Jewish refugees who came to Britain as domestic servants wrote and rewrote their stories. They did so initially to gain posts, to reassure relatives, to campaign for better treatment, and to awaken a wider public to the wider plight of the Jews. After the war their testimony was part of literacy practice, coming to terms with the past and present situation through forms of everyday autobiographical writing. Since the late 1970s they have been interviewed about their experiences either directly or indirectly and by a range of different heritage organisations. At times they have struggled to get their particular experiences heard against the assumptions of the interviewers, who have imposed their own agenda and interests. This partial silencing raises the question posed by Gillian Elinor when reflecting on the testimony collected for a project on cleaners, 'Stolen or Given: An Issue in Oral History'.[228] Yet, as a collectivity, the autobiographical material produced by refugee domestics is remarkable in its variety, scale, and inventiveness. Even so, it has never been totally free from the expectation of its audience. This was blatant in the 1930s in what could be, through letters and adverts, life-saving writing, but it has still been more subtly the case since 1945. In particular, the performance of gratitude to Britain, often genuinely held, has shaped testimony, sometimes limiting criticism and the ability to make contemporary comparisons.

In the case of recent migrant domestic workers, testimony is still relatively rare – in spite of the greater numbers – and has often been in legal form or in the form of media representations exposing the abuses of such work, particularly where the immigration status of those involved is extremely marginal. There has been a tendency, especially in the media, to present the women purely as victims and, as with the case of Jewish 'white slavery', to remove their agency by presenting them as purely subject to

---

225 See Ben Luke's interview with Ciara Phillips in *London Evening Standard*, 15 October 2014.

226 Laura Cumming in *Observer*, 5 October 2014.

227 Jonathan Jones in *Guardian*, 30 September 2014.

228 Gillian Elinor, 'Stolen or Given: An Issue in Oral History', *Oral History* vol. 20 no. 1 (1992), pp. 78–81.

forces beyond their control, such as human trafficking. This is even more the case for 'sex workers', the large majority of whom in western Europe are of migrant origin.[229] Presenting the migrant 'other' as 'helpless' and 'child-like', such 'discourses serve to reinforce notions of female dependence and purity that serve to further marginalise sex workers and undermine their human rights'.[230] As with the situation a century earlier, this is not to deny that trafficking is absent, but that those women who provide their labour are often aware of the 'choiceless choices' they are making. The testimony of marginal migrant women – whether domestics, au pairs, or prostitutes – can reinforce their 'victim' status. Like the refugee domestics, however, when given sufficient space, it can restore their wider humanity and agency.

Waling Waling and more recently J4DW have drawn on history to proclaim 'Slavery Still Alive'.[231] Both do so not simply to shock but also to 'demand to be recognized as *workers*'. As Bridget Anderson explains, there are several levels to this assertion. First, it

> asserted the dignity and value of their work, for themselves, employers and the wider public. They were not 'helping' but contributing socially and economically to households and wider society; they were not 'girls' but women (and men) who were often sustaining extended families back home.

Second, it placed them in the public realm as actors with a 'right to be heard and to be treated with respect, and it was accompanied by the demand that this labour be recognized as a route to formalized citizenship'.[232]

In this respect, the impetus to collect testimony has been part of that politicisation. A European Commission project in the 1990s led to group interviews of migrant domestics, attended by over 120 women and men. 'Self-moderated and taped', and held in 'workers' mother tongues', the participants were 'eager to share their experiences and learn of the situation of others'.[233] There was thus greater migrant agency present here than in the oral history projects that emerged in the late 1970s/1980s in Britain, which were the first to interview former refugee domestics. What is, however, still lacking in the testimony collected relating to contemporary domestic workers is detailed consideration of their life before migration.

229 Raymond, 'A Comparative Study'.

230 Jo Doezema, 'Loose Women or Lost Women? The re-emergence of the myth of "white slavery" in contemporary discourses of "trafficking in women"', *Gender Issues* vol. 18 no. 1 (2000), pp. 23–50.

231 Anderson, 'Mobilizing Migrants', p. 64.

232 Ibid., pp. 64–65.

233 Bridget Anderson, 'Overseas Domestic Workers in the European Union', in Janet Momsen (ed.), *Gender, Migration and Domestic Service* (London: Routledge, 1999), p. 118.

The distillation of their testimony, whether in media, legal campaigning, or academic work focuses on their (largely negative) experiences as foreign domestics. This extends into the cultural realm. As part of her Turner Prize entry, Clara Phillips included a soundscape: 'New things to discuss'. This included her notes from conversations, including with J4DW. While reflecting empathy with their campaigning, the snippets focus very narrowly on that aspect of the migrants' lives, however challenging and affirming of their resistance: 'I am a worker; I am human; Prevention of human trafficking; Slavery by another name; We are workers, not visitors.'[234]

Global inequalities, racist immigration controls and procedures, and the general pressure of late modernity have produced a huge gendered market in migrant labour in which categories of labour become blurred. For example, as in the 1930s, those coming as au pairs are not treated as equals but often as another means to obtain domestic labour alongside child care at a low rate of pay and with long hours of work.[235] The scale and extremity of the situation in the early twenty-first century may appear to make comparisons with the Jewish refugees of the 1930s unsustainable. Yet, as Raffaella Sarti has highlighted, the 'historical perspective does … allow scholars to appreciate what, today, is really "new"'. She adds that the 'current abundance of people willing to work as domestics, the "resurgence" of paid domestic work, the presence of educated and middle-class domestics … may simply be seen as a reversal within varying long-term trends, rather than something completely new.'[236] Sarti is one of the few scholars who has integrated, if briefly, the refugee domestics into a longer time frame. In this respect, the fact that many of those who came in the 1930s came from better-educated and more bourgeois backgrounds than their employers connects rather than separates them from a large number of contemporary domestic workers. In one survey, nearly half of Filipino migrant domestics possessed degrees.[237] Moreover, there is a further parallel: responsibilities to home were/are a huge part of both stories. In the 1930s this meant trying to find a way of helping those left behind in their attempts to leave. Today it is in the form of financial remittances which can be placed alongside overseas aid in their importance and are often used to look after and educate children left at home. Equally, placing the refugee domestics in longer-term patterns of female migration – as well as within the specific context of Nazi persecution – helps broaden Holocaust studies when comprehending the experiences of those who escaped from the abyss. It has been noted that the

---

234 Author visit, Tate Britain, 29 December 2014.

235 See Rosie Cox (ed.), *Au Pairs' Lives in Global Context* (Basingstoke: Palgrave Macmillan, 2015) and the ongoing research project in this area led by Nicky Busch and Rosie Cox.

236 Sarti, 'The Globalisation', p. 92.

237 Rhacel Parrenas, *Servants of Globalization: Women, Migration and Domestic Work* (Stanford: Stanford University Press, 2001), p. 19 and passim.

phrase 'slave labour' within the testimony of former refugee domestics such as Margot Allan references the horrors of Nazi work camps and ultimately the 'Final Solution'. With care, links can also be made productively between the Holocaust and slavery past and present, following the model of Michael Rothberg's 'multidirectional memory', which allows for 'a comparative space beyond competition'.[238]

This forensic exploration of the refugee domestics' testimony, as well as that of their predecessors and successors, reveals the importance of taking the life stories of such migrant workers seriously. How they constructed and reconstructed their experiences (and how they were represented and misrepresented by others) is extremely relevant to understanding contemporary migrants and giving them not only the space to speak but also the possibility of being listened to. As Spivak notes, 'it is important to acknowledge our complicity in the muting, in order precisely to be more effective in the long run'.[239] An example of the way forward is provided by Rhacel Parrenas and her study of Filipino domestics in Rome and Los Angeles. Based on 'in-depth interviews ... about the life history of subjects', it allowed the 'women [to] tell their own stories about their migration, family, community relations, and work experiences'.[240] Other studies have interviewed employers, providing the testimony that might allow the reflexive approach of Lore Segal and Ronald Fraser to be emulated in the future in allowing many voices, from different times, to be heard and engaged with.

Elizabeth Tonkin concludes, in her pathbreaking study *Narrating Our Pasts: the Social Construction of Oral History* (1992), 'That one's self is both variable and vulnerable may be disconcerting to consider, but it does not follow that selves are non-existent. We really have consciousness, we are really agents till death, of past-into-future.' She adds that 'knowledge and social life itself have to be passed on if they are to survive.'[241] For that reason alone, the life stories of migrant domestic workers, both 'then' and 'now', have been placed in dialogue here to recognise the importance of both their particular and universal experiences. Finally, such juxtaposition is utilised to help better understand the experiences of women who will inevitably follow in this exploitative and increasingly globally organised occupation.

---

238 Michael Rothberg, 'In the Nazi Cinema: Race, Visuality and Identification in Fanon and Kluger', *Wasafiri* vol. 24 no. 1 (2009), p. 19 and note 2 and idem, *Multidirectional Memory: Remembering the Holocaust in the Age of Decolonization* (Stanford: Stanford University Press, 2009).

239 Gayatri Chakravorty Spivak, 'History', in *A Critique of Postcolonial Reason: Toward a History of the Vanishing Present* (Cambridge, MA: Harvard University Press, 1999), p. 309.

240 Parrenas, *Servants of Globalization*, p. 18.

241 Elizabeth Tonkin, *Narrating Our Pasts: The Social Construction of Oral History* (Cambridge: Cambridge University Press, 1992), p. 136.

Part 2

Place, Performance, and Legality: Holocaust Survivors and Other Migrant Journeys in the Long Twentieth Century

Chapter 3

The Journeys of Child Refugees, Lost and Rediscovered

Place, Heritage, and Child Refugees

'The identity of places is very much bound up with the *histories* which are told of them, *how* those histories are told, and which memory turns out to be dominant.'[1] Doreen Massey's comments are especially salient with regard to the presence of refugees – how do we remember and historicise those who, by circumstances beyond their control, are transient and placeless? The previous Part of this book charted the slow, uneven, and incomplete process by which refugee domestics established themselves in Britain in their attempt to recreate a place called home (if, in many cases, only temporarily so, as they continued searching for a new life in the Americas, Israel, and elsewhere). In their testimony, the spectre of the Holocaust has grown as time has passed. Yet the actual journeys to destruction of friends and relatives left behind was rarely confronted, being too painful to contemplate.

In 2014 the 'Prime Minister's Holocaust Commission' announced its terms of reference to 'ensure that Britain has a permanent and fitting memorial to the Holocaust'. One of its key objectives was to include 'a clear focus on the role that Britain played through, for example, the Kindertransport, the liberation of Bergen-Belsen and the experiences of survivors now living in Britain'.[2] It is revealing that there is no mention made of the 20,000 Jewish refugee domestics in this self-congratulatory

---

1   Doreen Massey, 'Places and Their Pasts', *History Workshop Journal* no. 39 (Spring 1995), p. 186.
2   Official Publications: 'The Prime Minister's Holocaust Commission: Terms of Reference', 2014.

list, even though it brought double the number of refugees than the *Kindertransport* and ten times that of Holocaust survivors who came after the war. No doubt the exploitation associated with the early refugee years in service has made it problematic as a usable, self-eulogising past. It is a narrative that does not fully confirm Britain's self-image of being free, fair, and generous.

The ambiguity of the domestic permit scheme has led it to be inconspicuous, eclipsed especially by celebratory *Kindertransport* memory. It is thus not surprising that places and events that fundamentally query the self-assuredness connected to innate British decency, especially in relation to Nazism, the Second World War, and the nation's 'finest hour', have been further marginalised and subject to amnesia. The occupation of the Channel Islands from 1940 to 1945 is a major case in point. Only recently have questions been raised about collaboration with the occupying Nazi forces from the Islanders and, within that, the fate of the small number of Jews who were deported and subsequently murdered.[3]

In July 1938 Major General Sir Horace de Courcy Martelli, Lieutenant-Governor of Jersey, wrote to Sir Ernest Holderness of the Home Office's Aliens Department complaining about the activities of two local Jews. Martelli suspected they were 'engaged in importing Austrian Jews into the Island in the capacity of domestic servants for whom, unlike dentists, there is a very great demand'. Four Jews had already arrived and three more were in process 'when I intervened and refused leave to land'. Even with his role as heavy-handed gatekeeper, Martelli was not satisfied: 'In the meantime we have the 4 Austrian Jews or Jewesses here, possibly for keeps.' If they lost their jobs or fell ill 'they would have to be supported by the Island, so the problem is a serious one'.[4]

Holderness was not sympathetic either to the general argument of Martelli or to Jersey's specific refusal to allow entry to these three Jewish women. Indeed, as noted in the previous Section, Holderness acknowledged (and without any hint of embarrassment or disapproval) that the refugee domestics no doubt would take up other forms of employment in the future.[5] It is hardly surprising, however, given the prejudice expressed by Martelli in his belief that Jersey could not 'assimilate an indefinite number of German or Austrian Jews' (four being too many), that so few were to

---

3   The issue was raised provocatively by Madeleine Bunting, *The Model Occupation: The Channel Islands Under German Rule, 1940–1945* (London: HarperCollins, 1995). A more detailed and nuanced account is provided by Paul Sanders, *The British Channel Islands under German Occupation 1940–1945* (Jersey: Jersey Heritage Trust, 2005). More specifically, see Frederick Cohen, *The Jews in the Channel Islands during the German Occupation 1940–1945* (Jersey: Jersey Heritage Trust, 2000).
4   National Archives, HO 213/281 E409: Martelli to Holderness, 4 July 1938.
5   National Archives, HO 213/281 E409: Holderness to Martelli, 4 July 1938.

find refuge in the Channel Islands.[6] Indeed, in Jersey the Island's Defence Committee rejected 'all the applications from German Jews to the Bailiff'.[7]

Hardly any Jewish refugee domestics, therefore, were allowed entry to the Islands and one of those who was subsequently caught up in the Holocaust came there by accident. Therese Steiner (1916–42) was born in Vienna and brought up in a middle-class Jewish home, escaping to Britain in 1939. She expected to work as a dentist's assistant in Kent but in fact was treated as a nanny. Therese followed her employers on a holiday to the Channel Islands in late summer 1939. Once war was declared, however, she could not return to England with them: the Island's bureaucracy insisted on a strident reading of new alien regulations which forbade the entry of Germans and Austrians into Britain. Therese was stranded on Guernsey, where she became a nurse. She was deported from the Island in 1942 to France and subsequently transported from Drancy and murdered in Auschwitz. Another refugee, Auguste Spitz, who *was* working as a domestic in Guernsey, was on the same train on 20 July 1942 and was killed in Auschwitz (as was a third, Marianne Grunfeld, on a later transport). Of the 824 Jews on this three-day journey, including Therese and Auguste, only 14 (all men) survived the war.[8] One of these was Dr Andre Lettich, who provided an account of this particular transport. Its brevity and matter-of-fact style make it typical of so many reports of journeying to the abyss, or what the Nazis' victims, with the darkest black humour, described as the 'road to paradise':[9]

> We were loaded into cattle wagons, sixty-five to eighty people to a wagon, and the windows and doors were hermetically sealed. In the course of the journey, crammed against each other, we suffered terribly from thirst and we were forced to sacrifice the corner of the wagon for the necessities of nature.[10]

British xenophobia resulted in the state closing of its borders in September 1939 to 'enemy' aliens and, at a popular and press level, a campaign against those present (with specific animus against refugee domestics) in spring 1940, which culminated with their mass internment on the Isle of Man (or, for Therese Steiner, in Guernsey). On the Channel Islands, the antipathy expressed by Martelli had a more lethal impact. While some resisted and protected the small Jewish population, this was not the dominant response of the local population or the Island authorities.[11]

---

6   National Archives, HO 213/281 E409: Martelli to Holderness, 4 July 1938.
7   Cohen, *The Jews in the Occupied Channel Islands*, p. 12.
8   Ibid., p. 49.
9   *Polish Fortnightly Bulletin* no. 47 (1 July 1942), p. 2.
10 Bunting, *The Model Occupation*, p. 111.
11 David Fraser, *The Jews of the Channel Islands and the Rule of Law, 1940–1945*

Immediately after the war the British government carried out an investigation of what had happened in the Channel Islands. An opportunity was provided for self-criticism, but in Guernsey the 'three foreign Jewish women sent … to their deaths in March 1942 do not even appear'.[12] An MI5 investigation found that 'When the Germans proposed to put their anti-Jewish measures into force, no protest whatever was raised by any of the Guernsey States Officials, and they hastened to give the Germans every assistance.' In contrast, steps against the local Freemasons led to 'the Bailiff ma[king] considerable protests'.[13] Thereafter, as Madelaine Bunting argued in 1995, 'For the best part of forty years, little was known on Guernsey about the fate of Therese Steiner, Auguste Spitz and Marianne Grunfeld, and no one showed any inclination to find out more about this episode in the island's past.'[14]

It has taken third-generation British Jews of East European origin, such as Frederick Cohen and playwright Julia Pascal, to recover and commemorate these small-scale but neglected Holocaust journeys. Pascal's *Theresa* (1995) recovers the life and death of Therese Steiner, attempting to insert her into British and specifically Channel Island memory. Pascal was prompted by reading a 1989 newspaper article on the deportation of the three Guernsey women. It 'changed my life … . I was brought up with the myth that the British would never collaborate … what happened on the Channel Islands was a secret history full of shame, guilt and cover-up'.[15]

Locally, limited progress has been made in connecting Jersey and Guernsey to other murderous places such as Auschwitz. More widely, these deportations are regarded, at most, as minor footnotes to the wider history of the British Isles at war and the Holocaust. The deportation of the three Jewish women remains, as Laurence Rees notes, 'an indelible stain on [Guernsey's] past'.[16] A senior MI5 officer, Major Stopford, reflecting on his office's report, pondered that 'In view of the fact that the Channel Islands are the only piece of British territory to have been occupied by the enemy, the behaviour of the inhabitants merits careful thought.' The evidence they obtained made it 'impossible not to feel disquietened by the way the Islanders behaved'.[17] But it was this very unease (and the challenge

---

(Brighton: Sussex University Press, 2000), provides a detailed if somewhat overstated critique of Channel Island antisemitism.

12 Sanders, *The British Channel Islands*, p. 243.
13 National Archives, KV 4/78 and HO 45/22399: Report sent to the Home Office, 17 August 1945.
14 Bunting, *The Model Occupation*, p. 109.
15 Julia Pascal, 'Introduction', in idem, *The Holocaust Trilogy* (London: Oberon Books, 2000), p. 4. *Theresa* was written in 1990 and first performed in 1995.
16 Laurence Rees, *Auschwitz: The Nazis and the 'Final Solution'* (London: BBC Books, 2005), p. 185.
17 National Archives, KV 4/78: Stopford notes, 8 August 1945.

it offered to assumptions of innate British moral superiority as exemplified by the Second World War) that stopped consideration of the wider question raised by Stopford.

Instead, it is British journeys into the Holocaust as liberators that is increasingly recognised and celebrated, especially in relation to Bergen-Belsen concentration camp – again, highlighted in the 2014 Holocaust Commission. As will emerge, it was largely the emotional response through witnessing the horror images from the western concentration camps that brought about the Holocaust survivor journeys (forming the third and final element of the 'British role' outlined by the Commission) that will be the focal point of this chapter. While relatively minor at the time, the history of this movement is now (if gradually) becoming part of the local and national memorial landscape and, as with the Holocaust Commission, incorporated into political discourse.

This chapter analyses the experiences of and responses to Jewish child survivors of the Holocaust who came to Britain just months after the end of the Second World War. The focus is on Windermere and the Lake District, where the largest number of the children were initially settled. Through the exploration of place identity and Englishness, it analyses how the journeys of these children have been excluded and included in narratives of the past. Cultural theorist Stuart Hall has argued that '[M]ajority, mainstream versions of the Heritage should revise their own self-conceptions and rewrite the margins into the centre, the outside into the inside.'[18] Although the process is far from complete, recent progress in incorporating the remarkable saga of these children shows how this is made possible. This chapter will not only explore the particularity of these young survivors but also place them in a wider, neglected history of unaccompanied child migration in the twentieth century and beyond.

In 1945 and 1946 732 child survivors were airlifted to recuperate in Britain.[19] Compared with the *Kindertransport*, the story of the 732, misleadingly referred to as 'The Boys' (over 10 per cent were female), has until recently hardly been remembered, even though these movements

---

18 Stuart Hall, speech at national conference, 'Whose Heritage? The Impact of Cultural Diversity on Britain's Living Heritage', G-Mex, Manchester, 2 November 1999 reproduced in Jo Littler and Roshi Naidoo (eds), *The Politics of Heritage: The Legacies of 'Race'* (London: Routledge, 2005), p. 34.

19 The first, brief history of this movement was provided by Norman Bentwich, *They Found Refuge: An account of British Jewry's work for victims of Nazi oppression* (London: Cresset Press, 1956), pp. 74–77. Sarah Moskovitz, *Love Despite Hate: Child Survivors of the Holocaust and their Adult Lives* (New York: Schocken Books, 1983) was the first detailed study, focusing on the children who were sent to Weir Courtenay, a large house near Lingfield, Surrey, after the initial reception camps. The only detailed overview of the movement is by Martin Gilbert, *The Boys: Triumph over Adversity* (London: Weidenfeld & Nicolson, 1996).

shared elements of organisational structure and personnel.[20] While both of these movements have yet to achieve a critical and sustained academic historiography, the *Kindertransport*, as emphasised throughout this study, has become part of the stories Britain tells of itself and is now recognised internationally as one of the major acts of rescue during the Nazi era. But, with regard to the children who came after the Second World War, for many decades the near absence of memory work was as true in the places where they were originally looked after as it was at a national level in the UK and globally within Holocaust commemoration.

The reason for this lacuna, especially relative to the *Kinder*, is not accidental. These children, mirroring in this respect the refugee domestics, do not 'fit' easily into wider narratives of migrant journeys, Jewish or non-Jewish. It will be argued here that it is the childrens' 'otherness' to so many concepts – especially related to place as refracted through everyday experience, nationality, class, and religion – which explains their obscurity. Such invisibility exists in spite of the intense efforts that were made to help them at the time and the remarkable experiences and multi-layered identities of the children themselves. There are, however, prequels and sequels of such journeys which, while as obscure, help locate them in a wider context of forced migration, war, persecution, and childhood in the modern era.

In November 1938 the Home Secretary, Sir Samuel Hoare, announced to the House of Commons the scheme to bring 'Jewish and non-Aryan children' to Britain. He had been approached by leading members of the central refugee coordinating body, who had 'pointed back to the experience during the war, in which we gave homes to many thousands of Belgian children, in which they were educated, and in which we played an invaluable part in maintaining the life of the Belgian nation.' Hoare was in agreement and told his fellow MPs that 'we could find homes in this country for a very large number without any harm to our own population'.[21]

Referencing the Belgian refugees was politically astute but historically flawed. A very large number of Belgian children *did* come to Britain during the First World War – 18,500 under five and 32,500 aged from five to 15, according to a contemporary estimate in November 1915. At that point they represented roughly one-quarter of the Belgian refugees in Britain.[22] While a few were brought to Britain specifically to be schooled, there was

20 See, for example, the narrative provided by Bentwich, *They Found Refuge*, chapter 5, which presents the later scheme as a brief afterword (pp. 74–77). For the memoirs of another British Jewish refugee worker who was involved with both sets of children, see Elaine Blond with Barry Turner, *Marks of Distinction* (London: Vallentine Mitchell, 1988).

21 *Hansard* (HC) no. 341 cols 1473–1474, 21 November 1938.

22 T. De Jastrzebski, 'The Register of Belgian Refugees', *Journal of the Royal Statistical Society* no. 79 (March 1916), p. 36.

no generic scheme to bring in children and the vast majority of those that came were accompanied by their relatives. These young refugees were dispersed, along with their families, across Britain and educated in local schools.[23]

In terms of becoming a 'usable past', the Belgian example had some virtues. On the surface, the children were well-integrated and local antagonism was minimal. Their education, even without any specific language provision, was deemed a success by the educational authorities.[24] In reality, in deprived areas where they were concentrated, such as Earl's Court in London, there was friction, including some violence in 1916.[25] Moreover, during the second half of the war Belgian parents began to worry that the children were losing their linguistic and cultural identity and in response they set up specific primary and secondary schools.[26]

Any tensions were, however, conveniently forgotten, and the narrative presented by Hoare was a reassuring one, especially as the Belgians returned or, as we have noted, were encouraged/forced to go home shortly after the end of the war. The Belgian nation revived after 1918, bolstered by the resettlement of its exiles, who amounted to as much as one-sixth of its total pre-war population. There was thus no guilt necessary at the nature or speed of this repatriation. It was only those that had worked closely with them that were distressed about 'How [the returned Belgians] would survive the circumstances they would be called on to face – no work, no means, and with necessities at little short of famine prices'.[27] This, however, was far from what the nation that had offered refuge to the 'brave little Belgians' wished to dwell upon. Instead, as the first and totally sympathetic history of refugees in Britain benignly noted, it was better simply to narrate that 'after November 1918, nearly all the Belgians [simply] melted away'.[28] But what Hoare failed to acknowledge was that, while support for the Belgian refugees supposedly came from local voluntary contributions, the government provided most of the funding behind the scenes.[29] This was

---

23 See National Archives, ED 91/48 and ED 12/23 for local examples.

24 Government Belgian Refugees Committee, *First Report* (London: HMSO, 1914 Cd.7750), p. 29.

25 Katherine Storr, 'Belgian Children's Education in Britain in the Great War: Language, Identity and Race Relations', *History of Education Researcher* no. 72 (November 2003), p. 91.

26 Kevin Myers, 'The hidden history of refugee schooling in Britain: the case of the Belgians, 1914–18', *History of Education* no. 30 no. 2 (2001), pp. 161–162.

27 Katherine Storr, *Excluded from the Record: Women, Refugees and Relief 1914–1929* (Bern: Peter Lang, 2010), p. 99.

28 Franscesca Wilson, *They Came as Strangers: The Story of Refugees to Great Britain* (London: Hamish Hamilton, 1959), p. 215.

29 Peter Cahalan, *Belgian Refugee Relief in England during the Great War* (New York: Garland, 1982), chapter 3.

not what the British state intended with Jewish refugees from Nazism, including the children.

There *was*, however, a specific scheme for refugee children to come to Britain during the First World War. Significantly, it had been lost in collective consciousness by 1938: only the Belgians were recalled. In late 1915–early 1916, the British government, through its War Refugees Committee, allowed the entry of up to 600 Serbian boys who had initially found refuge in Greek territory behind the Allied lines in Macedonia. They were part of a pitiful movement of civilians behind the Serbian army retreating to the Adriatic in which a contemporary estimate put the refugee deaths en route at between 18,000–27,000. It was a journey subsequently named in Serbian collective memory as the 'Golgotha'.[30] In the end, just over 300 came to Britain from spring 1916. Funded and administered by the Serbian Relief Fund, financial and logistical problems limited the total to half that initially intended.[31] In France, a larger, state-funded operation brought ten times that number of Serbian boys. And it was from within these 3000 that most of the children coming to Britain were chosen.[32]

As with the Belgians, the Serbians were regarded as deserving victims of the war whose intense suffering was a symbol of enemy barbarism. Initial irritation over Serbia's 'responsibility' for the war was replaced by admiration for its bravery and resilience: 'When Englishmen were fired for enthusiasm for Belgium or Serbia ... they saw themselves as maintaining the rights not only of these nations but some common and fundamental interest of mankind'.[33] As the school which took the largest number of refugees commented,

> just as the prospective union of the Serb race was doubtless one of the causes that brought about the present War, it is to be hoped that it will be one of the first things to be consummated when the War is over.[34]

The Serbian Relief Fund, founded as early as September 1914, was one manifestation of this sympathy, as were the many British nurses (especially Scottish, reflecting – contemporaries suggested – an affinity with another small and much persecuted nation) and other relief workers who went to help in Serbia itself.[35] While, as with the Belgians, there was increasing

---

30 National Archives, MH 8/5: 'Serbian Work in Progress' (1916).

31 A brief overview is provided in National Archives, MH 8/5: circular letter of 25 March 1918 by the Serbian Relief Fund.

32 National Archives, MH 8/4: Serbian Relief Fund, *For Serbia* (London: Serbian Relief Fund, 1916?), p. 17.

33 Harry Hanak, *Great Britain and Austria-Hungary during the First World War* (London: Oxford University Press, 1962), pp. 38, 60.

34 *The Herioter* no. 10 (December 1916), p. 5.

35 Hugh and Christopher Seton-Watson, *The Making of a New Europe* (London:

irritation with these refugees, initial support built on a sense of empathy with the Serbian nation and the huge losses that had been inflicted on it through 'the evils of Germanisation'.[36] It was 'peculiarly appropriate' to help these youngsters, as 'It was the attempt of the Central Powers to crush little Serbia that originated the Great War.'[37]

As an illustration of that sympathy, when the first batch of 170 Serbian children arrived in Britain at the port of Southampton during April 1916, the town council happily provided lunch, treats, and accommodation for them. The ex-Mayor greeted the boys, and

> spoke in eulogy of the part which Serbia had played in the war and ... hoped that by the education they would receive in England the students would be able to assist in the regeneration of their country which would be looked up to by the other nations who honoured the cause of freedom.

From Southampton they progressed to Oxford University and were then distributed across the country.[38] More generally, the organisers attempted to foster a bond between Britain and Serbia and emphasised the role the former could play in the rebuilding of the latter. And it was for this reason that the scheme to bring the refugee boys to Britain was self-consciously gendered.

The narrative created by the Serbian Relief Fund focused on the decimation of the nation and how it was in danger of being emasculated. 'During the great Serbian retreat every effort was made to bring away as many of the boys as possible, and thus save the *country's future manhood* [my emphasis] from the tender mercies of the enemy.'[39] In the initial transports only a handful of girls were selected to come to Britain – unlike the children from the concentration camps, the male bias was deliberately intended. The aim was to educate and train these boys so that they would return to Serbia equipped not only with intellectual and practical skills but also with a strong and virile determination to rebuild the nation.[40] Leading female members of the Serbian Relief Fund, and especially Mrs Carrington

Methuen, 1981), p. 106; Hanak, *Great Britain*, pp. 67–68; Storr, *Excluded from the Record*, chapter 7. For testimony of these nurses, see M.I. Tatham, 'The Great Retreat in Serbia', in C. Purdom (ed.), *Everyman at War* (London: J.M. Dent, 1930), pp. 374–379 and Anne Powell (ed.), *Women in the War Zone: Hospital Service in the First World War* (Stroud: History Press, 2013), pp. 94–111, 158–206, 377–386.

36 National Archives, MH 8/5: 'Serbian Work in Progress in England', no date.
37 *George Heriot's School Roll of Honour 1914–1919* (Edinburgh: War Memorial Committee, 1921), p. 22.
38 *Southampton Times*, 6 May 1916 and Southampton City Council, Minutes of Proceedings, 1915–16, Finance Committee, 11 May 1916.
39 Serbian Relief Fund, *For Serbia*, p. 17.
40 Andrej Mitrovic, *Serbia's Great War* (London: Hurst, 2007), pp. 169–178.

Wilde, attempted in vain to bring a smaller colony of girls to Britain to be retrained, but there was neither the funds locally nor the will from the Serbian authorities to enable this to happen.[41]

Dispersed across England, Scotland, and Wales, the children were under the general care of a Serbian priest and a leading academic. Placed in local self-contained hostels, the ideal was to combine the best of 'British and Serbian methods [while] avoiding anything which could even remotely be regarded as denationalising'.[42] The rapid influx of Belgian children necessitated integrating them fully both in local schools and accommodation. The Serbians, much smaller in number, could be controlled more closely with their future role in the nation clearly in mind.

The 300-plus Serbian children were divided into 14 colonies across Britain. The choice of this word was itself significant: the children were regarded by the Serbian authorities as under their rule – they were in temporary exile abroad.[43] The majority were placed in schools across the country, mainly in secondary education. Over 60 went to universities ranging from Edinburgh University to the University College of Bangor and including Oxford and Cambridge, where the initial distribution of these youths had begun. Of these in higher education, 18 studied engineering, 13 agriculture, six forestry, six commerce, and five medicine.[44] Roughly half that number were sent to work in a variety of engineering works and farms, where the experience was far less happy – the adolescent boys complained of the work being too hard and unrewarding. Four boys at a munitions factory in Barnes wrote to the Serbian Relief Fund in summer 1918 complaining that, despite promises, it was not getting any easier and 'now we are getting weaker everyday'. Hoping for less demanding non-factory employment/ training, they were aware of the danger of appearing lazy, emphasising instead that in Barnes 'we can't learn anything that [will] be any use to us in Serbia'. Here, the voice and agency of these young refugees was clearly expressed, playing on the organisers' future ambitions for them. The Serbian Relief Fund took their pleas seriously and moved them on to more interesting and less arduous positions.[45]

Articulating a different perspective, factory managers complained about the work rate and reliability of the Serbian teenagers. In turn, the Serbian Relief Fund reminded them that many of these teenagers had already served

---

41 See the SSEES Library, London, Seton-Watson papers: Executive Minutes of the Serbian Relief Fund, 16 March 1916, 7/7/7 and 1 November 1916, 10 May 1917, 7/7/8 and 14 December 1919 in 7/7/9.

42 Serbian Relief Fund, *For Serbia*, p. 18.

43 Mitrovic, *Serbia's Great War*, p. 174.

44 Sidney Ball, 'Serbians at British Schools', *Times Educational Supplement*, 24 January 1918.

45 National Archives, MH 8/13: Letter of 29 August 1918. See also MH 8/12 relating to factories in Bradford and Letchworth.

in the Serbian army (some as young as 13) and then on the Western Front, and were therefore deserving of support and encouragement.[46] As with the Belgians, there were accusations of shirking. Peter Gatrell notes that there were insinuations that 'young Serbian refugees in Oxford deliberately evaded military service, but in fact they were too young to enlist'.[47] Such criticism, however, seems to have been aimed only at the older boys, and the Serbian children were treated largely with affection. A large number – 25 – were admitted to the ancient Heriot's School in Edinburgh. In the School Roll of Honour, published in 1921, it was emphasised that these Serbian refugees 'had conferred many advantages … in respect of the feeling of *camaraderie* they had inspired amongst the other boys'.[48]

On the surface, given the apparent success of this movement and the effort expended by the state through the War Refugees Committee, voluntary bodies such as the Serbian Relief Fund, and local initiatives through schools and hostels, it is surprising that the presence of these children had, by the 1920s, become utterly obscure in official as well as popular memory. As an illustration of local affection towards them, when the last Serbs departed the journal of Heriot's School commented that 'Already their well-known faces are being missed from the quadrangle … for they had formed close friendship with many of the Scottish boys.' In turn, the young refugees erected a plaque of gratitude and it was noted that they would not 'break their connection with this School – a connection they will always proudly cherish'.[49]

In 1937 the National Joint Committee for Spanish Relief proposed bringing Basque children from the Spanish Civil War to Britain. In a high level inter-departmental conference, the First Lord of the Admiralty asked 'what other cases there had been of bringing in refugees from other countries to England'. He was told by Sir Ernest Holderness that 'there had been no comparable problem'. Here is confirmation that the Serbs had simply been forgotten.[50] The reasons for this amnesia in the official mind and in public consciousness are complex, but several factors can be identified.

First, as noted, the numbers were small, especially compared with the Belgians, who dominated the consideration of the War Refugees Committee and who even then, as noted, were also largely forgotten. Government involvement, beyond a representative on the Serbian Relief Fund, was

---

46 See, for example, National Archives, MH 8/13: the letter from the Assistant Secretary of the Serbian Relief Fund to the manager of the Beverley Works, Barnes, concerning a boy Ikitch, who had served for both the Serbian army and the Middlesex Regiment, 21 October 1918.

47 Peter Gatrell, *The Making of the Modern Refugee* (Oxford: Oxford University Press, 2013), p. 35. See the heated correspondence in *Oxford Chronicle*, 21 July 1918.

48 *George Heriot's School Roll of Honour*, p. 23.

49 *The Herioter* no. 13 (July 1919), pp. 3–5.

50 National Archives, HO 213/288: Conference minutes, 13 May 1937.

minimal until 1918, when the Treasury was asked for a donation of £25,000 to continue the education of the children.[51] In contrast, key figures within the Jewish refugee movement of the 1930s, especially Otto Schiff, had gained experience with Belgian refugees. In September 1917 Mrs Emily Hamilton, who had befriended some of the refugees, wrote a letter of complaint to the Foreign Office, complaining that the Serbian Relief Fund was a front for converting the Serbian children to the 'perver[sion]' of Roman Catholicism. Remarkably, her bigoted allegations were taken seriously. What emerged from the correspondence was that the government knew next to nothing about these young Serbs and their treatment. And, revealing a wider antagonism to the arrival of refugees to Britain, a senior Foreign Office figure starkly minuted that 'We were ourselves always opposed to these boys being brought to England, but Mrs [Carrington] Wilde [of the Serbian Relief Fund] insisted upon it.'[52] Fellow refugee worker Francesca Wilson later recalled the pragmatic as well as the racialised discourse underpinning the reasons behind the British state's resistance to their entry:

> One of these was economy, the other the theory that life in England would be too comfortable for unsophisticated Serbs, that they would be ruined and spoiled by it, and unable to assimilate to modern ideas … . Another notion she had had to fight was that the Serbs would be wild and destructive.[53]

The Serbian authorities themselves were initially uneasy about bringing the children to Britain, as it reported 'a certain unwillingness amongst the refugees to go so far away'.[54] Not withstanding this hesitation, the scale of the refugee crisis was such that all places were soon considered by the Serbs. For the Foreign Office, however, Bonar Law was unconvinced: 'We should be careful not to encourage Serbians to come here – they would be a burden on us, as I am sure they w[ould] be unable to support themselves'.[55] As would happen with many subsequent refugee movements, the government eventually but only partially yielded to humanitarian pressure and allowed a small number of children entry on a temporary basis.

The second reason for the collective amnesia of these children was that, while locally in the 14 'colonies' the refugee presence was important, nationally the issue of Serbia and what became Yugoslavia was, by the

51   National Archives, T1/12514.

52   National Archives, FO 371/2894: Minute, AN (?), 21 September 1917 and correspondence.

53   Francesca Wilson, *In the Margins of Chaos: Recollections of Relief Work in and between Three Wars* (London: John Murray, 1944), p. 99.

54   National Archives, FO 371/2603: Letter from Serbian Legation, 5 January 1916 to Sir Edward Grey.

55   National Archives, FO 371/21282: Memorandum, 15 December 1915.

end of the war, less pressing. As Harry Hanak argued, 'By the summer of 1917 the average Englishman was more interested in the ending of the war than in liberating the southern Slavs.'[56] When introducing the refugees to Heriot's School, it was noted that before the war the Serbians 'were perhaps to most English-speaking people little more than names'.[57] That obscurity, bolstered by intense post-war xenophobia and anti-alienism, returned after 1918. Third, and providing an overarching link to the previous two, was the difficulty in placing these Serbian refugees in a meaningful context, especially as those who campaigned for them were, while vociforous and well-connected, relatively few in number. Nevertheless, by 1919, when it was being wound up, there had been some 50,000 subscribers to the Serbian Relief Fund over its five-year existence. Even with the factors outlined above, the later amnesia of the refugee children remains puzzling. The concept of place identity needs further consideration in addressing this conundrum.[58]

Peter Gatrell, the leading scholar of refugee movements of the First World War, notes how Serbian refugees 'made their way to Salonika, Corfu and Brindisi. Serbian schools and orphanages were established in Nice, Tours, Grenoble, and in France's colonies in North Africa.' He adds that 'A few even ended up as farm labourers in East Anglia.'[59] Gatrell's surprise at this last place of settlement reflects the apparent *out of placeness* of these Serbians in rural England. Similarly, a history of a Hampshire school, when covering the First World War, adds without comment the terse and isolated sentence: 'Five Serbian refugees were entered as pupils at Taunton's.' This was between references to a debate on conscription and the setting-up of a War Savings Association.[60] Here, recognition of the Serbians was of novelty value at most – they were like exotic birds that had been swept by the wind to unfamiliar shores.

John Hope Simpson's 1939 policy-orientated history of refugee movements explained why he had ignored 'the exile of Belgians and Serbians during the Great War'. These, he argued, were 'purely temporary movements'.[61] Yet, while it is true that most of these refugees did return home, some did not. Moreover, for all of them, and especially perhaps the children, many of whom were orphaned, their journeys were traumatic and rarely straightforward, reflecting the nature of forced migration as a whole. Many thousands of lives were lost in the process – perhaps as many as half those

56 Hanak, *Great Britain*, p. 77.

57 *The Herioter* no. 10 (December 1916), p. 4.

58 SSEES Library, London, Seton-Watson papers 7/7/9: R.W. Seton-Watson, circular letter, 30 December 1919.

59 Gatrell, *The Making of the Modern Refugee*, p. 29.

60 H. Spooner, *A History of Taunton's School 1760–1967* (Southampton: Taunton's School, 1968), p. 137.

61 John Hope Simpson, *The Refugee Problem: Report of a Survey* (London: Oxford University Press, 1939), p. 1.

Serbs embarking on the trek across the Albanian mountains. To dismiss them, as did Hope Simpson, is to neglect the experiences of millions of war refugees, including children, in the twentieth century and beyond. It runs the risk of ignoring the impact of such displacement on their individual and collective identity, especially in relation to 'home'. Furthermore, it could also lead to minimising the importance of their presence and the support (and occasional antipathy) towards them at a local level.

Typical in this respect was the settlement of Serbian refugees in the Kent coastal town of Faversham. There, in September 1918, a party of 57 boys and 25 girls arrived and were housed in a former Military Hospital, The Mount. They were given 'a tremendous welcome. It was memorable, like that accorded when other events aroused interest and admiration among the townspeople.' This group was of different makeup to the earlier arrivals – most of them were orphans and they had come from Salonika accompanied by members of the Serbian Relief Fund.[62] In this respect, as will emerge, their movement was even closer to that of the Holocaust survivor children in 1945.

Sydney Clark was a local boy and he experienced the Serbians at first not at The Mount but at Faversham Grammar School. They were taught initially in Serbian, but soon in English. One Serbian was in Sydney's form and two in his football team. They were, he remembered, 'physically and intellectually very robust, and competitive in their studies'. The children's leaving in August 1921 was marked by a 'special Farewell Service at the church ... Every returning Serbian was given a Souvenir Guide to Faversham, together with postcards with a map of Kent.' In return, the Serbian children sang '"Tipperary", a favourite with the British soldiers in the war that had led to their exile'.[63]

In 2002, Sydney Clark reflected that

> They had become part of our life in Faversham, and went home carrying the Scout Flag they had treasured in England ... . They left a Serbian flag in Faversham ... . And with many memories of The Mount, their home-from-home in exile, they travelled by way of Dover, Ostend and Brussels to Belgrade ... . I wonder if any still survive, despite another war and all the Balkans turmoil since? They had three years of peace in Kent.[64]

His history of The Mount during the twentieth century concentrates on its period hosting the Serbian refugee children, 'since that was the period

---

62 Sydney Clark, 'A Faversham Chameleon House', *Bygone Kent* vol. 23 no. 2 (2002), p. 99.

63 Ibid., p. 101.

64 Ibid.

when I became most intimately acquainted with the house and grounds and its use'. He notes the irony that this local knowledge of The Mount came, 'strangely enough, [when] the people there came from a far foreign land'.[65]

The Mount, as with the other hostels for the Serbian children, made them both invisible *and* prominent in the local landscape: they were a part of and yet apart from the world around them. Sydney Clark's printed remembrances have lifted them from obscurity in Kent and, as with the experiences of the refugee boys in Edinburgh, commemoration of the First World War's centenary have provided space for rediscovery.[66] As noted, the same has happened with the recovery of the Belgian presence in Britain. In both cases, but especially that of the Serbians, this process is partial and incomplete. These remain largely forgotten histories despite the intense local engagement with these refugees at the time. In Southampton, at Taunton's School, for example, its journal noted 'the exceptional interest displayed' in the arrival of five Serbians into the Sixth Form by 'smaller boys'. It was 'prompted by some extraordinary impulse to risk much in order to boast proudly that they have seen *them!*'[67] The importance for these war refugees themselves must also not be underestimated. But, in contrast to the refugee domestics, no later testimony is available to analyse the long-term impact of their stay in Britain.

To justify the scheme, and local support of it, great emphasis was placed on the transient nature of the Serbian presence. Thus, in extending a 'hearty welcome' to the children, Taunton's School wished them good luck and 'a happy *sojourn* [my emphasis] with us'. A reassuring narrative was constructed, expressing the 'hope that in more fortunate days of the future, when they will once more settle down in their far homes, they may have pleasant recollections of England'.[68] The Serbian boys were happy to reinforce the passing nature of their stay. Dimitrije Dulkanovitch, just 13 when 'I hurriedly left my native town of Cuprija', wrote in the magazine of Heriot's School, *The Herioter*, in 1918 that 'We have been exiled from our dear land of Serbia for more than three years, but now that our cruel enemies have been expelled from it, we naturally look with longing eyes for a glimpse of home.' To remove any lingering doubt, he concluded that

the chief joy for us is to know that our soldiers have fought so bravely and our generals have been so skilfull that Serbia is free once more,

---

65 Ibid.

66 See, for example, websites devoted to 'Edinburgh's War' at www.edinburghs-war. ed.ac.uk/schools/george-heriot's-school, and Kent and Medway History Timeline at www.kent.gov.uk, both accessed 10 February 2015.

67 'School Gossip', *Taunton's School Journal* no. 24 no. 190 (February 1917), p. 12.

68 Ibid.

and that a warm welcome awaits us from the dear ones from whom we have been separated for nearly four years.[69]

Indeed, it is notable that in all three personal accounts of the Serbians published in *The Herioter* from 1916 to 1918 a military-style narrative was constructed, including their personal role in the army as boy soldiers.[70] In contrast to the testimony of the Jewish domestics, who presented themselves as refugees, the Serbians in Edinburgh present themselves as exiles whose unbending loyalty to 'home' and desire to return is expressed through a martial discourse of masculinity. In contrast, a 1916 photograph of these boys in school uniform is revealing: they appear very young, small, and desperately mournful.[71] Included is Dimitrije, who had witnessed his father being killed in 1914 and his mother being wounded, losing an arm. Dimitrije was also injured and, separated from his family, he endured two years of forced flight 'through the wilds of Albania with its fierce and unfriendly inhabitants'.[72] Closer to the reality was a headline in a local Scottish newspaper when reporting their arrival in Edinburgh: 'Boys who have looked death in the face.'[73] As with all the autobiographical writing examined in this study, silences are as important as the stories that are told. Similar to the letters of complaint written by the Serbian teenagers in employment, the school boys melded their accounts to the expectations of their readers, stressing manliness and a desire to be part of a new, virile Serbia. In defending the youngsters to the Foreign Office, Emily Henderson did so on their behalf because they 'naturally are tongue tied'.[74] Henderson did not do justice to their articulacy, including in English, but she did pinpoint the restraints of them being able to speak freely.

By the early 1920s the Serbians had indeed left and memories of them began to fade. Those travelling back with them from the Serbian Relief Fund reported that there was some initial problems in getting their British school and university certificates recognised and some difficulty for the youngsters in finding suitable work. But there were success stories, including that of Vladimir Miselj, who became a leading figure in the Secretariat of the League of Nations.[75] More generally, these Serbs were survivors of the murderous ethnic cleansing that was so pronounced in Europe's rimlands during the First World War and whose journeys to

---

69 *The Herioter* no. 12 (December 1918), pp. 6–7.

70 *The Herioter* no. 10 (December 1916), pp. 7–8 and no. 11 (March 1917), pp. 4–5.

71 *The Herioter* no. 10 (December 1916), frontispiece.

72 *The Herioter* no. 12 (December 1918), p. 6.

73 *People's Journal*, 19 August 1916.

74 Henderson letter to Lloyd George, 21 September 1917 in National Archives, FO 371/2894.

75 SSEES Library, London, Seton-Watson papers, 7/7/9: Executive minutes of the SRF, 14 January 1919, 13 April 1921, 14 December 1921.

Britain and other places of asylum were often torturous.[76] Unlike many of those displaced by the horrors of the conflict, they did return home through the speedy liberation of Serbia and establishment of Yugoslavia. It is hard, as John Hope Simpson recognised, to place the Serbians and Belgians even within a history of modern refugee movements, let alone within wider trends in modern migration patterns. Yet this is no reason to ignore their experiences and responses to them, as temporary refugees, as children, and as part of a truly global refugee crisis created by mass ethnic cleansing.

The hope of the Serbian Relief Fund was to have extended the scheme, but it did not have the capacity to do so, as illustrated by its failure to bring girls and young women to Britain in meaningful numbers. While its loftier aims of restoring the 'manhood' of the Serbian nation could be only partially realised, and some of its work training schemes were naive, the educational experience of the young Serbs was clearly successful, as was their general integration into local society. Andrej Mitrovic, historian of the Serbian experience during the First World War, concludes that 'The schoolchildren and students in Britain lived in incomparably better conditions than those in France, probably because there were far fewer of them and because Britain was not directly exposed to war operations.'[77] Yet, for all its virtues, it did not become part of bureaucratic memory for those carrying out aliens policy in the UK.

When activists in 1937 again demanded that Britain be opened up as a temporary refuge for children, this time those suffering the aerial bombardment of Guernica in the Spanish Civil War, the government was opposed to their entry. What is revealing is that one of the most prominent charities set up after the war to deal with global issues involving young people – Save the Children Fund (SCF) – was also unsure. While its concerns were not those of the government, it reflected a greater sensitivity to what would later be termed the 'rights of the child'. In terms of continuity, although some of its earlier activists had been linked to the Serbian Relief Fund, again there was no direct reference made to these earlier refugee children.

The government's objections were a mixture of financial (concern that the maintenance of the Basque refugees would eventually fall on the state), political – the fear especially that the older children would stimulate anti-alienism – and concerns about health.[78] The Council of SCF was

---

76 Mark Levene, *The Crisis of Genocide* vol. 1 *Devastation: The European Rimlands, 1912–1938* (Oxford: Oxford University Press, 2014), Part 1.

77 Mitrovic, *Serbia's Great War*, p. 174. Even so, at least six of the children died of diseases, especially TB.

78 See correspondence in National Archives, HO 213/287 and 288, CAB 23/90A, and CAB 23/88.

initially unwilling to challenge state restrictionism, but for different reasons. It commented, with some justification, that 'the principle of evacuating children and adults to foreign countries from war and/or persecution areas require[d] considerably more study than the problem ha[d] at present received' (an observation that is still relevant, perhaps, eight decades on). Even so, it recognised the severity of the situation in Spain and could therefore not 'oppose the evacuation of children from Bilbao'.[79]

In early May 1937 the SCF position, outlined in a draft statement, was still opposed to the entry of the Basque children to Britain, arguing instead that they should be sent to south-west France. Britain was unsuitable, it argued, because of the length of the journey from Spain, its climate, the unsuitability of its food, its religion, and the lack of appropriate educational facilities. It also believed the campaign to bring the children was motivated by politics coming from those sympathetic to the Spanish Republican or Basque cause. Funding was a potential issue, but it also warned of logistical problems: 'provision must be made for repatriation with necessary guarantees', which would be especially difficult if parents had subsequently died. If the French option was not viable, it commented finally, then a neutral zone should be found where the children with their teachers could be made safe. This would 'prevent the creation of Refugees with all the dire consequences associated with a state of Refugeedom'.[80]

This statement was the work of the Fund's secretary, Lewis Golden. While SCF eventually and hesitantly supported the arrival of the 4000 Basque children, this was totally opposed by Golden, who told the Home Office that he 'could not emphasise too strongly that his Society which has upwards of 20 years experience in succouring refugee children in all parts of the world was absolutely opposed in principle to the removal of young children from their native country'. Golden continued in the most dramatic manner, stating that where 'this had been done the later results were too often deplorable'. He concluded that 'he would sooner see them die in their own land than rot slowly in exile where they deteriorate physically, morally and mentally'.[81]

Golden's (unsuccessful) intervention, for all its negativity, did show that some working with refugee children were, by the 1930s, aware of their cultural and psychological needs. Yet, while his comments on the negative characteristics associated with 'refugeedom' cannot be dismissed, the example of the Serbs (and the Belgians) in the First World War showed that such schemes for children were not inherently without redeeming features. In the particular case of the Basque refugee children, however, its implementation was far from unproblematic, as Golden had predicted.

---

79 National Archives, HO 213/287: Draft statement of Council, 10 May 1937.
80 Ibid.
81 Report of telephone conversation with Mr Golden, 4 May 1937 in Ibid.

The journey to Southampton on the *SS Habana*, with as many as eight times the number of passengers it could have comfortably carried, was miserable, and most of the children were violently sick. Moreover, beyond the initial positive welcome in the reception camps in Eastleigh, the 90 'colonies' set up to house them across Britain were uneven in the care and attention they gave to these already dislocated and often traumatised children.[82] The revival of the term 'colony' suggests a connection, even if indirect, to the Serbian refugees and the desire to keep a link to their homeland. In both cases, however, the psychological needs of these youngsters, who had experienced the trauma of war and persecution first hand, was rarely considered.

With regards to their initial selection, the British government insisted that they should be aged between five and 15, desiring that the older children should be female to avoid any hostility about the displacement of British workers. In Spain the children were picked through 'a quota system from amongst the Basque political parties'.[83] The children themselves had no say in this decision-making. As one bluntly recalled some 60 years later, 'We didn't come, we were sent. I didn't want to come. I grumbled a lot.'[84] While the memories of those recorded have largely been positive, testimony does tend to highlight their initial lack of agency: 'I wasn't asked if I wanted to go to England. I am sure that if I had been asked, I would have probably said, no.'[85] Without necessary training and support, those left in Britain (some 400 by 1945) struggled to establish careers and a sense of belonging. It has still been noted that in many cases their 'sheer determination and self-motivation … help[ed] them overcome, in later years, the disadvantages of their early years'.[86] But, even when parents survived, the separation was so prolonged that they regarded themselves as orphans. Valeriana recalls that her mother later remarked '"If I had known what this meant, I would never have sent you to England" … because she practically lost me as a daughter'.[87]

From the perspective of the state bureaucracy, this was not deemed a successful experiment. Returning to A.J. Eagleston's history of the Home Office Aliens Department, his final (damning) comment on the scheme was what 'emerges very plainly from the story … is that a great deal of caution

---

82 Adrian Bell, *Only For Three Months: The Basque Children in Exile* (Norwich: Mousehold Press, 1996).

83 Tom Buchanan, *Britain and the Spanish Civil War* (Cambridge: Cambridge University Press, 1997), p. 111.

84 Bell, *Only For Three Months*, p. 1.

85 Alicia Pozo-Gutierrez and Padmini Broomfield, *'Here, Look After Him': Voices of Basque Evacuee Children of the Spanish Civil War* (Southampton: University of Southampton Press, 2012), p. 36.

86 See Steve Bowles' film, *The Guernica Children* (2005/2007) and Pozo-Gutierrez and Broomfield, *'Here, Look After Him'*, p. 135.

87 Pozo-Gutierrez and Broomfield, *'Here, Look After Him'*, p. 156.

is necessary in admitting temporary refugees in any substantial number because whatever guarantees of removal may be given they are very likely to become permanent residents'. He added that, in spite of all parties wanting the Spanish children to return, 'more than 10% of the total number of refugees had to be allowed to stay in this country because they could not be repatriated at all'.[88] In contrast to detailed discussion of the Spanish children, Eagleston mentioned Jewish refugee children only in passing, failing to give the impression that they, too, were part of an organised scheme. He did emphasise that those escaping Nazism had to be 'emigrated when they reached 18 and that they were being retrained in agriculture and industry with 'no encouragement ... given to them to qualify for the professions or for "black-coated occupations"'.[89] As will be illustrated, these comments could easily be applied to the Jewish children that came after the war.

With both the Serbian children and the Basques their entry into Britain – in both cases due to war (global and regional) – was as much symbolic to those organising it as it was about need. As Tom Buchanan notes in relation to those evacuated from the Basque country in 1937, 'the children achieved more than any pamphlet or public meeting in bringing home the harsh realities of the war to the British people'.[90] Likewise, no opportunity was lost by those responsible for the Serbian refugees in making wider linkages and emphasising the need to protect 'civilised' values.

The experiences of the children themselves was varied, especially so in the case of the Basques. The neutrality and at times antipathy of the state ensured that their treatment would depend on voluntary organisations and individuals, many of which/whom were naive and inexperienced in dealing with the particular problems facing child refugees. The children had no say in whether they came to Britain or not, but, as with all the refugees studied so far, they asserted their agency where possible and were certainly not silent victims.

To summarise: from 1914 to 1939 a variety of child refugees came to Britain and often in significant numbers. Popular responses were largely positive and the presence of these child refugees became part of local place identity. The state, however, remained at best ambivalent and generally hostile to their arrival. It reflected an unease about aliens policies being undermined by humanitarian gestures rather than a concern for the well-being of the children themselves. The Jewish children who came in 1945, therefore, entered a country with a complex if not fully recognised tradition of dealing with young refugees. It was one built on sympathy but less so on empathy: the youngsters' particular needs were rarely recognised beyond a desire to impart practical skills linked to the workplace.

---

88   National Archives, HO 213/1772: A.J. Eagleston, 'The Control of Alien Immigration'.
89   Ibid.
90   Buchanan, *Britain and the Spanish Civil War*, p. 109.

Wandering Jews and the Importance of Being Wordsworth

In the analysis which follows, two particular contexts relating to place and identity will be emphasised to explore the processes of othering and inclusion in relation to these young Holocaust survivors. In this particular case, insights into the responses to these 732 children (that is, twice the number of the earlier young Serbian refugees) will be gathered especially through the mythical construct of the 'Wandering Jew' and its place in Christian and Jewish discourse. From the eighteenth century onwards, and especially through Romanticism, this figure was represented in an increasingly ambivalent manner.

Migrant journeys, whether forced or voluntary or a mixture of the two, are experienced at both a physical and a spiritual level. The discourse used to describe them from within and without has often utilised religious imagery, albeit often in a secular context. For Jewish journeys, the 'Wandering Jew' is a recurrent motif.[91] And, as this wider study covers both 'now' and 'then', it will also tease out the relationship between history and memory and between individual and collective constructions of the past and present. In so doing, it will confront the tensions in place identity generated by the meeting of the 'there' of the Holocaust and the 'here' of post-war Britain.

Here, the starting point for understanding contemporary responses to these children is William Wordsworth, the English Romantic poet who has come to symbolise and dominate the identity of the Lake District. He was not the first to write about Lakeland and to give it a distinct identity, but, as Melvyn Bragg notes, 'Wordsworth immortalised it.'[92] Since then, the Lake District has been advertised in the heritage industry as 'Wordsworth country' – a national park of some 900 square miles 'Described by many as the most beautiful area in England'.[93] Physically, the Lake District is located in the relatively young (1974) county of Cumbria (previously Cumberland, Westmorland and parts of Lancashire), or, as has been quipped with less administrative precision, 'Wordsworthshire'.[94]

As noted, it was in the Lake District that the largest group of these children – roughly 300 – were initially settled. They had been grouped

---

91 See Joseph Gaer, *The Legend of the Wandering Jew* (New York: Mentor Books, 1961) and Galit Hasan-Rokem and Alan Dundes (eds), *The Wandering Jew: Essays in the Interpretation of a Christian Legend* (Bloomington: Indiana University Press, 1986).

92 Melvyn Bragg, *Land of the Lakes* (London: Secker & Warburg, 1983). p. 198.

93 See, for example, 'What is Wordsworth Country?', in http://www.wordsworth-country.com/whatisit.htm, accessed 15 June 2010.

94 W. Darby, *Landscape and Identity: Geographies of Nation and Class in England* (Oxford: Berg, 2000), pp. 211–212. See also Dave Russell, *Looking North: Northern England and the national imagination* (Manchester: Manchester University Press, 2004), p. 54.

together after the war at Terezin and were flown from Prague to Crosby-on-Eden (near Carlisle) in the north of England. A second group was flown from Munich to Stonycross in the New Forest in the south of England.[95] Those in the north were bussed to Calgarth near Windermere and those in the south to a large stately home in Hampshire – Wintershill Hall in Durley. Even within the limited, though growing, recognition of this child refugee movement, it is the Windermere camp that is remembered, whereas the experiences in Wintershill Hall have been largely lost. It is true that the numbers in the Hampshire reception camp were approximately half those of Windermere.[96] Yet it is, perhaps, not so much size as the wider fame of the Lake District itself that has prompted the northern reception centre to be remembered at the cost of the southern.

Recent commemorative work, much of it prompted by the Heritage Lottery funded 'From Auschwitz to Ambleside', has focused on Windermere. This remarkable local history project has begun to reawaken local memories, even though none of the buildings where the children were housed survives.[97] Wintershill Hall, in contrast, having been a family home for many generations, including that of a branch of the prominent Anglo-Jewish (Sebag-) Montefiores from 1937 to 1946, is in a fine state of repair.[98] The absence of physical remains was one of a variety of factors hindering memory work in Windermere – the story of the children has been hidden within what has become 'The Lost Village of Calgarth'.[99] Contrarily, its clear presence in Durley, Hampshire – admittedly in what William Cobbett in his *Rural Rides* in 1823 described as 'one of the most obscure villages in this whole kingdom' – has not acted as a prompt to rediscover the narratives of the child survivors who

95 For the details of all the flights, see National Archives, HO 213/1797.
96 For Wintershill Hall see Mollie Panter-Downes, 'A Quiet Life in Hampshire', *New Yorker*, 2 March 1946 and Tony Kushner and Katharine Knox, *Refugees in an Age of Genocide: Global, National and Local Perspectives during the Twentieth Century* (London: Frank Cass, 1999), pp. 210–211.
97 Trevor Avery, *From Auschwitz to Ambleside* (Sedbergh: Another Space, 2008). Supported by the Big Lottery Fund 'Their Past Your Future', this project has led to exhibitions, school packs, and a website (http://www.anotherspace.org.uk/a2a/index.htm, accessed 29 June 2010). It also prompted the television documentary *The Orphans Who Survived the Concentration Camps*, BBC 1, 5 April 2010. Author site visit with Trevor Avery, 18 August 2009. There has been a basic archaeological mapping of the site to reveal the foundations of some of the major buildings.
98 Hilda Stowell, *Wintershill Hall Hampshire from the period of Roman Occupation to 1972* (Chichester: Chichester Press, 1972), p. 12. On the offer from James Sebag-Montefiore to provide his home, see University of Southampton Archives: Central British Fund council minutes, 22 October 1945, in CBF archives, File 9/179, microfilm collection.
99 Trevor Avery and Rosemary Smith (eds), *The Lost Village of Calgarth* (Sedbergh: Another Space, 2009).

were present there.[100] It suggests that other, more important, factors are at work in the Lake District when explaining the lacunae relating to the Windermere children. Put boldly, Wordsworth and the 'Lake poets' have, unsurprisingly, dominated the memory and identity of the district at the expense of alternative histories. It is, as a recent photographic essay of the landscape makes clear in terms of ownership, 'Wordsworth's Lake District'.[101]

The attention given to the Romantic writers in the Lake District explains superficially why the story of the child survivors has been forgotten at a local level. Yet the work of Wordsworth, especially his poem 'The Wandering Jew', as well as the writings of the other Romantics and their complex construction and reconstruction of this figure, also facilitates a way of confronting and re-remembering the experiences of the children.[102] It enables an analysis of the 'othering' process that has left these survivors, referencing anthropologist Mary Douglas and her work on the concepts of pollution and taboo, as 'matter out of place'. It reflects a wider tendency with regard to refugees, who, as Liisa Malkki reminds us, are 'liminal in the categorical order of nation-states'.[103]

Wordsworth's poem, written and published in 1800 when he had recently settled into the remote Dove Cottage in Grasmere,[104] reveals classic Romantic ambivalence towards the figure of 'the Jew'.[105] Within some Romantic writing, the figure of the 'Wandering Jew' was presented in all its hideous, unambiguous medieval and even pre-medieval form – as a grotesque male Christ-killer, his monstrosity given an additional gothic twist of criminality and alienness. In 1856 the American Romanticist Nathaniel Hawthorne, in his *English Notebooks*, described a Lord Mayor's

100 G.D.H. and Margaret Cole (eds), *William Cobbett: Rural Rides* (London: Peter Davies, 1930), p. 175 entry 6 August 1823 describing the parish of Durley. Jack Hecht, 'Revisiting Wintershill Hall', *Journal of the '45 Aid Society* no. 30 (2006), p. 21 is by one of the former 'Boys'.

101 Alex Black and Hazel Gatford, *Wordsworth's Lake District: The Landscape and Its Writers* (Sevenoaks: Salmon, 2001) – my emphasis.

102 Sheila Spector (ed.), *British Romanticism and the Jews: History, Culture, Literature* (New York: Palgrave, 2002); Judith Page, *Imperfect Sympathies: Jews and Judaism in British Romantic Literature and Culture* (New York: Palgrave Macmillan, 2004).

103 Mary Douglas, *Purity and Danger: An Analysis of the Concepts of Pollution and Taboo* (London: Routledge, 1996 [1966]), p. 41; Liisa Malkki, 'National Geographic: The Rooting of Peoples and the Territorialization of National Identity among Scholars and Refugees', *Cultural Anthropology* no. 7 no. 1 (February 1992), p. 34.

104 See William Knight (ed.), *Journals of Dorothy Wordsworth* (London: Macmillan, 1930), chapters 3–6, on Grasmere, 1800 to 1803; Jonathan Wordsworth, *William and Dorothy Wordsworth: The Dove Cottage Years* (Grasmere: Wordsworth Trust, 2008).

105 William Wordsworth, 'Song for the Wandering Jew', in E. de Selincourt (ed.), *The Poetical Works of William Wordsworth* (Oxford: Clarendon Press, 1952), pp. 158–159; Page, *Imperfect Sympathies*, pp. 175–176.

banquet in London's Mansion House where he confronted what he perceived to be

> the very Jew of Jews; the distilled essence of all the Jews that have been born since Jacob's time; he was Judas Iscariot; he was the Wandering Jew; he was the worst, and at the same time, the truest type of his race, and contained within himself ... every old prophet and every old clothesman, that ever the tribes produced; and he must have been circumcised as much [as] ten times over.[106]

In fact, the man was a distinguished gentleman, the brother of David Salomons, the Lord Mayor and pioneer for Jewish emancipation in Britain.[107] In spite of this reality, Hawthorne's prejudiced mind delighted in the sight of this man who justified 'the repugnance I have always felt towards his race'. His journal entry was, however, classically bifurcated, with Hawthorne extolling the dark, mysterious beauty of this 'Shylock's' female partner.[108]

Yet with Wordsworth – as with Hawthorne's fellow American Romanticist Herman Melville – there is an *identification* with the 'Wandering Jew' and the attraction of him as a part of nature, but also differentiated from the local landscape.[109] The very idea of alienation, of belonging, and not belonging, and the necessity of movement is at the heart of Wordsworth's poem. It begins with the harmony between motion and home achieved by nature:

> Through the torrents from their fountains
> Roar down many a craggy steep,
> Yet they find among the mountains
> Resting-places calm and deep ...

The poem closes with the tension caused by the failure of man to replicate this relationship and, from this, Wordsworth's identification with the figure of the legendary tormented Jew:

---

106 Randall Stewart (ed.), *The English Notebooks by Nathaniel Hawthorne* (New York: Oxford University Press, 1941), p. 321. See Regine Rosenthal, 'Inventing the Other: Ambivalent Constructions of the Wandering Jew/ess in Nineteenth Century American Literature', in Leonard Greenspoon and Bryan Le Beau (eds), *Representations of Jews Through the Ages* (Omaha: Creighton University Press, 1996), p. 177 for a careful analysis of Hawthorne's gendered bifurcated representation of Jews.

107 Todd Endelman, *The Jews of Britain 1656 to 2000* (Berkeley: University of California Press, 2002), pp. 106–107.

108 Stewart, *The English Notebooks*, p. 321.

109 See Rosenthal, 'Inventing the Other', pp. 181–184 for Melville.

Day and night my toils redouble,
Never nearer the goal;
Night and day, I feel the trouble
Of the Wanderer in my soul.[110]

There is, as Judith Page suggests, poetic sympathy for the 'Wanderer'. Nevertheless, as she adds, 'the figure is an almost pure idealization – there is no physical description of person or place – just a state of mind'.[111]

Wordsworth is now remembered as being essential to understanding the Lake District. He was at the forefront of the movement to preserve its 'true' character through his opposition to the railway spur that ends at Windermere but which he feared would extend as far as his beloved Grasmere. But Wordsworth was also an agent for change. His guidebooks and poetry inspired a popular interest in the Lake District. Their success promoted a desire to visit the area, including from the poor, who he believed would spoil its calm and tranquillity for the refined classes.[112] As one of his biographers notes, Wordsworth was not against railways per se: 'he had written a poem about them and used them with pleasure'. Nevertheless, he 'feared all the common people from Lancashire would come into his vale and ruin it'.[113] For Wordsworth and later for the artist and critic John Ruskin it has been suggested (again utilising the work of Mary Douglas) 'To facilitate working-class entry into the inner sanctum of ... Lakeland would be to condone "matter out of place"'.[114] Even so, Wordsworth 'later bought shares in the railway company which proved very profitable, and his objections were forgotten'.[115] This two-ness towards newcomers and change is evident also in the story of the child survivors in Windermere.

---

110 Selincourt (ed.), *The Poetical Works*, pp. 158–159.

111 Page, *Imperfect Sympathies*, pp. 175–176.

112 See his letters to the *Morning Post* in 1844 concerning the Kendal and Windermere Railway reproduced in William Wordsworth, *Guide to the Lakes* (London: Frances Lincoln, 2004), pp. 135–148. See also Hunter Davies, *A Walk Around the Lakes: A Visit to Britain's Lake District* (London: Frances Lincoln, 2009), pp. 130–131 for ascerbic comment on Wordsworth's hypocrisy in his attitudes to the masses.

113 Hunter Davies, *William Wordsworth: A Biography* (London: Weidenfeld and Nicolson, 1980), pp. 322–323.

114 Darby, *Landscape and Identity*, pp. 155–156.

115 'Explore the history around Kendal Railway Station', Kendal Station, site visit, 8 July 2010.

The Arrival of the Children

The Holocaust survivor children were sent to Calgarth, an industrial estate on the shores of the Lake. It is of great significance that this site was already regarded as alien to Windermere. During the war the estate had been constructed to build flying boats. The Calgarth 'village' consisted of the factory itself and temporary accommodation huts for its workers – over 1,500 at its peak.[116] As over half the workers recruited for the factory were 'outsiders' it was given the local nickname 'Chinatown'.[117] None of the workers were Chinese or indeed of immediate immigrant background. Nevertheless, their origins from the major industrial cities of the north-west of England made them alien and the moniker Chinatown literally orientalised their presence: the reference point, presumably, was the Pitt Street/Cleveland Square area of Liverpool, the Chinese quarter of the port since the late nineteenth century and perhaps the most 'exotic' place that local imagination could conjure up.[118]

In 1948 the Conservative travel writer S.P.B. Mais revisited the Lake District as part of his survey of the surviving heritage of England following the destruction of the war. Mais had been one of the key writers and broadcasters in the interwar years and during the conflict itself, popularising the English countryside and the physical evidence of the country's past.[119] He was now anxious to discover what damage had been done not only by enemy bombing but also through the needs of the war economy. When visiting Windermere he noted that the only change since the war was the addition of the flying boat factory. Mais stated that the 'locals' could not wait for the Calgarth estate to be demolished. As a true heir of Wordsworth, Mais claimed that 'The people of Windermere are rightly jealous of their land, and any attempt to spoil the fair face of their lake or its shores by any factory or hutment erection is hotly resented.'[120] There is a bitter irony here: Mais, bastion of a nostalgia-tinged English heritage, was at this stage confronting the news that his daughter had collaborated with the Nazis in occupied Paris, taking rich lovers who gave her gifts of art stolen from the Jews of the city. Her war years were

---

116 Allan King, *Wings on Windermere: The history of the Lake District's forgotten flying boat factory* (Sandomierz: Stratus, 2008); Liz Rice (ed.), *Flying boats & fellow travellers* (Sedbergh: Another Space, 2008).

117 Rice (ed.), *Flying Boats*, pp. 4, 5.

118 On the history of this minority, see specifically Maria Lin Wong, *Chinese Liverpudlians: A History of the Chinese Community in Liverpool* (Birkenhead: Liver Press, 1989) and, more generally, Colin Holmes, *John Bull's Island: Immigration & British Society, 1871–1971* (Basingstoke: Macmillan, 1988), pp. 32–33, 78–79.

119 Darby, *Landscape and Identity*, pp. 173–174.

120 S.P.B. Mais, *The English Scene Today* (London: Rockliff, 1948), p. 257.

thus – if only indirectly – linked to the lives of Therese Steiner, Auguste Spitz, and Marianne Grunfeld, who were deported from the city to their deaths in summer 1942.[121]

Mais was confident that demolition of the 'alien' estate at Calgarth would happen soon. To him, Windermere and the Lake District more generally had a greater significance and therefore restoration to the pre-war period was essential: 'Here if anywhere in England we can still recover that sense of freedom which has been lost in almost every other district.' To this place of 'harmony and serenity' which Wordsworth had 'perfectly' described, 'discriminating visitors' would always be welcome – like the poet and his opposition to the railway extension, the key was to ensure that newcomers appreciated the unchanging history of the Lake District.[122] In this Mais was not alone.

During the Second World War Jewish visitors to the area were often perceived as unwelcome and undeserving of its tranquillity and peace. The now famous Mass-Observation diarist Nella Last, who lived on the edge of the Lake District, was bemused to find her son moaning that Bowness, the town next to Lake Windermere, was 'stiff with Jews', urbanites from Manchester whom he regarded as 'parasitic'.[123] For Last's son, as for Mais, those coming in must not be allowed to undermine its traditions or landscape. The Jews of the world's first industrial city had no place through reasons of class, race, and region in Lake Windermere and its surrounds.[124] And it was to the temporary estate of Calgarth, within a place/space so culturally loaded – yet still functioning as a factory – that the War Office located billets for the child survivors in autumn 1945. As the Jewish organisers of the scheme noted, 'The hostel is unfortunately not a self-contained unit but is part of a bungalow camp. Some of the work people still live in some of the other houses.'[125]

But there was an even deeper pre-history in local memory with regard to Calgarth. In legend, repeated in many guides to and histories of Windermere and the Lake District, the story of the 'two skulls' and the 'world of shadows' was repeated:

To Calgarth Hall in the midnight cold
Two headless skeletons cross'd the fold … .
The skeletons two rushed through the yard,

---

121 Nicholas Shakespeare, *Priscilla: the Hidden Life of an Englishwoman in Wartime France* (London: Harvill Secker, 2013).

122 Mais, *English Scene*, p. 257.

123 Richard Broad and Suzie Fleming (eds), *Nella Last's War: A Mother's Diary 1939–45* (Bristol: Falling Wall Press, 1981), p. 83 entry for 3 November 1940.

124 Ibid. and Mais, *English Scene*, p. 257.

125 University of Southampton Archives: Central British Fund council minutes, 22 August 1945, File 9/145, CBF microfilm archives.

They pushed the door they left unbarr'd,
Laid by their skulls in the niched wall,
And flew like the wind from Calgarth Hall ... .[126]

In folk memory, the skulls of the 'wicked squire'd victims always come back' – it is a classic story of Gothic horror located in a decaying Elizabethan manor house and estate. If the estate was no more, memories of it had still existed when the factory at Calgarth had been erected.[127] It is with the two images of the ultimate alien presence of 'Chinatown' and that of the 'living dead', alongside a deep sympathy connected to their experiences, that contemporaries – Jewish and non-Jewish – would confront the presence of the children. Not surprisingly, given this heady mix of psycho-emotional baggage attached to the place and to the newcomers, it would take some time for those around them to adjust to both the normality and abnormality of these child survivors.

In the National Archives in Kew files relating to the scheme – clumsily, but revealingly, named the Committee for the Care of Children from the Concentration Camps (CCCCC), the struggle of Home Office officials to 'place' the children is neatly illustrated. Initially labelled 'Proposed scheme for bringing Jewish children from Bergen-Belsen Concentration Camp to UK for rehabilitation', the words 'Jewish' and 'Bergen-Belsen' were crossed out by Home Office officials.[128] For Britain and within British culture in 1945 especially, Belsen was *the* place of Nazi crimes and instantly connected to the horror images of the newsreels, radio broadcasts, newspaper reports, and exhibitions.[129]

Even months after their arrival in Windermere, newspapers referred to the 'Children from Belsen'[130]. The same was true in Wintershill Hall in Hampshire. The local newspaper reported their arrival with the headline 'From Belsen to [the] New Forest',[131] and the *Jewish Chronicle* summarised their double vulnerability with the title 'Belsen Orphans in England'.[132]

---

126 'The Armboth Banquet', reproduced in John Page White, *Lays and Legends of the English Lake District* (London: John Russell Smith, 1873), pp. 170–173.

127 W.G. Collingwood, *The Lake Counties* (London: Frederick Warne, 1932), p. 27. See also Peter Nock, *Tales and Legends of Windermere* (Windermere: Orinoco Press, 1989), pp. 5–7.

128 National Archives, cover of file HO 213/1797 GEN 323/6/11.

129 See Joanne Reilly, *Belsen: The Liberation of a Concentration Camp* (London: Routledge, 1998); Joanne Reilly et al. (eds), *Belsen in History and Memory* (London: Frank Cass, 1997); David Cesarani and Suzanne Bardgett (eds), *Belsen 1945: New Historical Perspectives* (London: Vallentine Mitchell, 2006).

130 Frank Davey, 'Children from Belsen have London feast', *News Chronicle*, 6 December 1945.

131 *Southern Daily Echo*, 31 October 1945.

132 *Jewish Chronicle*, 2 November 1945.

Dr Fridolin Friedmann, a former refugee from Nazism and a progressive Jewish teacher in Germany, was in charge of Wintershill Hall in Hampshire. Mollie Panter-Downes, the English journalist and writer who played a major role in the war communicating the 'Home Front' to an American audience, wrote a powerful report for the *New Yorker* on the children there. Interviewing Friedmann, he told her that

> You know, it's funny, the English press has called these children who have come over here Belsen children, but many have never been to that camp. Belsen and Buchenwald have taken all the limelight, but there were others far worse, far more horrible, which no one seems to know about. Many of our boys have been in four or five camps, and if you ask them, they say Treblinka, in Poland, was the worst.[133]

Such a realisation was a long time in coming in British society, and it was Belsen that for many years was the byword for Nazi crimes against humanity. But if Belsen was 'proof positive' of Nazi atrocities[134] – its intimate link to Britain revived again in the 2014 Holocaust Commission – the metaphors used to describe the sights and smells that confronted the liberators were other-worldly and essentially theological. Belsen was an evil place and it was especially 'Dante's inferno' that was evoked to describe the indescribable.[135] In short, a Christian construction of 'hell' was used to represent this place of Jewish suffering.[136]

Contemporaries provided two contesting frameworks to construct narratives of the children's experiences: first, truth versus atrocity propaganda, and second, the worldly versus the demonic. The tensions within both these tendencies made it difficult to understand the particular journeys experienced by these children and the problems they were now facing. Thus the official report of the Westmorland County Council noted that 'They have become less and less inclined to talk of the past, and the tendency to exaggerate their adventures is dying down': a well-meaning but revealing example of early British inability to confront the scale and horror of the Holocaust.[137] Elsewhere, the same report produced statements from three boys about their persecution during the war. These three were, it noted, in contrast to the others, 'the sons of educated parents

---

133 Mollie Panter-Downes, 'A Quiet Life in Hampshire', *New Yorker*, 2 March 1946.
134 This was the title of the Paramount News newsreel of Belsen. See Nicholas Pronay, 'Defeated Germany in British Newsreels: 1944–45', in K.R.M. Short and Stephan Dolezel (eds), *Hitler's Fall: The Newsreel Witness* (London: Croom Helm, 1988), pp. 42–44.
135 See Reilly, *Belsen*, passim.
136 Ibid.
137 J. Dow and M. Brown, *Evacuation to Westmorland from Home and Europe 1939–1945* (Kendal: Westmorland Gazette, 1946), p. 58.

and [therefore] able to give a reasonably dispassionate account of their experiences'.[138]

The reverse tendency of seeing the children as if they came from another planet – that of Belsen – also simplified their varied war experiences. In reality, as Friedmann highlighted, only a minority had been there. Moreover, some had survived outside the complex Nazi camp and ghetto system. It is even possible that a small number, the very youngest, were of semi-privileged *Mischlinge*, or 'mixed blood', background.[139] The varied experiences of these children, catapulted through ghettos, slave labour camps, in hiding, on the run, in concentration and extermination centres, and on the death marches,[140] reflected the nature of the Holocaust and Holocaust journeys, but they were not ones that fitted the simplistic understanding of early post-war Britain.[141] Moreover, their very survival made them atypical. Deborah Dwork, the leading authority on children and the Holocaust, suggests that 'only 11 percent of Jewish children alive at the beginning of the war survived its conclusion'. They totalled roughly 170,000: not a small number in itself, but representing just a remnant of a lost world.[142]

Even so, it should be noted that it was largely the harsh limitations imposed by the Home Office, again based on a narrow reading of what typified Jewish suffering during the war, that explains why only 732 and not the full quota of 1000 children could be found to meet the regulations. Indeed, the number brought over could have been even smaller. Imrich Yitzhaj Rosenberg was a prominent Zionist who had been involved with the Czech government in exile during the war. From 1944 he had official status as the Jewish delegate in dealing with the liberated territories of Czechoslovakia. In that role he came across the child survivors in Terezin. Initially he suggested that there were 50 orphans there and it was on this basis that negotiations were set up between the Czech government and the Home Office for their transfer. When 'the Home Office heard there were as many as 300 orphan survivors in the camp, arrangements became more complicated'.[143]

The process of narrowing the criteria for eligibility, continuing the pre-war process and with even smaller numbers envisaged, began with

---

138 Ibid., p. 52.

139 Interviews with the Author: discussions with Trevor Avery, Windermere, 11 December 2009 (with Aimée Bunting).

140 Deborah Dwork, *Children with a Star: Jewish Youth in Nazi Europe* (New Haven: Yale University Press, 1991), provides all these subheadings.

141 More generally, see Tony Kushner, *The Holocaust and the Liberal Imagination: A Social and Cultural History* (Oxford: Blackwell, 1994), chapter 7.

142 Dwork, *Children with a Star*, pp. xxxiii, 274 (note 27).

143 Corey Goldman, 'A Portrait of Imre Yitzhak Rosenberg', in Imrich Yitzhak Rosenberg and Corey Goldman, *A Jew in Deed* (Manotick, Ontario: Penumbra Press, 2004), p. 190.

the well-meaning if rather naive intervention of British Jewish refugee workers. In early May 1945 Otto Schiff of the Jewish Refugee Committee (a man, as noted, involved in such work since the First World War) wrote to Sir Alexander Maxwell, Permanent Under-Secretary at the Home Office. Schiff submitted a request from Leonard Montefiore to help some orphans. Montefiore was a leading British Jewish philanthropist who happened to be in Paris during spring 1945. A year later, Montefiore explained what had motivated his intervention:

> I saw some of the first arrivals brought by air direct from the camps. I have never seen anything so ghastly in my life. The people I saw were like corpses that walked. I shall never quite forget the impression they made.[144]

Montefiore wanted something done, arguing 'for the temporary admission to this country of about 1000 Jewish orphan children from the camps in Buchenwald and Belsen' – though initially he had more modestly thought that 'a few hundred' should be brought to Britain from these recently revealed Nazi sites of horror.[145] In later May 1945 Montefiore visited the Home Office himself. Here he was explicit about why the children should come from these particular camps. It was, he argued,

> right that England should do something to show sympathy, and also because … there is no better way of impressing on the British people the horrors of the concentration camps than by bringing some of the actual victims to this country.[146]

Maxwell was in agreement, but clear in his response that any scheme implemented would have to be restrained:

> It must, of course, be understood that this is an exceptional arrangement made for dealing with the specially pitiful condition of children found in concentration camps, and must not be taken as a precedent for requests to bring to this country other children or young persons, or older persons, who are in a distressed condition on the Continent.[147]

---

144 University of Southampton Special Collections: Leonard Montefiore, 'Address given to the Cambridge University Jewish Society, 18 October 1946' (Parkes Library).

145 National Archives, HO 213/1793: Schiff to Maxwell, 4 May 1945. On the lower number initially envisaged by Montefiore, see Vera Fast, *Children's Exodus: A History of the Kindertransport* (London: I.B. Tauris, 2011), p. 134.

146 National Archives, HO 213/1797: Alexander Maxwell, 24 May 1945, minutes of meeting with Leonard Montefiore.

147 National Archives, HO 213/1797: Maxwell to Schiff, 1 June 1945.

Maxwell's position reflected the nervousness expressed by civil servants and politicians before the Second World War about the entry of refugees, including children, on a temporary basis. The Home Office's willingness to provide (another) exception reflected a genuine empathy with these survivors of genocide. It was also hard to turn down Montefiore when in recent months the Home Office had allowed 'Young People from Occupied Countries' to recuperate in Britain for six weeks. Over 4000 had come from Holland alone in the period from February to August 1945.[148] Yet, while the Home Office was happy to make this gesture, other civil servants were more concerned. Maxwell was warned by the Colonial Office that he could not assume that these children would be subsequently allowed into Palestine. An apologetic response was sent to him stressing that 'the complications of Palestine immigration policy are so great that there is no alternative'.[149] But pressure from both Jewish and non-Jewish campaigners ensured that the children would still be allowed in Britain, albeit with very strict conditions of entry.

Slowly, once the Belsen/Buchenwald scheme was under way, it was extended to include children from other concentration camps, especially those from the east – initially it was limited to those from Germany alone.[150] Nevertheless, what constituted proof of persecution remained a problem and the regulations of who was eligible still focused on those who had been within the Nazi concentration camp structure. It is telling with regard to the power of the imagery associated with Belsen and Buchenwald that the organisation set up to deal with the scheme shortened its title simply to that of the 'Committee for the Care of Children from the Camps', lacking any geographic or historic precision.[151]

By January 1946 Schiff and other refugee workers asked for the scheme to include 'orphan or homeless children who have not necessarily been in a camp'. The Home Office civil servant noted that '*ex hypothesi*' such children could not be brought under the 'Distressed Relatives' scheme, which stipulated that those under its umbrella should have suffered in the Nazi camps. Nevertheless, they agreed to the extension because the numbers coming under the children's scheme had been so limited.[152] The reasons for this were partly the strict conditions and the focus on the camps but also the desire of the children to go to other destinations, especially Palestine and north America. Such decisions were not apolitical. As an exasperated Schiff told Maxwell, there was

---

148 National Archives, HO 213/1797: C. Robinson minute, 30 August 1945.
149 National Archives, CO 733/455/3: G.H. Gater to Maxwell, 26 May 1945.
150 National Archives, HO 213/782: W. Lyon memorandum, 25 February 1946, on 'Existing and proposed schemes for bringing children to the UK'.
151 See University of Southampton Archives: the minutes of this committee from 1945 to 1950 in file 198, Central British Fund microfilm archives.
152 National Archives, HO 213/1797: Prestige to Lyons, 12 January 1946.

little prospect of more children coming from Germany because the leaders of the camps ... are fanatical Zionists, who refuse to contemplate the possibility of children going anywhere except to Palestine. They would rather let them remain in the poor conditions obtaining in the camps ... than let them come to this country.[153]

Schiff was understating the agency of the children themselves. Unlike those already covered in this chapter – the Belgians, the Serbs and the Basques – they could refuse to go to certain places, even if ultimately they had limited options in a world in which free movement of peoples, especially Jews, remained so restricted. From later testimony it emerges that to some the appeal of Britain was that it was simply a way of getting out of the post-liberation camps – a stepping stone to more economically or ideologically desirable places (America and Palestine respectively). This was true of Solomon Freiman, who was born in a small village outside Warsaw in 1926. He escaped from the Warsaw ghetto and survived the war in hiding and then in slave labour camps. Transferred to Terezin, after liberation he heard of the English scheme through representatives of the Jewish Refugees Committee. He told them he wanted to go to Palestine but was informed that this would not be possible because of the White Paper quota. He still signed up, lying about his age and with the intention to move on to what he hoped would soon become the Jewish homeland.[154]

A more hesitant process brought Sidney Finkel (Sevek Finkelstein) and his brother to England on the same flight. Sidney was born in Lodz in 1931 and he, like Solomon, survived ghettoisation and slave labour camps before being liberated from Buchenwald. Remarkably, his elder brother, Isaac, and sister, Lola, also survived and they were reunited in Terezin. 'We were torn about the decision we had to make between immigrating to England rather than the Jewish state.' In the end 'Isaac made the decision that we would go to England because he felt that our hardships were great enough, and we deserved an easier more secure life.' Isaac was too old for the scheme but went as one of the adult helpers. Lola was also over-age but it was 'her intention to return to [a German displaced persons camp] and attempt to put her life back together'.[155] Sidney subsequently re-emigrated to America.

Chaim Ajzen from Bialobrzegi, a young survivor of Buchenwald, was also on this flight from Prague to Crosby-in-Eden. How he got on this transport reflects the ability of the children to subvert the rules

---

153 National Archives, HO 213/1797: Maxwell to Prestige, 10 January 1946.
154 British Library, 'Living Memory of the Jewish Community', Solomon Freiman interview, 22 September 1989, C410/052.
155 Sidney Finkel, *Sevek and the Holocaust: The Boy Who Refused to Die* (Matteson: Sidney Finkel, 2006), p. 81.

of bureaucracy and make their own way through immigration control procedures. When he and his friend Kopel Kendall heard of the possibility of going to England, the places on the initial flight were full up. Two boys on the list, however, had left for Poland and had not yet returned. Chaim and Kopel took their names and changed them back when they arrived at Windermere.[156]

With hindsight, some of the reasons for coming to England seem more thought through than was probably the case. The randomness recalled by Pinkus Kurnedz, another Windermere boy, was perhaps closer to the truth. When news of possibilities reached the young survivors in Terezin 'Some said Switzerland, others said America. As it turned out, I came to England.'[157] Ultimately, while they were not in reality free to go where they liked, the older children especially did play a major role in deciding where their lives would be rebuilt.

It was the stipulations of the Home Office and the choices of the children themselves, rather than the absolute dearth of other child survivors (as has been claimed in popular histories of the scheme), that explain the low figure of those who came under its auspices.[158] Moreover, as early as March 1946 the Jewish Refugee Committee proposed to limit the scheme to a ceiling of 800 'for financial reasons'.[159] Neither the refugee organisations nor the government wished to extend the scheme too broadly for both economic and political reasons. Thus a scheme to bring surviving relatives from the western camps to Britain was severely curtailed as, according to Alexander Maxwell:

> to admit for indefinite periods all 'relatives' who have had a bad time in a camp – brothers, sisters, brothers-in-law, sisters-in-law, uncles, aunts, nephews, nieces, and in some cases their minor children – would involve a substantial addition to our alien population at a time when there is a shortage of housing, food and supplies generally.[160]

It seems likely that it was the strict criteria imposed by the Home Office in conjunction with the refugee organisations that accounts for not only the small overall numbers taking up the scheme but also the low percentage of girls who came under this movement. Aside from those in the camps for 'privileged' Jews in Belsen and Terezin, where families might survive together, at least initially, the majority of girl survivors would have been

---

156 Written testimony quoted in Gilbert, *The Boys*, p. 272.

157 Ibid., p. 262.

158 Anton Gill, *The Journey Back from Hell: Conversations with Concentration Camp Survivors* (London: Grafton, 1988), p. 165.

159 National Archives, HO 213/782: Lyons memorandum, 25 March 1946.

160 National Archives, HO 213/618 E409: Quoted in H.H.C. Prestige memorandum, 21 September 1945.

in hiding throughout the war.[161] Some girls were also sent to Sweden to recuperate after the war and were thus not immediately available for the scheme.[162]

The *Kindertransport*, to which some of the personnel and much of the structure of the 1945/6 scheme owed so much, was interpreted very differently from its successor. The pre-war child refugees were seen, ultimately, as rescuable in body and soul, and the discourse that accompanied them was in many ways Christian. The children were to be 'saved'.[163] In contrast, the children in the 1945/6 scheme were seen by many as beyond redemption. The beauty and quiet of the Lake District would hopefully bring back physical health, but there was a sense that they could never recover sufficiently to be part of the nation. It was emphasised that the children, already checked to be free of infectious diseases, were sent to Britain only to recuperate, like those from Holland and elsewhere on the continent. They thus did not possess the temporary transmigrant status initially given to the *Kindertransport* – their legal position was even more marginal. Months before their arrival the Executive Committee of the Save the Children Fund noted that 'These children would be largely orphans or stateless, so there would be no question of returning them to Germany [*sic*] after two or three years.'[164] What the SCF did not recognise then was that the scheme was on the strict understanding, according to a leading Home Office official, 'that it [was] the responsibility of the refugee organisations to make arrangements for their emigration as soon as emigration becomes practicable'. Some, he added, 'might go to Palestine, some to Australia and some to the United States'.[165]

Their perceived rootedlessness and unEnglishness was internalised also by those in the CCCCC, who came largely from the liberal Jewish and Christian worlds. The leading force was Leonard Montefiore, a gentle man who in many ways became a father figure to the Windermere boys and girls. To him a sense of Englishness was ingrained and essential to his identity. He was a classic nineteenth-century figure, like his father before him, the founder of Liberal Judaism, Claude Montefiore, who described

161 Gilbert, *The Boys*, p. 2 states that the 'reason there were so few girls among the youngsters brought from Prague is that it was much harder for girls to survive'. Whilst this was true for the extermination and slave labour camps, it must be suggested that it was easier for reasons of disguise for girls to survive in hiding.

162 See also Carole Bell Ford, *After the Girls Club: How Teenaged Holocaust Survivors Built New Lives in America* (Lanham: Lexington Books, 2010).

163 See Tony Kushner, *Remembering Refugees: Then and Now* (Manchester: Manchester University Press, 2005), chapter 4.

164 University of Birmingham Archives: SCF Executive Minutes, 14 June 1945, A/2/1/1.

165 National Archives, HO 213/1797: Sir Alexander Maxwell to the Home Secretary, 12 May 1945.

himself as 'an Englishman of the Hebrew persuasion'.[166] In 1936 Leonard
Montefiore related how whenever he visited Woburn House 'and pass[ed]
the door of the Jewish Museum, I wonder whether my appropriate place
is not there rather than anywhere else in the building'.[167] At that stage
the collecting policy of the Museum was not to accept items that were
not at least 100 years old and elite in nature. He was a man out of time
and place and yet drawn to help those who had suffered the worst of
twentieth-century barbarity.

Expectations

In 1946, while addressing Jewish students at his old university, Cambridge,
Leonard Montefiore gave an impassioned speech about the children. He
referred to them in relation to his own congregation, the West London
Synagogue, the oldest reform community in Britain and still the movement's
leading place of worship and religious authority. Without any sense of
malice, Montefiore remarked that 'By no stretch of the imagination is it
conceivable that any of these children will become a member of [this]
Synagogue.'[168] Ironically, one of these children, Hugo Gryn, became the
best-known and most respected of West London's rabbis and more widely
the voice of moral authority in late twentieth-century Britain.[169] Indeed,
it was Montefiore who persuaded Gryn to come under the scheme.[170] So
why was it that Leonard Montefiore, such a friend to the children, could
not envisage them even becoming a member, let alone a leader, of his
synagogue?

Montefiore's roots were ultimately foreign, but they were to be found
in the early years of the readmission of the Jews to England and in the
elite Sephardi and western European Ashkenazi communities. 'Two of
the most distinguished of the old-established Anglo-Jewish families were
united in his ancestry' – the Montefiores and the Goldsmids.[171] The child
survivors in England were largely east European Jews and especially from
the *shtetls*, towns and industrial cities of Poland. They were thus separated
from Montefiore by class, politics, nationality, and religious practice. They
were not only defined by him as victims of persecution but as *ostjuden*;

166 Daniel Langton, *Claude Montefiore: His Life and Thought* (London: Vallentine
    Mitchell, 2002).
167 Leonard Stein, 'Memoir', in Leonard Stein and C.C. Aronsfeld (eds), *Leonard
    Montefiore 1889–1961: In Memorium* (London: Vallentine Mitchell, 1964), p. 13.
168 University of Southampton Special Collections: Montefiore, Montefiore, 'Address
    given to the Cambridge University Jewish Society', p. 10.
169 Hugo Gryn with Naomi Gryn, *Chasing Shadows* (London: Penguin Books, 2001).
170 Gill, *The Journey Back from Hell*, p. 165.
171 Stein, 'Memoir', p. 3.

they were, to him, of the same type as those who journeyed to Britain before 1914 in their hundreds of thousands and transformed Anglo-Jewry. 'The boys and girls who arrived at the aerodromes', Montefiore wrote in 1947, 'were remarkably similar in appearance to those who stepped off some immigrant ship from Libau or Riga way back in 1907 or thereabouts'.[172] 'If one could visualise their homes', he wrote in October 1945, 'it is most likely one would see an orthodox home, in the strictest and narrowest sense, orthodox in the sense that U.S. orthodoxy would seem a very wishy washy sort of orthodoxy'.[173] It is no accident that, alongside their alloted place in the religious sphere outside the ultra-anglicised and elite reform movement, they were also perceived by Montefiore in the economic realm solely as potential workers and artisans.

When told by the children that they wanted to train to become doctors or musicians, Leonard was firm in response: 'Think of something else.'[174] Apprenticeships in the workshops of Manchester and London working for those of east European Jewish origin was indeed the path of many. To the elite of British Jewry, the child survivors of the Lake District and Hampshire countryside were too 'other', too placeless, too radical, and too orthodox in origin to be fully anglicised. The hope was that they would quickly re-emigrate, thereby fulfilling the pledge to the British government that their stay would be temporary. If there *was* to be a place for them it was to be industrial towns of Britain alongside their fellow *ostjuden*. Again, Montefiore was clear in the 'tough love' philosophy of unreconstructed Victorian philanthropy and in cutting down 'unrealistic' expectations:

No doubt there have been certain disappointments. They thought England was a very rich country where all the things they had missed for so many years would be provided by the incredible number of incredibly rich Jews who lived here. They had not the faintest conception of economic conditions prevailing in this country.[175]

The children, he noted in early 1947, had to be told that it was

high time [they] should consider how to earn a living ... [T]hey are apt to consider any small talent they possess as the proof of their genius. They are disinclined to accept the fact that much seeming drudgery accompanies the first steps in any trade or occupation.[176]

---

172 Leonard Montefiore, 'Our Children', *Jewish Monthly* no. 1 no. 1 (April 1947), p. 19.
173 University of Southampton Archives: Leonard Montefiore, memorandum 15 October 1945 in Central British Funds committee minutes, file 9/169, CBF microfilm archives.
174 University of Southampton Special Collections: Montefiore, 'Address given to the Cambridge University Jewish Society', p. 5.
175 Ibid., p. 8.
176 Montefiore, 'Our Children', pp. 20–21.

Stereotypical assumptions, reflecting wider societal expectations, similarly conditioned the training the girl survivors received from the CCCCC. On the Surrey/Sussex border two neighbouring hostels were created for a number of the children once they had left Windermere and Wintershill Hall. The very young, including some who were babies, were looked after in Bulldogs Bank, where psychiatrist Anna Freud played a prominent role in their rehabilitation.[177] The older ones, including a high percentage of girls, were located in Weir Courtney, Lingfield, in the house of Jewish entrepreneur Sir Benjamin Drage. The possibility of bringing some of the youngest from Bulldogs Bank to Weir Courtney so that the girls could 'learn mothercraft' was raised several times by the CCCCC.[178] The girls from Weir Courtney were trained as secretaries, hairdressers, sales girls, and typists, with only one noted as 'working for [a] higher school certificate'.[179] The aim was to be 'realistic' with regard to the children's/young adults' futures and also to justify and limit the amount spent on them through instilling independence. By 1950 the CCCCC scheme had cost over £400,000.[180]

Child Perspectives

What of these 'Wandering Jews' themselves? The growing mythology of the movement, if on a smaller scale, replicates that now associated with the *Kindertransport*. Britain proved redemptive, and they recovered from their experiences and went on to have successful lives and new families there. None of this narrative (part of the official storyline as presented by Martin Gilbert's *The Boys*, whose subtitle, 'Triumph over Adversity', exemplifies such an approach) is without foundation.[181] But, just as the experience of the 100 girls has been airbrushed from this picture,[182] reflecting the

---

177 See Moskovitz, *Love Despite Hate*, passim.

178 University of Southampton Archives: CCCCC minutes, 2 January 1946, file 198/18, CBF microfilm archives.

179 In 1948 the children from Weir Courtney were transferred to Lingfield House, Isleworth. For examples of their occupations, see University of Southampton Archives: 'A Statement about Lingfield House', (1958?), file 200/72 in CBF microfilm archives.

180 University of Southampton Archives: Stephany to Montefiore, 8 February 1950, provides year by year figures, file 202/151 CBF microfilm archives.

181 Gilbert, *The Boys*.

182 *The Journal of the Holocaust Survivors '45 Society* no. 34 (2010) reveals the inclusion and exclusion that occurs at a general level. It includes an article by Zdenka Oppenheimer, 'Where the Daffodils Grow' (p. 58) which includes her experiences at Windermere and then Weir Courtney, Lingfield, Surrey. It also has on its last page (p. 102) a photograph of 'The Boys' in Windermere Autumn 1945, which contains 20 individual photographs, none of them girls.

wider marginality of women in Holocaust historiography,[183] and also the very young children,[184] so have the less palatable aspects of their years of reception and recovery in Britain. These lacunae reflect a wider tendency in the still limited study of children in the Holocaust in which critical perspectives have, understandably, been overwhelmed by sentimentality. 'From Victim to Champion', an advertisement for a talk from one of the former 'Boys', reflects the understandable desire for a happy ending.[185] This is not surprising, given both the overpowering loss created by the murder of one and a half million Jewish children and the achievements of the minority who survived.[186] It does mean, however, that particular effort is required to raise aspects of the children's early years in Britain that challenge the dominant and reassuring mythology, especially so with regard to their place identity.

Most of the children came to Windermere and Wintershill Hall with no personal possessions relating to their pre-Holocaust lives and families – some of the younger ones even without knowing their original name. Roman Halter, one of the older boys in the Lake District (aged 18 but, again, claiming to be younger), came from the small Polish town of Chodecz, with its 800 Jews. He had been a slave labourer in the Lodz ghetto and in August 1944 was subject to a forced march:

> We were starved and weak, clinging to our most precious possessions, a duvet, a water jar, a photo album, a blanket, a prayer book. I accidentally dropped my photo album and as I stooped down to pick it up, an SS man kicked it into a ditch.

He survived Auschwitz, Stutthof, and finally Dresden and made his way to the children's camp at Terezin 'with absolutely nothing'.[187]

Arek Hersh was born in the larger Polish Jewish community of Sieradz. Its ghetto was liquidated in 1942. His father had already been sent away and his mother and siblings deported to their death in Chelmno. Sent to the Lodz ghetto, his only possessions were 'six photographs of my family'. The 14-year-old Arek survived in the orphanage there and he, like Roman, then experienced the terrible journey to Auschwitz in 1944 when the ghetto was liquidated:

183 See, in contrast, Dalia Offer and Lenore Weitzmann (eds), *Women in the Holocaust* (New Haven: Yale University Press, 1998).

184 Tereza Ward, 'Erasure of Memory: Children Who Survived the Holocaust and their Struggle for Identity' (MA dissertation, University of Manchester, 2013).

185 Talk by Ben Helfgott at the Cape Town Holocaust Centre, 28 April 2011, leaflet in author's possession.

186 Dwork, *Children With a Star*, p. 256.

187 Roman Halter, *Roman's Journey* (London: Portobello Books, 2007), pp. 140, 321.

We were forced to get into line and shuffle forward as the wagons were filled up. At last our turn came and we were herded into a cattle wagon, packed like sardines, orphans and strangers alike ... . 'How will we breathe?' I thought. 'How will we sleep? What will we eat?'[188]

In his bag were the items he 'treasured most in the world, a number of family photographs'. One was of himself and his brother 'standing next to a tree in the park', another of 'my sisters, Mania and Itka, by the River Warta, three of the whole family with my parents sitting in the middle, two of my grandparents'. Arriving at Auschwitz, he was ordered to undress and discard everything:

They took away the only photographs I had left of my family, my only link with home, and standing in the large hall I began to weep. Of all the blackest days during the war, this was undoubtedly, for me, one of the blackest.[189]

At Windermere and beyond, Roman and Arek and the other survivors were encouraged to draw a line under their past and to focus on the future. In the short term it was a practical solution but it left the children, especially the younger ones, struggling with identity crises through what has been called a deliberate 'erasure of memory'.[190] This suppression incorporated not only the horror of their Holocaust journeys but also their life before the abyss. With uncertain legal status and few prospects, they had little choice but to cooperate – which they did, for the most part, with great energy. As early as 1949 in *Primrose Leaves*, a journal produced for themselves (if under the auspices of the organising bodies), Gina Weiss wrote from Canada that she felt 'homesick and wished I were back in England'.[191] Another 'old boy' suggested that settlement in Israel was difficult because they were 'Anglo-Saxons'![192] The progress of the boys' cricket team from bottom to third top was proudly announced in *Primrose League* and reveals neatly the emphasis that was placed on training them in Englishness and in taking pride in local identity.[193]

Such assimilation was not total and there were those such as Perec Zylberberg, who, with his sister Esther, maintained his Bundist politics, working to preserve Yiddish culture in all its forms.[194] It is revealing that the American correspondent of *Primrose Leaves*, Arnost Blobstein,

---

188 Arek Hersh, *A Detail of History* (Laxton: Beth Shalom, 1998), p. 108.
189 Ibid., p. 127.
190 Ward, 'Erasure of Memory'.
191 *Primrose Leaves* no. 1 no. 6 (August 1949), p. 5.
192 Ibid., p. 15.
193 Ibid., p. 12.
194 Perec Zylberberg, 'Recollections' (in possession of the author).

could write in 1950 that he was enjoying New York because of the Yiddish programmes on the radio and seeing people reading Yiddish papers on the trains: 'it makes one feel at home'.[195] This, clearly, was a reference to Eastern Europe and *not* England. Others, such as Dovid Herman, reviewing the films *That Others May Live* (on the Warsaw ghetto uprising) and *Long is the Road* (on the journey to Auschwitz) in *Primrose Leaves*, stated 'It's our story!'.[196] This was, however, a rare incursion into Holocaust memory and most of the energy of the journal was focused on future plans and 'so many dreams to be dreamt'.[197]

It was only much later, with a greater societal sensitivity towards the Holocaust, that some of these children began to challenge the deliberate strategy of amnesia that those administering their early years in England had imposed. Leading this process was Roman Halter, one of the oldest boys, who in the *Journal of the '45 Aid Society* (the organisation formed by the former children in the 1960s) suggested in 1981 that 'we should print ... photographs which illustrate various aspects of pre-war Jewish life in the areas which we were born'.[198]

It is significant that this did not subsequently happen, a result of both the totality of the Nazi destruction process and the psychological gulf between 'then and now' and 'here and there' for these survivors. Tellingly, the *Journal* has published and republished articles relating to their early days in England in what can be regarded as foundational documents of their new lives. Indeed, it has sometimes taken the efforts of the second generation to reconnect their parents to past places.

Naomi Gryn is a film maker and in the 1980s she took her father, Hugo, back to his home town of Berehovo in Carpathia. *Chasing Shadows* reflected both the lost and the traces of its Jewish community.[199] Hugo had kept one precious family photograph through various ghettos and forced marches, hiding it in a shoe. It was lost when his clothing was confiscated at Auschwitz. Four decades later, visiting Berehovo's synagogue, Naomi was handed a photograph of the town's Jewish Elementary School, class of 1942. 'I passed the photograph to my father. The colour drained from his face. Pointing to one of the children, he gasped, "That's Gabi in the back row." It was as if his brother had found a way to say hello.'[200] Such memories were not encouraged when the children came to England: 1945 was simply treated as 'year zero'.

So how did the youngsters view Windermere, a place they experienced initially in the glories of late summer? In the 'official' version the Windermere

---

195 *Primrose Leaves* no. 7 (Spring 1950), p. 5.
196 Ibid., p. 8.
197 *Primrose Leaves* no. 1 no. 6 (Autumn 1949), p. 2.
198 *Journal of the '45 Aid Society* no. 8 (March 1981), p. 3.
199 Naomi Gryn, *Chasing Shadows* (1989).
200 Gryn with Gryn, *Chasing Shadows*, pp. xxvii, 179.

camp has been described as 'paradise' – a biblical illusion to the Garden of Eden, if through a Christian or at least a non-Jewish discourse. It was far from the ironic use of the word for those who experienced the road to destruction mentioned earlier.[201] Windermere was similarly referred to as 'heaven'.[202] To David Jonisz, born in Serock, Poland, in 1927, who survived ghettos, slave labour camps, and finally Buchenwald before being sent to Terezin, Windermere was *ganeydn*, Yiddish for paradise, and he regarded the English people he met there as 'angels'.[203] Michael Perlmutter is even more Christological in his description: 'I was reborn in Windermere in 1945. The promise of England was a dream to a teenage boy who no longer believed he could believe in dreams. But it happened.'[204]

These were not simply later constructs of memory. Within only a few years of arrival the children were happy to provide the narrative of gratitude and rebirth expected by the organising bodies and to begin the process of historicisation, paving the way for Gilbert's celebratory account: 'And in years to come you will say: "Remember how it all began? With pride we remember what we have achieved from the outset and with thanks we remember our debt to [all the] representatives of British Jewry".'[205]

Even the difficult flight to England has been remembered with affection. The journey in old converted RAF Stirling bombers from Prague to Crosby-on-Eden, near Carlisle, had been rough, with most of the children being sick, replicating the Basque journey on the SS *Habana*, if, in this case, only for a couple of hours. For some, however, it was remembered positively as part of the general liberation process. Samuel Hilton recalls that it was his 'first time in a plane and I loved it … [and] one of the most vivid memories I have of the entire war and the Holocaust'.[206] In official memory work relating to these child survivors, a certain mythology has taken root about their journeys to England. Indeed, they have been provided with an additional element of glamour. Martin Gilbert related that 'On 14 August 1945 a dozen Lancaster bombers flew with their three hundred young passengers from Prague.'[207] He thereby mistakenly, but revealingly, connected these flights with an icon of the British military war effort (and

201 Rice, *Flying Boats & Fellow Travellers*, p. 6; *The Orphans Who Survived the Concentration Camps*, BBC 1, 5 April 2010 for the use of the word 'paradise'.
202 David Hirszfeld quoted in Avery (ed.), *From Aushwitz to Ambleside*, no page.
203 British Library: David Jonisz, 'Living Memory of the Jewish Community' collection, British Library Sound Archive, C410/177. Jonisz adds that he had little actual contact with English people for some time after arriving in the country and that this description was a form of idealisation.
204 Michael Perlmutter, 'The Bonds of Windermere', *Journal of the '45 Aid Society* no. 18 (December 1994), p. 8.
205 *Primrose Leaves* no. 6 (Autumn 1949), p. 2.
206 Quoted in Goldman, 'A Portrait of Imre Yitzhak Rosenberg', pp. 194–195.
207 Gilbert, *The Boys*, p. 280.

not with much older planes that were particularly unsuitable for the task of transporting children).[208] In contrast to the dominant later romanticisation of their journey, Sidney Finkel notes in his autobiography that, as they left Prague:

> I sat down on the floor in the belly of the plane with the others. There was no one among us who had experienced flying. As the plane taxied, I could sense the uneasiness that was present. I just kept my eyes shut and my hands clamped. I was telling myself not to be afraid; it would soon be over one way or another.

In spite of such efforts, the 14-year-old still struggled: 'I grew certain that we were going to go down each time the bomber would hit an air pocket. It was like being on the inside of a large metal tunnel, where every movement was like a sudden jolt.'[209]

It is significant that Sidney's counter-narrative was privately published and remains obscure in the history of the movement. Closer to the time, and further confirming Sidney's perspective, the psychoanalyst Anna Freud, in her study of six of the youngest children, highlighted their collective fear of planes. The success of encouraging the children to break with their past is revealed in the response of one of the young boys. Just a year and a half after his arrival in England, when asked how they got to Windermere, he responded 'One does not get there, everybody is borned there.' Life before the Nazis and persecution had literally been effaced from his memory, leaving only a general anxiety about flying.[210]

The first transport was delayed for several days and even after the arrival in Carlisle the journey did not run smoothly: the lorry transporting the children to Windermere broke down. Leonard Montefiore apologised to one boy, a 16-year-old, that his 'first evening in England should be spent on the road'. He later recalled the boy's response: 'Never mind … for me it is a privilege and a pleasure to sit on an English road, I ask nothing better.'[211] Such memories, some constructed over a 60-year period, at a basic level reflect the changing fortunes of the children, from persecution and brutal anonymity to rehabilitation and individual care. Yet the discourse used to describe that transformation also reveals the shaping of identities

---

208 It is interesting that Gilbert's narrative has affected the testimony of the former children who also claim they came in Lancaster bombers. See, for example, British Library Sound Archive C410/052 and 177.

209 Finkel, *Sevek and the Holocaust*, p. 83.

210 Anna Freud, 'An Experiment in Group Upbringing', *Psychoanalytic Study of the Child* no. 6 (1951), pp. 161, 165.

211 Description of the arrival of the children and lorry journey in National Archives, HO 213/1797: Leonard Montefiore to Carew Robinson of the Home Office, 17 August 1945; Gilbert, *The Boys*, p. 286.

thereafter and, in this case, the cult of gratitude expected of all refugees entering Britain.

The contemporaries confronting the children had to deal with the intense psychological problems still to be overcome. As a leaflet produced to raise money for '700 Concentration Camp orphans' acknowledged:

> If, at the age of 12 or 13, you had suddenly been flung into prison and came out again five or six years later, what would you want most? You would want to catch up with the time you had missed or thought you had missed. If then you had suddenly been flown to a foreign country and had to learn a foreign language, would it be odd if you felt a bit bewildered and thought that, after all, freedom did not bring the Paradise you had expected?[212]

Subsequent reflections on Windermere, to meet the desire for a 'rebirth', have tended to smooth away the tensions and difficulties that inevitably affected the children's initial months in England. The sentiments expressed in this leaflet were not always kept in mind when dealing with the young survivors.

The hope of the organisers was that the English countryside itself would act as a restorative aid to the youngsters' physical and mental recovery. 'We are rightly', Montefiore noted in October 1945, 'parking the children in country districts'.[213] By 1947, Montefiore himself acknowledged the sentimental naivety of the organisers, including himself, in this respect: 'We expected children, we had talked about children, and written about children. We had pictured under sixteens who could be sent to school or nursed back to health in the peace of an English countryside.'[214] Solomon Freiman recalls the shock of those receiving them in Windermere:

> We were a rough lot ... We would steal if necessary, they didn't know what they [were] dealing with. They thought we were children ... the girls who were looking after [us] were younger than us. Can you imagine, they wanted to bath us and all that sort of thing.[215]

Contemporary reporting of their arrival similarly emphasised the redemptive quality of the English pastoral and the pathos of the children. The London *Evening Standard* noted that 'The most pathetic of all victims of Nazi cruelty

212 Central British Fund, *This is Rehabilitation* (London: Central British Fund for Jewish Relief and Rehabilitation, 1946), no page. Pamphlet located in Parkes Library, University of Southampton.
213 University of Southampton Archives: Montefiore memorandum, 15 October 1945 in Central British Fund council minutes, file 9/169, in CBF microfilm archives.
214 Montefiore, 'Our Children', p. 19.
215 British Library Sound Archive, 'Living Memory of the Jewish Community', C410/052.

have arrived in this country to be helped back to health and hope.' These 'tragic' children would, it added, 'learn to live again in freedom amid the lovely scenery of the Lake District'. To reassure its readers, and following the same pattern as those responding to the Serbian, Spanish, and earlier Jewish child refugees, it concluded that this was to be a temporary stay 'while plans for their emigration are being completed'.[216]

The article shared S.P.B. Mais' belief that the countryside and especially the Lake District represented the essential characteristic of Englishness – freedom. But Mais had also insisted that only 'discriminating visitors' would be welcome in the Lake District. Like the industrial estate of Calgarth itself, the journey of the 300 children there was only temporary – they were, in Montefiore's words, only to be 'parked' in the Lake District and Hampshire, and not to be permanently settled there. By 1948, when Mais revisited the shores of Lake Windermere, there was literally no trace left of the children's stay in Calgarth.[217]

The local newspaper, the *Westmorland Gazette*, reporting their 'Arrival in Lakeland', highlighted how the children had 'escaped death from gas and burning and have now been removed to ideal surroundings for rest and recuperation'.[218] The landscape was truly inspiring, nature at its most intensely beautiful, combining England's longest lake and some of its highest mountains. Yet, although through Wordsworth it was seen as quintessentially English, it was also regarded as somehow foreign because of its extremes of natural formation. It was too wild and dangerous, evoking to some the continent of Europe and especially the Alps.[219]

The child survivors, too, regarded it ambivalently. They had been brought to the countryside to recuperate – to walk and climb, eat and sleep, and to regain their strength and sense of liberty. Nevertheless, they were accommodated and schooled in the middle of a small industrial estate. They appreciated its beauty and the chance to explore the local landscape. As Mayer Hersh recalls, 'we were walking around … whole areas, the Lake District and Bowness and Windermere and other places. We went for long walks and we really enjoyed it.'[220] Roman Halter regained strength through swimming in the lake and later took part in international events in the sport.[221] Even more spectacularly, Ben Helfgott, later leader of the '45 Aid Society, represented England in the Olympic Games as a weightlifter during the 1950s. He recalls the many games of football, volleyball, and hiking in

---

216 '300 of the Nazis' youngest victims here for health: Windermere Home', *Evening Standard*, 20 August 1945. This newspaper article was filed by the Home Office. See National Archives, HO 213/1793.

217 Mais, *The English Scene Today*, p. 257.

218 *Westmorland Gazette*, 18 August 1945.

219 Davies, *A Walk Around the Lakes*, p. 123; Russell, *Looking North*, p. 54.

220 Quoted in Avery (ed.), *From Auschwitz to Ambleside*, no page.

221 Gilbert, *The Boys*, p. 296; Halter, *Roman's Journey*, pp. 325–327.

the Lakes, part of what he refers to as the three-month 'dream' of being at Windermere.[222] Indeed, Ben Helfgott was always positive about his experiences in Britain – it was he who was the 16-year-old boy befriended by Leonard Montefiore at the roadside after the lorry had broken down.[223] In Wintershill Hall, Magda Bloom, who had survived Auschwitz and Belsen, and her friend Marta saw the house and its surrounding countryside as 'fairyland. It was a mild autumn. The trees were still green and there were roses everywhere ... we just revelled in being free.'[224]

The children were, however, also mourning for families and a world that had been destroyed and were deeply unsettled about their uncertain future. Some of the older ones, such as Roman Halter, had tried to return to their homes at the end of the war. It was not a happy experience. In Chodecz, Roman felt

> completely alone. Out of all the Jewish people of the town, I was, so far [in May 1945], the only one who had returned. How many others would come back? Chodecz seemed so different without the Jews, without their shops and businesses. It was unreal: no longer my home town.

While he knew he had to leave Poland, Roman was 'lost. I didn't know where to go from here.'[225]

From the temporary security of the initial settlements in England, rest and recuperation soon gave way to a sense of frustration and boredom in the remoteness of the places they had been sent. Samuel Finkel, brought up in the industrial city of Lodz, recalled that while he found the Lake District 'very beautiful, I had little appreciation for nature'.[226] Their physical recovery – at least in terms of weight – had largely occurred *before* they were flown to England – they were not the skeleton-like figures that many locals anticipated and now mistakenly re-remember.[227]

There was little to do, other than visit the local cinemas, and there was none of the excitement of the big city that had been briefly sampled in Prague. Recent oral history suggests among the older boys a desire to assert their manhood, even if this meant resorting to the unlikely fleshpots of Kendal, hardly the metropolis.[228] As Montefiore noted as early as October 1945, aside from smoking, 'I should be greatly surprised if they

---

222 Ben Helfgott, interview with Trevor Avery and Chris Atkins, 23 June 2008. I am very grateful to Trevor for sending me a copy of the transcript of this interview.
223 Ibid.
224 Zoe Josephs, *Survivors: Jewish Refugees in Birmingham 1933-45* (Birmingham: Meridian Books, 1988), p. 179.
225 Halter, *Roman's Journey*, p. 239.
226 Finkel, *Sevek*, p. 85.
227 See local testimony in Avery (ed.), *From Auschwitz to Ambleside*, no page.
228 Information related to the author by Trevor Avery.

had not formed other and far less innocent habits.'[229] The official local report covering their experiences noted that there was 'some evidence of homosexuality' and that the boys 'have been pestered by young English girls'.[230] It is likely that such advances were not simply one way and local tensions resulted in the sexual sphere.[231] Mutual attraction, however, was also present: Solomon Freiman, born in 1926, fondly recalls dating Christian girls in Windermere.[232] But it is no surprise, that given the quiet nature of the Lake District and the Hampshire countryside, that most were keen to leave for Manchester and London, or, in the case of Magda Bloom, Birmingham, as soon as they were able and allowed to do so.[233] All these cities provided not just economic opportunities but also thriving Jewish communities of east European origin within which the children could rebuild their lives.

Within Anglo-Jewry the children were an oddity. They were, as Montefiore noted, closer to those of east European origin than the more recent arrivals from central Europe in the 1930s. Even so, they were still distanced from the former by their scarring experiences during the war. Indeed, it was a few exceptional German Jewish refugees, such as Oscar Friedmann, who helped take care of the children in the two reception camps. The cultural and experiental distance articulated through the concept of place was illustrated neatly by Perec Zylberberg, who was at Windermere having survived the Lodz ghetto and a variety of Nazi concentration camps. Several years after Windermere, a club was set up for the children. Perec's suggestion of naming it the Klepfish Club, in honour of the young Bundist fighter of the Warsaw ghetto uprising, Michal Klepfish, was rejected by the British Jewish organisers. What sort of fish, they wondered, was a klepfish? It was eventually named the Primrose Club, far more English in its associations, though ironically popularised through his stately home, Hughenden, by Benjamin Disraeli – another Jewish outsider in British society.[234]

Only with the belated British recognition of the Holocaust from the 1990s onwards would some of these young survivors gain recognition inside and outside the Jewish community. Even then, those that never fully recovered have been forgotten by all but those in the small survivor community, a net that is itself far from inclusive, especially in relation to

---

229 University of Southampton Archives: Montefiore memorandum, 15 October 1945 in Central British Fund committee minutes, file 9/169 CBF microfilm archives.

230 Dow and Brown, *Evacuation to Westmorland*, p. 59.

231 Interviews with the Author: conversation with Trevor Avery, 8 July 2010 (with Aimée Bunting).

232 British Library: Solomon Frieman, 'Living Memory of the Jewish Community' collection, Sound Archive, C410/052.

233 Joseph, *Survivors*, p. 179.

234 Perec Zylberberg, 'Recollections', diary entry 21 October 1993.

gender and place.[235] In clinical fashion, Leonard Montefiore reported to Anthony de Rothschild, one of the biggest supporters of the Central British Fund for Jewish Relief (the umbrella organisation for the CCCCC), that, by 1950, 57 of the children still required financial support. This included 'twenty invalids', some of whom were in his eyes 'hopeless'.[236] The domestication of the Holocaust in late twentieth- and early twenty-first-century Britain has helped to bring home and naturalise these 'Wandering Jews' who came after the war. Some, indeed, have been honoured, allowing a life journey of one of the survivors to be described as one 'from the depths of humanity to the pinnacles of success, from Belsen to Buckingham Palace'.[237]

Yet there are still elements of their journey to Britain that there is a reluctance to accept – one largely relating to how 'other' they were regarded at the time. First, there is little or no recognition of the limitations imposed on their entry, confined by stay and numbers. As noted, those allowed in were kept at a low level partly for financial reasons – this was not a government-sponsored scheme but one funded privately by British Jewry with support from the Quakers and Save the Children Fund – hence the decision after a few months to cut the absolute ceiling to 800. Apart from finance, it reflected political reasons – the government feared antisemitism and did not see Jewish refugees, including child survivors, as racially desirable. In 1945, even post-Belsen, the 'Jew' was still perceived as alien to British or more specifically English national identity.[238]

Second, the children themselves were sometimes and not surprisingly more difficult than the ideal of innocent but suffering victims that contemporaries desired. It is a wider expectation, Christological in inspiration, that expects nobility through suffering, even and perhaps especially through the Holocaust. It is worth remembering as a corrective that Britain's most notorious landlord, Peter Rachman, was a survivor (one of his henchmen, the former *Kinder* Norbert Rondel, had a long criminal record for violence), as was the gangster Maurits de Vries, who helped run Amsterdam's red light district after the war.[239] If none of the Windermere or other children

---

235 It is interesting that of the 26 accounts assembled by the Child Survivors' Association of Great Britain, only a couple relate to the 'Boys' scheme. Many of these 26 were from western and central Europe and came to Britain beyond 1946. Roughly half were female. See their *Zachor: Child Survivors Speak* (London: Elliot & Thompson, 2005).

236 University of Southampton Archives: Montefiore to Rothschild, 13 December 1950 in file 112/49, CBF microfilm archives.

237 Paul Oppenheimer, *From Belsen to Buckingham Palace* (Laxton: Beth Shalom, 1996), p. 191.

238 See Kushner, *The Holocaust and the Liberal Imagination*, pp. 234–235.

239 Shirley Green, *Rachman* (London: Michael Joseph, 1979). There are various Dutch documentaries on de Vries.

gained such infamy, the cases of Rachman, de Vries, and others show that not all survivors had the warmth, humanity, and vision of Hugo Gryn. Leonard Montefiore lamented in 1950 about the 'hard core' cases of the children under his care: 'we have half a dozen tough guys who have no great enthusiasm for work in any shape'. Another, aged 15, 'has all the makings of a delinquent. A typical case for Basil's [Henriques] Juvenile Court.'[240] One young female survivor had a young child and kept herself financially afloat through prostitution, providing a desperately sad link to Eastern European Jewish female migration before 1939. Yet, as Elaine Marks of the CCCCC remembered, overall 'court appearances were infrequent and … we never had to deal with a really serious crime'.[241]

The Importance of Place

The forgotten 'Wandering Jews' of Windermere found themselves, like the literary mythic figure confronted by the Romantics, subject to fascination and sympathy, fear and rejection. They were sent to England on a wave of repulsion following the concentration camp revelations, ones that created intense horror but also misunderstandings about the complexity and range of the Nazi genocidal machine. As figures escaping from the furnace of hell, they were expected to find and often genuinely regarded the English countryside and especially the Lake District as its opposite – paradise. But if this sublime example of English nature was meant to help the youngsters to recuperate, the experience showed that Englishness itself was far from porous. The West London Synagogue, for example, was a place where resources might be found for the children, but it was never perceived as somewhere where they might worship, let alone lead a service.

Told not to exaggerate, or to keep quiet, it is not surprising that, after the initial efforts to help them and the genuine kindness that was shown to the children in their first settlement at Windermere and Hampshire, thereafter their greatest strength was within the group itself. But rather than gain, as Wordsworth and other Romantics had fantasised, from perpetual wandering and the freedom that allegedly brought, most of the former children settled permanently in particular places – in Britain, Israel, north America, and elsewhere – and attempted where possible to rebuild families around them, thereby re-establishing a 'place called home'.[242] Writing from America as early as 1950, one of the former children, Ernest Sunog, lamented that while he was getting on well 'there was something which isn't the same

240 University of Southampton Archives: Montefiore to Anthony de Rothschild, 13 December 1950, file 112/49–50, CBF microfilm archives.

241 Blond with Turner, *Marks of Distinction*, pp. 93–94.

242 See, for example, the reminiscences and life stories presented in the *Journal of the '45 Aid Society*.

as it was in the *old country* [my emphasis]'.[243] His geographical point of reference was England and not eastern Europe. But if they became rooted in cities such as Manchester and London, increasingly those who were originally flown to the north of England have returned to visit Windermere. In so doing, they have provided memories that are increasingly providing a more inclusive history of Windermere and the stories the Lake District tells of itself.

Black photographer Ingrid Pollard was born in Guyana in 1953 and came to Britain three years later. Her exhibition *Pastoral Interludes* (1984) explores the English countryside and 'feeling I don't belong'. Evoking Wordsworth especially, the texts accompanying her photographs question the nature of Englishness and exclusion. The first image in this exhibition featured Pollard resting alone against a drystone wall. The accompanying text reveals her ambiguity towards the beauty of the landscape and her place within it:

> it's as if the black experience is only lived within an urban environment. I thought I liked the LAKE DISTRICT, where I wandered lonely as a Black face in a sea of white. A visit to the countryside is always accompanied by a feeling of unease, dread ... .[244]

The cultural anthropologist Wendy Joy Darby, exploring the Lake District during the 1990s by taking part in rambler groups, queried the absence of ethnic minorities within them. It was explained to her that 'their particular absence in the Lake District [was because] this was not a place that held "their" history ... Blacks and Asians were seen to be urban.'[245] Ingrid Pollard's *Pastoral Interludes* and John Kippin's photograph 'Muslims at Lake Windermere' (1991), showing men praying in a corner of a field near the Lake with the women and children around them, are thus political interventions challenging notions of English exclusivity within the landscape. As John Taylor suggests in *A Dream of England* (1994), with these photographs 'the meaning of the countryside is in transition'.[246]

Since the early 1990s the desire to open up heritage within major national organisations to people of all backgrounds has indeed intensified. In 2003, for example, it was stated that 'English Heritage seeks to understand the diversity of this country's heritage and promote a more inclusive past ... [It] values the heritage of the different cultures that have been woven into our shared

243 *Primrose Leaves* no. 7 (Spring 1950), p. 6, copy available at the Jewish Museum, London.

244 Phil Kinsman, 'Landscape, race and national identity: the photography of Ingrid Pollard', *Area* no. 27 no. 4 (1995), pp. 301–302.

245 Darby, *Landscape and Identity*, p. 245.

246 John Taylor, *A Dream of England: Landscape, Photography and the Tourist's Imagination* (Manchester: Manchester University Press, 1994), p. 258 and colour plates 16, 23.

history over hundreds of years.'[247] Nevertheless, exclusion based on narrow definitions of Englishness, past and present, has far from disappeared.[248] While roughly 10 per cent of the English population is non-white, just 1 per cent of visitors to the national parks of England are people of colour. Is this part of what Trevor Philips, once head of Britain's Equality Commission, provocatively refers to as the 'passive apartheid' of the English countryside, or are more complex factors at work in explaining this apparent imbalance?[249]

If the Lakes and their poet laureate, Wordsworth, remain 'quintessentially English',[250] his evocation of the 'Wandering Jew' also enables a connection to be made between Ambleside and Auschwitz, between the 'now "lost" village of Calgarth Estate ... and one of the defining moments of modern human history – the Holocaust'. It is, as the local heritage project states, 'a journey through time and space'.[251] Moreover, there are other forms of inclusion that his poetry has promoted and can promote. Wordsworth's 'tenderness towards his children' was articulated through 'some of his finest poems [which] pre-emptively record early death and the sorrow of losing a child'.[252] It was thus no coincidence that Liza Shleimowitz, whose mother was raped and both parents brutally murdered by nationalist antisemites in the Ukraine during the early 1920s, should identify with Wordsworth's poetry, and especially the 'Lucy' poems and their enigmatic portrayal of loss. Liza, with her siblings, was left in the Atlantic Park transit camp, near Southampton, after being rejected at Ellis Island as a result of racist American immigration policies during the 1920s. These children and others from the camp were soon successful in local schools. A Hampshire teacher recalled the 'children were lively and intelligent ... [They] made very good scholars and enjoyed the English way of life.'[253]

Liza's notebooks from her English lessons, which she took with her to South Africa, where she eventually found a home, include lovingly transcribed verses from the poem, the only surviving writing that is in English:

> She dwelt among the untrodden ways
> Beside the Springs of Dove,

---

247 English Heritage, 'England's heritage – your heritage' (2003).

248 See the comments of Jo Littler, 'Introduction: British heritage and the legacies of "race"', in Jo Littler and Roshi Naidoo (eds), *The Politics of Heritage: The Legacies of 'Race'* (London: Routledge, 2005), pp. 1–19.

249 Homa Khaleeli, 'Why don't black people camp?', *Guardian*, 9 July 2010.

250 Ibid., p. 29.

251 Trevor Avery, press release, 2010, announcing the semi-permanent exhibition 'From Auschwitz to Ambleside' at Windermere Library, organised by Another Space.

252 Margaret Drabble, 'Foreword', in *The Romantic Poets: William Wordsworth* (London: Guardian, 2009), p. 6.

253 Winifred Dominy, letter to *Hampshire Magazine*, June 1971, p. 24.

A maid whom these were none to praise
And very few to love ... .
She lived unknow[n] and few could know
When Lucy ceased to be;
But she is in her grave, and, oh,
The difference to me![254]

The Lake District, as the rest of the English countryside, has many different histories, and even those that dominate, such as the narratives relating to William Wordsworth, enable plural readings. Furthermore, ethnic minorities themselves are developing complex relationships with the place. At an extremist level it emerged that the failed English suicide bombers of 21 July 2005 had been camping in Baysbrown Farm, Langdale (less than ten miles from Windermere), just a year earlier. They had trained or bonded in other rural parts of Britain. Was this a form of (perverse) integration in outdoor pursuits or an attempt to hide their activities in remote areas, or both? If it was a desire for invisibility, it failed, as they made themselves – as a group of young Muslim men in the Lake District – highly visible to the police and British security world.[255] As one local resident of Langdale sardonically noted, 'Frankly, I would have thought they would have stood out.'[256]

Whether the story of the child survivors will remain marginal as 'matter out of place ... not [to] be included if a pattern is to be maintained',[257] or, alternatively, will become integrated, is still unclear. The creation of a museum of their experiences in Windermere Library indicates the inclusion that is increasingly taking place. Since a BBC television documentary in April 2010, *The Orphans Who Survived the Concentration Camps*,[258] there has 'developed an irresistible demand from far and wide for a locally based exhibition and resource where people could come and learn about the story'.[259] Subsequently 'From Auschwitz to Ambleside' has evolved into 'the Lake District Holocaust Project'. The aim,

---

254 School notebooks formely in possession of Cyril Orolowitz, Cape Town, the son of Liza, and since his death deposited at the University of Cape Town archives.

255 Sandra Laville, '21/7 bombers: ringleaders slipped through police net', *Guardian*, 10 July 2007. See also the online *Grough* magazine 14 August 2006, 4 September 2006, 16 and 17 January 2007 and 10 July 2007 at http://www.grough.co.uk/magazine/category/magazine/ for the local elements of this story, accessed 13 October 2011.

256 Quoted in Ian Cobain and Richard Norton-Taylor, 'Training camps for terrorists in UK parks', *Guardian*, 14 August 2006.

257 Douglas, *Purity and Danger*, p. 41.

258 Produced by Gillian Bancroft and shown on BBC 1, 5 April 2010. It averaged 1.848 million viewers according to figures provided for Another Space.

259 Another Space press release, 26 July 2010, 'Lakes Holocaust Story Finds Home In Windermere'.

through 'educational activities, exhibitions, events and archive research', is to 'commemorate the profound connection between the Lake District and the Holocaust'. So far, however, local responses to this initiative remain ambivalent.[260]

Through the English Romantics, notes Wendy Joy Darby, 'The Lake District was made into an icon, a window through which a greater reality or truth could be perceived, be it of God or England – although the two were not necessarily different from one another.'[261] Thereafter, the Lake District has continued to be made and remade. Arthur Ransome's novels, starting with *Swallows and Amazons* (1930), have, for example, become 'identified with a particular vision of England: a pastoral, old-fashioned utopia set in the Lake District sometime between the wars, with its roots in the Edwardian heyday of the British Empire'.[262] This is not far removed from Darby's 'Wordsworthshire', 'compounded of drifts of daffodils, lakeside strolls, the ever-hovering presence of the National Trust's long-ago comforting world of Peter Rabbit and Mrs Tiggy Winkle, and high teas taken in gleaming dark wood interiors set with chintz and lustreware'.[263]

It is hard to imagine that the story of the Holocaust survivor children would fit into such limited readings of Wordsworth's Lake District. Nor, for that matter, would that of Liza Shleimowitz and her consolation found in Wordsworth's poetry in an English transmigrant camp. The same has been true of the Dadaist Kurt Schwitters, who left Nazi Germany in 1937 to escape arrest as a 'degenerate artist'. He settled in Ambleside, next to Lake Windermere, at the end of the war and remained in the area until his death in 1948. It has been noted that now 'there are no signs of his ever having been [in the Lake District]. While there is a plethora of shops and cafes bearing the names of the Lake Poets and Beatrix Potter's rabbits, you will find none bearing his name.'[264] But such heritage struggles over the meaning of place are part of a bigger battle over national identity at both a political and a cultural level, and in which exclusion in the early years of the twenty-first century still remains the dominant force.

Progress *has* been made in this most important of English localities, such as Ingrid Pollard's 'witty series of pictures that put black people into the

---

260 'From Auschwitz to Ambleside', Windermere Library, visited 12 July 2011 and on continuing local ambivalence to the project, Trevor Avery in discussion with author and Aimée Bunting, 12 July 2011.

261 Darby, *Landscape and Identity*, p. 87.

262 Roland Chambers, *The Last Englishman: The Double Life of Arthur Ransome* (London: Faber and Faber, 2009), p. 3.

263 Darby, *Landscape and Identity*, pp. 211–212.

264 Russell Mills, introduction to Barbara Crossley, *The Triumph of Kurt Schwitters* (Ambleside: Armitt Trust, 2005), p. 6. His Ambleside collage the Elterwater Merzbarn, was moved to Newcastle in 1963 and in 1970 his body was taken from Ambleside churchyard to his birth town of Hanover.

frame of Wordsworth's Lake District',[265] and the work of Another Space's 'From Auschwitz to Ambleside', whether in exhibition, website resource, or BBC television documentary. Early in this chapter the thoughts of cultural critic Stuart Hall were referenced with his vision for a more inclusive heritage that would 'rewrite the margins into the centre, the outside into the inside'. This is not special pleading, as Hall makes clear, but the necessity of

> representing more adequately the degree to which 'their' history entails and has always implicated 'us', across the centuries, and vice versa. The African presence in Britain since the sixteenth century, the Asian since the seventeenth century and the Chinese, Jewish and Irish in the nineteenth have long required to be made into a much more 'global' version of 'our island story'.[266]

With this in mind, embracing the local, national, and global as well as the particular and the universal, this case study of the young survivors will close with two of these former children and how they have taken their experiences and wider Jewish narratives to make messages for all humankind. They are ones that expose the danger of being other and the vulnerability the process of othering causes more generally.

Ben Helfgott has done more than anyone to keep these 'children' together in Britain and beyond. He has helped create a world of mutual support but one which reaches out beyond the confines of this small community: 'I believe our story is "pour encourager les autres" because every day there is someone who feels helpless, feels a need for support, especially the young with specific difficulties.'[267] One of these was Vesna Maric, who came to Britain in 1992 as a teenager fleeing persecution in Bosnia-Herzegovina. She relates how when she arrived in England the expectation was 'something a little more like "proper" refugees: people suffering, hardship visible on their faces, clothes torn and wrinkled, children's eyes crusted with tears'. Instead, there was a determination 'not [to] advertise our misery'. Vesna and her party were taken to the Lake District to recuperate, where they were treated with kindness but also with some fear and condescension. As she concludes, 'It's not easy suddenly becoming a refugee.'[268] And Vesna's story brings us to Auschwitz survivor Hugo Gryn, who came over in the last major flight of children in February 1946 and became lifelong friends with Ben Helfgott. His last speech, in 1996, referred to asylum-seekers, those

265 Naseem Khan, 'Taking Root in Britain: the process of shaping heritage', in Jo Littler and Roshi Naidoo (eds), *The Politics of Heritage: The Legacies of 'Race'* (London: Routledge, 2005), p. 134.

266 Hall, 'Whose Heritage?' in Littler and Naidoo (eds), *The Politics of Heritage*, p. 31.

267 Ben Helfgott, letter to Trevor Avery, 2008, in the Another Space project, 'Avenue of Exile'.

268 Vesna Maric, *Bluebird: A Memoir* (London: Granta, 2010), p. 29 and passim.

contemporary 'Wandering Jews' without the safety of the concept of home either through time or place. He likened them to the Jews on board the *St Louis* in 1939, wandering the oceans of the world in search of refuge. More generally Hugo Grynn reflected that

> It seems to me that true religion begins with the law about protecting and shielding the alien and the stranger ... . There are so many scars that need mending and healing it seems to me that it is imperative that we proclaim that asylum issues are an index of our spiritual and moral civilisation.

He concluded that 'How you are with the one to whom you owe nothing, that is a grave test and not only as an index of our tragic past.'[269] In this respect, it is intriguing to reflect on how some of these Holocaust survivors casually changed their age in Prague in order to qualify for the CCCCC scheme. To return to Solomon Freiman's testimony: 'up to 16 [I] can go to England. So I registered. I was eighteen. OK [now] I'm under sixteen.'[270] Today, even the suspicion of a young asylum-seeker making such a deception would guarantee instant deportation – often based on spurious medical advice. Indeed, in autumn 2016, in an atmosphere of intense xenophobia and racist violence following the successful 'Brexit' campaign, politicians and the popular press railed against the entry of unaccompanied minors to Britain from the Calais 'Jungle': 'There's not a young child, or a female of any age, among them.'[271] What was already a tokenist refugee policy was too much for the right-wing newspapers to stomach.

And, as the final examples of this chapter will reveal, the world of colonies and hostels for young refugees has changed to one of detention centres. From being part of the local landscape, their place has increasingly gone beyond the public gaze. In turn, such geographical remoteness and physical restriction reflects a growing discourse of criminality in dealing with the presence of unaccompanied child migrants.

Placing Contemporary Child Refugees

The entry of the Serbians and Spanish refugees, then *Kindertransportees* and Holocaust child survivors, was due to strong intervention from prominent campaigners whom sceptical governments felt they could not resist. In all four cases, although agreement was reluctantly given, it was on an understanding that the stay would be strictly temporary.

---

269 Hugo Gryn, *A Moral and Spiritual Index* (London: Refugee Council, 1996).
270 British Library National Sound Archive, C410/052.
271 *The Sun*, 19 October 2016.

The partial exception to this pattern was the *Kindertransport*, which the prime minister welcomed as a specific way of addressing the persecution of the Jews. This was *not* a state-sponsored scheme, but it was one that was proudly announced in the House of Commons. And, as Louise London has highlighted, while the Home Secretary, Samuel Hoare, was uncertain about it (fearing popular antagonism to increased refugee entry), Neville Chamberlain was more generous. There was thus an unresolved tension around whether the children coming to Britain were to be there only temporarily (as reflected on their official documentation) or would eventually become a permanent part of the population.[272]

The idea of individuals sponsoring and hosting children was an indication that a long-term home was also being considered. The *Kindertransport* was the first time this had happened in Britain (the Belgians *were* partly housed privately, but in family units and on a temporary basis) and it raises a wider issue about the politics of place and the presence of refugee children. The first *Kindertransportees* in late 1938 were accommodated, as was Lore Segal, in a reception centre (a summer holiday camp) in Dovercourt, Kent, and then distributed around the country, mainly to private homes.[273] Hostels were provided for the others, reflecting not an absence of offers from within the Jewish and non-Jewish world but the snobbery of the Refugee Children's Movement. It was reported to the Save the Children Fund in May 1939 that in fact 'there were a large number of homes for Jewish children in this country, but they were mostly of a poor class and unsuitable'.[274] For the substantial minority placed in hostels, experiences varied as much as for those living with families.

With the earlier Serbs and Spanish refugees, the hostels/colonies were regarded as a way of keeping the 'home' identity of the children strong before their return. They also provided an easier way of administering these schemes from a practical perspective. Lack of resources and the speed with which suitable buildings and staff were found inevitably resulted in some being better than others (the Serb colony in Southampton was, for example, closed down after 'a case of scandal').[275] With the *Kinder*, the orthodox Jewish authorities were keen to keep the young refugees under their auspices in hostels to preserve their religious identity, sometimes to the discomfort of children who came from secular backgrounds. The reverse also happened to those who came from very traditional families.[276] Those

---

272 Louise London, *Whitehall and the Jews* (Cambridge: Cambridge University Press, 2000), p. 105.

273 Barry Turner, ... *And The Policeman Smiled. 10,000 Children Escape from Nazi Europe* (London: Bloomsbury, 1990), chapter 4.

274 Executive Committee, 16 May 1939, SCF (Save the Children Fund) archive, A/2/1/1.

275 National Archives, T1/12514: confidential report 27 June 1918.

276 Jennifer Craig Norton, 'From Dependence to Autonomy: *Kinder*, Refugee Organizations, and the Struggle for Agency', *Prism* no. 5 (Spring 2013), pp. 54–60.

coming under the CCCCC scheme were also sent to hostels in the major commercial/industrial cities after their initial settlements in Hampshire and the Lake District. Here the wider goal was to help their integration back into 'normal' society, especially in the employment market. The setting-up of these hostels/colonies was thus partly about control – keeping the survivors together for both bureaucratic and ideological reasons. As a result the children were often resentful of their lack of financial and general independence from the organising committees. These hostels were, however, part of the local world and the children themselves found ways of venting their frustrations and asserting their agency, even if the power structure tended to mute their voice. Such marginality reflected a wider issue concerning contemporary understanding of the 'rights of the child'.

As will become apparent, more recent and sophisticated interpretations of such rights have not so far helped the vastly increased number of unaccompanied refugee children who have been rendered placeless and voiceless by the world's most powerful nation, America. Even so, the 'top down' interpretation of such rights until the second half of the twentieth century reflected and reinforced a tendency to regard children as passive victims, unable to determine their own destiny.

Save the Children Fund (SCF) was established as a British organisation in 1920. As noted in its 1938 *Annual Report*:

> The question of refugee relief again takes us back to the early days and to the fundamental purpose of the Save the Children Fund. It is one of the tragedies of our history that, after nearly twenty years, we should still be compelled to offer charitable aid to children in the same categories as their fathers whom we helped after the Great War.[277]

In 1923 the Save the Children International Union was formed, with its secretariat in Switzerland. It was from there, a year later, that the Declaration of Geneva concerning the 'Rights of the Child' was formulated through the League of Nations. These 'were not rights to "do" or to "act" independently as individuals; instead they were rights to "receive" in the form of things that should be done for and to the child'. Mankind, it pronounced, 'owes to the Child the best that it has to give'.[278]

At this stage, who was to interpret what was 'best' was left vague, falling between the state and the voluntary sector, and it could be interpreted in many different ways by those exercising power over children. It led, for

---

277 University of Birmingham Archives: Save the Children Fund, *Annual Report 1938* (London: SCF, 1938), p. 13 in SCF archive, A/680.

278 Cynthia Cohen, 'United Nations Convention on the Rights of the Child', in Kathleen Alaimo and Brian Klug (eds), *Children as Equals: Exploring the Rights of the Child* (Lanham: University Press of America, 2002), p. 50.

example, to hundreds of thousands of children – both orphans and those placed in care – in Britain being sent to the 'white' colonies, where a frightening number were subject to sexual, physical, and economic abuse for 'their own good'. While such schemes had operated to north America from as early as the seventeenth century, they grew through the nineteenth century as Britain exported those it regarded as a waste of resources while adding to the 'right' racial stock of Canada, New Zealand, Australia, and Rhodesia. Only with the last-mentioned, which was among the smallest of the schemes, did the children themselves possess any choice in whether to go.[279]

After 1945 Australia was the major destination and where, largely through the auspices of religious charities, the rape and exploitation of their charges was systematic. Those children with relatives still alive, including their parents, were denied all knowledge of their family heritage. The concern expressed by some contemporaries, including at a parliamentary level, about whether such schemes were in the children's interests was ignored. For example, in 1953 the Home Office was concerned about the further extension of the scheme through the 'Overseas League'. It raised the proposed regulations of the Children Act 1948, which would have granted greater protection (reflecting its status as the first British legislation that moved towards accepting the individuality of the child). But, as a civil servant from a rival department noted, these were 'no nearer the light of day than they were two and a half years ago'.[280] The schemes were halted as late as the 1960s and it would be another 30 years before the abuse was exposed.[281]

More generally, it was not until the United Nations 1989 Convention on the Rights of the Child (UNCRC) that the individuality and autonomy of the child was recognised, including 'the child's right to free expression and association'. As Kathleen Alaimo notes, 'The UNCRC brings to the table a new recognition of the child's right to a voice.'[282] Article 12 insisted on the 'the views of the child being given due weight in accordance with the age and maturity of the child' and the 'opportunity to be heard in any judicial and administrative proceedings'.[283] This was a long way removed from the treatment of refugee children observed throughout this chapter. It reflected not only the earlier limitations of the first Conventions but also the failure to recognise the particular issues affecting refugee children, who were rendered doubly vulnerable without the protection of their families. They were and remain placeless and isolated.

---

279 Margaret Humphreys, *Empty Cradles* (London: Doubleday, 1994).

280 National Archives, MH 102/2049: K.R. Crook to R.L. Dixon, Commonwealth Relations Office, 29 July 1953.

281 Humphreys, *Empty Cradles*.

282 Kathleen Alaimo, 'Historical Roots of Children's Rights in Europe and the United States', in Alaimo and Klug, *Children as Equals*, pp. 18–19.

283 Ibid.

In summer 1939 the Save the Children International Union proposed a major conference on the problem of refugee children. The fear of controversy in this tense moment of global politics led to delay – as did interest groups, who were concerned only about specific refugee children. SCF was still keen for the conference to go ahead, aware of the scale and urgency of the problem. Its Executive Committee agreed that 'While admitting the conditions of the child refugees varied considerably, it was felt that there was no reason why the conference should not deal with all categories, under separate heads if necessary.'[284] In the end, war intervened and the conference failed to materialise, but child refugees did not disappear: indeed, their numbers were to increase drastically.

The clumsiness of Lewis Golden's SCF intervention with the Spanish Civil War refugees in 1937 obscured his perspicacious and progressive understanding of the psychological as well as the practical issues facing children taken from homes and families through war and persecution. Some two decades on, little progress had been made in understanding the specific needs of young refugees. This was illustrated when Britain faced a new influx of refugees, this time fleeing from the Soviet invasion of Hungary in 1956. The recently formed British Council for Aid to Refugees (BCAR) was appalled to find that while the number of unaccompanied children was relatively small – a dozen or so – there were initially no facilities (educational or otherwise) for children in the hastily assembled reception camps for the Hungarians. BCAR's representative asked the authorities for this thereafter to be considered in advance rather than when the children arrived 'bewildered and unhappy'.[285]

Indeed, it was not until 1994 that the UNHCR first formalised specific guidelines for the protection and care of refugee children, somewhat belatedly recognising that half of the world's forcibly displaced were under 18 years of age.[286] Three years later it highlighted the growing issue of unaccompanied children seeking asylum in further guidelines.[287] These acknowledged that 'Because of their vulnerability, unaccompanied children seeking asylum should not be refused access to the territory.' Indeed, it added that 'Children seeking asylum, particularly if they are unaccompanied, are entitled to special care and protection.'[288] The right of the child

---

284 Executive Committee minutes of SCF, 16 May 1939 and 6 June 1939 in SCF papers A/2/1/1.

285 SCF archive, A53, 'Hungarian Refugees 1956/57'.

286 UNHCR, *Children on the Run: Unaccompanied Children Leaving Central America and Mexico and the Need for International Protection* (Washington, DC: UNHCR, 2014), p. 56 note 3 for a summary of such guidelines.

287 UNHCR, 'Guidelines on Policies and Procedures in Dealing with Unaccompanied Children Seeking Asylum' (UNHCR, February 1997) available through the UNHCR website, accessed 20 March 2015.

288 Ibid., pp. 1–2.

to give their testimony was part of this greater awareness. It argued that through sensitively conducted interviews, ideally carried out by those of the same cultural background and mother tongue, 'his/her story and all relevant information will help to ensure that subsequent actions are taken in the "best interests" of the child'.[289]

When these guidelines were produced in 1997 the UNHCR noted that 'In recent years, States [had] expressed concern about unaccompanied children seeking asylum either at their borders or at some later time after entry.'[290] In the second decade of the twenty-first century, that concern, especially in America, where it became a heated political issue, had turned to a moral panic as numbers began to double from year to year. In 1990, for example, 8,500 'minors' were detained by the US Immigration and Naturalization Service, of whom up to 70 per cent were unaccompanied.[291] The number of unaccompanied children grew slowly until 2011/12, when it surged to over 20,000, doubling in 2013 and reaching 90,000 the year after, with no sign of the numbers decreasing.[292] As President Obama conceded in 2014, the influx represented an 'urgent humanitarian situation requiring a unified and coordinated Federal response'.[293]

The majority of these children fleeing to America came from El Salvador, Guatemala, and Honduras, totalling over 21,000 in 2013.[294] The reasons behind these frightening statistics are complex, but, rather than poverty, fundamentally the children are fleeing violence – often drug-/crime-related. It is also clearly gendered: boys were intimidated into joining gangs and girls faced sexual violence/coercion. Of 404 children interviewed by the UNHCR, 58 per cent were regarded as having 'potential international protection needs'.[295] In 2006, however, only 13 per cent of such children were put into that category.[296]

In desperation, parents and guardians believed that the children undertaking what has been described as a 'treacherous journey' was

---

289 Ibid., pp. 7, 8.

290 Ibid., p. 4.

291 Liza Navarro, 'An Analysis of Treatment of Unaccompanied Immigrant and Refugee Children in INS Detention and Other Forms of Institutionalized Custody', *Chicano-Latino Law Review* no. 19 (1998), p. 589.

292 Vox, '14 facts that help explain America's child-migrant crisis', 29 July 2014, http://www.vox.com/2014/6/16/5813406/explain-child-migrant-crisis-central-america, accessed 10 February 2015.

293 Quoted by Elizabeth Kennedy, 'No Childhood Here: Why Central American Children are Fleeing Their Homes' (American Immigration Council Perspectives, July 2014), p. 1.

294 UNHCR, *Children on the Run*, p. 4.

295 Ibid., p. 6.

296 Ibid., p. 24.

their best chance of a peaceful future.[297] Kevin, a teenager in Hondurus, summed up the hopelessness of his situation at home through the words of his grandmother: 'If you don't join, the gang will shoot you. If you do join, the rival gang will shoot you – or the cops will shoot you. But if you leave, no one will shoot you.'[298] Thousands have died en route through further violence or accidents in transit, especially riding atop trains. 'Their journeys may be as harrowing as the experiences they are fleeing, with children often facing sexual violence or other abuses as they travel.'[299] Leaving is 'often a last resort' and for parents and guardians there is great distress in 'weighing the risks of an incredibly dangerous journey to the U.S. versus an incredibly dangerous childhood and adolescence in [countries such as] El Salvador'.[300] PBS news reported how, in December 2013, 'dozens of mothers [from Guatemala, Honduras, El Salvador and Nicaragua] converged on the central Mexican town of Tequisquiapan, where they laid pink paper flowers on a lonely stretch of train tracks to mourn their lost children.'[301] In other cases, parental abuse was the reason for flight – one in five in the case of Salvadoran children.[302]

As with contemporary domestic workers, testimony has been produced by these children: they are not silent victims. But, like the millions of these exploited women, it is in the form of evidence collected by humanitarian organisations or legal bodies working on the children's behalf. Typical of this material is that of Mario, a 17-year-old from El Salvador:

I left because I had problems with the gangs. They hung out by a field that I had to pass to get to school. They said if I didn't join them, they would kill me ... . They beat me up five times for refusing to help them.

When they killed his friend and, finding that the police were unwilling to do 'anything to help, I had to leave'.[303] A 16-year-old girl from the same country interviewed by the UNHCR related how a gang member warned her that she 'would be killed if she resisted his sexual advances'.[304]

Leslie Velez, senior protection officer at the UNHCR, is co-author of *Children on the Run*. Asked who it was within the family to make the decision to flee, and how much agency the children themselves exercised,

---

297 Lisa Frydman et al., *A Treacherous Journey: Child Migrants Navigating the US Immigration System* (San Franscico: Center for Gender & Refugee Studies/Kids in Need of Defense, 2014), p. ii.
298 UNHCR, *Children on the Run*, p. 36.
299 Frydman et al., *A Treacherous Journey*, p. ii.
300 Kennedy, 'No Childhood Here', p. 3.
301 P.J. Tobia, 'No country for lost kids', *PBS Newshour*, 20 June 2014.
302 UNHCR, *Children on the Run*, pp. 6, 33.
303 Ibid., p. 32.
304 Ibid.

she responded that 'is there really a choice here? [This is] in the context of entrenched poverty in which criminal gang armed actors can really act with impunity. This is a bad recipe.'[305] It remains that very few of these children have claimed or received asylum from the US immigration authorities: 'Through the first nine months of fiscal year 2014, only 108 unaccompanied children have been granted asylum [in America]. And as of March [2014], only 1100 children were waiting for their asylum applications to be processed.'[306]

UNHCR guidelines state clearly that 'Children seeking asylum should not be kept in detention', adding that this is 'particularly important in the case of unaccompanied children'.[307] Where states do 'regrettably' detain children, they should do so in accordance with Article 37 of the Convention of the Rights of the Child. This stipulates that 'detention shall be used only as a measure of last resort and for the shortest appropriate period of time'. The UNHCR guidelines add that if children are detained in airports, immigration-holding centres, or prisons, 'they must not be held under prison-like conditions'. The approach should be '"care" and not "detention"'. In terms of place, 'Facilities should not be located in isolated areas where culturally-appropriate community resources and legal access may be unavailable.'[308]

In no respect does the treatment of the tens, now hundreds, of thousands of unaccompanied children who have reached America (and many other countries), reflect these guidelines. Instead, they are being treated as an immigration problem rather than as vulnerable children requiring particular care. In America many of the children are housed in Border Patrol processing centres which have been described as 'essentially prisons' or in 'makeshift facilities in military bases'.[309] In 2002 the Homeland Security Act handed over responsibility for 'Special Immigrant Juveniles' to a new agency, the US Immigration and Customs Enforcement (ICE).[310] But even before this bureaucratic change, through a variety of centres, camps, and facilities, American immigration authorities had 'a history of housing immigrant minors in disgraceful conditions,

---

305 Brian Renwick, 'Why 90,000 Children Flooding Our Border is Not an Immigration Story', 16 June 2014, http://www.nationaljournal.com/domesticpolicy/why-90–000-children-flooding-our-border-is-not-an-immigration-story-20140616, accessed 10 February 2015.

306 Dara Lind, '14 facts that help explain America's child-migrant crisis', http://www.vox.com/2014/16/5813406/explain-child-migrant-crisis-central-america-unaccompanied-children-immigrants-daca, accessed 6 February 2015.

307 UNHCR, 'Guidelines on Policies and Procedures', p. 10.

308 Ibid., pp. 10–11.

309 Lind, '14 facts'.

310 Angela Lloyd, 'Regulating Consent', pp. 238–9.

without access to education, health care, legal services, or other basic necessities'.[311]

Writing as early as 1998, Lisa Navarro noted that such child detention reflected 'a clear congressional desire to discourage immigrant minors from entering the United States illegally'.[312] Detention followed by deportation is thus there not only to manage the problem of numbers but also to act as a deterrent to stop the flow of children. While Barack Obama expressed concern on humanitarian grounds about unaccompanied child migrants, it remains that his administration

> touted a strategy of 'aggressive deterrence', one centred around the idea that if Central American parents know for certain that their children will be sent home almost as soon as they arrive, they'll decide against sending them in the first place.[313]

The reality, however, is that deportation, apart from to Mexico, is not easy to achieve. Unaccompanied children languish in unsuitable facilities for weeks and months – well beyond the regulatory 72 hours.

The treatment of unaccompanied migrant children is a problem beyond the USA (as noted, totalling 80,000 on the continent of Europe alone in 2016) and the conditions of detention are even more inappropriate in transit countries such as Indonesia, Turkey, Greece, Libya, and Egypt. Since the beginning of the twenty-first century Human Rights Watch (HMW) has 'documented serious violations of children's rights arising from immigration detention of children. Children may be arbitrarily detained, held in cells with unrelated adults, and subjected to brutal treatment by police, guards and other authorities.' As HMW concludes, such poor and dangerous conditions 'fall far short of international standards governing appropriate settings for children deprived of their liberty'. Rather than detain such children and adding to their loss of education and strains on their mental health, it argues, states should provide them 'with opportunities to find some normality in their uprooted lives'.[314]

The crux of the matter has been whether the states regard those coming in primarily as vulnerable children or as potential unwanted migrants.[315] There are few domestically in America and beyond who regard unaccompanied child migrants in the words of the UNHCR's Leslie Velez as 'not a migration story [but] a humanitarian crisis'.[316] Such interventions are

---

311 Navarro, 'An Analysis of Treatment', p. 590.

312 Ibid., p. 604.

313 Josh Voorhees, 'What Immigration Crisis?', *Slate*, 20 August 2014.

314 Alice Farmer, 'The impact of immigration detention on children', *FMR* no. 44 (September 2013), pp.14–16.

315 Lloyd, 'Regulating Consent', p. 261.

316 Resnick, 'Why 90,000 Children'.

important in restoring to the forefront of a heated debate the 'child's best interest'. For those for whom there is 'nowhere else to go',[317] detention in remote places renders these children inconspicuous as well as adding to their trauma. The huge numbers of these children on a worldwide basis points to a larger problem and one that the narrow confines and historic context of the 1951 Geneva Convention on Refugees is failing to confront.

War and genocide in the twentieth century and beyond have left the child especially vulnerable. In its most extreme form the percentage of Jewish children murdered reflected the determination of the Nazi state to ensure that there would be no future generations of this 'race' to survive. Yet less systematic ethnic cleansing has also had a drastic impact on children, as has all forms of conflict, including civil war. The more recent internal crises of crime and poverty in countries such as El Salvador, Honduras, and Guatemala has created a fresh situation in which there is 'no childhood' and where there is 'no place for children'.[318] What is also new is that when fleeing to countries of safety or transit, these unaccompanied child migrants find that through mass detention there is still 'no place for children'. As will be detailed in the following chapter, the image of the three-year-old Syrian Kurd Alan Kurdi dead on a Turkish beach in September 2015 shocked the world and led to a wave of international sympathy towards refugees. It remains that the numbers of child refugees continues to rise, including those who are unaccompanied, and sadly there have been other 'Alan Kurdis' since September 2015 who have drowned attempting to reach freedom and the chance of a better life. Since the tragedy of the Kurdi family and thousands of others, the ease with which the West again is turning its back on and erecting barriers against the entry of defenceless refugees recalls the last statement of Hugo Gryn. The child survivor and ex-Windermere resident feared that 'mean spirited responses' to asylum seekers were 'part of the process which is the hardening of the caring arteries'.[319]

Conclusion

If the global history of forced migration is still a forgotten story, then that of child refugees suffers from a double marginality. To take the British example alone, the narrative of unaccompanied child migrants coming into and out of the country starts at least with the early modern period. Although the stories of Huguenots' ship journeys hidden in barrels may be apocryphal, there were certainly children, such as Henri de Portal, who came to England

---

317 Lind, '14 facts'.
318 Kennedy, 'No Childhood Here', pp. 3–4.
319 Gryn, *A Moral and Spiritual Index*.

on their own.[320] It has already been noted that the first unwanted children sent from England to the 'new world' left in the seventeenth century. There are now more unaccompanied child refugees in twenty-first century Britain than came through the celebrated *Kindertransport*, with over 3000 arriving every year.[321] The lack of facilities and care for them in Britain is reflected in the remarkable statistic that over 900 children from 2010 to 2015 have simply 'gone missing', leaving them vulnerable to 'domestic servitude, the sex trade or ... ending up on the streets'.[322] Unaccompanied children have been part of the migratory experience – forced or otherwise – since the days of antiquity and the myth of Moses found in his reed basket. Such journeys were/are often traumatic, but their troubling nature is no excuse for it not being part of both migration studies and the history of childhood and of global, national, and local responses to refugee crises which need to recognise the particular needs of the young.

More specifically, this chapter has shown that throughout the twentieth century and now into the twenty-first century, while the concept of the 'rights of the child' have grown in sophistication – especially in allowing the voice of the child to be heard and considered – this is yet to impact on the treatment of those who are most vulnerable, having already lost their homes and security. Here, in case studies ranging from the Serbians through to the child survivors of the Holocaust, the desire (if sometimes naively expressed and implemented) to help refugee children has been illustrated. Attempts, however crude and misguided, were made to recreate a place called home, if often only on a temporary basis and without full understanding of the need to preserve their past cultural, religious, and political identities. And in terms of local identity in places such as Faversham and Windermere, with the Serbian and Jewish orphans respectively, the presence of these children made a deep impact on those coming into contact with them. This was equally true of the children themselves, marked in memory work by the return in recent years of the Holocaust survivors to their Lake District sojourn.

Now, in the twenty-first century, the number of forced migrant children (both internally and externally displaced) approximates, according to the UNHCR for 2013, over 25 million of a global total exceeding 51 million. Already by then these figures reflected a growth in numbers and percentage, partly due to the Syrian refugee crisis: they have continued to increase more recently, adding a further 10 million in the following three years,

---

320 Elsie Sandell, *Southampton Through the Ages: A Short History* (Southampton: G.F. Wilson, 1960), p. 93.

321 Lisa Nandy, *Going It Alone: Children in the Asylum Process* (London: Children's Society, 2007), p. 2. Of these, 94 per cent have their asylum claim rejected.

322 Maeve McClenaghan and Tracy McVeigh, 'Fears as more children seeking asylum are lost', *Observer*, 6 December 2015.

with children accounting for at least half the rise.[323] Only a fortunate few of these minors are treated with the sensitivity required relating to their age and the trauma they have experienced. To take Britain alone, the number of young asylum-seekers who are officially 'lost' during the second decade of the twenty-first century exceeds the total of Serbian and Holocaust survivor children brought to the country in the First World War and immediately after the Second. Across Europe as a whole, at the start of 2016, it has been estimated that 'at least 10,000 unaccompanied child refugees have disappeared', some of whom are being sexually and economically exploited by criminal gangs.[324] These are shocking statistics and details and damning with regard to the region's more positive historic responses to child refugees.

The reasons for the departure of contemporary unaccompanied refugee children are immensely varied, as are their geographies, and collectively they do not fit the neat storylines that contemporaries constructed in the earlier case studies explored in this chapter. The suffering experienced, however, through trauma, violence, loss, and displacement, remains constant. But if there is a direction in these disturbing examples, it is a negative one that increasingly points towards the global placelessness of these children. There is a danger that, with regard to not only their treatment but also the memory and representation of them, they will become invisible.

Returning to historical geographer Doreen Massey and her reflections on places and their pasts with which this chapter opened:

> The description, definition and identification of a place is ... always inevitably an intervention not only into geography but also ... into the re(telling) of the historical constitution of the present. It is another move in the continuing struggle over the dilineation and characterisation of space-time.[325]

In this respect, the battle to restore the childhood of young forced migrants and to create a shared narrative of their experiences is also one to regain their (safe) place in the world. It is to bring past and present into dialogue in an attempt to ameliorate the grim prospects of the future.

---

323 Figures from UHNCR website, accessed 31 March 2015.
324 Mark Townsend, 'At least 10,000 refugee children "have vanished"', *Observer*, 31 January 2016.
325 Doreen Massey, 'Places and Their Pasts', *History Workshop Journal* no. 39 (Spring 1995), p. 190.

Chapter 4

The Ship and the Battle Over Migrant 'Illegality'

Space, Illegality, and Naming

How long have immigrants been labelled 'illegal'? To reappropriate Martin Luther King's words in Montgomery, Alabama: 'How long? Not long.' The slogan 'no one is illegal' has been taken up by pro-migrant groups, especially those campaigning on behalf of asylum-seekers and others detained or awaiting deportation in the West. It is used to highlight the common humanity of those placed beyond the law with regard to their national/ international status.[1] In this respect, the children's character Paddington Bear, who came to England as a stowaway on board a ship from 'Darkest Peru', has become 'amongst immigration lawyers a walking, talking, ursine pin-up for *humanising* our work'.[2] Yet had Paddington (who arrived in the London docks in the 1950s) come just half a century earlier, he would have had no need to enter as an 'illegal immigrant'. Indeed, until the late nineteenth century onwards (and especially since the First World War), the introduction of border controls, with concomitant legislation and state bureaucracy, linking the act of migration with legal legitimacy was largely unthinkable. If the idea of 'open borders' is now regarded as utopian (or dystopian, from a restrictionist's perspective), for the vast majority of human history it has been the natural order of the world.

In her *Excitable Speech: A Politics of the Performative*, Judith Butler refers to the 'jarring, even terrible, power of naming ... the power of the

---

1 See, for example, Steve Cohen, *Deportation is Freedom! The Orwellian World of Immigration Controls* (London: Jessica Kingsley, 2006), p. 10.
2 Colin Yeo, 1 December 2014, in https:///www.freemovement.org.uk, accessed 6 May 2015.

name to inaugurate and sustain linguistic existence, to confer singularity in location and time'. It is 'the vulnerability to being named [which] constitutes a constant condition of the speaking subject'.[3] Butler adds with regard to 'hate speech' that

> Clearly, injurious names have a history, one that is invoked and reconsolidated at the moment of utterance ... The name has ... a *historicity*, what might be understood as the history which has become internal to a name, has come to constitute the contemporary meaning of a name.

It is the 'sedimentation of its usages ... a repetition that congeals, that gives the name its force'.[4]

In the case of 'illegal immigration' or 'illegal immigrants', the terminology is relatively new – it came into bureaucratic use during the 1930s. Once coined, however, it developed its own life beyond the time and place of its origins, thereafter gaining momentum. And, if its linguistic coinage owed much to the unique situation of Britain's Palestinian Mandate and, within it, a specific local colonial crisis, it had predecessors in Western countries of immigration. These can be identified, for example, among those who aimed to stop the entry of 'undesirable aliens' to Britain or likewise Americans seeking protection against 'the scourings of foreign disease, pauperism and crime'.[5] What such descriptions had in common was the *de-humanising* of migrants. As *Public Opinion*, an American journal, warned during the 1880s, when local nativism was growing in strength, there had been 'an invasion of venomous reptiles' representing 'Europe's human and inhuman rubbish'.[6]

The designation 'illegal immigrant' was novel, therefore, but it drew upon an evolving tradition of xenophobic and racist discourse. In Butler's words, 'no term or statement can function performatively without the accumulating and dissimulating historicity of force'.[7] When, immediately after the First World War, a handful of aliens landed in Britain without permission, the London *Evening Standard* warned against it being the beginning of a 'huge influx of undesirables from Eastern Europe'. Britain had no room for 'parasitic citizenship'.[8] What the Home Office then labelled

---

3   Judith Butler, *Excitable Speech: A Politics of the Performative* (New York: Routledge, 1997), pp. 29–30.

4   Ibid., p. 36.

5   John Higham, *Strangers in the Land: Patterns of American Nativism 1860–1925* (New York: Atheneum, 1978), p. 52.

6   Ibid., p. 55.

7   Butler, *Excitable Speech*, p. 51.

8   *Evening Standard*, 23 February 1920.

the 'illicit traffic in aliens' would, in a colonial context, seamlessly become branded as the crime of organised illegal immigration.[9]

What *was* innovative during and immediately after the Nazi era was the type of location where the struggles over migrant restriction took place. It has been suggested by Matthew Gibney that in the twenty-first century the implementation of immigration controls has shifted in location – and significantly so:

> The traditional view of entrance as something operated at the state's borders, train stations and airports by domestic immigration officials increasingly appears quaint and outdated. It is now *beyond* the boundaries of the state, on the high seas, in foreign countries, or in vaguely defined territories (like Australia's excised zones) that exclusion from admission occurs.[10]

This chapter will conclude with an examination of the often catastrophic journeys that 'irregular migrants' are taking across the oceans in the twenty-first century – the responses to which closely fit Gibney's paradigm. But what he calls 'new places' of control can be identified much earlier.[11] They were created and employed by the British Palestinian authorities throughout the Nazi era – and then immediately after it – when dealing first with Jewish refugees and then survivors of the Holocaust. Ironically, they were largely implemented in a locus now infamous for tragic migrant journeys – the Mediterranean.

In Part 1 of this study, the secondary refugee journeys of those such as Hanna Spencer who came as domestic servants to Britain (as well as those whose parents did, such as Lore Segal), were documented. Michel Foucault's concept of 'different spaces' – heterotopias – was utilised to analyse the shift in their identity as they moved from 'old world' to 'new world'. Foucault posits that 'the ship is a piece of floating space, a placeless place, that lives by its own devices, that is self-enclosed and, at the same time, delivered over the boundless expanse of the ocean'. Not only is the 'sailing vessel is the heterotopia par excellence' it is 'the greatest reservoir of imagination'.[12]

---

9   National Archives, HO 144/1624/400005: William Haldane Porter to Mr Henderson, 29 December 1919.

10 Matthew Gibney, 'Beyond the bounds of responsibility: western states and measures to prevent the arrival of refugees', *Global Migration Perspectives* no. 22 (January 2005), p. 9. For comment on this observation, see Robert McKenzie and Alessandro Triulzi, 'Listening to Migrants' Narratives: An Introduction', in idem (eds), *Long Journey. African Migrants on the Road* (Leiden: Brill, 2013), p. 2.

11 Ibid., p. 4.

12 Michel Foucault, 'Different Spaces', in idem, *Aesthetics, Method, and Epistemology* (London: Allen Lane, 1998), pp. 184–185.

As will be noted in the major case studies of this chapter, twentieth- and twenty-first-century sea journeys by desperate migrants have often been likened (by those both sympathetic and unsympathetic to those undertaking them) to the 'Middle Passage' and the horrific world of transatlantic slavery. It is debatable whether the playfulness of Foucault's heterotopia, where in 'civilizations without ships the dreams dry up', is appropriate to describe the misery and loss of life of those in the twenty-first century who travel 'port to port' (or, frequently, fail to do so when their vessels sink).[13] Yet the concept of 'different spaces' – if employed more bleakly – *is* still potentially helpful. And it is so not only when considering political responses to migrants by sea and attempts to interrupt their movement but also in considering the perspectives of those trying to escape from war, oppression, and economic deprivation.

Returning to Judith Butler and her reflections on hate speech, while acknowledging that 'to be named by another is traumatic', she highlights how 'that trauma constitutes a strange kind of resource'. It is an 'act that precedes my will, an act that brings me into a linguistic world in which I might then begin to exercise agency … . A founding subordination, and yet the scene of agency' which leaves the future 'partially open'.[14] Power relations, developing Foucault, are thus crucial to her analysis. Thus, even if the state/authority/society/culture imposes a name, the oppressed subject, while restricted, can still use performative acts against it as a point of resistance. From there it can construct its identity more positively.

As will become apparent in the major case studies of this chapter, those attacked can attempt to diminish the force of negative naming by creating their own counter process of nomenclature. Thus Dalia Ofer notes: 'The variety of names given [to] illegal aliyah (immigration) [to Palestine] reflects its many facets.' From the Zionist perspective, these included:

> *ha'apala*, connoting surmounting obstacles to reach the high ground; aliyah bet – 'class B immigration' [as opposed to 'class A' which was approved by the Palestinian authorities] – to designate an underground operation; [and] 'independent' or 'special' aliyah – terms used to emphasize the positive validity of Jewish immigration to Palestine.[15]

Others challenged official discourse by referring to 'so-called illegal immigration'.[16] Whether or not this option of resistance through self-appellation is open for contemporary migrants in the Mediterranean

---

13   Ibid., p. 185.
14   Butler, *Excitable Speech*, p. 38.
15   Dalia Ofer, *Escaping the Holocaust: Illegal Immigration to the Land of Israel, 1939–44* (New York: Oxford University Press, 1990), p. v.
16   I.F. Stone, *Underground to Palestine* (London: Hutchinson, 1979 [orig. 1946]), p. 223.

– given their relative powerlessness – will be raised in the last substantive section of this chapter. Yet, even with those Jews attempting to reach Palestine during and after the Nazi era, *who* exercised authority has to be kept in mind. As Ofer concludes, there was one, final term to describe potential migrants to Palestine: 'illegal immigration – the preferred British designation'.[17] Indeed, the focus of this chapter will largely on where power rested – the (colonial) state apparatus.

The earlier chapters of *Journeys from the Abyss* have analysed in turn the freedom or otherwise of forced migrants to speak and then their attempts to (re-)establish a place called home. In this final chapter issues of narrative voice and of place will continue to be explored, but they will put alongside those of space and identity, all refracted through the politics of naming. It has been suggested that 'the name performs *itself*, and in the course of that performing becomes a thing done'.[18] The veracity of this observation will be tested throughout the discussion, exploring the role also of international bodies as well as the nation state and the agency of the migrants themselves.

The battles over migrant journeys – both physical and rhetorical – that took place and are taking place involved and involve both international law *and* military/humanitarian intervention. The labelling of the migrants concerned has been at the heart of such struggles. In juxtaposing the journeys from Nazism with contemporary 'boat people', and the memory and representation of them, the space for the migrants to represent and speak for themselves will not be ignored. Indeed, the discussion will be directed by studying the performativity of a wide range of historical actors, expressed through many different activities and articulated in a variety of media. Following Andrew Parker and Eve Kosofsky Sedgwick, who build on Derrida and Butler, performativity here is defined as 'the ways that identities are constructed iteratively through complex citational processes'.[19] The complexity in this case is particularly pronounced, reflecting, on the one hand, the many transnational contexts and, on the other, multiple narrative voices that interweave discourses from the ancient to the modern and from the religious to the secular.

---

17 Ibid.

18 Judith Butler summarising the work of J.L. Austin's *How to Do Things With Words* (1962) in her *Excitable Speech*, p. 44.

19 Andrew Parker and Eve Kosofsky Sedgwick, 'Introduction: Performativity and Performance', in idem (eds), *Performativity and Performance* (New York: Routledge, 1995), pp. 1–2.

Palestine and Jewish Refugees: The 1930s

The attempt of Jewish refugees to reach Palestine by sea before September 1939 has already been touched upon in the Introduction. It is a story, when compounded with the stories of those that tried to gain entry during and after the Second World War, that has become of mythical importance in the state of Israel itself and more generally across the Jewish diaspora. Told briefly, the narrative constructed empowers agency and heroism upon those that both undertook and organised these emotionally driven and increasingly desperate life-saving journeys. Inevitably it also casts those that opposed them – whether the local Arab population or the British Mandatory government – as villains of the piece. Thus in *The Secret Roads* (1954), one of the first historical overviews of 'illegal' Jewish immigration, Jon and David Kimche acknowledge that 'It was almost inevitable that in the course of the narrative the British should come off second best. The part of the hunter ... does not lend itself easily to sympathetic recapitulation.'[20] There is little space left for ambiguity among all the historical actors. The reality, however, is that the Jewish movement to Palestine during the 1930s was complicated by the origins of the migrants, the nature of their journeys, and the response of the British authorities and local population to them. And, as early as 1933, the politics of naming with this migrant movement was becoming a site of contestation in itself.

In 1920, as part of their new Mandatory powers bestowed upon them by the San Remo conference, the British authorities instituted the first Immigration Ordinance for Palestine. Clearly modelled on earlier alien legislation in Britain and elsewhere, it prohibited the entry of 'lunatics', those rejected on medical grounds, and criminals. The immigrant had to be in possession of a passport or permit endorsed by the British authorities.[21] The Ordinance was 'neutral' and did not specifically identify Jewish immigrants, but it was supplemented by a separate agreement that was made for those whose application was 'supported by the Zionist Organisation up to an agreed number'. They could 'receive visas from British Consular Officers throughout the world'. For these Jewish immigrants, possession of capital or the prospect of employment (both of which it was hoped would lead to self-sufficiency) was the key to the numbers to be let in: the Zionist Organisation (and later the Jewish Agency) was responsible for the maintenance of those it had approved.[22]

The aim was that those coming into Palestine would be productive

---

20 Jon and David Kimche, *The Secret Roads: The 'Illegal' Migration of a People 1938–1948* (London: Secker and Warburg, 1954), p. 13.

21 Details of the ordinance in *Jewish Chronicle*, 22 October 1920.

22 Mr Harmsworth, Under-Secretary of State for Foreign Affairs, in *Hansard* (HC) no. 133 col.1766, 27 October 1920.

immigrants in what was in effect (if not technically) part of the British empire – indicated by the early decision to pass bureacratic control from the Foreign to the Colonial Office. The needs of the country – as defined by the British authorities – were paramount in determining who would be allowed entry. In 1934, for example, Arthur Wauchope, the High Commissioner for Palestine, was asked by the leader of the Jewish Agency for fresh permits to be granted. Wauchope responded: 'by what ways could you make me feel assured that these would be the type of labourer we want most ... and at the same time most likely to be permanently absorbed?'[23] Also following the pattern of aliens legislation in the metropole itself and executed by the Home Secretary, the High Commissioner could arbitrarily prohibit from entry anyone he regarded as undesirable.[24]

If the 1920 Immigration Ordinance was produced in a moment of optimism by the British authorities in Palestine, as the interwar period progressed conflicting forces – local labour needs, Arab responses (including major unrest and violence in 1929 and 1936 to 1939), world Jewish opinion, and the need for new opportunities/asylum for persecuted and marginalised Jews – would increasingly reveal the fragility of the situation. A managed immigration policy at the will of volatile economic and political considerations was bound to be messy, inconsistent, and subject to rapid change.

But, as with the early years of the 1905 Aliens Act, it is an indication of the bureaucratic laxness of the early days of the 1920 Ordinance that it was not until 1926 that any measurement was made of Jewish emigration from Palestine. With the fluidity of Jewish movement in and out of Palestine, all numbers for the interwar period were regarded by officials in Whitehall as approximate, none more so than for the classification 'Jewish illegal immigrants'. In the words of the Colonial Office, by its 'very nature' this category was hard to quantify. When asked, for example, for statistics 'concerning the number of illegal Jewish immigrants' entering Palestine from 1919 to 1945, the Colonial Office emphasised that any figures were 'conjecture' and 'purely an estimate [which] cannot be regarded as an authentic official statement'.[25]

With Arab unease about the levels of Jewish immigration to Palestine continuing to grow, an attempt was made in November 1933 to tighten up procedures, especially for those without permits to work (including individuals who had entered on tourist visas, those who had married purely to gain entry, or whose permission to be in the country had lapsed). The number of people affected was small. Fewer than 100 Jews were deported from August to December 1933, which was just over half the corresponding

---

23 National Archives, CO 733/254/10: Wauchope to Shertok, 3 July 1934.
24 Mr Harmsworth, Under-Secretary of State for Foreign Affairs, in *Hansard* no. 133 col. 1766, 27 October 1920.
25 National Archives, CO 733/454/2: Minutes and drafts, December 1945.

figure for Arabs, whose immigration to Palestine was also increasing at this point.[26] It is revealing that the terminology to describe those whose paperwork was not in order still remained uncertain in the first year of Nazi power. Naming of them, however, was itself a source of controversy.

In late 1933, trying to assure the establishment leaders of British Jewry, including moderate Zionists, that the new measures were benign and would be implemented gently, the High Commissioner for Palestine and the Secretary of State for the Colonies emphasised how few were being affected. They also used a variety of terms to describe those who were being pursued. These included 'illegitimate immigrants',[27] 'illegal settlers',[28] and people engaged in 'illicit settlement'.[29] There was also some use of the phrase 'illegal immigrants', but this tended to focus on 'individuals illegally crossing the frontier and on tourists entering the country and remaining illegally there'.[30] Such reassurance was largely successful. The specific and occasional twinning of 'illegal' with 'immigrant' was not yet seen to be a major assault in word or deed by those supporting Jewish migration to Palestine. Indeed, Selig Brodetsky, the British Zionist leader, in a statement made at the 34th Annual Conference of the Zionist Federation held in London during December 1933, made light of its usage.

Brodetsky drew attention to the 'question of the so-called "illegal immigration"', but he was quick to minimise the significance of this coupling: 'This is one of those unfortunate phrases leading to misunderstanding.' It was not, he quietly corrected, '"illegal" immigration' but instead '"un-authorised settlement"'. Brodetsky conceded that the issue had been 'used against us in the last two months' – that was since November 1933. But, in consensual mode, he added that the British government had never forbidden visitors who then applied to stay. It was a 'perfectly regular procedure'. Recently, however, some Jewish migrants had opened up businesses or found jobs without obtaining the necessary paperwork. It was right that these people should be regularised and, if they did not have means to support themselves, be removed from the country.[31]

If there was tension over 'illegal immigration' then it was largely contained – even if some Zionists in Palestine itself, especially from the Revisionist right, objected to what they alleged were the initial heavy-handed methods that were used against those existing outside bureaucratic regulations. For the most part, the tightening up of procedures and their

26 National Archives, CO 733/255/5: Arthur Wauchope to Lord Reading, 12 January 1934.

27 Ibid.

28 National Archives, CO 733/255/5: A phrase used by Sir John Maffey, 29 January 1934.

29 National Archives, CO 733/255/5: Telegram from Wauchope, 22 January 1934.

30 National Archives, CO 733/255/5: Telegram, Secretary of State for the Colonies to Maffey, 8 January 1934.

31 National Archives, CO 733/255/5: Brodetsky statement, 25 December 1933.

implementation was handled discretely and sparingly. Nevertheless, albeit somewhat tentatively, the rhetorical device of linking 'illegality' to immigration had been established, resulting in some local police intervention. Over the next couple of years, with increased Jewish migration to Palestine from Germany (but more significantly from Eastern Europe and Iraq), and growing animosity from Palestinian Arabs, usage of the term would intensify and develop an increasingly conspiratorial tone: the words 'illegal' and 'immigrant' were now contiguous.

Although the issue was not a major source of controversy in 1934, in the following year Jewish immigration to Palestine was again causing concern to the British colonial authorities. And, by 1935, 'Jewish Illegal Immigration' had become bureaucratically standardised with capitalisation to ensure the firmness and certainty of this new label. It went alongside belief that it was in the form of organised 'traffic', as opposed to the spontaneous movement of individuals.[32] Detention pending deportation was now used by the British authorities as a more public act of deterrance, aiming to appease the local Arab population and showing that it was taking the 'problem' of Jewish immigration seriously. What was not yet set in the construction of an official British discourse defining 'illegality' was the type and place of Jewish journeys being undertaken.

With Biblical and classical textual precedents, journeying over sea has mythical importance for migrants and those responding to them. For the forcibly displaced, including refugees, the Exodus story has particular symbolic significance and meaning. To work more generally, such a narrative requires a particular place of persecution and a difficult journey (both physically and spiritually) to the 'Promised Land'. If the Jewish flight from Egypt was, as is quipped, executed as 'Red Sea pedestrians', it is the ship in Jewish and Christian tradition, especially the latter, that is linked more powerfully in evoking the notion of the escape to freedom and prosperity. More recently, in a world of international control of migration and the desperation of those trying to escape it, (aside from crossing oceans) hiding in or under lorries, container vessels, and trains has become the dominant form of 'illegal' movement. It is represented negatively by most of the media and sympathetically only by a small number of film directors, artists, and playwrights who recognise the humanity and individuality of those undertaking these often lethal migrations.[33]

In this respect, some of the migrant journeys to Palestine worrying British officialdom in 1935 do not fit easily into such narrative expectations: they were not especially dangerous (but would become so several years

---

32 National Archives, CO 733/276/6: Wauhope to J.H. Thomas, Principal Secretary of State for the Colonies, 9 December 1935.

33 See the excellent cultural analysis provided by David Farrier, *Postcolonial Asylum: Seeking Sanctuary Before the Law* (Liverpool: Liverpool University Press, 2011).

later) and they were by car across easily crossed borders. Furthermore, these Jews were not escaping Nazi persecution but increasing intolerance and diminished economic opportunities elsewhere, including beyond Europe. First were those from Arab lands who were entering Iraq through its eastern frontier and then progressing to Palestine.[34] Second were Jews from Eastern Europe – mainly Poland but also Rumania and Hungary, countries where state discrimination and popular violence against Jews was growing throughout the 1930s. These migrants travelled to Turkey, then Syria via train and from there to Palestine. It was the view of the High Commissioner that both these types of movement were organised and involved 'smugglers'.[35]

At this stage German Jewish immigration to Palestine was, in contrast, largely 'legal' and not of particular concern to the British authorities. Thus by December 1935, of 139 detained 'illegal Jewish immigrants pending deportation', only two were of German nationality.[36] In turn, these measures prompted hunger strikes from those imprisoned in the notorious Acre gaol. The High Commissioner wanted firmness, fearing that, if those detained were released, 'such deterrent measures against illegal immigration ... will be largely stultified'.[37] Some within the Colonial Office were more cautious, anticipating a critique of immigration detention policies that has been made ever since. An official minuted that while the actions of the 'illegal' immigrants had caused some of the problems, the length of detention was unjustifiable. To him, '8 months appears unduly long'.[38]

This study opened with the Royal Commission on Palestine, which began its work in 1936, marking the increasing dilemma the British authorities faced in satisfying both Jewish and Arab demands over the territory and migration to it. Jews from many different parts of Europe and the Middle East were attempting to enter Palestine. Arab unrest was growing and again becoming violent. What especially annoyed some senior officials in the Colonial Office was that, while the Commission's *Report* recommended stricter numerical controls of Jewish movement to Palestine, it included a section on the 'legalization of illegal immigrants'.[39] H.F. Downie, Head of its Middle Eastern Department, was outraged to find that this heading was included in a 'list of proposals for the *prevention* of illegal immigration'. Downie added that 'One would have supposed that legalization could

34 National Archives, CO 733/276/6: Wauhope to Thomas, 9 December 1935.
35 National Archives, CO 733/276/6: 'Memoranda: Illegal Immigration into Palestine', December 1935.
36 National Archives, CO 733/276/6: Wauhope to Thomas, 12 December 1935.
37 National Archives, CO 733/276/6: Wauchope telegram to Secretary of State for the Colonies, 17 February 1935.
38 National Archives, CO 733/276/6: H. Morgan minute, 3 May 1935.
39 Secretary of State for the Colonies, *Palestine: Statement of Policy* (Cmd. 5513, London: HMSO, 1937), pp. 289–290.

only encourage the entry of more illegal immigrants'. He pressed for stronger measures of deportation, as legalization 'would only increase the exasperation of the Arabs'. Downie realised that the removal of those Jews who had been in Palestine longer without the correct paperwork 'would raise equal difficulties'. Nevertheless, he urged 'resist[ance against] Jewish pressure for early action'.[40]

Of particular concern to leading Zionists in 1937 were the cases of 'illegal' immigrants who were not allowed to 'bring their wives and children into Palestine'. Downie stated that 'I must confess that I cannot feel much sympathy with them. They entered Palestine knowing that they were breaking the law.' It was 'open to them, if they wish to rejoin their families, to go back to Poland or whatever country they came from'. Downie thus rejected what he called the 'sob stuff' coming from prominent Zionist leaders – a phrase that queried the reality of Jewish persecution in Europe.[41]

The Introduction to this study emphasised the need to avoid hindsight and with it the teleological distortion of the Holocaust's inevitability – that is, viewing 1933 from the prism of Auschwitz. When, in December 1942, Downie's counterpart in the Foreign Office, J.S. Bennett (who had earlier been a colleague of his in the Colonial Office), minuted that he was concerned that the new Colonial Secretary, Oliver Stanley, was taking 'Jewish Agency "sob stuff" at its face value', the context had shifted markedly, while the peculiar and insensitive language remained the same.[42]

The information reaching the Western Allies about the implementation of the 'Final Solution' was, by late 1942, both extensive and authoritative. Stanley's supposed generosity related to the intended rescue of a small number of Jewish children in risk of being sent 'East'.[43] In 1937 the situation was not so dire for the Jewish men whom Downie wanted to deport back to Eastern Europe. Even so, antisemitism through state discrimination and public violence was becoming part of everyday life, especially for the Jews of Poland and Romania. Downie, however, had constructed a narrative about Jewish immigration to Palestine that was to be persistent among many of his fellow senior civil servants in both the Foreign and Colonial Offices – the key departments alongside the Palestinian authorities in this question. He had promoted an unusual but powerful form of 'hate speech' to undermine any Jewish claims of 'deserving' victim status.

During the early stages of the war, responding to Zionist criticism of Britain's handling of Palestine and questions of immigration, Downie

---

40 National Archives, CO 733/331/3: Downie minute, 16 October 1937.
41 National Archives, CO 733/331/3: Downie minute, 26 October 1937.
42 National Archives, FO 921/10: Minute 7 December 1942.
43 Ibid.

minuted in March 1940 that 'This sort of thing makes one regret that the Jews are not on the other side in this war.'[44] A year later, a more sympathetic Foreign Office official noted in exasperation, responding to yet another paranoid paper by Downie, that it could only be understood by taking into account 'Mr Downie's inward and spiritual conviction that illegal immigration is only the outward and visible sign of a world-wide scheme to overthrow the British Empire.'[45] By the middle to late 1930s attempts were being made to organise Jewish immigration to Palestine outside the quota system by both mainstream and Revisionist Zionist bodies. Yet, rather than ad hoc responses to the increasing vulnerability of Jews in Eastern and Central Europe, Colonial Office officials were convinced that it was something more sinister relating to the power, rather than the powerlessness, of the Jewish world. And, as with anti-alienism in the Metropole from the 1880s to the 1920s, the greatest animus of British officialdom was reserved for the *ostjuden* who were seen as undesirable and dangerous immigrants. It was a fear that persisted throughout the Nazi era and beyond.

In January 1938 the Colonial Office wrote to Wauchope that 'The pressure from Eastern Europe is steadily increasing.' With the offending paragraphs of the Royal Commission *Report* in mind, it emphasised again that deterrence was the only answer: 'undoubtedly the main factor which keeps illegal immigration to its present level is the knowledge of the disabilities which beset the illegal immigrant.' There was, if somewhat perversely, an awareness that the situation in Poland and Romania with increasing discrimination against the Jews 'might ultimately render immigration uncontrollable'. A firm hand was thus needed before the situation worsened and, with it, the chances of Arab cooperation. It was also feared that opening the doors to Palestine would only further encourage the Polish and Romanian governments to get rid of their unwanted Jewish populations.[46] By then, rather than the muddled storylines of diverse illegal immigration journeys that had been constructed in mid-decade, a clear narrative had emerged in the official mind. It placed the emphasis solely on arrival by ships chartered to take Jews to Palestine and which were part of an international financial and political racket.

In summer 1939 the Colonial Office produced an extensive departmental paper on 'Illegal Jewish Immigration'.[47] It was prompted to do so by hostile press coverage, especially in America, of the Palestinian authorities and its

---

44 Quoted by Bernard Wasserstein, *Britain and the Jews of Europe 1939–1945* (Oxford: Clarendon Press, 1979), p. 50.

45 R.T.E. Latham minute, 27 April 1941 quoted in ibid.

46 National Archives, CO 733/364/4: Orsmby Gore to Wauchope, 13 January 1938.

47 National Archives, CO 733/394/3: 'Palestine. Notes in Illegal Jewish Immigration', July 1939.

treatment of those trying to reach its shores by boat and, more generally, in relation to the British government's 1939 White Paper, which set a maximum of 75,000 Jewish immigrants for the next five years.[48] In June 1939, for example, the *New York Times* covered the story of a 'Greek cattle boat', the *Liesl*, which carried 906 Jewish refugees from Poland, Romania, Germany, and Czechoslovakia, including 300 women and 60 children. While they had been allowed to land, their numbers were to be deducted from the official Jewish immigration quota. Exempting the British soldiers and police from criticism in their treatment of this 'human contraband', the animus of the article was against higher officialdom:

> Destitute refugees forced to leave their homes in Central and Eastern Europe seek any haven they may possibly enter. In desperation they board unseaworthy cargo and cattle boats bound for Palestine, where most of them have relatives willing to care for them but [are] prevented by restrictions laid down by the Palestine Government.[49]

While the Colonial Office shared the view that the vessels involved were dangerous and the conditions on board horrific, it was deeply concerned that the British government's perspective was being derided as inhuman by the outside world. Indeed, it was warned by the Palestinian intelligence services that 'The danger of Illegal Immigration being used as a political weapon with the sympathy and resources of World Jewry behind it cannot be too strongly stressed.'[50] To counter this possibility, the Colonial Office paper began by emphasising that 'An intensive campaign of attempted illegal immigration into Palestine is now under way.' It recognised that 'Reports of the adventures of ships engaged in this traffic have considerable news value', but expressed the frustration that they 'usually contrive to slur over the essential point that these people are knowingly trying to evade the law of Palestine'.[51]

The 1939 Colonial Office paper set the template for what would be an even more intensive performative struggle over the rights and wrongs of immigration policy in Palestine. Like many defending immigration controls before and after, emphasis was placed on 'the interests of the inhabitants' as against the 'entry of myriads of immigrants' who would, unless stopped, 'flood the country indiscriminately' through 'mass invasion'. Control of illegal immigration was especially necessary in Palestine, which was 'only about the size of a small county in New York State'. Against this reality,

48 *Palestine: Statement of Policy* (Cmd. 6019, London: HMSO, 1939).
49 Joseph Levy, '900 Seized in Palestine', *New York Times*, 2 June 1939.
50 National Archives, CO 733/396/5: Palestinian CID report, 17 May 1939.
51 National Archives, CO 733/394/3: 'Palestine. Notes in Illegal Jewish Immigration', July 1939.

'The idea is fostered by Jewish circles that they are justified in trying to break the law by virtue of some super-legal higher morality'. Jews did this by citing the persecutions in Greater Germany and 'the desperate plight in which many European Jews now find themselves'. But, playing into a Semitic discourse of selfishness, criminality, and insularity, the paper highlighted how Jews were 'thinking only of themselves, and fail to realise that what they are doing is fundamentally anti-social'. And, no doubt revealing the influence of Downie, who was one of the paper's main authors, it continued that it was in fact 'as anti-social as the German persecution of which they complain'.[52]

While it was true that conditions on board the ships were 'miserable', and that the ships were 'old and small, grossly overcrowded, and short of provisions and medical supplies', it was, argued the Colonial Office, 'necessary to be clear about one thing. This illegal immigration traffic is a dirty, sordid, crooked business.' Moreover, in relation to the morality of the issue, it had to be

> remembered [that] by no means all the intended illegal immigrants are refugees. A considerable number of them come from countries such as Poland and Rumania, and cannot plead that they are driven by desperation and have no alternative but to make the attempt to get into Palestine illegally.[53]

There were other voices within government circles that queried such assumptions about the motives for such Jewish migrant undertaking these journeys to Palestine. Closer to the ground was R.D. Macrae, the British Consul in Galatz, Romania, who had investigated the role of Greeks involved in the commercial venture of Jewish illegal immigration. Unlike those in the Colonial Office, Macrae recognised the dire circumstances of the Jews of both Central *and* Eastern Europe, who were 'either persecuted or living in fear of persecution'. Using a historical analogy that would be amplified after 1945 with regard to 'illegal' Jewish immigration, Macrae argued that 'This trade is, in fact, one of the most brutal that has been devised since the abolition of slave-trading, and is particularly reprehensible as it is based on the exploitation of misery.' These pirate vessels and their conditions, he added, 'outrage not only all the clauses of the Convention for the Safety of Life at Sea, but every law of human decency'.[54]

Such alternative perspectives were largely ignored and ridiculed by the Colonial Office, including the 'rather surprising suggestion [made by a diplomat] that a number of Jewish illegal immigrants should be admitted to

---

52 Ibid.
53 Ibid.
54 National Archives, CO 733/394/3: Macrae to Bucharest Embassy, 17 June 1939.

Palestine on humanitarian grounds'.[55] Instead, the High Commissioner and the Colonial Office spent their energies in vilifying the illegal immigrants. In the words of Wauchope, in summer 1939 there was an 'uncontrolled spate of immigrants of doubtful antecedents at the expense of more deserving cases'.[56]

In 1939, to act as a deterrent and to defuse tension in Palestine, the Colonial Office also explored the possibility of implementing a policy of 'Disposal of Illegal Immigrants'. The Secretary of State mooted the idea of finding an 'island or other suitable place (either in British territory or to be leased from a foreign Power) where they could be maintained temporarily pending their absorption as refugee settlers elsewhere'.[57] So animated were these officials that it was only the economics rather than the morality of this solution that stopped it being pursued rigorously. It was not, however, totally dismissed as a possibility: the 'disposal' of 'illegal' immigrants was to return to the agenda and be implemented during the war and immediately after it.

Meanwhile, all effort was made by the new interdepartmental committee on 'Jewish Illegal Immigration' (a symbol itself of the speed with which this term had become bureaucratically regularised and prioritised) to halt the flow of Jewish migrants at source.[58] If this failed, the next tactic was to stop at sea all ships inside territorial waters around the Palestinian coast. With regards to the last mentioned, the committee acknowledged the problem of exceeding the three-mile limit imposed by international law. It referred, however, to the recent example of the United States during Prohibition and the searching and seizing of vessels on the high seas to push the boundaries of control. Again this historical analogy reinforced the criminality of this migration – in terms of both the organisers and their human 'cargo'. With the example of Prohibition clearly in mind, those organising the trade in illegal immigration were described by British officialdom as 'Jew-runners' engaged in 'Jew-running'. It was another example of newly forged hate speech based on long-standing discourse. It was, as with the smuggling of alcohol across borders, regarded as an essentially criminal racket importing undesirable goods which would bring only harm to the receiving society.[59] The parallels with contemporary boat migrants will be explored later. At this stage it is simply necessary to highlight how closely responses to Jewish

---

55 National Archives, CO 733/364/5: Downie to Downing Street, 25 July 1938.

56 National Archives, CO 733/364/5: Telegram to the Secretary of State for the Colonies, 5 July 1939.

57 National Archives, CO 733/364/5: Memorandum, 'Disposal of Illegal Immigrants', 12 July 1939.

58 This Committtee was dissolved in October 1947. See National Archives, ADM 1/20685.

59 National Archives, CO 733/364/5: Committee on Illegal Immigration, 10 July 1939.

refugees at sea some 80 years earlier follow the same pattern of negative naming and criminalisation.

Even as late as 1939, what was still largely missing was any bureaucratic recognition of the increasing desperation of Jewish migrants in Europe. It has been noted that, up to the mid-1930s, the number of 'illegal' Jews entering Palestine from Germany was mimimal. By the outbreak of war, however, over 70 per cent of all 'illegal' immigrants were from Greater Germany. In 1938 and 1939 some 40,000 Jews reached Palestine, just over 17,000 of whom were categorised as 'illegal'. To put this in perspective, the number of 'illegal' immigrants for the whole period from 1920 to the end of the Second World War was only twice that number. The Revisionist Zionists were responsible for organising the large majority of German and Austrian Jews and the mainstream Zionists those from the East.[60]

For the Palestinian authorities and the Colonial Office, having to their own satisfaction dispensed with the ethics of the question, 'illegal' immigration became a matter simply to be policed through military and security measures. Colonial Office files from 1938 through to 1948 are thus dominated by intelligence reports listing ship movements and their attempted journeys to Palestine. Routes, funding, ownership of vessels, and numbers and types of Jews on board were described with reflections only on how they could be stopped or diverted. In this respect, they have a surface resemblance to later Zionist accounts such as the semi-official *Haapala: Clandestine Immigration 1931-1948* (published first in Hebrew and then English by the Israeli Ministry of Defence and the Israel Defense Forces Museum in 1987), which catalogues boat journeys in chronological order.[61]

Where these rival narratives fundamentally part company is in how these journeys were interpreted. *Illegality* – from the ownership of the vessels, the tickets sold, and, of course, the arrival in Palestine – dominated Colonial Office descriptions. But, from the Zionist perspective, the emphasis was placed on persecution as the main impulse to migration: there was no choice for those attempting to reach Palestine before the war. 'Unless as many Jews as possible emigrated to Palestine the outcome would be tragic.' And, because the crisis was, by the mid-1930s, so intense, 'The conclusion was obvious – clandestine immigration had to be organized.' Moreover, it was more than a pragmatic solution in the search for a place of asylum: 'For these immigrants the Land of Israel represented the final haven of refuge after escape or expulsion from Europe over which gathered the clouds of the approaching storm.'[62]

60 Figures from Ofer, *Escaping the Holocaust*, pp. vii, 14.
61 Mordechai Naor, *Haapala: Clandestine Immigration 1931–1948* (Tel Aviv: Ministry of Defence Publishing House, 1987).
62 Ibid., pp. 3, 7.

In Israeli/Zionist accounts, the agency of Jews was emphasised by focusing on collective action controlled from above. The result is that 'illegal' immigration has been presented in such memory work in a top-down form, downplaying the role and personal testimony of the individual beyond the organisers of this movement. Thus the 'heroes of this "army" were the tens of thousands of anonymous immigrants – men, women and children who fought for their right to immigrate into Palestine. But the "army" needed leaders to guide and direct it.'[63] In contrast, the immigrants were depicted in official British discourse as (at best) naive victims of racketeers exploiting their situation for financial or ideological gain or (more often) criminals and chancers who were denying genuine refugees the chance to get to Palestine legitimately through the British quota system.

For very different reasons, therefore, contemporary documentation tends to silence the ordinary refugee journeying to Palestine. As with contemporary foreign domestic workers, when these migrants speak, they 'perform' within legal/security processes instituted by those hostile to them or, alternatively, through narrow statements of victimhood reproduced by those more sympathetic to their cause. A letter from a young Romanian Jew from Bukovina to his parents, which was subsequently published in the *New York Times*, reflects the latter tendency: it reads as a collective account with no attempt made to convey his own feelings or any sense of intimacy with his mother and father. The author, whose identity is kept anonymous, finally arrived in Palestine in mid-June 1939 following a journey that had started some four months earlier.[64]

His letter describes how he was one of 40 young Romanian Jews attempting to reach Palestine. They assembled first in Bucharest, joining a larger number of Polish Jews and travelling to Greece, where their ship sank as a result of the captain's negligence – this was no doubt the *Chepo*, referred to by Abba Eban mistakenly as the *Capo* in the first paragraphs of this study and as the *Gippo* in other accounts.[65] They were then transferred to another vessel (the *Katina*) carrying an even larger group of Jews, in this case Czechoslovakian: 'These unfortunate people had been on the sea for seven weeks, had had to fight with illness and were full of vermin. Besides they had no more food on board.' Now numbering 1200 people, they travelled to Crete and from there to the shores of Palestine, where roughly half the passengers – children, women, and the elderly – were landed. An attempt the next night to land the remaining passengers was repelled by the coast guards, who fired on the ship. It returned to Greece in a journey lasting another week. Eventually they were landed in Palestine but intercepted and taken to Haifa, where some were arrested and then

---

63 Ibid., p. 55.
64 'Road of Refugees to Palestine Hard', *New York Times*, 2 July 1939.
65 Naor, *Haapala*, pp. 19–20.

released, it was suggested, only after the intervention of a kindly British police official.[66]

The article emphasised the sheer misery of this tortuous journey. It was framed as such by the *New York Times* with its stark title: 'Road of Refugees to Palestine Hard'. While its subheading described him as an 'illegal emigrant', reflecting the strength of British colonial discourse, there was no doubting where the readers' sympathies should lie. The account 'tells of woes and suffering of hundreds at sea in crowded ships. Without food for days'.[67] The assumption is that no-one would undertake such a haphazard and dangerous journey unless forced to so by their dire circumstances. Even so, there is no background given to the individual who had penned the account or to his fellow Jewish passengers – whether they be Romanian, Polish, or Czechoslovakian. In contrast, Colonial Office files represent those on board the *Chepo* either as numbers[68] or simply as 'illegals' encouraged to leave by their country of birth: 'their passports are not in order [and the] Roumanian authorities have not effectively hindered embarkation'.[69]

And, while they are sometimes named, the exclusive focus on the journey to Palestine is true of the small number of Jewish migrants interviewed or interrogated by the British authorities during the late 1930s and the Second World War. These include the statement of an anonymous Jew who is simply described by the Palestinian intelligence services as an 'illegal immigrant who entered Palestine on 30 [November 1938]'. He/she describes travelling with a party of 560 Jews from Vienna, first on small boats up the Danube to Budapest and then to Galatz in Romania. They then went on board the *Geller* with provisions for only 15 days. The chaotic nature of these journeys on boats (which were elderly, unsuited to passenger usage, and often with inadequate supplies of food, water, and medical supplies) was true of the *Geller*. The irregularity of these vessels was also manifest in their random naming, sometimes changed to avoid detection by the Palestinian authorities but often reflecting their decayed state and frequent changes of ownership. The anonymous informant helpfully added for the benefit of the Palestinian intelligence services that 'I believe the [*Geller*] to be now [the] *Marsalla*'.[70]

The first attempt to land in Palestine was aborted as a smaller transfer boat failed to turn up. After days with the ship floating between Rhodes and Cyprus, they were moved to another vessel carrying what he/she described as 'the second part of the consignment of illegal immigrants

66 'Road of Refugees to Palestine Hard'.
67 Ibid.
68 National Archives, CO 733/396/5: Intelligence report 27 February 1939.
69 National Archives, CO 733/394/1: Telegram of Sir R. Hoare, British Embassy in Bucharest, 24 February 1939.
70 Undated statement in ibid.

from Vienna'. This time they were greeted and they arrived on the beach in Netanya via rowing boats, 'ten persons in each'.[71] Close to 1200 Jews from Vienna arrived in Palestine through the journeys described by the informant but no indication is given of their specific background. Instead, it is the details of how the journey was organised that interested the Palestinian authorities. The testimony was performed by the informant to meet this desire. Anxious to please, the person making it – who presumably had been arrested on arrival – conveniently did not even query the badge of 'illegal immigrant'. Moreover, by focusing on the mechanics of the journeys – who was organising and paying for them, the ship owners, and the attitude of the countries that were part of this trade – the motives of the masses taking part in them were completely sidelined.[72]

In May 1939 an intelligence report noted briefly that the refugees had 'literally "nothing to lose"' in undertaking these difficult and dangerous journeys. Even then, this rare insight was a prelude to a longer diatribe against those responsible for organising them, who, it alleged, were motivated by 'the prospect of financial gain' or the possibility of making political and financial profit for their own [Zionist] party'. While the 'genuine desire to assist refugees' was mentioned, it was clearly not regarded as possessing much credence compared with the other two factors.[73]

The Second World War

With the outbreak of war and the fast-deteriorating situation of European Jewry, the discourse of the Colonial Office on 'illegal' immigration not only persisted but intensified in its animosity. Indeed, the conflict allowed ever more conspiratorial aspects to develop. The belief that the Nazis were encouraging such migration to cause maximum damage and embarrassment to the British in the Arab world was given fresh impetus. It was therefore suggested that there were Nazi agents among the Jewish migrants who were now not only illegal but also 'enemy aliens'. Bennett wrote in June 1940 after the entry of Italy into the war that 'the boats with illegal immigrants run risks [to us] far greater than before'.[74] The German government, he added a few weeks later, was largely behind this 'traffic' and they were no doubt doing so with the aim of 'securing the infiltration of Fifth Columnists'. This last phrase was underlined by his fellow Colonial Office colleagues and became a standard feature of the Department's argument against any liberalisation of immigration entry. It was, he added, 'of greater importance

---

71 Ibid.

72 Ibid.

73 National Archives, CO 733/396/5: CID report, Jerusalem, report on the 'Organization of Illegal Immigration', 17 May 1939.

74 National Archives, CO 733/429/1: Luke minute, 20 June 1940.

than any other aspect of the question, and we cannot afford to let any humanitarian considerations stand in the way of measures dictated by the most imperative security considerations'.[75]

Increasing emphasis was placed on deterrent but, rather than detention in Palestine, officials believed that using other territories, especially within the British Empire, could now be employed – the more unattractive the better. Bennett explored the various options for transferring 'illegal' immigrants arriving in Palestine elsewhere. In the recent past, the idea of sending them to 'tropical African territories' had been 'dropped on climatic grounds' and to neighbouring Cyprus because of local political considerations. Sending them to Britain was ruled out because of difficulties of transport as well as there being, it was alleged, too many aliens in Britain already. Indeed, with regard to the last possibility, Bennett's colleague Stephen Luke, whose hostility to Jewish immigrants was even stronger, annotated Bennett's minute with the aside 'I can think of nothing to commend it!'[76]

The High Commissioner for Palestine wanted to pursue the possibility of sending them to Australia and Bennett regarded this as the best option, adding a punitary twist to this possibility. He suggested that anyone landing illegally in Palestine would be imprisoned for five years 'followed by Deportment [*sic*] to Queensland'. Echoing an earlier colonial mindset, Bennett suggested that the promoters of 'illegal' immigration and the captains of the ships should be sent to Australia for 'penal servitude and hard labour'.[77] Not to be outdone, Luke added a comment that, while extreme, typified the overall Colonial Office view of how these Jewish migrants, especially now in wartime, should be regarded and treated:

> I cannot see why tropical countries should be ruled out on grounds of health: if these people wittingly set out to break our laws they must take their chances of where they are sent to. They have a simple issue ... to stay at home [or not]. Unless they know they will be sent to a disagreeable place they [will not] be discouraged.[78]

It would be easy to dismiss these minutes as irritated senior civil servants letting off steam, but the infamous cases of the *Patria* and the *Struma* in the war reflect how the impulse behind them could tragically be put into practice. The stories of these ships have been told many times before,[79] but

---

75 National Archives, CO 733/429/1: Luke minute, 24 September 1940.
76 Ibid.
77 Ibid.
78 National Archives, CO 733/429/1: Luke minute, 30 September 1940.
79 See Artur Patek, *Jews on Route to Palestine 1934–1944: sketches from the history of Aliyah Bet: clandestine Jewish immigration* (Krakow: Jagiellonian University Press,

will be covered again briefly, as they were integral to the wider narrative of 'illegal' immigration. Looking back, they represented a new stage in the official animosity to 'illegal immigration' that had developed throughout the 1930s. And, looking forwards, the notoriety of these ships provided an outlet for propaganda against the British in war and post-war Zionist rhetoric. The fate of the two ships was also at the forefront of official thinking with regard to Britain's international reputation. As the flow of 'illegal' Jewish immigration increased early in 1946, it was noted that 'Both the Colonial Office and the Government of Palestine have unfortunate memories of the "Struma" and "Patria" incidents and the storm of world-wide protests and internal disturbance which was their outcome.'[80]

Although there was a flurry of 'illegal' immigration to Palestine in the first months of war, the flow slowed down by summer 1940 only to pick up again in the autumn – much to the concern of the High Commissioner and Colonial Office. Inevitably the journeys, on increasingly unsafe vessels in a time of total war, became more and more dangerous and the conditions within them appalling. Two such ships – the *Milos* and the *Pacific* – arrived early in November 1940 carrying around 1800 Jews from Greater Germany between them. Sticking to the deterrent/punishment plan, the decision was made to transfer them to the island of Mauritius in the Indian Ocean on a larger vessel, the *Patria*. A third ship, the *Atlantic*, with roughly 1800 on board, arrived later, even though it had set off before the other two. Horribly overcrowded, it anchored first in Crete and then ran out of fuel on the way to Cyprus. It has been noted in relation to its condition: 'After a time the *Atlantic* recalled a metal shell rather than a real ship.'[81] The disabled ship, in which seven of its passengers had died of typhus, was towed by the British Navy into Cyprus and from there 'under British naval escort, [it] set off for Haifa'.[82] On arrival, transfer of its passengers to the *Patria* began but was largely incomplete before disaster struck.

While all the Zionists within Palestine were united in their disgust at the move to deport those on board, moderates and militants were in disagreement over the tactics to be employed against the authorities. Some in the *Haganah* (the Jewish military underground movement in Palestine) wanted a decisive response and on 25 November 1940 a bomb that had been planted earlier was detonated with the intention of immobilising the *Patria*. The planned explosion led to calamity – the ship sank rapidly. Roughly 200 immigrants out of the 1900 on board and 50 British crew drowned.[83]

2012), chapter 5; Ofer, *Escaping the Holocaust*, pp. 31–39; Wasserstein, *Britain and the Jews of Europe*, pp. 67–73, 143–157.

80 National Archives, CO 537/1794: Mathieson minute, 26 March 1946.
81 Patek, *Jews on Route*, p. 116.
82 Ibid., p. 118.
83 Ibid.

Before the sinking of the *Patria* and the arrival of the *Atlantic*, the Jewish Agency had urged that the men, women, and children from the *Milos* and *Pacific*, a 'considerable proportion of whom' had been in concentration camps, should be allowed to stay in Palestine. To turn such refugees away, it pleaded, 'would be a measure of inhumanity'.[84] After the explosion, the British Cabinet decided not to deport the survivors of the ship to Mauritius, justified as a 'special act of clemency'. This was not, however, a recognition of their persecution in Europe, but 'having regard to the sufferings which these immigrants had undergone in the S.S. PATRIA'.[85] This clemency did *not* extend to the passengers on board the *Atlantic* who had avoided being transferred. Instead, they were to be deported to Mauritius for the remainder of the war.[86]

Five of the Jewish survivors gave evidence to the *Patria* Commission set up by the British government in January 1941. Their testimony did not dominate the proceedings – there were 58 witnesses in all – and, as with the earlier migrant from the *Geller*, it focused purely on the ships they travelled in and the routes undertaken as 'illegal immigrants'.[87] By then, and in the light of the *Patria* and investigations of the passengers on board all three ships, the Foreign Office began to fundamentally query the Colonial Office and its claim – without any supporting evidence – that enemy agents were arriving on 'illegal immigrant ships'.[88] Downie responded that, while no such cases had been found, 'illegal immigration [was itself] a conspiracy against the declared policy of His Majesty's Government and against the law of Palestine'. He added that the 'deportation policy now in force is but the climax of a series of preventive measures which have grown increasingly severe as the difficulties of suppressing the traffic became apparent'.[89]

The ending of Nazi emigration policy towards the Jews in autumn 1941 and the move towards the 'Final Solution', alongside restricted routes of escape, inevitably limited the number of Jews able to reach the shores of Palestine. The cases of the *Salvador* and the *Struma* reflected this harsh reality for European Jewry. The *Salvador*, formerly the SS *Tzar Krum*, carried around 350 Jews mainly from Bulgaria and it set off from Varna in December 1940. Unseaworthy, it was wrecked not long into its journey, with 'over two hundred of the passengers drowned. Among the dead were seventy children.' Bernard Wasserstein in his pioneer account of Britain and the Holocaust quotes the head of the Foreign Office Refugee Section in

84 National Archives, CO 733/429/1: 'Refugee Ships in Palestine', 12 November 1940.

85 National Archives, FO 371/25124: Cabinet comclusions, 27 November 1940.

86 Aaron Zwergbaum, 'Exile in Mauritius', *Yad Washem Studies* no. 4 (1960), pp. 191–257.

87 See its report of 31 January 1941 in National Archives, CO 733/446/4.

88 National Archives, CO 733/445/16: T. Snow to Downie, 14 January 1941.

89 National Archives, CO 733/445/16: Downie to Snow, 8 February 1941.

response to news of its sinking: 'There could have been no more opportune disaster from the point of view of stopping this traffic.'[90] Deterrence was still the main strategy of control.

A month later, the Foreign Office heard reports that another ship carrying 'illegal' immigrants was due to leave Varna. In a telegram to its representative in Sophia it noted that the 'S.S. Strouma [now more commonly known as the *Struma*] is due to leave ... with 500 Jews for Palestine'. Blaming the Bulgarian authorities for the 'terrible loss of life' on the *Salvador*, it recommended that 'If the [*Struma*] is overcrowded and has insufficient life-saving apparatus you should refer Bulgarians to relevant articles of International Convention for the Safety of Life at Sea.'[91] A year later, the same ship – in reality 'an ancient converted yacht' – embarked on a fresh journey that was to end in an even greater tragedy at sea.[92]

The *Struma* left Constanza in December 1941 with 769 Jewish refugees on board, victims of rapidly escalating Romanian state persecution. When it arrived in Turkish waters A.W.G. Randall, head of the Foreign Office's Refugee Department, perceived a 'terrible dilemma'. In his mind it was one as much for the British government as it was for those on board:

> if the Turks send the refugees back to the Black Sea they may be wrecked or in any case will presumably go back to the very hard conditions in whichever part of German-controlled Europe they have come from. If, however, they are sent on to Palestine ... they will be an impossible burden for the High Commissioner ... .

Reviving a theme that his office had rejected as nonsense just a year earlier, Randall added that the refugees 'may also be a means of introducing enemy agents'. And, again echoing earlier concerns, he argued that allowing them in would encourage further movements.[93] C.W. Baxter of the Foreign Office's Eastern Department concurred: 'If we were to accept these people, there would of course be more and more shiploads of unwanted Jews later!' Yet, rather than being self-interested, Baxter argued that encouraging such movements would bring 'more sufferings to the Jews as a whole' because of the conditions and dangers of such journeys.[94] Anthony Eden, the Foreign Secretary, then wrote to Churchill confirming that policy would be maintained: the survivors of the *Patria* were the 'only exception' to the policy of not giving 'illegal immigrants' permission to stay in Palestine.[95]

---

90 Wasserstein, *Britain and the Jews of Europe*, p. 77. See National Archives, FO 371/25242 W12451.

91 National Archives, CO 733/445/15: Telegram to Rendel, 1 January 1941.

92 Wasserstein, *Britain and the Jews of Europe*, p. 143.

93 National Archives, FO 371/32661: Randall minute, 12 February 1942.

94 National Archives, FO 371/32661: Baxter minute, 12 February 1942.

95 National Archives, FO 371/32661: Eden to Churchill, 13 February 1942.

Nevertheless, there was concern about Britain's reputation if another disaster was to occur at sea. E.A. Walker, also of the Foreign Office's Refugee Department, warned that

> The Black Sea is rough at this time of the year & the "Struma" may well founder. I do not [at] all like the idea that we may be acting as accessories in bringing about the death of these miserable people.[96]

Such concerns were noted and, although the Colonial Office was opposed, it was agreed that an offer should be made to the Turkish government to allow entry to Palestine for those on board the *Struma* aged between 11 and 16. The Turks rejected this possibility and the ship was forced back to sea, where it was sunk by a torpedo later identified as Soviet. All but one of its passengers drowned.[97] Luke of the Colonial Office remained unmoved. On hearing the news, he repeated the standard response of his Department and the need for maintaining 'effective control of immigration'. He expressed

> the gravest objections to illegal immigration during war time as a menace to security ... . [T]he Gestapo are known to assist the Jews in organising and despatching parties of illegal immigrants ... there has been specific report of Nazi agents on the 'Struma'.[98]

As part of this discourse the one survivor of the *Struma*, David Stolar, was interviewed, his statement conforming to such earlier Jewish migrant testimony as obtained by the Palestinian authorities. He related the journey of the ship from Romania and the weeks stranded in Turkey followed by the torpedoing of the vessel. Again, there was nothing within this testimony explaining his motives for undertaking this perilous journey. It was left to the Jewish Agency (and the elements of the press in the democratic world that were sympathetic to the Jewish cause) to explain the background of its victims.

The Jewish Agency was aware that, alongside security, 'the shortage of supplies in Palestine' was the reason given to refuse permission to continue the journey of the *Struma* there. Indeed, its passengers were perceived by the High Commissioner as likely to be an 'unproductive element in the population'.[99] The Jewish Agency responded that two-thirds of those on the *Struma* were fit and willing and able to work and fight. It added, 'To use the argument of "short supplies" against admitting some two hundred

96   National Archives, FO 371/32661: Walker minute, 24 February 1942.
97   Wasserstein, *Britain and the Jews of Europe*, pp. 151–152.
98   National Archives, CO 733/446/10: Luke memorandum, 25 February 1942.
99   National Archives, FO 371/32661: Telegram to the Colonial Secretary, 17 February 1942.

elderly people [that is the remaining third] fleeing from torture and death reflects on the intelligence, as well as the heart, of those who advance it.'[100] The reality of persecution by the Nazis and their satellite states was not, however, a factor that the Colonial Office and the Palestinian authorities were willing to consider when dealing with 'illegal' Jewish immigration.

While there was a minor revival of such migration to Palestine in 1944, the construction of it as a security threat/burden by the British authorities ensured that the overall numbers would be pitiful in relation to the crisis of European Jewry during the war. For the whole of the conflict it is generally estimated at between 16,000 and 17,000.[101] At the end of 1945 the Commissioner for Migration and Statistics in Palestine produced a numerical account of Jewish 'illegal' immigration since 1920. His terse comment that the 'Lack of transport has made emigration insignificant during the years of war' reflected one reality. It also ignored both the intensity of Nazi persecution and the efforts made to deter and repel Jewish migration to Palestine, especially through the use of other spaces such as the island of Mauritius.[102]

While humanitarian concern was not totally absent, officials in their ever-hardening attitude towards 'illegal' immigration argued that holding firm against it was in the interests not only of the British war effort and the Palestinian Arab population but also of the Jews themselves. In this respect, a joint paper of the Foreign Office and the Colonial Office on 'Jewish Illegal Immigration into Palestine', which was agreed at the start of 1940, set a template for the rest of the war (and beyond). Those undertaking the journeys were 'largely political. Illegal immigration to Palestine is not primarily a refugee movement.' The Gestapo, it added, were 'known to assist the Jews in organising and despatching' the boats. It concluded that 'The problem is thus an organised invasion of Palestine for political motives, which exploits the refugee problem and unscrupulously uses the humanitarian appeal of the latter to justify itself.'[103] The only solution was to combat it through diplomatic, security, and, ultimately, military means. And the discourse of illegality, racketeering, and false morality, having shown itself to be flexible and persistent during the war itself, proved to have an even longer performative life beyond 1945.

---

100 National Archives, FO 371/32661: Executive of the Jewish Agency, 'The "Struma" Disaster, 25 February 1942.

101 Patek, *Jews on Route*, p. 101.

102 National Archives, CO 733/454/2: 'Jewish Illegal Immigration', December 1939.

103 This statement was agreed December 1939 to January 1940: National Archives, FO 371/25241.

The Post-war Era

The last journey of the *President Warfield*, renamed *Exodus 1947* when it was transformed into one of the largest ships transporting 'illegal' immigrants to Palestine during the last years of the British Mandate, has become a central plank in constructing the mythological origins of the state of Israel. In the words of Israeli novelist Yoram Kaniuk: 'After *Exodus* came the War of Independence. The first chapter ended, and a new chapter began.'[104] Moreover, it became so controversial that the very nature of Britishness and Jewishness was bitterly contested by the opposing sides. While on one level simply a drama at sea over several months, *Exodus 1947* brought forth memories of other epic and tragic migrant journeys – ancient and recent, Jewish and non-Jewish.

At a mundane level, this ship was one of many (over 60) carrying 'illegal' immigrants attempting to reach Palestine from August 1945 to May 1948 and the foundation of the State of Israel. Slow to pick up after the war, with chaos and prejudice still impacting on the remnants of European Jewry (only 4000 arrived in the last five months of 1945), it was part of the rapid increase in such migration during the following two years (roughly 23,000 in 1946 and 29,000 in 1947). Indeed, 'Approximately 55% of all clandestine immigrants arrived in Palestine between 1946–1948.'[105] In terms of scale, two later ships were to carry more passengers – the *Pan York* and the *Pan Crescent* carried over 15,000 between them. The notoriety/fame of *Exodus 1947* was not, however, due to numbers alone. Articulating the Zionist reading of the ship's wider significance, Mordechai Naor notes how

> Over 100 ships reached the shores of Palestine during the years of organized clandestine immigration, but none was as famous as *Exodus 1947* ... [M]ore than any other vessel, it exemplified the struggle of the immigrants and the Yishuv for free immigration.

He concludes that 'British obstinacy and indifference to the Holocaust survivors also reached its peak in the story of the Exodus.'[106] In an earlier such interpretation (1954), Jon and David Kimche argued that after *Exodus* 'victory was now at last in sight', requiring only 'the knock-out blow, the culminating effort which would exploit the breach which the *Exodus* had made in the British line of defence'.[107] Half a century on, it was argued that enough time had passed for the story to have 'now entered the academic

---

104 Yoram Kaniuk, *Commander of the Exodus* (New York: Grove Press, 1999), p. 206.
105 Naor, *Haapala*, pp. 105, 108–114.
106 Ibid., p. 73.
107 Kimche and Kimche, *The Secret Roads*, p. 192.

phase' and for a more sober analysis to take place.[108] But just five years later (2010), the tone of a new and extensive study of the *Exodus* suggests that mythology is still to the fore. It was 'an event unparalleled in history; a precursor for the foundation of a nation and its people'.[109]

Told succinctly, the *President Warfield/Exodus 1947*, having left France in July 1947 with over 4500 Jews on board, was confronted by British forces as it moved towards Palestine, leaving three dead, many injured, and the ship damaged. The ship was then escorted to Haifa under British control. At Haifa, almost all of those on board (with the exception of those in great need of medical attention) were transferred by the British authorities to three ships – the *Runnymede Park, Ocean Vigour* and *Empire Rival* – and then returned to Europe.[110]

After an extended stay in the port of Port-de-Bouc, where the vast majority of the refugees refused to accept the French offer of asylum, the ships moved on via Gibraltar to Hamburg, where they arrived on 8 September 1947. Following a brief and minor struggle, the 4000-plus Jews on board finally disembarked in the German port. Sent by the British to two refugee camps in Schleswig Holstein, Poppendorf (which held 3400 of them) and Amstaw (a further 1000) through 'Operation Oasis',[111] the *Exodus 1947* refugees were given privileged status by the Zionist movement. Most were, in the following months, surreptitiously sent to Palestine as special immigrants.[112] Such a performative act was in final defiance of the British authorities over this notorious episode. As a member of the Foreign Office's Refugee Department summarised in March 1948: 'The line taken by HMG when these Jews were returned to Germany was that they would go to the bottom of the queue and there has been no official suggestion that they have any priority whatsoever for entry into Palestine.'[113]

There were many such confrontations between the British authorities and 'illegal' Jewish immigrants in the immediate post-war period: the island

---

108 Fritz Liebreich, *Britain's Naval and Political Reaction to the Illegal Immigration of Jews to Palestine, 1945–1948* (London: Routledge, 2005), p. 252.

109 Gordon Thomas, *Operation Exodus* (London: JR Books, 2010), p. xv.

110 Official British government figures indicated that of the 4493 passengers on board the *President Warfield* when it arrived at Haifa, three were dead and a further 62 were sent to hospital. National Archives, FO 371/61818 E6711: Duff Cooper memorandum, 25 July 1947. For a thorough and detailed study of the diplomacy surrounding the *Exodus* affair see Arieh Kochavi, *Post-Holocaust Politics: Britain, the United States & Jewish Refugees, 1945–1948* (Chapel Hill: University of North Carolina Press, 2001), esp. pp. 266–275.

111 See National Archives, FO 945/762 for 'Operation Oasis'.

112 For a detailed and thoughtful account, see Aviva Halamish, *The Exodus Affair: Holocaust Survivors and the Struggle for Palestine* (London: Vallentine Mitchell, 1998).

113 National Archives, CO 537/3953: J.H. Moore of Foreign Office to J.D. Higham of the Colonial Office, 17 March 1948.

of Cyprus became a holding camp for the thousands who were caught attempting to reach the shores of Palestine – as noted, this option had been considered earlier as a deterrent to further movement and as a place of remote immigration procedure. Yet both at the time and subsequently the journey (or, more strictly, journeys) of *Exodus 1947* was given special attention. After the *President Warfield* left France, Ambassador Duff Cooper in Paris told the French Foreign Minister that the British government 'intended to make an example of this ship'.[114] But, for Zionists, it was, according to the journalist Ruth Gruber – one of its most famous chroniclers – 'The Ship that Launched a Nation'.[115] As Israel reached its fortieth anniversary in 1988, its journeys were given privileged status in national commemorations. Ervin Birnbaum, who as an 18-year-old Czech-born survivor had been on board the ships, was clear about the 'message' of *Exodus 1947*: 'It shows that we cannot depend on anybody but ourselves. We had only one place to go and that place was, and still is, Israel. We cannot go to the moon and no other country wants us.'[116]

The story of *Exodus 1947* has largely been told/performed within an American and Israeli/Zionist context. In contrast, there has been very limited British input into the narrative of a journey and a ship that very quickly became a 'symbol and even a myth'.[117] In 1988 the *Sunday Times* ran a major feature: 'EXODUS: A Voyage of Hope and Pain which led to Milk and Honey'. But this was a rare return to the story in Britain, even more so as it reproduced, uncritically, a simplistic Zionist narrative.[118] Thereafter, it has appeared only occasionally and mainly as a sensational episode allegedly exposing 'Britain's Holocaust shame'.[119] Whereas the story, covered in the previous chapter, of the young Holocaust survivors in the Lake District and beyond is slowly becoming recognised at a national level, as time passes the journey of *Exodus 1947* has become increasingly obscure in British memory. 'The entire incident' of *Exodus 1947*, it was suggested in the late 1990s, 'became the material for literary and cinematic exploitation that still resonates'.[120] Its vibrations continue to be felt, however, largely outside the country that controlled the Mandate in Palestine.

---

114 National Archives, FO 371/61815 E6218: Duff Cooper to Foreign Office, 12 July 1947.
115 Ruth Gruber, *Exodus 1947: The Ship that Launched a Nation* (New York: Union Square Press, 2007).
116 Lee Levitt, '"Exodus" survivor relives the drama', *Jewish Chronicle*, 29 April 1988.
117 Halamish, *The Exodus Affair*, p. xv.
118 *Sunday Times*, magazine, 15 May 1988.
119 Robert Verkaik, 'The Voyage of the Exodus', *Independent*, 5 May 2008 relating to the release of government papers on the episode.
120 A.J. Sherman, *Mandate Days: British Lives in Palestine 1918–1948* (London: Thames and Hudson, 1997), p. 207.

On the surface, the national balancing act between memory and forgetting appears unremarkable. From a contemporary British perspective it reflected a form of defeat and an unhappy end to its quasi-colonial rule. In the Zionist rhetoric of Arthur Koestler, writing just two years after the turning back of the *President Warfield*: 'It was indeed an exploit as pointless as it was symbolic. His Majesty's Government seemed to have taken it upon themselves, by reversing the *Exodus*, to turn back the tide of history.'[121] Similarly, the Kimche brothers, writing from London and Jerusalem, a few years later called it an episode 'which shocked the world by [Britain's] sheer uncomprehending stupidity'.[122]

British amnesia also reflected realities of post-1948 diplomatic power politics in the Middle East and differing Anglo-American relations with Israel. As will emerge, however, there are nuances that make the remembering of *Exodus 1947* multi-layered and complex: such memory work and performativity has been subject to contestation within and between the various nation states intimately involved in its journeys. Furthermore, the telling and retelling of its story reveals much about minority–majority relationships and the construction of Jewish identities in the post-war era. And, as with so many quintessential forced migrations, earlier religious and secular reference points have been used to construct and perform the scripts of its remarkable journeys.

For America, and especially American Jews, there were direct connections to the ship. The *President Warfield*, a large wooden pleasure steamer operating in the American Great Lakes, was named after an entrepreneur 'known only to the world of finance and certain hunt club circles around Baltimore and the Chesapeake Bay country'. The ship had been utilised briefly by the American forces in the latter part of the war, carrying supplies and then troops across the channel to and from France.[123] Moreover, most of its crew after it had been bought and refitted by the *Haganah* were young American Jews. They were radicalised by the fate of European Jewry during the war and anxious to help the survivors. 'It was the experience with the refugees of Europe that decided him', according to his brother, that led Bill Bernstein to join the ship.[124] Bernstein was to be one of the three fatalities on the *President Warfield*, hit on the head by the British landing crew and never to recover from the blow. Equally important for the American Jewish crew was seeking out adventure in the name of a good cause. Finally, American Jewish organisations helped with the financial underpinnings enabling mass Jewish immigration from Europe

---

121 Arthur Koestler, *Promise and Fulfillment: Palestine 1917–1949* (London: Macmillan, 1949), p. 151.
122 Kimche and Kimche, *The Secret Roads*, p. 175.
123 David Holly, *Exodus 1947* (Boston: Little, Brown, 1969), p. 7 and chapter 4.
124 Halamish, *The Exodus Affair*, p. 18.

to Palestine (much to the annoyance and disgust of British politicians and media) as well as the arming of the Jews already there.[125] Not surprisingly, with such linkages many American Jews developed close emotional bonds with the journey of *Exodus 1947*.

Ruth Gruber, born in Brooklyn in 1911, was one of the first reporters to give the ship prominence in articles that were published in the *New Republic*. Significantly, however, they were rejected by the *New Yorker* for being 'too Jewish'. It was an indication that early post-war America far from embraced ethnic particularism.[126] Gruber's articles formed the basis of the first book devoted to the subject, published in 1948.[127] Within the American Jewish sphere, Gruber's work was followed in a fictional form, with equally mythic and melodramatic underpinnings, in Leon Uris' *Exodus* (1958), later transformed into a Hollywood blockbuster (1960). To Uris, a journalist, war novelist, and 'western' screenplay writer, '*Exodus* [was] the story of the greatest miracle of our times, an event unparalleled in the history of mankind.'[128]

The fact that the novel was one of the major bestsellers in twentieth-century America and that the film version produced by the émigré, Otto Preminger, achieved equal success, points to the appeal of the story to an American audience beyond its (sizeable) Jewish minority, highlighting 'the concept of an organic link between American democracy and the new Jewish state'.[129] Indeed, it has been argued that 'In essence, Uris waves both the Israeli and the American national flags ... prais[ing] the American way of life and the values of the American society.'[130] As the *Los Angeles Times* noted in 1960, 'It's the story of our own Revolutionary War against the British, transposed to Palestine.'[131] Similarly, in his account of an 'illegal' journey that took place a year before the *Exodus*, American Jewish journalist I.F. Stone concluded that if it and other ships were 'illegal, so was the Boston Tea Party'.[132] It was also hugely influential in a very different sphere of the Cold War – the USSR.

---

125 Derek Penslar, *Jews and the Military: A History* (Princeton: Princeton University Press, 2013), chapter 7.

126 Gruber, *Exodus 1947*, p. 192.

127 Ruth Gruber, *Destination Palestine: The Story of the Haganah Ship Exodus 1947* (New York: Current Books, 1948).

128 Frontispiece to the Corgi edition, 1961.

129 On this appeal and Uris' and Preminger's desire for it to reach the widest audience, see M.M. Silver, *Our Exodus: Leon Uris and the Americanization of Israel's Founding Story* (Detroit: Wayne State University Press, 2010).

130 Rachel Weissbrod, '*Exodus* as a Zionist Melodrama', *Israel Studies* no. 4 no. 1 (1999), p. 134.

131 Quoted in Amy Kaplan, 'Zionism as Anticolonialism: The Case of *Exodus*', *American Literary History* no. 25 no. 4 (2013), p. 873.

132 Stone, *Underground to Palestine*, p. 224. On official attitudes towards Stone,

For Zionist Jews across the Soviet Union,

No book caught the imagination ... like Leon Uris's novel *Exodus* ... . For the handful of Zionists in the Soviet Union ... the book was pure sustinence – many tears fell on the thin typewritten pages. And it served as a remarkable recruitment tool.

The book 'spread like a virus ... . Copies proliferated everywhere. One major source was the prison camps.'[133] External supporters smuggled in suitcases with 'dozens of [translated] copies'.[134] The book even had an afterlife for those who managed to escape. Arriving in America as a ten-year-old with his Russian–Jewish family, Gary Shteyngart remembers how for his parents owning a property in suburban New York was their 'first step to Americanism'. In this new home pride of place went to a 'special hardcover copy of Leon Uris's *Exodus*'. Even so, 'Except for Leon Uris and his tales of Israeli derring-do, our house [was] Russian down to the last buckwheat kernel of kasha.'[135] Tellingly, in contrast to the hunger with which Uris's *Exodus* was consumed in America and by Soviet Jewry, *To the Quayside* (1954), a novel by the British–Jewish novelist, Louis Golding (aided by Emanuel Litvinoff), the latter part of which gave a detailed and didactic account of *Exodus 1947*, made little or no impact in Britain and was soon forgotten.[136]

Both Gruber and Uris created a natural bond between the Jewish and American causes, appealing also to Jews still persecuted in the diaspora. Furthermore, and echoing contemporary Zionist propaganda – if with far less venom – they presented Britain as traitor, denying the persecuted Jews a deserved and overdue homeland which had been pledged in the Balfour Declaration. It is a country that Gruber portrays as having betrayed its history and ideals, becoming instead a collapsing and corrupt empire: 'The *Exodus* showed how weakened Great Britain had become. This was not a

---

see National Archives, CO 537/2384.

133 Gal Beckerman, *When They Come For Us We'll Be Gone: The Epic Struggle to Save Soviet Jewry* (New York: Houghton Mifflin Harcourt, 2010), pp. 27–29.

134 Ibid., p. 99.

135 Gary Shteyngart, *Little Failure: A Memoir* (London: Hamish Hamilton, 2014), p. 137.

136 Louis Golding, *To the Quayside* (London: Hutchinson, 1954). I am grateful to Gavin Schaffer to bringing this novel to my attention. This book was the last in a series under Golding's name which outlined a history of the Holocaust. Weakness in plot, as well as the lack of national context in which to operate, partly explain the obscurity of this novel. For a more positive reading of the series, and this novel in particular, see Paul Nugat, 'From Magnolia Street to the Quayside', *Jewish Quarterly* no. 1 no. 4 (spring 1954), pp. 81–84. For Litvinoff's involvement, see his obituary in *The Times*, 3 October 2011. His obituarist is more charitable towards this book, describing it as 'the most interesting' of the works ghosted for Golding.

single misguided act by unfortunate and unhappy civil servants in the field. This was part of a tragic pattern of corrosion and decline.'[137]

The power associated with the performance of naming has been highlighted in the introduction to this chapter – one that is clearly illustrated in the case of *Exodus*. Gruber especially pointed to the politics of nomenclature regarding the ships, noting how the *Runnymede Park*, named after the place where the Magna Carta had been signed, was now undermining English commitment to human freedom – the spirit of which was now taken over by the ship's passengers.[138] Uris also played on this connection, renaming one of the ships returning the refugees back to Europe the *Magna Charta*.[139] There are 'decent' British individuals in both Gruber's and Uris' accounts. In both their works, however, in general the British officials and soldiers are represented as being either at best indifferent towards the Jews or, at worst, antisemitic towards the refugees under their charge. In terms of the 'baddies', Arabs, British, and Nazis become melded, the first two categories, remarkably, presented often as negatively as the last.[140]

Bartley Crum was a relatively junior and maverick member of the American team at the Anglo-American Committee of Inquiry into the Problems of European Jewry and Palestine (1946).[141] In his introduction to Gruber's account of *Exodus 1947* Crum suggested that Britain, by blockading Palestine and turning back the Jewish refugees, had created 'slave ships'.[142] He thus bluntly attempted to subvert Britain's self-image as the country of freedom and emancipation. Sympathetic to the Zionist cause, he was also responding to contemporary discourse in Britain which defended the actions of the British Navy and blamed the organisers of the 'unsavoury trade in immigrants' for the hardships caused. In April 1947, for example, the naval correspondent of *The Times* claimed that the Jewish immigrants had been

> crowded into insanitary ships totally unfitted to carry them in any tolerable degree of safety, regardless of what happens to them, so long, presumably, as the passage money contributed by pious sympathisers is paid to the sea-gangsters who run this modern slave traffic – the conditions in most of the ships can be compared only to those of the slavers of the last century.[143]

---

137 Gruber, *Destination Palestine*, p. 121.
138 Ibid., p. 117.
139 Uris, *Exodus*, p. 152.
140 Weissbrod, '*Exodus* as a Zionist Melodrama', p. 131.
141 More generally see Amisam Nachman, *Great Power Discord in Palestine: The Anglo-American Committee of Inquiry into the Problems of European Jewry and Palestine 1945–46* (London: Frank Cass, 1987).
142 Gruber, *Destination Palestine*, p. 14.
143 *The Times*, 9 April 1947.

Such linkages have been noted before the Second World War among hostile civil servants, but they were more sustained after 1945. It even extended into the legal sphere. Desperately exploring ways of circumventing international law and the freedom of the seas beyond the three-mile territorial restriction, the exception of intercepting ships suspected of carrying slaves in the nineteenth century (and alcohol during prohibition) was raised by the Admiralty in 1947. While such interceptions were still deemed unlawful, it said much about official thinking that the connection to such illegal cargo – human or contraband goods – could still be made.[144] Furthermore, *The Times'* correspondent was not alone in making use of a negative discourse which linked Jews to immoral, internationally organised financial activities. Duff Cooper, while claiming that he 'sympathised with the Jews', regarded the organisation of illegal immigration as a 'money-making racket'.[145] Over 40 years later Captain Brian de Courcy-Ireland, in charge of *HMS Ajax*, which helped intercept *Exodus 1947*, provided a similar conspiratorial narrative in his autobiography: 'From all over Europe ... from the ghettos, refugee camps, ex-concentration camps and hiding places, the remnants of the Jewish people were trying to find their way by whatever means they could towards the Promised Land.' But whatever sympathy de Courey-Ireland had was removed by the action of the sinister forces in charge of this illegal movement. The survivors, he added,

> allowed themselves to be driven like cattle by determined ruthless fanatics intent only on getting as many of them as possible into Palestine ... . They were often exploited, robbed and treated with ruthless callousness by the 'organisation'; and yet they came.[146]

More generally, the Foreign Office was adamant that the poor conditions on the ships were the fault of the Jewish organisers and not the British government in forcing this migration 'underground'. Its briefing to embassies across the world when dealing with the press, therefore, emphasised 'the inhumanity of the Jewish organisers in their gross overcrowding of the President Warfield'. The Foreign Office added hopelessly that 'The number of passengers on this tiny ship might usefully be compared to that normally carried by the "Queen Elizabeth" or other vessels of her size.' It concluded that 'You should contrast this with British treatment exemplified by use of three ships each larger than the President Warfield for their return.'[147]

---

144 See National Archives, ADM 1/235261.

145 National Archives, FO 371/61818 E6643: Duff Cooper to the Foreign Office, 23 July 1947.

146 Captain S.B. de Courcy-Ireland, *A Naval Life* (Poulton: England Publishing, 1990), p. 344.

147 National Archives, FO 371/61816 E6398: Harold Beeley briefing, 19 July 1947.

With so much at stake in this performative war, both sides evoked the memory of the most despicable symbol of forced migration, the 'Middle Passage', to make their case for occupying the moral high ground. Thus Bartley Crum was clear that these were *'Britain's "slave ships"'* [my emphasis].[148]

Jewish leaders on board the *President Warfield* were aware of the bandying about of the 'slave ship' allegation and they brought their own heightened rhetoric to bear on the subject. In broadcasts on the ship it was emphasised that the 'naval might' of Britain was being turned against women and child survivors. In contrast, during 'the years of the rivers of blood no ships were available to help and rescue Jews'. Alongside the 'whole fleet [of] cruisers and destroyers' barring the entry of the Jews to 'their Homeland' was 'an evil propaganda campaign against the rescuers, you describe them as slave merchants, unscrupulous people, hell ships'. In fact, the broadcasts claimed that it was the British who were

> the damned slave merchants. You traded with Jewish blood during the war and you are continuing to do so now. You are paying with red Jewish blood for black oil. You describe our ships as 'hell ships', you say that they are overcrowded, too small and the conditions in them are inhuman. You have suddenly donned sacred garments which you have ignored when we were burning in the furnaces of hell.[149]

In Britain Abraham Abrahams, the Revisionist Zionist editor of the *Jewish Standard*, also used the memory of the war to debunk what he saw as British hypocrisy 'on the subject of hell-ships', referring to the example of the *S.S. Dunera* and the removal of Jewish refugee internees in Britain to Australia in 1940. Indeed, his extravagance of language and polemical use of history almost outmatched his Zionist counterparts on the *President Warfield*. The previous chapter emphasised the symbolic importance of the 'Wandering Jew'. Abrahams also evoked this powerful Semitic construct, but he did so by trying to reclaim it for the Jewish cause. He concluded that:

> The Jews in the DP camps have passed through even worse than a 'Dunera' voyage. Only those who understand this can appreciate why many thousands of them would prefer to travel ... on rafts ... than on well-found boats and expose them eternally to one 'Dunera' after another throughout successive generations.[150]

148 Crum in Gruber, *Destination Palestine*, p. 14.
149 National Archives, FO 371/61822 E7699: Translation by CID Palestine Police, 21 July 1947: 'Listen to the voice of the refugee's ship "Exodus 1947"'.
150 A. Abrahams, 'On the subject of hell-ships', *Jewish Standard*, 1 August 1947.

Alongside slavery-related metaphors, 'hell ships' evoked the Second World War and Japanese atrocities. American and British prisoners of war were transported to work as slave labourers by the Japanese in unmarked freighters that were subject to attack – hence what soon became known among the Western Allies as 'hell ships'. Not only were the British being accused of cruelties associated with the 'Middle Passage' – they were also being linked in extreme Zionist propaganda with what was perceived as the 'inherently' cruel Japanese 'race'.[151]

Chaim Weizmann, soon to become Israel's first president, when addressing the Anglo-American Committee was also critical of the nation which he admired so much and with whom he had tried hard to reach rapprochement:

> When a refugee today comes to Palestine, on a leaky boat after a long hard journey, he finds, off the coast, a British destroyer anxious to have a good look at him; when he lands on the beach, he meets British soldiers, again anxious to see that, if possible, he shouldn't land.[152]

Weizmann diplomatically acknowledged 'the forbearance which some authorities have shown', but his emphasis was on what he termed the Jewish 'right to survive'. His testimony thus focused on *why* Jewish refugees were risking these difficult journeys. In the process, and in contrast to his portrayal of recent British responses, Weizmann made a reassuring connection between the Jewish present and the American past, again using the metaphor of the ship, and one imbued with a powerful national–religious symbolism:

> All these difficulties and discouragements which face them after their escape from the jaws of death, these people are ready to accept and endure, because this leaky boat on which this boy or girl travels is their *Mayflower*. It is the *Mayflower* of the whole generation of young Jews eager to reach these shores.[153]

In a different national context, Leon Uris was particularly anxious to show a commonality between American and Zionist ideals. He therefore saw no tension with regards to the loyalty of American Jewry in its collective support for the creation of a Jewish state. In his fictional account of *Exodus 1947*, the 'Jewish-American captain [of one the 'illegal' immigrant ships in

---

151 See http://www.west-point.org/family/adbc/hellship.htm, accessed 13 January 2010.

152 Chaim Weizmann, *The Right to Survive: Testimony before the Anglo-American Committee of Enquiry on Palestine* (London: Jewish Agency for Palestine, 1946), pp. 11–12.

153 Ibid.

the novel] … waxes eloquent about his allegiance to America and desire to remain an American citizen'.[154] The enthusiastic reception of both Uris' book and the later film revealed that American society had indeed taken the story to heart. Nevertheless, it should be noted that Preminger's version was less overtly Zionist, with the story becoming more universalist (and less anti-British and anti-Arab), and thereby designed to appeal to the widest possible audience.[155] Hollywood's defensiveness when embracing Jewish themes – a feature of the 1930s and the Second World War – had not totally disappeared.[156] The book and the film paved the way for later memorialisation of *Exodus 1947* in the mainstream of the nation's heritage sites, including the Smithsonian Institute in Washington, DC, maritime museums, and, embracing the elite military sphere, marine academies.[157]

In Israel, not surprisingly, the identification with *Exodus 1947* has been even more intense than in America. With the need to emphasise *Jewish* agency in the formation of the state, the organisation of illegal immigration played and continues to play a key role in Israeli mythology. Indeed, as part of the core foundation stories of the nation, the memory of the ship/ships has become precious. It thus has been performed/contested by rival Zionist factions, as well as leaders of the ships, anxious that their role in the epic story not be lost or marginalised. 'No sooner had the immigrants landed in Germany, than the various parties and movements set to writing down the history of the Exodus Affair to ensure their part in the glory.'[158]

Early Narratives and Later Memory Work

Ruth Gruber noted that when the ships returning the Jewish refugees to Europe arrived back in France 'Already the *Exodus* was losing reality, becoming a phantom ship on which the weird people of history were creating a new mythology.'[159] Certainly the phenomenal success of Uris' book added confusion, as its 'key story episodes often bear nominal resemblance to "real life" events'. There is ship called *Exodus* in the novel, but another fictional vessel, *The Promised Land*, more closely follows the

---

154 Weissbrod, '*Exodus* as a Zionist Melodrama', p. 134.
155 Ibid., pp. 139–140. See also Silver, *Our Exodus*, pp. 204–207.
156 K.R.M. Short, 'Hollywood Fights Anti-Semitism, 1940–1945', in idem (ed.), *Film and Radio Propaganda in World War II* (London: Croom Helm, 1983), pp. 149–160.
157 Gruber, *Exodus 1947*, p. 189.
158 Halamish, *The Exodus Affair*, p. 267. For examples of populist accounts of 'illegal' Jewish immigration, including *Exodus 1947*, from Zionist perspectives, see Bracha Habas, *The Gate Breakers* (New York: Herzl Press, 1963) and Ze'ev Venia Hadari and Ze'ev Tsahor, *Voyage to Freedom: an episode in the illegal immigration to Palestine* (London: Vallentine Mitchell, 1985).
159 Gruber, *Exodus 1947*, p. 146.

journey of the former *President Warfield*.[160] It is possible to argue that this myth-making process began as soon as the *President Warfield* first left France. Mordechai Roseman (or Rosman in contemporary documents and Rosemont in later accounts), a former Jewish resistance fighter in eastern Europe and partisan, became one of the self-appointed leaders of the refugees on the ship. He was, it was grudgingly acknowledged by British intelligence, 'a young, capable and energetic fanatic'.[161] As noted, the *President Warfield* was just one of many ships attempting to take Jewish refugees to Palestine after 1945, albeit taking the largest number attempted so far. But Roseman made clear on the eve of its embarkation from Marseilles early in July 1947 that it had a much more significant and, indeed, historic role to play:

> Today we are about to board a ship, through which the Jewish nation is fighting for its existence. We shall march upright to victory, hand in hand with the rest of the Israeli people – leading them, at their side and in their defense, the way our comrades in the underground and the ghettos did before us, in the mission to save Jews and struggle for the honor of the Jewish people.[162]

Roseman was thus writing the story of *Exodus 1947* even before it had happened, emphasising the collective role of those on board and their agency in determining their own fate and that of the Jewish future.

In her study of performativity and Japanese–American internment during the Second World War, Emily Roxworthy highlights how some internees within the huge camp in Manzanar, California, 'Aware that the practice of Japanese culture rendered them un-American in the performative logic of U.S. citizenship ... yoked their fates together, not in resigned acceptance of the dominant policies that enforced their exile, but in reasoned resistance to them'.[163] Power rested with the American authorities, but the Japanese–Americans developed and performed their own transnational identities in the internment camps. Likewise, Roseman and others confronted their naming as 'illegal' by asserting their own identity and agency. Aboard the ships, the Jewish passengers were told 'you are already citizens of *Eretz Israel*, whatever the English say'. They were presented with a 'blue certificate printed in Hebrew on one side and English on the other' entitled a 'Permit To Enter Palestine'.[164] In similar vein, it was necessary, argued Roseman on

---

160 Silver, *Our Exodus*, pp. 61–62.

161 National Archives, FO 945/762: 'Report on Operation "Oasis", September 1947.

162 National Archives, FO 371/61822 E7699: Broadcast of 21 July 1947.

163 Emily Roxworthy, *The Spectacle of Japanese American Trauma: Racial Performativity and World War II* (Honolulu: University of Hawaii Press, 2008), p. 147.

164 Stone, *Underground to Palestine*, pp. 176–177.

Exodus 1947, for the passengers to 'take upon ourselves any directive, task and mission' and to be prepared 'for our meeting with the motherland and even to cruelly push away from her'.[165]

Reflecting on the conditions on the *Runnymede Park*, its British captain, A.C. Barclay, was aware that they were far worse than those on the *President Warfield*. In the latter ship 'they were more crowded but they probably had better facilities for laying down, and they undoubtedly had better food and better cooking facilities than we have ever given them here'.[166] The *Haganah* had prepared the *President Warfield* for a journey which was intended to be short and which, until the British navy interrupted its progress, was relatively uneventful (although rougher seas on the fourth day and the death of a young woman giving birth provided drama and tragedy). One of those on board kept a diary in which the French passenger noted that 'the only bad thing ... was the sleeping quarters ... [so the] resourceful amongst us slept on the various decks in their clothes. The weather is excellent. The voyage will only last about 6 or 7 days'. She/he later commented that 'The sea is as calm as a lake and one can hardly believe that we are on a ship', adding 'One cannot believe that one is on an illegal boat sailing to an unknown destination, one is on a boat of pleasure-seekers going to spend their holidays together.'[167] Deborah Zuckerfein, who was pregnant, and Bracha Michaeli, both Jewish refugees from Poland, similarly recall that the only memorable features of the journey before the ship was intercepted was the heat and, because of the overcrowding, the lack of space to sleep: 'we couldn't even turn from side to side'.[168] In contrast, Roseman insisted in advance that the *President Warfield* was to have a monumental purpose: 'Throughout the journey we shall exhibit the pioneering spirit and moral strength of our movement, we shall set an example to ourselves and to our fellow passengers.'[169]

Aviva Halamish, in her study of the 'Exodus Affair', has highlighted that 'when the story of illegal immigration was put down in writing [in the first decades of the Jewish state], the immigrants themselves all but disappeared.'[170] This top-down approach, highlighted earlier for both the 1930s and the Second World War, was apparent even on board the *President*

165 Reproduced and translated in Halamish, *The Exodus Affair*, p. 51. The veteran French socialist leader, Leon Blum, also evoked the memory of the Warsaw ghetto rebellion. See his article in *Le Populaire*, 1 August 1947, translated in National Archives, FO 371/61820 E6993.

166 University of Southampton Archives: Report, 3 August 1947, Barclay papers, MS 87 folder 1.

167 National Archives, CO 537/2400: Diary entries of 11, 12, and 13 July 1947, translated from French.

168 Both interviewed on *People of the Exodus*, BBC 1, 15 May 1973.

169 Halamish, *The Exodus Affair*, p. 51.

170 Ibid., p. 271.

Warfield with regard to the renaming of the ship. Several days after its initial departure from France, *Haganah* organisers in France agreed that it was to be known as *Exodus 1947*. The commander of the ship, Yossi Harel, was informed of this decision.[171] This dramatic renaming was not communicated to the passengers, who had come up with alternatives. The American crew members were keen on *Roosevelt*, possibly in honour of the late president's wife, Eleanor, who was 'much admired by the Jews of the United States'. Some of the passengers preferred *Mordechai Anielewitz*, one of the leaders of the Warsaw ghetto uprising in April 1943 and providing a parallel to the controversy over the Klepfish/Primrose Club for the child survivors and the honouring of Jewish resistance during the Holocaust. These were ignored, but it was not until the ship came into conflict with the British navy that the new name was unveiled and it sailed into Haifa with a 'large banner at her center declaring that she was HAGANAH SHIP: EXODUS 1947'.[172]

Thereafter, so great was the aura associated with this journey that all three ships returning to Europe with the former *President Warfield* passengers became collectively known, in the Zionist and pro-Zionist world and well beyond it in the western media, as *Exodus 1947*. This process of naming and renaming further added to the ship's/ships' mythology. As a piece of performative propaganda, this particular branding was an act of genius on the part of the *Haganah*. As one of the ship's first historians, David Holly, romantically noted:

> At the climax of a tumultuous career – at a magnificent moment of victory rising from defeat – the ship was to expunge [Solomon Warfield's] name from her side in a gesture of supreme defiance. The gesture was destined to change the world.[173]

To understand the whole episode, it is of critical importance to acknowledge that the journeys of the ships carrying 'illegal' immigrants took place in an atmosphere in which extreme rhetoric played a critical role. In *How Societies Remember* Paul Connerton insists that 'An image of the past, even in the form of a master narrative, is conveyed and sustained by ritual performances.'[174] The stories constructed and reconstructed around the journeys of *Exodus 1947* confirms his analysis. This was especially true of the weeks in which the ships were in motion or in port: for

---

171 See Linda Grant's obituary of Ike Aronowitz (or Aharonovich), Harel's captain in *The Guardian*, 28 December 2009.

172 Halamish, *The Exodus Affair*, pp. 68–69. See also Kaniuk, *Commander of the Exodus*, p. 131, on other names that were suggested by the passengers.

173 Holly, *Exodus 1947*, p. 7.

174 Paul Connerton, *How Societies Remember* (Cambridge: Cambridge University Press, 1989), p. 70.

sheer drama and propaganda effect ... illegal immigration by sea was unmatched. Regardless of the outcome, every incident was newsworthy .... clashes between the wretched refugees ... and robust British soldiers ... could not have been scripted and staged better for atrocity propaganda.[175]

As Lieutenant Colonel Gregson, who was in charge of the operation to remove the Jewish passengers at Hamburg, cynically noted: 'If one is an actor there is no point in putting on your show if there is no audience and the same applies to the immigrants.' At Hamburg, he was convinced, the problems of disembarkation started only when the press appeared.[176]

This is not to deny that violence occurred, but that it was kept under restraint by both sides as part of a performative struggle and the desire not to provide negative publicity to the eagerly awaiting media. As it was, the physical conflict that did take place on both sides should not be minimised. The British seaman responsible for the death of one of the refugees was casual, and casually prejudiced, in his report about the incident. Faced with 'opposition in the shape of big Yids' when boarding the ship, he stopped a 'lad of 17 or 18 from collecting my scalp with a meat axe' by shooting him in the stomach.[177] The seaman was later commended for bravery and put forward for a commission. In a semi-official history of *The Royal Navy and the Palestine Patrol* (2002) it is acknowledged by the author that alongside ten serious injuries and the death of Bernstein 'two male immigrants died of gun shot wounds, one being a 15-year-old youth who had not been the target'.[178] Such clinical, unemotional reports ignore the impact on many of the ordinary refugees aboard the *President Warfield* – for them, the attack was terrifying. Bracha Michaeli recalled of the boarding operation that she 'was very afraid because I was only 17 then and I did not know what would become of us'.[179]

Holly's melodramatic opening to his narrative of *Exodus 1947* undoubtedly overstates the importance of the ship's new moniker. But the evocative name did help draw the attention of the world to its progress. Indeed, the issue of nomenclature was such that the British government was forced in vain to insist on the original appellation of the ships, especially the *President Warfield* and the largest of the three returning to Europe,

---

175 David Charters, *The British Army and Jewish Insurgency in Palestine, 1945–47* (Basingstoke: Macmillan, 1989), p. 70.

176 National Archives, FO 945/762: Lt. Col. Gregson, report on disembarkation at Hamburg.

177 Report of Ordinary Seaman Wade reproduced in de Courcy-Ireland, *A Naval Life*, p. 397.

178 Ninian Stewart, *The Royal Navy and the Palestine Patrol* (London: Frank Cass, 2002), p. 125.

179 Testimony from *People of the Exodus*, BBC 1, 15 May 1973.

the *Runnymede Park*. Thus in a 'narrative of events' relating to the former compiled in mid-August 1947, it was referred to by the Royal Navy as the 'Jewish Illegal Ship PRESIDENT WARFIELD' and nowhere in the report by the name with which it had already become globally notorious.[180] In search of a suitable label once the refugees had been divided between three ships, the Foreign Office propagandists came up with the solution of referring to them collectively as the 'Ex-President Warfield'.[181] Indeed, one official was strongly reprimanded for referring to the ship by the wrong title. In the first draft it was noted that 'we should surely not refer to the "President Warfield" by her Jewish name of "Exodus"'. By the final draft this wording had become even stronger: 'it seems inappropriate to refer to the "President Warfield" as the "Exodus", a name subsequently given to this vessel by Zionist propagandists'.[182] By then – the second half of September 1947 – it was largely a futile exercise, as the rest of the world had accepted the name *Exodus 1947*. But in British eyes this was anathema. Even into the twenty-first century the journeys of *Exodus 1947* are collectively catalogued under the heading '*President Warfield*' in the National Archives at Kew.[183]

Exodus 1947 was, in essence, a secular, politicised journey but through the ship's renaming it evoked 'the epic Jewish adventure of all time' – that of the Biblical escape from Egyptian slavery and through the wilderness to the Promised Land.[184] As Jeremy Leigh suggests, 'even before their departure, the leader Moses had elevated the journey to the level of founding myth for the nation.'[185] This was exactly how the *Haganah* leaders hoped the organised journeys of the illegal Jewish immigrants would be perceived and remembered.[186] In the Book of Exodus, chapter 13, Moses implores his people to 'Remember this day, on which you went free from Egypt.' The journey of 40 years was designed to strengthen the people of Israel and, likewise, those on *Exodus 1947*, however circuitous, would empower the commitment of all Jews to the Zionist cause and would win over non-Jewish moral support. To those on board, it had a status between the religious and the secular, between the 'now' and the establishment of the Jewish state and the 'then' of Biblical times:

---

180 National Archives, ADM 1/20685: Captain R. Watson, 10 August 1947 report.

181 National Archives, FO 1032/871: Minute, 20 September 1947.

182 National Archives FO 371/61825 E8233: J. Cable memorandum, 10 September 1947 and B. Bullows to H. Ashley Clarke, 23 September 1947.

183 National Archives accessed 7 September 2009.

184 Ervin Birnbaum, 'On The "Exodus: 1947"', *Jewish Frontier* vol. 24 no. 5 (May 1957), p. 15 – one of the first published accounts by one of the passengers.

185 Jeremy Leigh, *Jewish Journeys* (London: Haus Publishing, 2006), pp. 74–75.

186 *The Times*, 22 August 1947, editorial 'The Jews at Port de Bouc', while hostile to the organisers of illegal immigration, was sympathetic to the Jewish refugees on board and their frustrations at being 'turned back on the very coast of the promised land', showing a partial success for Zionist propaganda.

All of us, old and young, orthodox and unorthodox, Russians and Belgians, men and women, all of us are instilled with the same desire 'to see a country again that they have never seen'. That nostalgia they have been singing in their prayers for two thousand years and now they are going to reconquer the country as was done once before ... by the Master Moses.[187]

Such a sense of purpose was long-lasting for its former refugee passengers. In the words of Noah Kliger, a Strasbourg-born Auschwitz survivor who became part of the crew of the *President Warfield*, 'It happened only 40 years ago, but it feels like 4,000.'[188]

In subsequent memory, the *specifics* of the particular journeys of the four ships collectively known as *Exodus 1947* would matter less. Uris' 'loose grasp of history' and his melding and confusing of nomenclature was only the most blatant and influential example of this process.[189] It is perhaps not surprising, therefore, that the *President Warfield* itself was left to rot in Haifa, where it 'remained ignominiously abandoned'. The ship was accidentally set on fire in 1952 and then 'disappeared beneath the waves like so much discarded rubbish'.[190] It now rests on the seabed outside the port. While there were some veterans during the 1950s who attempted to found a museum based around the story of these journeys, it was not realised until the late 1970s with the creation of the Clandestine Immigration and Naval Museum in Haifa.[191] Similarly, the Atlit Detention Camp, which was opened by the British in 1939 to house 'illegal immigrants' close to the port of Haifa, was neglected and in a state of almost irreversible decay when it was belatedly made into a visitor centre close to half a century later. A problem then emerged: 'Of the original ships of the "illegal immigration", not a trace could be found.'[192] It was thus decided to purchase a ship 'that resembled them as much as possible' and the *Galina* was duly purchased via the internet by veterans of this movement from a colourful 'sea dog' in Riga.[193] It remains that the journeys of *Exodus 1947* and that of the other 60-plus 'illegal' *Haganah* ships feature prominently in the Clandestine Immigration and

187 National Archives, CO 537/2400: French passenger diary, 12 July 1947.
188 Kliger's story is narrated in Sarah Honig, 'Beyond the Barbed Wire', *Jewish Chronicle*, 9 October 1987.
189 Silver, *Our Exodus*, p. 61.
190 Honig, 'Beyond the Barbed Wire'; Gruber, *Exodus 1947*, p. 188.
191 Author interview with Nir Maor, director of this museum, Haifa, 18 December 2016.
192 Yossi Feldman, 'The *Galina* – a Reconstructed Model of a *M'apilim* ship', in Mordechai Naor (ed.), *The Atlit Camp* (Tel Aviv: Yehuda Dekel, 2010), p. 7 and author site visit to the visitor centre, 16 December 2016.
193 Ibid. and interview with Rina Offenbach, scholar at the Atlit Immigration Detention Camp, 16 December 2016.

Naval Museum in Haifa.[194] Although the surviving and much smaller *Af al pi chen*, which brought just over 400 'illegal immigrants' to Palestine in September 1947, is the main exhibit in the museum, it is the *Exodus 1947* ships that have been the focus of subsequent memory work. Indeed, there is a direct link, as *Af al pi chen*, which translates as 'In spite of all that', was named in defiance after the *Exodus 1947* passengers were turned back to Europe.[195] Historians now dispute the centrality of illegal immigration in the power politics of late Mandate Palestine and the eventual formation of a Jewish state. Yet at the level of popular mythology in Israel and in the wider Jewish diaspora these journeys, and especially that of *Exodus 1947*, still play a self-affirming and comforting role. There is thus an attempt at continuity in stressing Jewish self-determination in the Clandestine Immigration and Naval Museum with the *Haganah*-led ships of 1946 and 1947 melding into that of the Israeli navy.[196] As the director of the museum, Nir Maor, explains, it was not only the practical maritime experience and the boats themselves that were a direct legacy from the period of 'illegal immigration' and the formation of the Israeli Navy. The example of these ships boosted morale and self-belief immediately before and after the creation of Israel.[197] Narrated through the prism of the nation state and with a redemptive ending, there is no link made or possible with the transnational journeys over the same seas made by desperate migrants some half century later.

One legacy of such exclusive memory work has been an enduring hostility towards Britain and its alleged antipathy towards helping the persecuted Jews of Europe, and especially those trying to reach Palestine. To re-emphasise, the journey of *Exodus 1947* was as much a performative battle over propaganda as it was a military confrontation. British forces may temporarily have won the latter, but they largely lost the former – both in summer 1947 and thereafter. To Yossi Harel, the Jerusalem-born commander of the ship, the symbolism of it being turned back represented a moral victory. Harel's aim was to protect the Jews and thus he quickly surpressed resistance when the British navy boarded the *President Warfield*.[198] Harel's desire to avoid major bloodshed was much to the frustration of his captain, Ike Aharonovich, who wanted to stage a pitched battle, even if it would have led to a 'Masada at sea'.[199]

194 Gruber, *Exodus 1947*, p. 188.

195 Author site visit to the Clandestine Immigration and Naval Museum, 18 December 2016.

196 See the section on Haifa museums in http://www.tour-haifa.co.il/eng/modules/ article/view.article.php/c21/76, accessed 2 September 2009. The permanent exhibition of this Museum has been re-worked and opened late in 2015.

197 Author interview with Nir Maor, Haifa, 18 December 2016.

198 See Kaniuk, *Commander of the Exodus*, passim.

199 Yoram Kaniuk, 'Obituary: Exodus Captain Ike Aharonovich was Israel's most daring sailor', *Haaretz*, 25 December 2009.

If the journey of the *St Louis* in 1939 has become focused on the failings of American refugee policy (while it was the Cuban government that turned the ship away, it then sailed along the coast of Florida with the thwarted aim of landing there), the popularised story of *Exodus 1947* presents Britain as the guilty party. Indeed, it has been suggested that the journey of *Exodus 1947* and other such ships 'were morality plays staged for the world press in the no-man's-land of the sea, between a continent of loss and the shores of salvation. These spectacles recalled, reframed, and redeemed the sad story of the *St Louis*.'[200] Why, however, is it that self-criticism has been possible in the world of American heritage with regard to the *St Louis* and not in Britain in respect of *Exodus 1947*?

To the British, the campaign against Jewish illegal immigration was a military operation and one designed to ensure, through keeping the balance of local population, 'the maintenance of law and order' in Palestine. It was also carried out to make sure 'that nothing is done to prejudice the eventual decision of the United Nations' concerning the future of that country.[201] The naval attack on the *President Warfield* was thus significant to the British authorities on a symbolic level – a firm and efficient operation, it was hoped, would act as a deterrant to potential future immigrants. It was also believed by the Admiralty that the military operation had been a great success, in which casualties and damage on all sides were kept to a minimum.[202] The Royal Navy's confrontation was thus described with total neutrality: 'a naval operation of some complexity was necessitated; moreover those aboard offered violent opposition to the naval boarding party. Three persons succumbed to injuries sustained.'[203] This official discourse continued earlier strategy, which was to strip the issue of wider politics and morality. In 1948 the Admiralty published for its own use an account of 'The Campaign Against Massed Illegal Jewish Immigration into Palestine', which was designed as a manual for future such operations. On the *President Warfield*, it simply noted that the use of destroyers 'had a considerable [impact] in lowering the morale of the Jews'.[204]

Such military narratives persisted beyond the specific dynamics of the immediate post-war period. It was at the heart of the only major British documentary on the subject, 'People of the Exodus', broadcast on BBC television in 1973.[205] As late as 2002, the First Sea Lord of the Admiralty

200 Deborah Dwork and Robert Jan Van Pelt, *Flight from the Reich: Refugee Jews, 1933–1946* (New York: W.W. Norton, 2009), pp. 334–335.
201 National Archives, CO 537/2403 : 'Statement of His Majesty's Government', August 1947.
202 National Archives, ADM 1/20685: Admiralty report, 15 September 1947, 15 September 1947.
203 National Archives, FCO 141/14284: Intelligence report, 17 July 1947.
204 In National Archives, ADM 239/412.
205 *People of the Exodus*, BBC 1, 15 May 1973 in the long-running 'Tuesday Documentary'

could write that the interception of 'sea-borne illegal immigration into Palestine 1945–48' was 'well-executed and successful'. It helped towards 'the best solution that could be found at the time, and maintained the Navy's high standing and unique reputation'.[206] These narrow interpretations, either at the time or subsequently, were not and have not been widely shared. In 1947 British actions were condemned by the outside world. What especially annoyed and worried British officials and politicians was the nature of the rhetoric that accompanied the journeys of *Exodus 1947*, which it believed induced an undeserved sympathy for those undertaking them. It has been noted that both 'sides' compared the journeys of these ships to those in the slave trade. There was, however, a more immediate point of reference in the battle to appear virtuous. In essence, it was a performative war of words that was based on two very different constructions and readings of the Second World War.

At the point when the three *Exodus 1947* ships left Port-de-Bouc en route for Germany, the Foreign Office's German section sent a telegram to its Lubeck officers stating that it would be 'useful for our propaganda purposes if the following information could be ascertained when screening the Jews on arrival'. These were as follows:

(A) Where the Jews come from. This may be difficult, but it should be possible to distinguish certain groups according to origin.

(B) Which, if any, of the Jews have been in German concentration camps or have suffered at German hands.

(C) How many of them have fought for the Allies during the war.

(D) Whether there are any persons amongst them known to be connected with terrorist activities.[207]

British officials were aware that sending the *Exodus 1947* passengers to Germany was a potential disaster in terms of the nation's reputation for fairness, one that was likely to be fully exploited by Zionist propaganda. They were fearful that those on board would be presented as defenceless recent victims of Nazi racialism and not as illegal immigrants, some of whom were not even European – there were, for example, north African Jews on the ship, including the Tunisian Arlette Guez, who later published

---

series. The military narrative was emphasised by contemporary film footage and also the use of model ships to illustrate the boarding of the *President Warfield*.

206 Admiral Sir Nigel Essenlough, 'Foreword' in Stewart, *The Royal Navy and the Palestine Patrol*, p. ix.

207 National Archives, CO 537/2401: Telegram, 28 August 1947.

her memoirs of this epic journey. Indeed, the presence of Guez reflected the heterogeneous nature of such migration before the war.[208] Yet, rather than merely being an act of wilful insensitivity, to the civil servants and military involved with this case there was simply no alternative but to stop their entry. As illustrated, attempting to discredit the deserving nature and persecuted state of these Jewish migrants was a continuous feature of British policy before, during, and after the Second World War.

It has recently been revealed that the British Secret Intelligence Service (SIS) launched 'Operation Embarrass' in late 1946, which aimed to locate and immobilise any potential ship to be used for the purpose of illegal immigration to Palestine. Five ships were disabled, but the Foreign Office did not approve a similar mission against the *President Warfield*, wanting to avoid any unnecessary casualties and the bad publicity that had followed the *Patria* and *Struma* (and perhaps aware that there were too many ships available in the post-war era to make the operation fully successful). The SIS agents working on 'Operation Embarrass' were clearly frustrated by the Foreign Office's reluctance. One of them was convinced that the failure to sink the *President Warfield* in its French port presented the Zionists with a 'first rate propaganda weapon and even among our friends sympathy was shown towards the illegal immigrants'.[209] As Arthur Koestler noted in 1949, 'Each stage of the journey was spot-lighted by the world Press; for weeks on end Britain was the target of more humiliating comment by her friends and foes alike than at any other time in recent history.'[210]

With only a half-hearted attempt at sabotage, and with the Cyprus camps more than full, the options available to the British government were limited. Those on board the three ships had largely refused to disembark in France and there was, of course, no possibility that they would be allowed to return to Palestine. Moreover, no suitable British colonial territory was available. Thus the British Zone of Germany represented the 'only territory under British jurisdiction outside Cyprus where such a large number of people can be adequately housed and fed at short notice'. The Foreign Office then attempted to occupy the moral high ground by suggesting that 'there are several thousand Jews in Germany today who would by now have been legally admitted to Palestine if they had not been pushed aside by the stream of illegal immigrants.'[211]

The Foreign Office's desire to find out how many of those on board the three ships were what would now be called 'Holocaust survivors' was not

---

208 Arlette Guez, *La passagère de L'Exodus* (Paris: Editions Robert Laffont, 1978).

209 Keith Jeffery, *MI6: The History of the Secret Intelligence Service, 1909–1949* (London: Bloomsbury, 2010), pp. 691–694; idem, 'British secret service blew up Jewish ships taking war refugees to Palestine', *The Times*, 18 September 2010.

210 Koestler, *Promise and Fulfillment*, pp. 150–151.

211 National Archives, CO 537/2401: Foreign Office draft publicity release, 21 August 1947.

accidental. Throughout the Zionist world, but especially in its extremist, Revisionist form, Britain's operations against illegal immigration, and especially the actions taken against *Exodus 1947*, were couched in the language of the 'Final Solution', emphasising that those on board were victims of the Nazis. Indeed, the struggle between the commander and captain of *Exodus 1947* was not about whether the memory of the Holocaust should be performed and instrumentalised or not but which message should be taken from the catastrophe. Aharonovich, born in Lodz in the early 1920s, was angry at the Jews 'for not fighting for their lives', while Harel responded that he did not 'bring the ship [to the shores of Palestine] so that 4,500 Holocaust survivors would be killed'.[212] On a practical level, Harel was one of the leading figures in the 'illegal' immigration movement to Palestine from 1945 to 1948, the commander of various ships that brought 24,000 to its shores, or over a third of the total in these years, and he cared for those under his charge.[213]

Against this pragmatic approach, Aharonovich wanted to wage war over the Jewish image – he wanted to risk a bloody fight to show that Jews could be tough 'heroes'. That he was not imagining the slight of Jewish cowardice is shown in contemporary intelligence reports on the *Exodus 1947* ships which referred to Jews as 'excitable creatures'.[214] Gregson commented that he rejected the use of 'tear smoke' on the *Runnymede Park* as the 'Jew is liable to panic and 800–900 Jews fighting to get up a single stairway to escape … could have produced a deplorable situation'. In contrast, Gregson believed that in removing the refugees 'No other troops could have done as well and humanely as these British ones did.'[215] Here he was reproducing not only a canard from the Home Front, when Jews were widely blamed for the Bethnal Green Tube disaster of March 1943, but also a longer tradition of accusing 'aliens' of 'feminine' hysteria when faced with danger.[216] This was true of the *Titanic* disaster of 1912 and unfounded claims about Italian pusillanimity (whereas in reporting of its sinking all British passengers and crew showed true 'Anglo-Saxon' fortitude). More recently, selfishness and unmanly behaviour had been attributed to the 'enemy aliens' – Italians and German refugees – on board the *Arandora Star* in 1940 when it was attacked by torpedo, leading to the deaths of over 600 of these men.[217]

212 Kaniuk, 'Obituary'.

213 Eli Ashkenazi, 'Yossi Harel, commander of Exodus, dies at 90', *Haaretz*, 28 April 2008; Kaniuk, *Commander of the Exodus*, passim.

214 National Archives, FO 945/762: BAOR telegram, 4 September 1947.

215 Gregson report in ibid. Gregson briefly appeared in 'People of the Exodus' but with far more conciliatory testimony.

216 Tony Kushner, *The Persistence of Prejudice: Antisemitism in British Society during the Second World War* (Manchester: Manchester University Press, 1989), pp. 125–126.

217 Tom Kuntz (ed.), *The Titanic Disaster Hearings: The Official Transcripts of the 1912 Senate Investigation* (New York: Pocket Books, 1998), pp. 209, 220, 484–485; for

Similarly, when those sent to Mauritius at the time of the *Patria* disaster were returned to Palestine in 1945, the Admiralty did not think 'it would be safe to allow 1300 hysterical refugees to travel with only a crew'.[218] But if there was internal dissent about military tactics within the Zionist leadership on *Exodus 1947*, this did not extend to propaganda against the British.

The Foreign Secretary, not known for his tact or diplomacy, was particularly defamed: 'Hitler lives again in Bevin' was the truth according to one American Zionist placard against his policy of returning the ships to Germany.[219] In the Poppendorf and Amstaw camps the refugees themselves came up with even more juvenile propaganda in the form of a ditty, the colloquialisms of which were designed to appeal to an American audience:

Bevin and Hitler are the same
Fie upon English concentration camp,
Fie upon you hooey English,
Hooey English Hitler's Policies ...[220]

Those passengers on board the *President Warfield* had made similar linkages as it approached Palestine. An appeal was broadcast on behalf of its passengers to the United Nations demanding that it witness the results of 'British brutality'. The British, it claimed,

acted and act according to all the Nazi methods. They insult, beat, and shoot into our ships which are crowded with women and children. These Britishers hold Jews in concentration camps in Cyprus without any justice or trial exactly as the Germans did in Europe. We repeat, come and see with your own eyes how Great Britain is reproducing the evil which the United Nations is striving to exterminate.[221]

A.C. Barclay, the sympathetic British captain of the *Runnymede Park*, in a secret report warned Whitehall officials when the ships were in Port-de-Bouc that the Zionists in the region were 'artists in propaganda, and there is no doubt they are making and will make full use of the golden opportunity to vilify our name on humanitarian grounds'. His ship had 'already been called a floating Auschwitz'. Rather naively, though illustrating his empathy for those on board, he added, 'and I think the title is not far off the mark,

British popular press reporting, such as 'Aliens Fight Each Other in Wild Panic', see Peter and Leni Gillman, *'Collar the Lot': How Britain Interned and Expelled Its Wartime Refugees* (London: Quartet Books, 1980), pp. 196–197.
218 National Archives, CO 537/2370: Eastwood, 5 April 1945.
219 National Archives, CO 733/491/2: Note to Foreign Office, 5 September 1947.
220 Reproduced in National Archives, FO 1032/871.
221 Translated from Hebrew in National Archives, CO 537/2400.

except that the treatment is more humane'.[222] It is significant with regard to instrumentalising the memory of the Holocaust that the description 'floating Auschwitz' came from France, where this death camp had already achieved notoriety and many French–Jewish (and also non-Jewish) victims had been murdered.[223] In extremist Zionist circles in America the ships were dubbed 'British floating Dachaus', a reflection of the emphasis on the western concentration camps, especially those liberated by American troops.[224] In Britain the Foreign Office struggled to contain false rumours that the refugees, once embarked from Hamburg, would be sent to Belsen.[225] Belsen had been transformed into a large displaced persons camp but was notorious in society as a whole after its liberation by British soldiers. Indeed, the tendency in Britain to regard Belsen as symbolising the worst of all Nazi camps has been noted in the previous chapter in attempts to 'place' the war experiences of the child survivors.

There *were* victims of Belsen on *Exodus 1947*, such as Miriam Bergman, a Berlin Jew born in 1928 who was there from when it was a camp largely for so-called 'privileged' Jews through to the indescribable horror of its last days.[226] But, for the British intelligence world, Belsen for those on board the ship and other 'illegals' was now being performed for the media by the refugees on board without actual experience of the camp (though in reality many had survived camps whose main purpose was extermination). It was claimed that the Jewish passengers 'had been told carefully and repeatedly how to behave' by their leaders, including the '"six years in Belsen" story'.[227] The Jews would always 'play ... to the gallery' and one particular passenger was accused of waiting to be photographed so that he could present himself 'with his hands in the air Belsen-wise' (presumably a form of supplication, emphasising pitiful victim status).[228] In fact, proclaimed an agreed statement for worldwide circulation put out by the Foreign and Colonial Office, 'No country in the world has been a better or more consistent friend of the Jewish people than Britain.' It had rescued tens of thousands of Jews and 'In Britain there are no programs [sic].' But, in response to its

---

222 University of Southampton Archives: Report of Captain Barclay, 3 August 1947 in Barclay papers, MS 87, folder 1.

223 Pieter Lagrou, 'Victims of Genocide and National Memory: Belgium, France and the Netherlands, 1945–1965', *Past & Present* no. 154 (February 1997), pp. 181–222.

224 The description is taken from propaganda from *Americans for Hagana* no. 1 no.2 (15 August 1947), reproduced in National Archives, CO 537/3953. For cultural meanings attached to this camp, see Harold Marcuse, *Legacies of Dachau: the uses and abuses of a concentration camp, 1933–2001* (Cambridge: Cambridge University Press, 2001).

225 See National Archives, FO 371/61822 E7488.

226 Thomas, *Operation Exodus*, pp. 12, 77–78, 92–93.

227 National Archives, CO 537/2374: Report on the *Guardian*, 22 April 1947.

228 National Archives, CO 537/2373: Report on *San Filipo*, 14 April 1947.

272 Journeys from the Abyss

'patience, forbearance and humanity', the Jews had attacked British soldiers and civilians – 'outrage more worthy of Nazis than of the Jewish victims of Nazis'.[229]

A perverse reading of recent history was performed by those in Whitehall and the British intelligence world. As Downie had attempted to do before and during the war, Jews were being presented, rather than victims of the Nazis, as behaving like them: it was thus important, especially for an American audience, to make 'Analogies between the Zionist movement and the Nazi movement'.[230] There was thus exasperation that the American government and public viewed the situation of 'illegal' immigration too sentimentally – as 'a spontaneous movement of desperate Jews, fleeing from intolerable conditions and persisting, despite incredible hardships, until they reach the Promised Land'. To counter such tendencies, the Foreign Office, with the assistance of MI5, sent the British Embassy in Washington advice on the appropriate script to be performed for an American audience:

> We ... want to show that the movement is a coldly organised one, starting in the depths of Russia and making use of deceit, forgery and bribery to attain its ends. We should above all put over the fact that American charitable instincts are being abused and that the people running the movement are making suckers out of American officials.[231]

The reference to Russia attempted to play on Cold War paranoia. Elsewhere, intelligence material blamed the increasingly violent antisemitism in post-war Poland and Rumania on the activities of Jewish communists. It again denied that the Jews were genuine victims and, instead, placed them as a source of danger.[232] In terms of the politics of the ships' renaming, it is also revealing that MI5 failed to engage with the Holocaust as a Jewish tragedy. In a contemporaneous report to the *Exodus 1947* journey it noted that the *Haganah* vessels were named only 'after Zionist heroes', including Theodor Herzl and Charles Orde Wingate. Tellingly, it included 'Rebels of the Ghettoes' in that category, in spite of the fact that many of these were non-Zionists, especially the Bundists.[233] The struggle over 'illegal' immigration was thus presented as one between underhand and

229 National Archives, CO 537/1797: Announcement, 11 August 1946.
230 National Archives, FO 371/52633: Beith minute, 8 October 1946.
231 National Archives, FO 371/52633: Rundall note, 27 September 1946. For further comment and contextualisation, see Steven Wagner, 'British Intelligence and the "Fifth" Occupying Power: The Secret Struggle to Prevent Jewish Illegal Immigration to Palestine', *Intelligence and National Security* no. 29 no. 5 (2014), p. 713.
232 National Archives, CO 537/1798.
233 National Archives, KV 3/56: MI5 paper on 'Jewish Illegal Immigration to Palestine', 14 July 1947.

devious Zionists (some under Communist control) and the forbearing and (too) tolerant British. And, further distancing themselves from the emotionally laden names given to the ships by the *Haganah*, the Admiralty simply referred to them collectively as 'illegals'.[234] Such single-word and dismissive nomenaclature anticipated the treatment of migrants by those operating immigration controls later in the century, denying the individuality of those attempting to breach 'Fortress Europe' and other parts of the West.

In contrast, the Zionist leaders on board the *President Warfield* were keen to emphasise that British policy had longer roots than the immediate post-war tension. Anticipating the more polemical attacks on Allied responses towards the Jews during the Nazi era which emerged from the late 1960s onwards, they 'condemn[ed] Great Britain for actively assisting in exterminating six million Jews'. In another melding of time, the 'then' of the Holocaust was linked to the 'now' of British efforts to stop Jewish refugees reaching Palestine:

> When the white smoke of our cremating people rose in a protest to the very dome of heaven through weeks and months there was not a single British plane which sought to bomb the scenes of horror, but now – against us – the tattered remnants – planes are available to bar our way to safety.[235]

Nowhere within this vindictive broadcast, most probably penned by Roseman, was there an attack on American inertia or antipathy towards helping Jews during the 1930s or the Second World War: the focus was purely on Britain. Linking Britain directly to the Holocaust was, as Roseman acknowledged 60 years later, 'hyperbole drafted then for political reasons'.[236] Thus, rather than the *St Louis*, it was the ships turned away from Palestine during the Second World War that were the focus of the animus: 'You have barred the ways of salvation to those who might have escaped … . You have done so to Struma, Patria, San Salvidor, Berl-Boll and Mafrock, all of which were driven by you to the depths of the sea.'[237] Significantly, in terms of memory work, a fragment of the *Patria* has subsequently been salvaged and is on display at the Clandestine Immigration and Naval Museum – again utilised performatively as a symbol of Jewish self-determination and outside indifference.

---

234 National Archives, ADM 1/235261.
235 National Archives, CO 537/2400: Broadcast from the *President Warfield*.
236 Lili Galili, '60 Years later, veteran rues loss of "Exodus Spirit"', 1 August 2007, *IDISHLAND*, in ar.groups.yahoo.com/group/IDISHLAND/message/23547-Argentina, accessed 1 January 2010.
237 National Archives, CO 537/2400.

Returning to the *President Warfield* broadcast, as a final insult, rather than being portrayed as glorious and brave, Britain's role in the Second World War was presented as essentially selfish. British condemnation of the Jewish illegal ships for their inhumane conditions was hypocrisy:

> You have suddenly donned sacred garments which you have ignored when we were burning in the furnaces of hell … . [W]ere you so strict as to whether your ships and fishing boats were overcrowded, too small and the conditions in them inhuman during *your* Dunkirk … You've done everything to save Britishers, but where *our* Dunkirk is concerned you suddenly appear in the impersonation of saints who care for our fate [my emphasis].[238]

In partial contrast, the passengers of the *Runnymede Park*, or at least their leaders, were also willing to evoke the memory of the Holocaust. They did so tactically in order to promote a possible anti-German alliance with the British soldiers, who were, they claimed, threatening to use force to remove them at Hamburg. The British had returned the Jews 'back to our enemies, back to the murder people'. Using language that was in turn universalistic and particularistic, the Germans, the passengers argued in their hand-written letter to the soldiers, 'wanted to annihilate the world, and basically destroyed our parents and children and exterminated more than a third of our people'. Rather than being essentially self-interested, as the earlier broadcast on the *President Warfield* had suggested, Britain should be proud of its war record, but it was in danger of tarnishing its memory:

> Today you are compelled to do the same thing the Germans did before, against whom you fought so heroically. Put not shame on your glorious tradition of the fight against fascism. Put yourselves on the side of the victims of Hitlerism![239]

In Leon Uris' *Exodus* one of the central characters, Brigadier General Bruce Sutherland, had earlier been involved in the liberation of the Nazi concentration camps, subsequently giving evidence about this traumatic experience at the Nuremberg Trials. It enables Sutherland to make an identification with the plight of the Jews on the immigrant ships and to be critical of his own government: 'I saw those people at Bergen-Belsen. Must be the same ones who are trying to get into Palestine now … . We have broken one promise after another to those people in Palestine for thirty years.' Few of the British in the novel, however, could make such

---

238 Ibid.
239 University of Southampton Archives: Letter in Barclay papers, MS 87, folder 1.

connections. As one of Sutherland's friends remarks, 'you and I see eye to eye on this, but we are in a minority'.[240] In this respect, Uris's portrayal was not totally without truth.

Few in Britain outside the Jewish minority would link the events in Palestine *sympathetically* to the treatment the Jews had recently received in Nazi Europe. It is true that Foreign Office files do contain correspondence from ordinary people appalled at the return of the Jews to Germany. It was, according to a Mr V.C. Osborne – describing himself as a 'Cockney and life long voter for the Labour Party' – 'diabolically wicked'. He asked 'Have not these people suffered enough?' and added 'Was it all humbug when the House of Commons stood in silence at the murdering of the Jews during the War?'[241] An elder of the Society of Friends wrote to the prime minister stating that 'Surely there can be no purpose in sending these people back to the country of horrors from which we, ourselves, liberated them.'[242] These, however, were relatively isolated views from non-Jews who were willing to connect the British war effort and the plight of European Jewry to post-war policy. The *Manchester Guardian*, deeply sympathetic to the Jewish plight and ceaseless campaigner for the refugee cause, claimed that there was 'sympathy which people everywhere feel for the Jewish survivors of Nazi persecution'. It reluctantly acknowledged, however, that it was 'rarely expressed in practical terms'.[243]

Indeed, one general reason for this lack of empathy and connection was the national framework within which British memories of the Second World War were constructed. Jewish suffering would remain largely outside this exclusive narrative for many decades after 1945 – the Imperial War Museum, for example, contained little or no information on the Holocaust until the early 1990s and then it was included only in relation to the liberation of Belsen. The addition of a large (greater in size than that devoted to the Second World War), separate, and permanent exhibition on the Holocaust in this museum in 2000 reflected the belated and intensified British interest in the catastrophe of European Jewry, as explored in chapter 2. This confrontation was partly inspired by the example set by the USA, which had increasingly engaged with the Holocaust since the 1980s. It also reflected the growing self-confidence and interest in the subject of British Jewry and a more pluralistic approach to the past in an increasingly multicultural society.

---

240 Uris, *Exodus*, pp. 29–30. Peter Kosminsky's *The Promise* (Channel 4, 2011), also has a Belsen liberation connection through its main character who later serves as a soldier in Palestine.

241 National Archives, FO 371/61820 E7071: Mr Osborne to the Foreign Secretary, 22 August 1947.

242 National Archives, FO 371/61820 E7071: Dora Catford to the Prime Minister, 23 August 1947.

243 'An Act of Folly', *Manchester Guardian*, 22 August 1947, editorial.

Even so, it is a British-linked event – the liberation of Belsen concentration camp – that is still at the forefront of such Holocaust remembrance, as noted in relation to the Holocaust Commission initiative (2014 onwards). In contrast to *Exodus 1947*, it presents Britain as the ultimate friend rather than the enemy of the Jewish survivors.[244] It has taken a new generation of British–Jewish writers since the late 1980s, such as Linda Grant, Bernice Rubens, and Jonathan Wilson, to write about the British Mandate in Palestine and to do so in a critical fashion.[245] This new representation of the troubled relationship between the British and Jewish worlds reflects James Young's observation that a 'society's memory ... might be regarded as an aggregate collection of its members' many, often competing memories'.[246]

It is possible – though not inevitable – that more pluralistic memory work will emerge in British culture with regard to the last days of the British Mandate and this will enable a wider and more open confrontation with the story of *Exodus 1947* as part of the country's relationship both with the Holocaust *and* with dangerous migrant journeys by sea.[247] So far, engagement with this particular migrant past has largely been confined to the British Jewish cultural and progressive elite, even if their work has gained critical acclaim. This is especially true of Linda Grant and her novel *When I Lived in Modern Times* (2000) and Peter Kosminsky's controversial television drama *The Promise* (2011). Both explore the porousness of the boundaries between Britishness and Jewishness and the sympathy as well as the enmity present in the difficult post-war years leading up to the creation of Israel.[248] Kosminsky, who has specialised in making films about 'uncomfortable subjects' in the recent British past, was prompted to make his epic programme after having been contacted by a former soldier in the British army who had served in Palestine. The old soldier pointed out to Kosminsky the amnesia concerning his experiences and

---

244 Tony Kushner, 'The Holocaust and the Museum World in Britain: A Study of Ethnography', in Sue Vice (ed.), *Representing the Holocaust* (London: Vallentine Mitchell, 2003), pp. 13–40.

245 See Axel Stähler, 'Metonymies of Jewish Postcoloniality: The British Mandate for Palestine and Israel in Contemporary British Jewish Fiction', *Journal for the Study of British Cultures* no. 16 no. 1 (2009), pp. 27–40.

246 James Young, *The Texture of Memory: Holocaust Memorials and Meaning* (New Haven: Yale University Press, 1993), p. xi.

247 There is, for example, only passing mention of the movement of illegal Jewish immigration to Palestine in the Imperial War Museum's permanent exhibition. It is within the section devoted to 'Conflicts since 1945' and within that to 'Post-War Palestine'. Author site visit, 1 April 2010. The Second World War Galleries will be replaced and re-open in 2020 as will the Holocaust Exhibition.

248 Linda Grant, *When I Lived in Modern Times* (London: Granta, 2000) which won the Orange Prize for fiction that year; Peter Kosminsky, *The Promise* (Channel 4), 6, 13, 20, and 27 February 2011.

those of his 100,000 fellow troops: 'When they came back to Britain, no one wanted to know; pulling out of Palestine was a terrible humiliation, a total defeat.'[249] Thus Kosminsky has claimed that *The Promise* 'is a British drama made primarily for and about Britons'.[250] It is still significant that it has taken someone of British–Jewish origin – and that an outsider to it – to confront and problematise a period of history that does not fit into narrative expectations of national destiny, remaining for many matter out of place and time.

The other factor explaining the lack of sympathy towards European Jewry in Britain was more immediate and related to the simultaneous terrorist campaign carried out by Zionist extremists inside and outside of Palestine. It was thus a disaster for mainstream Zionists from a propaganda and diplomatic perspective that, as the story of *Exodus 1947* was becoming of increasing international concern, terrorist activities reached a new level. Outrage over the infamous hanging of two British sergeants early in August 1947 precipitated antisemitic rioting in several British cities, namely Glasgow, Manchester, and, most intensively, Liverpool.[251]

In France, British Foreign Office representatives warned that sending the *Exodus 1947* passengers back to Europe was likely to lead to 'lurid anti-British propaganda'. French public opinion would probably be 'receptive [to it] in view of German persecution of Jews under occupation. [The man] in street is totally ignorant of Palestine problems and sees only in these illicit immigrants survivors of a persecuted race seeking refuge in their national home.'[252] In Britain knowledge of the Palestine crisis was perhaps equally lacking, but events there, as Mass-Observation surveys in 1947 violently illustrate, confirmed and intensified antisemitism:

> Jewish sufferings during the war are not often mentioned as a reason for sympathising with Zionist aims. When this does crop up ... it is by no means always as an argument for a National Home. Sometimes Concentration Camps are even mentioned in an anti-Semitic context – 'Hitler was right, exterminate the lot' – is the attitude then.[253]

The Gates of Zion, the journal of the Central Synagogue Council of the Zionist Federation of Great Britain and Ireland, was not being overly pessimistic when it editorialised that *Exodus 1947* showed that the tragedy

---

249 Peter Kosminsky, interview by Rachel Cooke, *Observer*, 23 January 2011.

250 Peter Kosminsky, interview with Simon Round, *Jewish Chronicle*, 4 February 2011.

251 Tony Kushner, 'Anti-Semitism and austerity: the August 1947 riots in Britain' in Panikos Panayi (ed.), *Racial Violence in Britain in the Nineteenth and Twentieth Centuries* (London: Leicester University Press, 1996), pp. 150–170.

252 National Archives, CO 537/2400: Paris to Duff Cooper, 18 July 1947.

253 Mass-Observation Archive, FR 2515, 'Report on Attitudes to Palestine and the Jews', September 1947, The Keep.

of Jewish homelessness had 'still not aroused the conscience of the non-Jewish world'.[254]

Peter Absolon was a young British officer in charge of the overnight guard of *Exodus 1947* when the ships arrived in Hamburg, and witnessed and was involved with the disembarkation of the passengers. Absolon, later an Anglican priest and active in Christian–Jewish dialogue, was haunted by the episode for many decades. His unpublished account, written in 1997, the fiftieth anniversary of the events, outlines the antipathy (and, to a lesser extent, the sympathy towards) the Jews on board at that time in British society.[255]

The concept of the 'queue' has an important role in constructing and contesting Britishness and it played a key role in piecing together the 'official' narrative of illegal immigration to Palestine. At Hamburg, echoing the comments of Ernest Bevin, the British soldiers were informed that those on the *Exodus 1947* ships 'were jumping the queue'. Absolon noted that such comments helped 'mollify the misgivings of squeamish soldiers as "Queue jumpers" received no sympathy from our people in those days. In any case, we knew that British servicemen were being killed by Jewish extremists in Palestine.' He added that this

> gave a sort of legitimacy to the anti-semitic feelings which were endemic at that time and which had not yet been modified by stories of the death camps. The words 'holocaust' and 'shoa[h]' had not been given their special meaning, and the enormity of what had happened had penetrated no further than the tops of our heads.[256]

Later that night in the Officer's Mess, Absolon confessed that he 'felt sorry for the Jews' on board, but found that no one concurred: 'One officer declared that it was a pity Hitler didn't finish off all of them.' Tellingly, although Absolon felt that few would have shared such antisemitic sentiments fully, 'no-one, including me, challenged that odious statement'.[257] In the 1973 BBC documentary *People of the Exodus*, the British forces are presented as carrying out their difficult task without any malice towards the Jewishness of the refugees. Absolon's account suggests that this reassuring narrative has to be queried.[258]

---

254 *The Gates of Zion* no. 2 no. 1 (October 1947), p. 1.

255 Peter Absolon, 'Exodus Hamburg 1947' (unpublished typescript, Parkes Library, 1997).

256 Ibid., p. 1. Bevin, in an unscripted comment at a press conference in autumn 1945, had warned Jewish displaced persons that 'they should not push themselves to the head of the queue'. See Alan Bullock, *Ernest Bevin: Foreign Secretary* (London: Heinemann, 1984), pp. 164–169 for a relatively sympathetic treatment of his Jewish/ Palestinian post-war policy.

257 Absolon, 'Exodus Hamburg 1947', p. 2.

258 *People of the Exodus*, BBC 1, 15 May 1973.

The young Absolon confronted the forced disembarkation of the Jews through a religious discourse. The passengers, having survived the 'worst pogrom in history', then 'endured the privations of the ship "Exodus" which had brought them into sight of the Promised Land', and were now being brought back to the 'land of their oppressors'.[259] Absolon regarded the shrill chants of 'Gestapo! Gestapo! Gestapo!' aimed at the British soldiers as 'comic craziness'. But no one, he admits, was laughing.[260] Having fought a long and bitter war 'alone', according to its own mythology, the British soldiers were in no mood to accept such taunts or to consider, as Absolon did, that while he had joined the army in the war to 'take the side of good against the bad', being involved with *Exodus 1947* had 'placed me, firmly and ingloriously, on the wrong side'.[261] And, as the detailed research of Mass-Observation among ordinary people revealed, the response of the soldiers in Hamburg was reflected more generally in British society.

Absolon, in identifying with Jewish suffering in the tense summer of 1947, was a relatively isolated voice, and, alongside British Jewry, largely powerless to influence wider opinion in Britain. In late August 1947 the Sunderland Jewish Ex-Service Men & Women's Association wrote to the Colonial Secretary imploring him not to send the *Exodus 1947* passengers to Germany. Their 'only crime', it insisted, was to

> survive Belsen, Jachau [*sic*], Buchenwald & Ravensbruck, and as a consequence no longer wish to expose themselves and their children to the possibilities of a reoccurence of such atrocities in a Europe in which anti-semitism is still rife and on the increase.

This group then evoked the loyalty and war efforts of Jews to the Allied cause in their attempt to change British policy. It would be for the

> sake of the 60,000 Jewish Ex-Service Men & Women who served in H.M. Forces in the 1939–45 War, for the 30,000 Jews from Palestine who volunteered to serve along with the other Allies, and for the sake of those thousands of Jews who served in the Marquis and other underground movements of the Allies.[262]

It and other such appeals by British Jews were either politely – or not so politely – ignored in Whitehall.

---

259 Absolon, 'Exodus Hamburg 1947', p. 3.
260 Ibid., p. 4.
261 Ibid., p. 9.
262 National Archives CO 733/491/2: T. Buck to the Colonial Secretary, 29 August 1947.

The collective journeys of *Exodus 1947* were at least partly determined by the British authorities. Radio reporting of them, especially that of BBC correspondent Godfrey Talbot, carefully conformed to the government's official narrative. This was especially so with his broadcasts when the ships arrived at Hamburg:

> Already it is a matter of history that these Jews, who got through and out of France with forged papers, were in Palestine waters transferred from their unseaworthy ship 'PRESIDENT WARFIELD' to three British transports; and that they refused to land in the South of France, though themselves denying tales that their vessels were hell-ships.[263]

Moreover, most of the British press and population were supportive at the time of the treatment of these 'illegal immigrants'. Subsequently, however, these astonishing migrant journeys have little or no place in the collective memory of the nation. Those such as Peter Absolon who agonised over his role in them found themselves effectively silenced and left to come to terms with their responsibility on their own.[264]

More typical was another of the British military actors, though a more senior one, Captain de Courcy-Ireland, a naval veteran of the Battle of Jutland.[265] He was eager to forget his role in intercepting and escorting the refugees in 1947: 'I had had more than enough of Jews.' Some 12 years later and in retirement, de Courcy-Ireland was irritated to be visited by a man, 'George Cassidy', claiming to be an American. Cassidy interrogated the former naval captain about what the latter insisted on calling the '*President Warfield* business'. The 'real' identity of his visitor, however, was given away. 'Cassidy' spread his hands 'in a gesture one could hardly describe as either American or Irish'. The Jews, concluded de Courcy-Ireland, 'have very long memories'. He also disapproved of the largely innocuous 1973 BBC documentary *People of the Exodus* and refused to take part. No doubt Brian de Courcy-Ireland wished for the '*President Warfield* saga' to return to the obscure status it occupied in British society and culture after 1947.[266] He need not have worried. Lacking a context in which it could easily fit and be related to, and largely avoiding controversy, the documentary received very little contemporary attention.[267] Screened to coincide with the

---

263 Godfrey Talbot, 'The Truth about the Jews at Hambourg', BBC North American Service, 16/17 September 1947. See also his BBC Home Service broadcast, 9 September 1947 in BBC Written Archives Centre, Radio Talks, 1926–70. My thanks to James Jordan for these references.

264 Absolon, 'Exodus', p. 9.

265 See his obituary in the *Independent*, 29 November 2001.

266 de Courcy-Ireland, *A Naval Life*, pp. 394, 400, 401, 402.

267 There were the briefest mentions in advance from *The Times*, 15 May 1973 and the *Jewish Chronicle*, 11 May 1973, but neither newspaper provided a follow-up

twenty-fifth anniversary of Israeli independence, it attempted to present a diplomatic compromise which both 'sides' could accept – the British were restrained in their military interventions and, while the *Exodus* refugees were temporarily thwarted, soon a Jewish state would be created.[268]

No immediate or even medium-term memory work was prompted by *People of the Exodus*. It remained forgotten for close to 40 years and was then rediscovered by Adam Curtis, a BBC journalist. Curtis, while interested in the documentary as a piece of history, also highlighted what he perceived to be its relevance to contemporary issues in the Middle East.

> As you watch the film it raises complex reactions and thoughts in your mind. But it is ironic that, although the two events are in many ways completely different, the Israelis are now preventing Palestinians and supporters of Hamas from doing what the Israeli defence organisation – the Haganah – tried to do over 60 years ago.

Significantly, his blog in June 2010 was greeted with polemical statements either expressing outrage at contemporary Israeli actions or suggesting that his historical comparison was 'a disgrace to humanity'.[269] Few wanted to explore sensitively, as did Curtis, the links between 'now' and 'then'.

At the time, the *Exodus 1947* ships returning to Europe were presented as fundamentally unBritish. The *Daily Express*, which frequently lapsed into antisemitic discourse when reporting the situation in Palestine,[270] covered their journeys as they moved from France en route to Gibraltar and then to Germany. On its front page, accompanied by a photograph, it tersely reported that 'Three dirty steamers slid through the English Channel

---

review. It was not mentioned in the weekly television reviews in *New Statesman*, *The Listener*, or *The Spectator*.

268 *People of the Exodus*. A similar narrative is reproduced in the conclusion to Stewart, *The Royal Navy and the Palestine Patrol*, p. 174. In spite of provocation by the Jewish survivors and the Jewish terrorists in Palestine, 'members of Boarding Parties remained fair minded, were not given to excessive force, and once opposition ceased did what they could to ease the lot of the immigrants, provide first aid and make friends. During 50th anniversary reunions of illegal vessel crews in Israel in 1997, the Royal Navy's unique forbearance was acknowledged and praised.'

269 See www.bbcco.uk/blogs/adamcurtis/2010/06/21_miles_off_the_coast_of_pale.html, accessed 31 October 2011.

270 It was the *Daily Express*, 1 August 1947, that printed the photographs of the 'Hanging Sergeants', precipitating the antisemitic riots in Britain. More generally for its provocative journalism in connecting Jews to terrorism, see David Cesarani, *Major Farran's Hat: Murder, Scandal and Britain's War Against Jewish Terrorism 1945–1948* (London: Heinemann, 2009), p. 118 and passim. Its reporting of the *Exodus 1947* journey emphasised the role of American–Jewish funding of the 'illegal' movement and the unfairness of anti-British Zionist propaganda. See editorial comment in *Daily Express*, 5 and 9 September 1947.

yesterday carrying 4,300 illegal Jewish immigrant back from Palestine to Germany. They were escorted by three British destroyers, gleaming white against the rust of the cargo ships.'[271] It is worth contrasting this report and its Manichean colour coding with the opening statement of Peter Absolon:

> Through the night I patrolled the quayside where the three white ships lay. The only sounds from the ships were the usual hissings, creakings and splashings. In the belly of each ship there were cages, and the cages were full of silent Jews.[272]

But it was the treatment in the *Daily Express* that was dominant in British culture and society, part of a discourse that presented the *Exodus 1947* ships and their passengers as foreign, other, and racially undesirable.

As the ships approached Hamburg, Sir Alan Cunningham, High Commissioner for Palestine, was worried that there would be disturbances back in the country he controlled if the passengers were forced to disembark in Germany. Cunningham wondered if they could not be sent to the United Kingdom and from there back to France. His suggestion was rejected by the Colonial Office, fearing that Britain would become a 'staging post on the way to Palestine – another Cyprus in effect'. The presence of its passengers in Britain would also not be welcomed more generally, reflecting a wider animosity towards the entry of Jewish refugees after the war and the concern that domestic antisemitism was growing out of control.[273] As the ships waited in Port-de-Bouc all British colonial territories were ruled out – as they had been earlier – viewed as unsuitable destinations for the Jewish immigrants either through climate, lack of facilities, or local animosity. This included Northern Ireland, where bringing them 'would undoubtedly meet with opposition from [the local] Government'.[274] In the end, the decision to send the *Exodus 1947* refugees back to Europe was justified legally using powers of refoulement under earlier aliens legislation and procedures.[275] The 'illegality' of the immigrants concerned provided the corresponding moral justification for this action, one that, with their eventual disembarkation in Germany, was roundly criticised across the world.

271 *Daily Express*, 4 August 1947.

272 Absolon, 'Exodus', p. 1.

273 Undated report of meeting between the Parliamentary Under Secretary of State for the Colonies and the High Commissioner for Palestine concerning the immigrants on the *President Warfield* in National Archives, CO 537/2402. See also Bullock, *Ernest Bevin*, p. 449 and National Archives, CAB 128/10, 66th meeting, 31 July 1947 on Britain and the passengers.

274 National Archives, FO 371/61822 E7488: Undated memorandum, 'Accommodation of Illegal Immigrants from the "President Warfield"'.

275 See National Archives, CO 537/2373.

While *Exodus 1947* has become famous in America, Israel, and in the Jewish diaspora more generally, in Britain, which was so intimately involved with its journeys, there was a complex process of amnesia surrounding the ships. They passed briefly and closely to its shores late in August 1947, but that was as near as Britain came to accepting either its passengers or their collective story. Only one family from *Exodus 1947* came to Britain – they had been taken off one of the ships at Gibralter as their baby was seriously ill. The family came to Southampton on a hospital ship. Tellingly, however, as soon as the baby recovered the family were sent to join the other refugees in the German camps set up for the purpose of looking after these 'illegal' immigrants.[276]

Unlike the journeys of the *Kinder* and, more recently and less completely, those of the young survivors, the narrative of *Exodus 1947* cannot (yet) be made into a usable British past – it remains as obscure as those of the refugee domestics in popular memory. The marked nature of these binary processes of remembering and forgetting have occurred largely because of the centrality of the Second World War in the construction of national identity and self-image. The Jewish child refugees of both the immediate pre- and the post-war era who came to Britain can be fitted into a redemptive narrative of a liberating nation – if less easily for the later arrivals. This is not the case with the last years of the Mandate in Palestine. As Ernest Bevin told the American Ambassador on 2 August 1947, 'We were disillusioned and disappointed by our thankless task as Mandatory, and might be forced to give up the charge. The Palestine situation was poisoning relations between the United States and Great Britain.' This was the day after antisemitic riots had started in Britain following the hanging of two British sergeants in Palestine and which the Foreign Secretary also highlighted.[277]

Even within British Jewry, the memory of *Exodus 1947* is confused and linked too closely to the formation of the Jewish state – the *Jewish Chronicle*, its major newspaper, when marking Israel's fortieth anniversary, redated its journeys to 1948.[278] It has perhaps taken the anger at the alleged hostility of the media in Britain to Israel in recent years to promote what was the first British Jewish literary response to the *Exodus* affair since 1954 – Bernice Rubens' *The Sergeants' Tale* (2003). As with Louis Golding's/ Emanuel Litvinoff's earlier novel, it is a limited late work of a fine writer, in this case crudely confronting and stereotyping British antisemitism in late Mandate Palestine.[279] Whether the journeys of *Exodus 1947* can be

---

276 See National Archives, FO 945/762: Foreign Office report, 10 October 1947 concerning the Segall family.
277 National Archives, FO 371/61821 E7167: Beesley minute, 4 August 1947.
278 *Jewish Chronicle*, 29 April 1988.
279 Bernice Rubens, *The Sergeants' Tale* (London: Little, Brown, 2003).

remembered with greater subtlety in the Jewish and non-Jewish worlds in America, Israel, and Britain especially is hard to predict. It will need not only the passage of time but also a greater sensitivity to the suffering and sensitivity of others, especially forced migrants occupying liminal spaces. Ultimately it will require a breaking-down of the certainties and exclusions involved in the construction and reconstruction of national and ethnic identities.

In the dominant Israeli narrative, for example, the dominant presence of Jewish isolation during the Holocaust and the antipathy towards its survivors as typified by the treatment of 'illegal immigrants' by the British authorities largely precludes consideration of other migrant journeys – that of the Palestinians in 1947 and 1948. Roughly three-quarters of a million Palestinians left or were forced out of their homes during the last months of the British Mandate and the creation of the Israeli state. In his *Strangers in the House: Coming of Age in Occupied Palestine* (2002), lawyer Raja Shehadeh powerfully evokes the loss and dislocation among his professional and educated family. His parents moved from Jaffa to Ramallah and Raja's grandmother's summerhouse. Raja notes that 'Its proximity to the deep-set Ramallah hills could have made for a pleasant life.' This was not the case, however: there was 'the nagging feeling of being in the wrong place. I was always reminded that we were made for a better life – and that this better life had been left behind in Jaffa.'[280]

Raja is fully aware that his family's experiences were relatively fortunate within the *Nakba* or Palestinian tragedy:

> Thirty thousand refugees had poured into Ramallah, and most of them had to take shelter in tents that were provided by relief organizations. Comparatively speaking, my father's circumstances were less desperate. At least he had a roof over his head, although it belonged to his mother-in-law.

They were still refugees, however, and, as he relates, 'what began as a temporary stay in Ramallah became a permanent one. Three years later I was born in that same summerhouse across the hills from Jaffa.'[281]

There are few in either the Israeli or the Palestinian worlds who are able to consider the recent (or ongoing) homelessness of each other's experiences. In early summer 2010 a flotilla of small vessels carrying aid to Gaza was attacked by Israeli commandos, leaving nine dead. The action led to international condemnation. Interventions such as those of Adam Curtis, which connected this incident to Britain's response to illegal immigration before

---

280 Raja Shehadeh, *Strangers in the House: Coming of Age in Occupied Palestine* (London: Profile Books, 2002), p. 3.
281 Ibid., p. 9.

1948, were rare. It is no accident that the one British commentator who did make the linkage was Linda Grant. Her writings have, as noted, explored the troubled relationships and differing narratives of the late Mandate era and, as has Peter Kosminsky more crudely, attempted to establish a dialogue between them. 'Perhaps', she concludes, 'like the Exodus in 1947, the Gaza aid flotilla will be the tipping point in the long agony of the Palestinian people.'[282]

Yet rather than connect, much of the rhetoric and performance relating to the flotilla divides and inflames, much as did the propaganda used by both sides in 1947 with *Exodus 1947*, when slavery and the Second World War were the points of reference. Exclusive narratives also dominated cultural forms relating to the journeys of the 'illegal' Jewish immigrants of 1947, stridently so in Uris' *Exodus*. The novel contains crude Orientalist portrayals of Arabs as dirty and unmanly. Uris had no sympathy for the Palestinian refugees, stating that their problems were caused by the Arabs themselves. Their initial movement was not forced, he claimed, and now they were 'kept caged like animals in suffering as a deliberate political weapon' by the Arab world.[283] In 1961, responding to Uris' dismissal of the Palestinian tragedy, Erskine B. Childers highlighted in the *Spectator* what he called 'The Other Exodus'. Childers claimed it was 'clear beyond all doubt that official Zionist forces were responsible for expulsion of thousands upon thousands of Arabs, and for deliberate incitement to panic'.[284] Such controversies continue to dominate the divided and divisive historiography of Israel's formation and its often explicit link to contemporary politics.[285]

More recently, in attacks on Israel's Palestinian policy, distorted and offensive linkages to Nazism or South Africa have been made by those searching emotively for historical parallels. Alternatively, the Holocaust has been evoked to curb any criticism of Israel and to give the state moral authority.[286] On both 'sides' such polemical interventions, however heartfelt and well-meaning, help to avoid the need for dialogue and mutual understanding. The flotilla in 2010 was no exception. The late Swedish author Henning Mankell joined the flotilla in Cyprus and was poorly treated by Israeli forces after being captured. He provocatively finishes his diary of the journey by stating 'Demolishing a system of apartheid takes time. But not an eternity.'[287] For others, the story of *Exodus 1947* provides

---

282 Linda Grant, 'This vivid act of piracy may yet turn the tide of opinion', *The Guardian*, 4 June 2010.

283 Uris, *Exodus*, pp. 552–3.

284 Erskine B. Childers, 'The Other Exodus', *The Spectator*, 12 May 1961.

285 Silver, *Our Exodus*, pp. 170–171.

286 For sensitive analysis of Holocaust memory in politics, see Brian Klug, *Being Jewish and Doing Justice: Bringing Argument to Life* (London: Vallentine Mitchell, 2010), chapter 5.

287 Diary translated from Swedish and reproduced in *The Guardian*, 5 June 2010.

an alternative reading of Israel's foundation than that provided by Mankell: 'The sunken *Struma*, *Mefkure*, and *Salvador* accompanied it. In all, 115,000 Jewish refugees who succeeded against all the odds accompanied it. They were the sacrifices, they were the scarred refugees, and they are the Jewish state.'[288] With so much at stake, it is not surprising that the journeys of *Exodus 1947* were recalled only within the confines of the progressive British–Jewish world during and after the summer of 2010 and the Gaza crisis. In contrast, Peter Kosminsky's *The Promise* was dismissed by the *Jewish Chronicle* as 'Shameful poison' and 'institutionalized, pre-meditated antisemitism'.[289]

Performing Lampadusa

Politics and suspicion have acted as a barrier between Jewish and Palestinian mutual awareness of and sensitivity to refugeedom in past and present. As Bashir Bashir and Amos Goldberg suggest, this need not necessarily be the case. They argue that the 'Palestinian and Jewish refugees of the Nakba and the Holocaust not only serve as disruptive and alarming reminders of the exclusionary forces of identity politics in Israel/Palestine'; more positively, they are 'also … a challenge to the statist mainstream Palestinian and Israeli politics that view exclusive and separate ethnic nation-states as the ultimate and desired institutional frame within which the political rights of the respective peoples are realised and protected.' From this inclusive perspective, they suggest that 'Consequently, one could view the refugee as a herald of alternative and creative forms of politics, ones premised on partnership, cooperation, joint dwelling and integration rather than on segregation, balkanization, separation and ghettoization'.[290] If making such linkages, however desirable, seem unlikely given the dismal politics of the contemporary Middle East, it is equally hard to envisage the *Exodus 1947* story being placed alongside more recent narratives of forced migration across the 'merciless sea'. So far, the exclusive tendencies and partial amnesia associated with its journeying have largely precluded such comparisons. But in the spirit of the challenge (and opportunity) offered by Bashir and Goldberg, who note that 'An empathetic view of the refugee disrupts the validity of the foundations of the political order that created her in the first place and now abandons her to her fate', the final section of this chapter will explore the possibilities further.

---

288 Kaniuk, *Commander of the Exodus*, p. 207.

289 Editorial, *Jewish Chronicle*, 4 March 2011.

290 Bashir Bashir and Amos Goldberg, 'Deliberating the Holocaust and the Nakba: disruptive empathy and binationalism in Israel/Palestine', *Journal of Genocide Research* no. 16 no. 1 (2014), p. 92.

In autumn 2015 Philip Hoare used the 'horrors of slavery', the 'coffin ships' of the Irish famine, and those transported to Australia by the British as 'historical parallels' when powerfully evoking the traumatic journeys of those attempting to cross 'the Mediterranean in search of a better life'. To him, these extreme examples from the past 'underline the desperation of the situation' today. British amnesia of 'illegal' Jewish migration to Palestine curtails juxtaposition with contemporary tragedies associated with the 'sea of despair' – one which Hoare may well otherwise have added to his list of maritime human misery. Hoare concludes: 'Slaves and transportees had no choice but to leave. The hungry and dispossessed have a choice, but it is hardly much of one.'[291]

As noted, it has been estimated that from 1933 to 1948 108,000 Jewish 'illegal' immigrants came to Palestine in 116 vessels.[292] In 2014 alone double that number of undocumented migrants came to Europe by sea, thousands drowning in the Mediterranean attempting to do so. A year later, and outside Europe, the crisis of boat people off the Indoniasian coast became scandalous, but nothing compared to what would become the global migration story of 2015, as will be outlined shortly. Earlier, within the Indian Ocean, Australia's treatment of asylum-seekers attempting to reach its shores provoked international criticism with the sinking of the *Palapa* in 2001, a tragedy that was a portent of what was to follow in the new millennium. A small fishing boat, it carried over 400 asylum-seekers, mainly Afghans, journeying from Indonesia and attempting to reach Christmas Island, which belonged to Australia. The Australian government was determined that those on board, rescued from the sea by the Norwegian vessel the *Tampa*, would not enter its territory. After weeks at sea, they were detained in newly created 'off-shore processing centres'. Christmas Island and other places en route, Caroline Moorehead notes in her exploration of modern refugeedom, *Human Cargo* (2005), were '"excised" from Australia for the purposes of migration. Australia had effectively, by a stroke of its pen, shrunk its borders.'[293]

Moorehead is one of the few who has been aware of the historical precedent explored in this chapter, stating that this 'Pacific Solution' of relocating refugees 'was not new – the British blockade of Palestine ... had refused to let Jewish refugees land and pushed them to Cyprus'.[294] It is significant that even then she confines such policies to the pre- rather than the post-war era, reflecting the vague memories associated with this

291 Philip Hoare, 'Sea of despair', *Guardian*, 22 April 2015 and idem, *The Sea Inside* (London: Fourth Estate, 2013).

292 Naor, *Haapala*, p. 105.

293 Caroline Moorehead, *Human Cargo: A Journey Among Refugees* (London: Chatto & Windus, 2005), p. 108.

294 Ibid.

troubled policy. The final section of this chapter will further explore such parallels between journeys out of the Holocaust and contemporary boat migrants. It will query whether or not they are ethically appropriate and analytically helpful with regard to the pursuit of comparative history and political intervention.

Introducing *Human Cargo*, Caroline Moorehead defines an 'illegal immigrant' as a 'person residing in a foreign country without permission'. As her narrative progresses, incorporating the harrowing personal testimony of refugees who have risked their lives in dangerous sea and land journeys, she returns to that definition. She interrogates it especially in relation to the Australian homeland of her father, Alan. A leading writer, he continuously explored the nature of Australianness, a tradition that his daughter was continuing through her examination of Australia's treatment of desperate sea migrants. There, such boat people, regardless of their status, were labelled by the Liberal government of the 1990s as 'illegals'. For Caroline Moorehead, 'The use of the word "illegals" suggests criminals, people who have done wrong, terrorists, certainly people not entitled to anything. They are seen as "queue jumpers", stealing the places of the good refugees who have been patiently waiting their turn ... .'[295] This process of 'othering' through the discourse of 'illegality' blatantly replicates that of the British official mind in the context of Jewish migration to Palestine during the 1930s and 1940s. The closeness in language reinforces the validity of Judith Butler's analysis of hate speech and how its sedimentation through repetition 'gives the name its force'.[296] Initially Britain provided Palestine with its alien legislation, but it was from this quasi-imperial space that the term 'illegal immigration' came back to the Metropolis and, from there, to global usage in rhetoric and policy by the end of the twentieth century.[297]

Moorehead's *Human Cargo* was an important statement about the nature of debates about world asylum-seekers which have grown increasingly animated in the early twenty-first century. By the time of its publication the island of Lampedusa had become infamous in this respect, a notoriety that has grown exponentially in the subsequent ten years. Lampedusa, as Moorehead poetically suggests, is 'where Italy ends and where Africa begins'.[298] Famous largely for its connection to the author of *The Leopard*, Guiseppe Tomasi di Lampedusa (whose ancestors had a long connection to the island, but who himself never visited, residing in Sicily), it is a small, sparsely populated and bare island (a result of misguided nineteenth-century deforestation) where fishing and tourism were the mainstays of

---

295 Ibid., p. 104.

296 Butler, *Excitable Speech*, p. 36.

297 More generally see Georgina Sinclair and Chris Williams, '"Home and Away": The Cross-Fertilisation between "Colonial" and "British" Policing, 1921–85', *Journal of Imperial and Commonwealth History* no. 35 no. 2 (2007), pp. 221–238.

298 Moorehead, *Human Cargo*, p. 51.

the economy until the migrant crisis. It had minor military importance in the twentieth century, especially as a post-war NATO base. Within Jewish folklore the island was much celebrated for the incident in 1943 when a British RAF pilot, Sydney Cohen, allegedly single-handedly (and accidentally) achieved the surrender of the Italian garrison there, having crash-landed – a story which somewhat embellished his role. This feat was commemorated at the time and subsequently in the *King of Lampedusa*, a play that revived Yiddish theatre in Britain and beyond to counter the image of the cowardly, unmanly Jew that, as noted, infused discussion of 'illegal' immigration to Palestine. And ominously, in relation to its later function as a reception and then a detention camp for migrants in the late twentieth and early twenty-first century, Lampedusa had a pre-history, serving as 'a penal colony during the late nineteenth and early twentieth centuries'.[299]

In this respect it has a similar history to other remote islands as racialised spaces used to relocate those deemed as 'matter out of place'. Robben Island, for example, was a penal and leper colony before it became notorious for incarcerating opponents of apartheid. Moreover, Lampedusa's role in the processes of modern migration is not out of place in its history from antiquity onwards. As Stefano, the fisherman hero of Anders Lustgarten's play *Lampedusa* (2015), explains:

> This is where the world began. This was Caesar's highway. Hannibal's road to glory. These were the trading routes of the Phoenicians and the Carthaginians, the Ottomans and the Byzantines … . We all come from the sea and back to the sea we will go. The Mediterranean gave birth to the world.[300]

Moorehead described Lampedusa in the first years of the twenty-first century: 'Spring and summer, on the long calm days, it is where the refugees arrive almost daily in their battered and crumbling boats, frightened, unsure, expectant.' More clinically, she added that

> Experts in asylum matters who study the flows of refugees and their journeys to the north, call it the blue route after the waters of the Mediterranean, and it has become a lucrative source of the estimated $5 to $7 billion revenue from the world's traffic in smuggled people.[301]

Until the tragedies of 2015 no place came to symbolise more the intense human tragedy and drama of modern migration, evoking sentiments of

---

299 Nick Dines et al., 'Thinking Lampedusa: border construction, the spectacle of bare life and the productivity of migrants', *Ethnic and Racial Studies* no. 43 no. 3 (2015), p. 443, note 8.
300 Anders Lustgarten, *Lampedusa* (London: Bloomsbury, 2015), p. 3.
301 Moorehead, *Human Cargo*, pp. 51–52.

pity, shame, and fear in equal measure. Politicians, NGOs, artists, and the media, as well as the islanders and migrants themselves, have confronted and represented the recent and ongoing story of Lampedusa. And, as with Palestine and 'illegal' immigration, questions of performativity have been central in establishing meaning for Lampedusa.

In their 2014 literary guide for travellers to Sicily, Andrew and Suzanne Edwards contrast its major town, Palermo, with its 'remains of a splendid Arab-Norman past', with the less happy reflection of 'modern-day relations with North Africa' – that of those 'intent on escaping the harsh realities at home':

> The most obvious demonstration of these events has been the refugee centre on the Sicilian island of Lampedusa, one of the nearest landfalls to Tunisia. Many have risked life and limb, often falling prey in the process to unscrupulous people – traffickers whose last priority is their victims' safety ... .[302]

Also in the realm of the holidaymaker, in 2015 TripAdvisor produced a list of the top ten beaches in Europe. The first three were in the Mediterranean, with Rabbit Beach, Lampedusa, ranked the highest.[303] As is happening in other parts of the 'blue route' – most recently the Greek islands – the misery of migration at its most desperate is coinciding in time and place with the pursuit of tourist pleasure. Affluent Western visitors are witnessing the victims of dictatorship, failed states, civil war, ethnic cleansing, religious intolerance, and basic deprival of life chances. They are thus inadvertently becoming co-presents to those suffering the most extreme problems of the contemporary world. While official Italian tourist information continues to insist that Lampedusa is 'one of the most-frequented destinations of sun-worshippers, scuba-divers and nature lovers', in reality this 'glorious sun-bleached island' is still firmly associated with human migration in its most basic and deathly form.[304]

There are no definitive figures for those who have died migrating to Europe using the Mediterranean. Using media and NGOs, the monitoring group Fortress Europe argued that between 1993 and 2011 close to 20,000 died en route. Since then the numbers have gone up alarmingly – estimated at 3419 for 2014 and 300 higher for 2015.[305] The problem of

---

302 Andrew and Suzanne Edwards, *Sicily: A Literary Guide for Travellers* (London: I.B. Tauris, 2014), p. 230.

303 *The Metro*, 18 February 2015.

304 http://www.italia.it/en/travel-ideas/the-sea/the-island-of-lampedusa.html, accessed 19 June 2015.

305 *The Guardian*, 2 April 2015; www.Migration.iom.int/Europe, accessed 27 December 2015. See also UNHCR figures reproduced in *The Times*, 5 October 2016.

using such information, however, is that 'Some places receive more ... attention than others because they have developed into "border theatres".' Of all these, Lampedusa until 2014 was the most prominent example.[306] Without its connection to boat migrants, 'Lampedusa would be just one of the many minor Italian islands living on fishing and tourism'.[307] Its recent connection to migration began slowly and then transformed the island. At times during the twenty-first century migrants have outnumbered residents (5800) and an infrastructure involving a large-scale policing and humanitarian presence has also impacted on the everyday life of Lampedusa.

It is often assumed that desperate migrants have *chosen* to come to Lampedusa as the piece of European land closest to Africa. While in the early stages of this movement in the 1990s there was an element of truth in such assumptions, it has not been the case subsequently. Since the early twenty-first century, it has been emphasised that migrants 'did not arrive of their own accord': they thus did not choose Lampedusa, but were directed and diverted there by the Italian authorities as a way of controlling the flows of migration which were both increasing in numbers and diversifying in places of origin.[308]

In 2013 close to 15,000 migrants were processed through Lampedusa, most fleeing from Eritrea.[309] The numbers in the early 1990s were much smaller, but in 1996 they merited the construction of an informal reception centre, largely run by local volunteers trained by the Italian Red Cross.[310] Two years later, reflecting the growing anxiety about such migration, this voluntary centre was replaced by an official one near the airport. It accommodated up to 150 people and was surrounded by barbed wire: 'inmates were forbidden from moving freely around the island. After a period (during which they were given almost no information about asylum procedures) boatpeople were "distributed" by plane to other facilities in Sicily or mainland Italy or deported to Libya.' In turn, a new detention (rather than reception) centre opened in 2007, designed for up to 800 internees and largely invisible within Lampedusa town, the only settlement on the island.[311]

---

306 Tara Brian and Frank Laczko (eds), *Fatal Journeys: Tracking Lives Lost during Migration* (Geneva: International Organization for Migration, 2014), p. 93.

307 Paolo Cuttitta, '"Borderizing the Island. Setting and Narratives of the Lampedusa "Border Play"', *ACME* no. 13 no. 2 (2014), p. 214.

308 Dines et al., 'Thinking Lampedusa', pp. 432–433.

309 Zed Nelson, 'A long way home', *The Guardian*, 22 March 2014.

310 Heidrun Friese, 'Border Economies: A Nascent Migration Industry Around Lampedusa', in Lisa Anteby-Yemini et al. (eds), *Borders, Mobilities and Migrations: Perspectives from the Mediterranean 19–21st Century* (Brussels: Peter Lang, 2014), p. 121.

311 Ibid., p. 122; author site visit, 6 August 2015.

Lampedusa had become a 'border zone',[312] a place which had 'essentially become detached from the rest of Italy'.[313] It is, in the words of Alison Mountz, one of many 'stateless spaces'.[314] The Sicilian Channel had, in effect, 'become an outer border of the European Union',[315] and Lampedusa was the focal place/non-place where attempts were made at controlling the flow of unwanted 'illegal' migrants. Then, on 3 October 2013, 'the world witnessed the most dramatic human disaster in the Mediterranean Sea since the Second World War'.[316] A small fishing boat left Libya carrying over 500 largely Somalian and Eritrean refugees. The vessel caught fire just half a mile from Lampedusa and only 155 survived, with the rest drowning. This was far from the first instance of mass migrant death at sea, and it has been surpassed by even greater tragedies thereafter. The response to it, however, marked a rupture: 'its scale [was] too great for us to ignore'.[317]

The disaster led to an international outcry, led by Pope Francis in what was his first official engagement. He visited the island, where both the survivors and the bodies of some (but not all) of the dead had been brought, and responded that 'The word disgrace comes to mind. It is a disgrace.' He also urged 'Let's unite our efforts so that tragedies like this don't happen again.'[318] While in 2014, through a variety of governmental and private initiatives, some 170,000 migrants were rescued in the Mediterranean,[319] less than 18 months after 3 October 2013 several similar boats capsized close to Lampedusa, with over 300 migrants feared to have drowned.[320] These, however, were overshadowed by an even larger catastrophe in the spring of 2015. In May 2015, a boat carrying over 800 migrants sank with just 28 survivors.[321]

In 2015 over one million migrants have attempted to reach Europe across the Mediterranean. Of these, 'only' 150,000 arrived in Italy from Africa, but the danger of this route is emphasised by the numbers continuing to drown in the 'Blue Desert'. The International Organization of Migration estimate that, of roughly 3700 recorded deaths, close to 2900 have been en route to Italy via Lampedusa/Sicily. In contrast, there were 'just' over 700

---

312 Cuttitta, '"Borderizing" the Island', p. 205.
313 Dines et al., 'Thinking Lampedusa', p. 433.
314 Alison Mountz, *Seeking Asylum: Human Smuggling and Bureaucracy at the Border* (Minneapolis: University of Minnesota Press, 2010), p. 129.
315 Timothy Raeymaekers, 'Introduction: Europe's Bleeding Border and the Mediterranean as a Relational Space', *ACME* vol. 13 no. 2 (2014), p. 165.
316 Ibid.
317 'Europe's Immigration Disaster', *Dispatches*, Channel 4, 24 June 2014.
318 *The Guardian*, 4 October 2013.
319 *The Guardian*, 8 April 2015.
320 *Metro*, 12 February 2015.
321 *The Guardian*, 23 May 2015.

deaths for the 800,000 plus who have attempted to reach Greece.[322] It is perhaps the comparative 'safety' of the sea journeys to the Greek islands that has persuaded some, especially Syrian refugees, to shift from the 'high-risk, central Mediterranean to the less risky eastern Mediterranean route' from 2015.[323] At the start of 2016, with European Union attempts to cut off journeys from Turkey to Greece, there were fears that the central Mediterranean route would become dominant again. These have subsequently been realised. At the time of writing (November 2016), the loss of life for 2016 is already anticipated as higher than that of the previous year. While the total number of boat migrants has declined because of the closing of the Turkish route, those leaving from the more dangerous journey towards Italy via Lampedusa/Sicily has increased.[324] Anticipating this possibility, then British prime minister David Cameron was reported as demanding that EU leaders increase the number of patrol ships in order to turn 'back boats of refugees as soon as they set off on perilous journeys across the Mediterranean from Libya'.[325]

With reference to the island's recent traumatic history, Paolo Cuttitta has referred to the 'Lampedusa "Border Play"', one that has been 'performed' from 2004 onwards and, up to 2014, consisted of 'five acts'.[326] Cuttitta is far from insensitive to the sufferings of the migrants linked to the island, noting that 'Lampedusa is the place where hundreds of migrants have touched Italian soil only as dead bodies.'[327] He is aware of the dangers of studies that ignore the 'agency and the subjectivity of migrants', pointing out in his case study that, alongside the role played by those managing and policing the border,

> Lampedusa has ... been a place of riots, of self induced injuries, of protests and escapes, during which migrants also happened to join the local population in rallies against the Italian government, as well as to clash with groups of local inhabitants.

---

322 'Irregular Migrant, Refugee Arrivals in Europe Top One Million in 2015', International Organization for Migration, 22 December 2015, in www.Migration. iom.int/Europe, accessed 27 December 2015.

323 Philippe Fargues, '2015: The year we mistook refugees for invaders', *Migration Policy Centre: Policy Brief* no. 12 (December 2015), p. 2.

324 See *The Times*, 5 October 2016. In early November another huge migrant disaster occurred with the loss of over 200 people when two migrant boats – inflatable dinghies – sank. The survivors were brought to Lampedusa. Most were from West Africa. See BBC News, 3 November, http://www.bbc.co.uk/news/world-africa-37861700, accessed 7 November 2016.

325 Rowena Mason, 'Cameron wants EU to turn back more refugees', *Guardian*, 18 March 2016.

326 Cuttitta, '"Borderizing" the Island', p. 207.

327 Ibid., p. 197.

More fundamentally, he highlights how 'each sea crossing testifies the motivation and strength of migrants trying to realize their migratory projects'.[328] His focus, however, is the 'performance' of migrant control.

Even with the vastly expanded numbers of boat migrants in 2014 and 2015, those travelling across the sea are still in the minority compared to those going across land or flying. But, as Cuttitta argues, 'if the border … is a suitable theatre for the "political spectacle", the sea border is the ideal stage for political actors to perform the "border play".'[329] The five acts identified by Cuttitta on Lampedusa consist of 'toughness', when, from October 2004 to March 2006, roughly 2200 migrants were returned from the island to Libya. The second 'act' was 'humaneness', following the success of a more progressive Italian coalition government in April 2006, and the number of such deportations was reduced. The detention centre was reformed and made more open to public scrutiny, but at the same time all efforts were made in cooperation with the Gaddafi regime to stop migrants leaving from Libya. This lasted until late 2008, when a third 'emergency' act was started.[330] The 'tough border' was re-established with increased migration and the detention centre soon became overcrowded, with over 1800 occupants, more than double its capacity, housed there by January 2009. Periods of internment increased, leading to hunger strikes and an attempt to set fire to the buildings. It was followed by a fourth act – 'zero immigration' – starting from May 2009 with 'push-back operations from the high seas' and the closing of the detention centre. This continued until 2011, when the number of migrants increased rapidly following the 'Jasmine Revolution', when thousands of Tunisians left their country. With the detention centre still closed, 4000 migrants were left sleeping on Lampedusa's streets and their numbers – over 6000 – 'exceeded that of the local population'.[331]

The tragic events of October 2013 and February 2015, with many smaller incidents between and following, have added further 'acts' to the narrative, but Cuttitta identifies astutely how Lampedusa is used not only to implement controls in a location 'more "border" than other Italian and European border places' but also as the place where this 'border' is performed to the outside world, including to would-be migrants.[332] There is a parallel here to *Exodus 1947/President Warfield* which the British and Palestinian authorities wanted to make into a salutary example as well as a specific case of refused entry to 'illegal' immigrants. Similarly, in 2016, the Australian immigration authorities commissioned a multi-million pound

328 Ibid., p. 199.
329 Ibid., p. 206.
330 Ibid., pp. 207–208.
331 Ibid., pp. 210–211.
332 Ibid., p. 212.

film, *The Journey*, to put off would-be migrants. A 'lavish production', it depicts 'hopeful asylum-seekers [from Afghanistan] who meet tragic fates crossing the Indian Ocean'.[333] In all these cases, security and economic fears have run alongside humanitarian concern. In the case of the Jewish 'illegal' immigration, the British tried (and largely failed) to impress the world that those embarking on such journeys, and especially the organisers, were doing so at the expense of genuine, legitimate refugees. Today, similar dynamics are at work, with the focus of European and other Western organisations and politicians being on the 'criminal' smugglers and the need to curtail their activities, including by the destruction of the boats used to carry the migrants. If those used to transport Jewish migrants in and after the Nazi era were larger vessels well beyond their useful life, many of those today are tiny, described as being like the ones 'children used to play with on the beach. They are really just toys.'[334] Returning to Lampedusa, since Cuttitta wrote, the detention centre has become closed to visitors and supporters of the migrants, isolating them from the largely positive response of the islanders to their presence. In a further attempt to render the migrants invisible, the coastguard boats bringing in the migrants and then sending them on to Sicily arrive and depart late at night.[335]

Self-consciously, Cuttitta's Lampedusa 'play' provides only a walk-on part for the migrants themselves. To conclude this section, their perspective and performativity will now be added, alongside the wider representation (including self-representation) of their experiences and those of the island/ islanders as a whole. It will be argued that, comparing the situation to the 1930s/40s, there is both change and continuity in how the migrant voice is incorporated. The major limitation then and now is the focus on the journey itself, with little attention given to the individual's life before it was undertaken. Typical in this respect is the substantial investigation: *Fatal Journeys: Tracking Lives Lost during Migration* (2014), published by the International Organization for Migration (IOM). Within it testimony is sparse and used to highlight a specific perspective. The report closes with the words of Kasseh, a 15-year-old Ethiopian boy who, with his friends, left a farming community in search of better-paid work. After a series of horrendous experiences, in which some girls in his group were abducted, Kasseh was eventually reunited with his family in Ethiopia. Rather than 'journeys of hope', he reflects that they were ones of disaster:

> My only dream now is that somebody may stop these 'trips' that are full of pain and suffering for poor people. My only truth now is tell my

---

333 *The Guardian*, 29 March 2016.
334 Montse Sanchez, a human rights worker, quoted in *The Guardian*, 3 June 2014.
335 Tony Kushner, discussion with local activist, Paola Larosa, Lampedusa, 5 August 2015.

friends about what happened to me and warn them not to go through what I went.[336]

As an intergovernmental organization, IOM campaigns for 'humane and orderly migration' and thus it is not surprising that Kasseh's testimony should be instrumentalised with this objective in mind, as a cautionary tale for those thinking of embarking on a journey that in reality would be chaotic and dangerous. Elsewhere in *Fatal Journeys* it is emphasised that of the 40,000 migrant deaths in transit recorded (and two-thirds are not), for as many as one in five the region (let alone the country) of origin is unknown.[337] That so many deaths literally leave no trace in a world of instant communication and constant surveillance reflects the utter obscurity and marginality of so many migrants today. The Mediterranean, in the words of Caroline Moorehead, 'is not a deserted sea. Its waters are among the busiest in the world, criss-crossed by fishing boats, naval vessels and cruise ships, along with the patrol boats of the various coastguards.'[338] Even so, thousands have drowned in it. Against that invisibility is the desire of many NGOs, journalists, campaigners, academics, and others to restore individuality to the migrant.

During the Nazi era the *Manchester Guardian* was unmatched globally for its daily coverage of the plight of the Jews. Before and after, it was not only Jewish refugees that this newspaper championed, and this empathy and support of the forcibly displaced has continued into the twenty-first century. Confronting the crisis of the boat people in the Mediterranean in spring 2015, and the paucity of the European Union's responses to them, it emphasised the common humanity binding 'us' and 'them':

> A proud father who is fleeing persecution, a mother who wants to give her family a chance – every migrant who risks their lives in the Mediterranean has a story that any European would recognise … . [I]n any discussion of what should be done, that particularity is the most important thing to remember.[339]

Effort has been made to record the 'individual stories of hope and fear' of those that have survived the nautical disasters, including those from the sinking near Lampedusa in October 2013. One of these was Fanus, an 18-year-old Eritrean woman whose story was told in words, photographs,

---

336 Brian and Laczko (eds), *Fatal Journeys*, pp. 174–175.

337 Ibid., pp. 15, 24.

338 Caroline Moorehead, 'Missing in the Mediterranean', *Intelligent Life Magazine*, May/June 2014.

339 Editorial: 'A thousand individual stories of hope and fear have been lost. Europe must act', *The Guardian*, 22 April 2015.

and documentary by filmmaker Zed Nelson.[340] She had paid close to £1000 for the journey that so nearly led to her death. Travelling with her best friend, 'Like almost every other passenger, they had left Eritrea, fleeing the military dictatorship and forced conscription. Fanus had paid smugglers to get her over the border and on through the Sahara to Libya.' The Mediterranean crossing was thus just 'the final leg of a dangerous, expensive journey in search of asylum in Europe'. Her narrative focuses on this and her other failed attempts to escape Eritrea and how 'My parents sold everything they had to raise the money' – in all, it cost over £2000.[341]

In Stockholm some six months after her traumatic arrival in Lampedusa, Fanus (her real name was withheld to protect her family), reflected with horror on how she got there from Africa: 'I don't want to look back and remember my journey, nobody should have to go through what we did. I wouldn't wish it on my worst enemy.'[342] But even this truncated account of her life story, with the focus on the Lampedusa disaster and her life as an 'illegal' immigrant after it, is exceptional. Fanus burnt her fingertips so as to avoid police recognition. The wider aim was to avoid return to Italy as place of first arrival under the Dublin Treaty in processing asylum-seekers. Others avoided telling the authorities of their journey to Lampedusa for the same reason. Meron Estefanos, an Eritrean activist who has supported those who survived the October 2013 disaster, relates that 'They are afraid if they tell their story, there is a risk they will be sent back to Italy so for that reason people choose not to mention they survived the boat tragedy. They pretend they came a different route.' In speaking out, having reached Sweden 'illegally', Fanus 'decided to take her chances. "If they want to send us back to Italy, we'll tell them Italy did not treat us right, We just have to be honest."'[343] But it is not only that aspect of their life stories that such migrants have performed differently from reality – their places of origin and reasons for leaving have also often been shaped to reflect the reality of European asylum procedures.

From the moment immigration controls were systematically introduced in the late nineteenth century migrants have shaped both their testimony and their paperwork to improve their chances of gaining entry. The latest manifestation of this 'game' (one that can mean life or death) is migrants performing what they hope will be the right narrative for those whose job it is to keep borders as restrictive as possible. As Caroline Moorehead noted in 2005, when covering the life of asylum-seekers in the north-east of England:

---

340 Nelson, 'A long way home'; 'Europe's Immigration Disaster', *Dispatches*, Channel 4, 24 June 2014.
341 Nelson, 'A long way home'.
342 Ibid.
343 Ibid.

Refugee life is rife with rumour. Among those who wait to be interviewed for refugee status, word circulates about how some nationalities are more likely to get asylum than others, about how some stories are more powerful than others, and some more likely to touch the hearts of the interviewers.

She adds that the 'buying and selling of "good" stories, stories to win asylum, has become common practice in refugee circles, among people terrified that their own real story is not powerful'. She concludes: 'How easy, then, how natural, to shape the past in such a way that it provides more hope for a better future.'[344] In the ten years since she published *Human Cargo*, the level of control and culture of disbelief has grown and, alongside it, the construction of migrant narratives to resist such tendencies.

Perhaps the most desperate attempt to 'perform' refugeedom is the desire to show innocence through the presence of young children on these boats. Abdul Azizi, and 26 other refugees from Afghanistan and Syria, boarded a boat from Turkey aiming for Greece. After two hours their engine failed and a Greek coastguard vessel ordered them to return to Turkey. 'We said the boat had broken down. And we took the babies and held them above our heads, to show that there were children on board. But they didn't listen'. Their boat was towed towards Turkey and then began to sink:

> The women and children were in the [hold] and we went to try and get them … . Everything happened so quickly. There was no time to save our children. We had arrived in Europe. We were refugees. But in a flash I had lost my child and my wife.[345]

In this vein, there are even more horrific stories. The 300-plus victims of the October 2013 Lampedusa disaster included 'a baby boy still attached to his mother by the umbilical cord'.[346] As noted, after 1945 Jewish survivors of the Holocaust performed their persecuted state through adopting, according to the British authorities, a 'Belsen' pose. In the first decades of the twenty-first century the climate of distrust is such that migrants have to exhibit their children to show they are not a threat to the receiving countries. No children under 12 reached Lampedusa following 3 October 2013. And then, at the beginning of September 2015, the world was shocked by Nilufer Demir's photograph of three-year-old Alan Kurdi washed up on the Turkish coast and cradled by a Turkish policeman.[347] If only briefly, the conscience

---

344 Moorehead, *Human Cargo*, p. 136.
345 Testimony in *The Guardian*, 3 June 2014.
346 *The Guardian*, 11 October 2013.
347 See *The Guardian*, 28 December 2015 for the background to the taking of this photograph.

of the world, which Pope Francis had valiently tried but largely failed to call to action in October 2013, was stirred by the death of this child, his brother, Galip, and his mother.

In the case of Jewish migration to Palestine during the 1930s/40s testimony extended only to routes taken, framed within a discourse of either legality/illegality or of organised resistance to British restrictionism. With contemporary boat people, there has been greater sensitivity from the media and NGOs in showing the individuality of the migrants, acknowledging their agency and explaining why they have been forced to break the law to continue their journeys. The concern has been with the present, understandable when for so many it has been and continues to be uncertain. But it reinforces the tendency to treat refugees as people 'with no history, past experience [and] culture'.[348] Even in respect of the journey itself, the media tend to present simplistic maps of 'migrants' routes directly connecting the Mediterranean Sea to sub-Saharan Africa'. As Luca Ciabarri, an ethnographer, concludes, 'what emerges are different seasons and histories of migration, each rooted in specific historical conjunctions, characterized by a different intertwining of social dynamics and different power relationships'.[349]

In much of the literature on refugees and forced migration in the late twentieth and early twenty-first centuries the work of Italian philosopher Giorgio Agamben on *homo sacer* (sacred man) and the concept of 'bare life' has been utilised and critiqued.[350] Agamben outlines why the refugee represents 'such a disquieting element in the order of the modern nation-state ... above all because by breaking the continuity between man and citizen ... they put the originary fiction of modern sovereignty in crisis'.[351] The concept of 'bare life' with regard to refugees does reflect a reality: the tens of thousands of deaths in the Mediterranean and elsewhere illustrate how even sheer survival can be tenuous. But, as many have noted, it can also remove all agency from refugees and, in the case of Lampedusa, this has been and continues to be a powerful factor.

In the detention centres of the island and in its everyday life the migrants have both resisted and formed alliances with the local inhabitants. In February 2014 this led to the creation of the Charter of Lampedusa, which was not 'intended as a draft law' but as the expression 'of an alternative vision' where 'Differences must be considered as assets,

---

348 Peter Gatrell, *The Making of the Modern Refugee* (Oxford: Oxford University Press, 2013), p. 284.

349 Luca Ciabarri, 'Dynamics and Representations of Migration Corridors: the rise and fall of the Libya–Lampedusa route and forms of mobility from the Horn of Africa (2000–2009)', *ACME* vol. 13 no. 2 (2013), pp. 246–262.

350 Giorgio Agamben, *Homo Sacer: Sovereign Power and Bare Life* (Stanford: Stanford University Press, 1998 [1995]), pp. 126–135.

351 Ibid., p. 131.

a source of new opportunities, and must never be exploited to build barriers.'[352] Such bonds have been celebrated as well as problematised in Emanuele Crialise's prize-winning Italian film *Terraferma* (2011), Anders Lustgarten's play *Lampedusa* (2015), and, most recently, Gianfranco Rosi's documentary *Fire at Sea* (2016), which won the Golden Bear award at the Berlin International Film Festival. It is also recognised movingly at an everyday level through the island's cemetery, where plots and headstones have been donated locally to bury both named and unnamed migrants washed up on its shores.[353] Lampedusa has also acted as a source of transnational identity for those who have found asylum beyond its shores. It has led to groups such as 'Lampedusa in Berlin' and 'Lampedusa in Hamburg' using the solidarity of this experience to campaign for better treatment of migrants at all stages of the journey.[354]

While *Terraferma*, *Lampedusa* and *Fire at Sea* are (sympathetic) artistic portrayals by non-migrants, those who have passed through the island or supported them there have made a determined effort at self-representation, including in the form of heritage performance. An alternative museum and archive of Lampedusa, Porto M, has been created on the island itself, made up of fragments of ruined boats and lost belongings of the migrants. The work of an anarchist collective, 'Askavusa' (Barefoot), it highlights the everyday possessions of the migrants. To ensure there is no exploitation, no images of the migrants (who may or may not still be alive) are included and the overall narrative is to present the issue as a global one rooted in inequality.[355] It provides a stark alternative to the nationally exclusive approach of the Clandestine Migration Museum in Haifa, while on the island itself it complements but also critiques Mimmo Paladino's 2008 'Porta di Lampedusa – Porta D'Europa' memorial, situated away from the town and close to the airport runway. Paladino's work demands that the door of migration should be kept open, though in terms of scale its portal is relatively small compared with the monument as a whole, suggesting perhaps a managed, rather than an open border, approach. It thus follows the philosophy of the IOM rather than Askavusa.[356]

The migrants themselves, in addition to their political interventions, have with their supporters created an online archive to document their experiences in passing through Lampedusa, utilising private documents

352 'The Charter of Lampedusa', http://www.bilding-fuer-alle.ch/political-program-charter-lampedusa, accessed 22 June 2015.

353 Crialise's film won several prizes at the Venice Film Festival; Tony Kushner, site visit to Lampedusa cemetery, 5 August 2015.

354 Dines et al., 'Thinking Lampedusa', p. 436.

355 Tony Kushner, site visit to Porto M and discussion with the Askavusa collective, Lampedusa, 6 August 2015.

356 Tony Kushner, site visit, 5 August 2015; 'The port of Lampedusa, an unfinished work', www.segreteria@aminiforaafrica.it, accessed 2 August 2015.

such as diaries, as well as films and oral history. They have thus helped to ensure that their voices are preserved and their testimony available not simply through the limitations of media, government, and non-governmental organisations.[357] In this respect, one of the most powerful forms of migrant self-representation has been produced through this initiative: Zakaria Mohammed Ali's documentary *To Whom It May Concern* (2012). Ali, a Somalian journalist and political refugee, had been interned at the island's detention centre in 2008. Four years later he returned as a 'free man' to Lampedusa with his friend and fellow migrant, Mahamed Aman. His film focuses on the traces of the migrant presence on the island and emphasises the importance of past lives before the journeys were undertaken as well as the dangers and losses (not just death at sea but also with regard to identity and status) of those undertaking them. It is thus a memorial to the multi-layered nature of migrant experiences – before, during, and after – and how they are affected yet not simply determined by the negativity of immigration procedures. Ultimately *To Whom It May Concern* is a statement about the importance of memory, which Ali defines as 'the only bridge which connects human beings to their past'. It highlights, through the Lampedusa detention centre, how Western bureaucracies attempt to erase memory through the violence of destroying paperwork (whether personal photographs, certificates, or diplomas) confirming who the individuals were before they made the journeys across desert and sea. By returning to Lampedusa, Zakaria and Mahamed illustrate how they have not been defined by their detention and the desire to render them 'illegal'.[358] If *Exodus 1947* was performed both at the time and subsequently as an epic narrative, it is already clear that Lampedusa has become a part of a global story, and one which the migrants themselves, in spite of their ongoing marginality, are playing a key role in emphasising their common humanity.

Conclusion

Why the island is called 'Lampedusa' is unclear. Greek origins are suggested, with three possible connections – 'rock', beacon', and 'crab'. All three in combination provide a neat summary of its complex past and present. In turn, the island has been a military base for various empires and it has continued this fortress role as a border for the European Union. It has also been a place of local welcome to newcomers escaping danger and a place of livelihood for its fishermen. Population movements in and out of the island, forced (including for slavery inflicted on the locals by Barbary pirates) and voluntary are integral to its remote history, linked to and apart from

---

357 Material available through www.archviomemoriemigranti.net.
358 *To Whom It May Concern* (Archivio Memorie Migranti, 2012).

Europe. The boat people and the treatment of them, including deportation and return, as well as empathy towards them, are part of a deep history and not alien to it, a point highlighted in Rosi's *Fire at Sea*.

In the politics of performativity involving both *Exodus 1947* and contemporary boat people, history matters. On one level, they share a common bureaucratic past and the construction of the 'illegal immigrant' or, more crudely and commonly today, the 'illegals'. The ahistorical tendency in migration studies has led to the missing of this connection and the origins of 'Migrant "Illegality"', which are dated much more recently, for example to American treatment of Mexicans and others and only from the 1970s.[359] Moreover, this chapter began by highlighting how from the late nineteenth century, the label of 'illegality' has easily slipped into denying the common humanity of migrants. Again, this racist tendency has not disappeared.

In April 2015 Katie Hopkins, a columnist in Britain's best-selling newspaper, *The Sun*, penned an article with the headline: 'Rescue Boats? I'd use gunships to stop illegal migrants. Make no mistake these migrants are like cockroaches.' Her Biblical discourse did not stop there, referring to British towns as 'festering sores, plagued by swarms of migrants and asylum-seekers'.[360] Despite an online petition exceeding 200,000 signatures calling for her sacking and criticism from Zeid Ra'ad Al Hussein, the United Nations Human Rights High Commissioner, that she had utilised language 'reminiscent of anti-Semitic Nazi propaganda' and the Rwandan genocide, Hopkins remained in post.[361] The reason why became apparent a few months later.

Revealingly, her hate discourse was regarded as acceptable by both the newspaper itself and by the then prime minister, David Cameron. On 24 July 2015 *The Sun*'s front page was devoted to a story from Calais describing how 'Illegals swarm into Britain on empty Channel freight wagons', with an editorial criticising Cameron for inaction.[362] Less than a week later the prime minister responded on national news, performing prejudice to the allegedly hostile public by referring to 'a swarm of people coming across the Mediterranean, seeking a better life, wanting to come to Britain'.[363] The acting leader of the Labour Party replied that Cameron should 'remember he is talking about people and not insects'.[364] And, as radical Church of England minister Giles Fraser commented, the refugees of the Bible are never described in such language: 'the only reference to swarm in Exodus

---

359 Nicholas De Genova, 'Migrant "Illegality" and Deportability in Everyday Life', *Annual Review of Anthropology* no. 31 (2002), pp. 419–447.

360 *The Sun*, 17 April 2015.

361 *The Guardian*, 20 and 24 April 2015.

362 *The Sun*, 24 July 2015.

363 Cameron to ITV news, 30 July 2015, reported favourably in *Daily Mail*, 31 July 2015.

364 Harriet Harman quoted in *The Guardian*, 31 July 2015.

is the "swarm of flies"', adding 'Little wonder people felt insulted by that'.[365] Migrants responded similarly: Berekat, a young Eritrean in the Calais camp, asked of Britain's political leaders, 'Why are you closing the door? We're not animals, barbarians.'[366]

David Cameron has pledged £50 million of government funding for the memorial and educational work of his Holocaust Commission, which emphasises the need to learn the 'lessons of the Holocaust'. It would seem that no connection was made by Cameron to the restrictionism that Jewish refugees faced in the Nazi era and his inflammatory outburst against recent asylum-seekers. But there is still a linkage, even if Cameron did not have the awareness to realise it: in the twentieth and twenty-first centuries, hate language to describe migrants as illegal and inhuman continues the persecution and misery from which they fled. In the words of a Sudanese asylum-seeker in Britain interviewed by the BBC: 'there I was attacked by bullets and here by words'. He explicitly had in mind the prime minister's insect/swarm analogy.[367]

David Cameron was at the forefront of promoting 'British values', and the Learning Centre of his Holocaust Commission will be part of this enterprise. Certainly, part of modern British history has been a strong strain of xenophobia tinged with many different forms of racism. Indeed, Hopkins, *The Sun*, and Cameron have their historical precedents. In 1903 the leading anti-alien William Evans-Gordon quoted with approval the bishop of Stepney, who blamed the poverty of East London on 'foreigners coming in like an army of locusts'.[368] Two years later, as the Aliens Bill was being fiercely debated, Robert Sherard, a journalist obsessed with the threat posed to British manhood by the Jewish white slave trade, warned readers of *The Standard* about the diseased and useless Jewish immigrants who 'swarm over to England'.[369]

The British case is important, for no other country possesses such a strong belief in its own tolerance and decency – past and present. In this respect, the rebuke of the prime minister and home secretary for fuelling 'a xenophobic climate in Britain' by Nils Muižnieks, the Council of Europe's human rights commissioner, is especially pertinent. Muiznieks criticised the language of these leading politicians, especially Cameron's use of the term 'illegal immigrant' with its connotations of criminality. 'People are not illegal', he noted, their 'legal status may be irregular, but that does

365 Giles Fraser, 'A church in the wild', *The Guardian*, 5 August 2015.

366 Quoted by Matthew Taylor and Josh Halliday, 'It's easier if you say we're bad, not human', *The Guardian*, 31 July 2015.

367 Sudanese asylum-seeker interviewed on BBC Breakfast News, 12 November 2015.

368 William Evans Gordon, *The Alien Immigrant* (London: Heinemann, 1903), p. 12.

369 'The Home of the Alien', *The Standard*, 5 January 1905.

not render them beyond humanity' – an observation that this volume will return to at its close.[370]

It is not only, however, the sphere of hate speech that provides a bridge between 'now' and 'then'. Through the 1930s/40s and today analogies have made been made between contemporary journeys and traumatic ones of the past. Slavery references have been common, but so have ones to the Irish famine and the infamous 'coffin ships'. That there are few if any links made between the boat migrants of the twenty-first century and the 'illegals' of the 1930s/40s reflects the self-contained nature of Holocaust studies (and, within it, Jewish refugee studies from that era) *and* the ahistorical nature of migration studies. Such exclusive readings of the past hinder the universalism proclaimed in the Charter of Lampedusa that 'As human beings we all inhabit the Earth as a shared space.' It stands for 'global freedom for all', recognising that 'The history of humanity is a history of migration.'[371]

Responding to the treatment of migrants in the twenty-first century, including in his adopted homeland America, with regard to its treatment of those at its border with Mexico, Auschwitz survivor and Nobel Peace Prize winner Elie Wiesel has commented that:

> You who are so-called illegal aliens must know that no human being is 'illegal'. That is a contradiction in terms. Human beings can be beautiful or more beautiful, they can be fat or skinny, they can be right or wrong, but illegal? How can a human being be illegal?[372]

How long have migrants been labelled 'illegal'? The answer, as this troubling account highlights, is historically not too long, but ethically, far, far too long.

---

370 Alan Travis, 'Human rights official attacks PM's rhetoric on migrants', *The Guardian*, 24 March 2016.

371 The Charter of Lampedusa.

372 Elie Wiesel, quoted in http://www.dailykos.com/story/2012/4/20/1084905/-No-Human-Being-is-Illegal, accessed 3 June 2017.

Conclusion

We know that the emigration of approximately 350,000 Jews from Germany and German-occupied Czechoslovakia before the war was forced ... . The flight of the Belgian and Parisian Jews in 1940 and the evacuation of Soviet Jews a year later was compounded with the mass migration of non-Jews.[1]

It seems that Raul Hilberg's reflections on Jewish emigration during the Nazi era connects it to wider movements of refugees, the numbers of which would not be exceeded until the twenty-first century. Yet rather than link Holocaust studies with migration studies, Hilberg (a Jewish refugee himself), was doing the reverse. His aim was to show what he believed was the particular and peculiar path of non-resistance followed by the Jews during the years of persecution. Indeed, Hilberg's chronological overview continued by emphasising Jewish passivity as the murderous assault intensified during the war:

We know that only a few thousand Jews escaped from the ghettos of Poland and Russia; that only a few hundred Jews hid out in the large cities of Berlin, Vienna and Warsaw; that only a handful of Jews escaped from camps.

Hilberg concludes 'In the main, the Jews looked upon flight with a sense of futility. The great majority of those who did not escape early did not escape at all.'[2]

Journeys from the Abyss has queried Hilberg's analysis at many different levels. It has done so not only in relation to the number and percentage of

---

1   Raul Hilberg, *The Destruction of European Jews* vol. 3 (New York: Holmes & Meirer, 1985), pp. 1035–1036.
2   Ibid, p. 1036.

305

Jews who were able to flee but also with regard to the importance of their own agency. As Gunnar Paulsson notes in his remarkable reconstruction of wartime Warsaw and its hidden Jews, a space and time which he describes as a 'secret city', Hilberg 'treats the reactions of the two million or so people who fled or went into hiding – surely the most reasonable and human of all responses to an overwhelming hostile force – briefly and dismissively'.[3] Yet it remains that, in spite of previous and subsequent scholarship, Hilberg, described as 'the seminal figure in modern Holocaust historiography',[4] set a model which has proved extremely durable. The enormity of the Holocaust has led to a tendency to place it outside of history and therefore beyond comparison. In terms of Jewish refugees during the Nazi era, this has meant an emphasis on the impossibility of escape and, for those that did manage to do so, a failure to connect to other migratory movements, whether before, during, or after.

This study has not attempted to understate the specificity of the Jewish refugee plight in the 1930s and 1940s, including the responses of receiving societies to their possible or actual entry. But by placing the experiences of and reactions to such Jews in the context of the long twentieth century, and thus of other traumatic migrations, it is a contribution to the demysti-fication of one important aspect of the Holocaust. It is especially necessary because it can aid understanding not just of Jewish refugees but also more generally of those attempting to make new lives away from life-threatening circumstances before 1933 and after 1945. As the number of forcibly displaced worldwide currently is estimated at a record level (59.5 million, according to UNHCR estimates, at the close of 2014 and a figure that grew rapidly throughout the subsequent year to around 70 million),[5] it is clear that the problem of refugeedom has anything but disappeared since the Second World War.

Comparative studies, especially in areas where ownership and contes-tation of a traumatic past are intensely emotional, run the risk of dismissing other experiences as 'not as bad' or of 'less significance'. This has been especially the case with the Holocaust – even in the context of studying its place in the history of genocide. And such emotional tensions when connecting a 'migrant now' to a 'Jewish then' have been especially raw in the question of contemporary boat people.

As noted, Australia has been at the forefront of controlling the entry of 'illegal' immigrants beyond its formal borders, setting an example that Europe has followed. Through the first two decades of the twenty-first

---

3   Gunnar Paulsson, *Secret City: The Hidden Jews of Warsaw 1940–1945* (New Haven: Yale University Press, 2002), p. 9.
4   Ibid, pp. 9–10.
5   Figures from http://www.unhcr.org.uk/about-us/key-facts-and-figures.html, accessed 25 July 2015.

century Australia continued and intensified its earlier actions in diverting desperate refugees elsewhere, resulting in boats sinking and asylum-seekers drowning. For some, echoing the response of senior British civil servants 60 years earlier, such tragedies, while unfortunate, act as a deterrent to others considering these dangerous journeys with Australia as their desired destination. Others have been less convinced and have utilised a particular reading of the Jewish past to make contemporary moral interventions.

In 2010 the B'nai B'rith Anti-Defamation Commission drew a direct parallel with the tragedies of the *St Louis* and the *Struma* during the Nazi era and those trying to get to Australia in the twenty-first century:

> As Jewish Australians, many of us descended from those lucky survivors who did get refuge in Australia, we are tremendously pained to see asylum seekers a generation later drowning and suffering. Most ... who come without visas are found to be legitimate refugees when their claims are processed.

It concluded 'That we are prepared to leave them in dangerous seas, on inadequate boats and in offshore detention centres after they have already suffered so greatly is unconscionable.'[6]

But the response from other Australian–Jewish organisations to such use of history was unambiguously hostile. It was

> truly unfortunate that a Jewish organisation would make such an odious comparison of the plight of current refugees with Holocaust survivors ... . The current asylum seekers have not been marked out for, or subjected to, genocidal mass murder ... and do have choices.[7]

And, according to the president of the Australian Association of Jewish Holocaust Survivors & Descendants, it was 'an unacceptable dilution of the singularity of the Holocaust'.[8]

Taking the examples explored in this study, including those of boat refugees, it could, ironically and disturbingly, be argued that contemporary migrants face far more difficult and dangerous journeys than Jews who managed to escape Nazi persecution from 1933 to 1945 or those survivors who left Europe after the war. Put crudely, hundreds of Jews died at sea searching for asylum in the 1930s and 1940s, and not the tens of thousands that have died and continue to die in the twenty-first century. The higher

---

6   Deborah Stone, 'Voyage of the Damned – Take Two', 16 December 2010, quoting Anton Block of the B'Nai B'rith Anti-Defamation Commission, in http://www.jwire.com.au/voyage-of-the-damned-take-two, accessed 30 January 2015.

7   Dr George Foster, 26 December 2010, in ibid.

8   Anna Berger, 27 December 2010, in ibid.

comparative death rate is certainly true with regard to the child migrants and boat people studied in Chapters 3 and 4 of this study.

Moreover, their treatment – as exemplified by the conditions of modern-day domestic service – is far more severe than that faced by the Jewish refugee women featured in Chapters 1 and 2. While those in the 1930s occasionally likened their status to slavery, it is doubtful whether their undoubtedly exploitative treatment would have been legally defined as such, as is the case today. Most Jewish refugees also eventually found places and spaces that could in some ways be called 'home'. They faced uncertain legal status, internment, deportation, and displaced persons camps, as well as the dislocation and loss that is at the heart of any refugee experience. But, for the most part, they were not kept in camps for generation after generation, as has been the plight first of Palestinians after 1948 and then other refugees across the world, especially within its poorest regions, thereafter. In 2015 one-sixth of the Syrian population, or four million people, are refugees outside its borders, mainly languishing in neighbouring (and often unstable) states that are unable to cope with such huge numbers of people. While the number of Syrians reaching the West has grown spectacularly in 2015 – they make up the large majority of the 800,000-plus refugees who have reached Greece – most remain outside Europe. Furthermore, four million remain internally displaced in Syria itself.

It is, of course, true that European Jewry during the Second World War (at least from autumn 1941 onwards) faced systematic mass murder: their horrific journeys were dominated by those *towards* destruction rather than away from it, following the appalling example of the Armenian Genocide in the First World War. Genocide is rarely *the* major cause of mass migration today but ethnic cleansing, political oppression, bloody civil wars, coercion (often gender- and age-specific) from military forces and gangs, ecological disaster, extreme poverty, and diminished life chances certainly are. Both then and now, the majority did not and do not move: there are inherent restraints in doing so. Aside from rootedness and local responsibilities, lack of resources alongside the enormous dangers involved and barriers imposed puts off the large majority. But for those brave or, relatively speaking, 'privileged' enough to undertake such journeys, there is no real choice. In the words of Ethiopian refugee Dagmawi Yimer, who arrived in mainland Italy via Lampedusa, 'This journey is a worse punishment than prison. And yet we leave because there's nothing else to do.'[9] It is a sign of the desperation involved that even knowledge of the death rate en route and the exploitation and abuse experienced routinely does not put off the migrants, many of whom repeatedly try to leave. As the Kenyan-born Somali refugee Warsan Shire writes in *Home*:

---

9   Dagmawi Yimer, 'Our Journey', in Alessandro Triulzi and Robert McKenzie (eds), *Long Journey: African Migrants on the Road* (Leiden: Brill, 2013), pp. 233–253 (p. 253).

no one leaves home unless
home is the mouth of a shark ...
you have to understand,
that no one puts their children in a boat
unless the water is safer than the land ...[10]

This study has emphasised, even in a world of increasing control and construction of ever larger categories of 'illegality', the individual and collective agency of the migrant – including with regards to the 'performativity' of their plight in a variety of cultural formats and related memory work. The ability to control their fate has varied according to specific political and economic contexts, as well as general factors such as race, nationality, class, gender, age, politics, disability, religion, and sexuality. Yet, even in the most oppressive situation, the importance of recognising the individuality of the migrant needs to be highlighted – whether in the academic sphere or in politics and society as a whole.

In July 2015 Angela Merkel, the German chancellor, was confronted by Reem, a young Palestinian girl facing deportation. Reem wanted to stay in Germany to complete her studies alongside her new friends in Rostock. Merkel responded honestly, if clumsily:

> Sometimes politics is hard. You are in front of me and you are a very nice person, but in Palestinian refugee camps in Lebanon there are thousands and thousands of people. If we say that you can all come and you can all come from Africa ... we can't manage that.[11]

Politicians and the media tend to refer to asylum-seekers and other migrants as 'masses', often using metaphors of the sea or infestation to emphasise the threat they might represent to receiving societies. Each one, however, has a unique story to tell.

With this in mind, *Journeys from the Abyss* has emphasised the autobiographical praxis of migrants throughout its challenging case studies. It has done so in a critical fashion to reveal both the restraints operating on 'speaking freely' and the complexities, contradictions, and silences that are at the heart of all life stories. In contrast, Merkel's embarrassment at Reem's subsequent tears and distress is not her particular failing but that of western society as a whole, which, for over a century, has legislated that some (now most) migrants are somehow 'illegal', less human and therefore undesirable. Indeed, Merkel may have been influenced more by this conversation with Reem than her first reaction suggests, reflecting also on her country's traumatic and caustic past.

---

10 Warsan Shire, 'Home', reproduced in ibid, p. xi.
11 Quoted in *Metro*, 17 July 2015.

Awareness of the Holocaust, it is widely believed (though never convincingly documented), led to various forms of human rights initiatives in the immediate post-war era. In fact, since 1945 more effort has gone not on protecting human rights internationally but on restricting migration and intensifying barriers against the 'illegal immigrant' – a term which, as noted, was formalised and institutionalised by the British authorities in the context of Jews attempting to reach Palestine during the 1930s. These Jewish refugees were also detained in 'placeless' places such as Cyprus and Mauritius, which were the forerunners of Nauru or Lampedusa in the unhappy history of modern immigration control procedures – what migration historian Aristide Zolberg has referred to as 'remote control'.[12] Yet, for all the restrictions and hostility Jewish refugees faced during the Nazi era, many still found safety and protection.

Indeed, when the period of mass migration from the late nineteenth century to today is taken as a whole, Jewish refugees are located in an ambivalent position. On the one hand, Jews, and especially those from Eastern Europe, were regarded along with other racialised groups as a danger to the state. On the other, they were privileged in having the presence of Jews already established in receiving societies who aided (though certainly not unambiguously) their arrival and integration. In the Nazi era German-origin Jews were seen as more desirable both by the Jewish elites and by a variety of states. Both before, during, and even after the Second World War, the British and other liberal democratic governments were anxious about the arrival of *ostjuden*, and this concern was largely shared by established Jews who were lobbying and advising politicians and civil servants. Even with this major caveat, the Jewish refugees had co-religionist champions in the western democracies who were close to state power. Although the influence of this elite (and its willingness to use it) can be overstated, its access to national and international bodies at least partly explains the comparatively more favourable attitude towards Jewish refugees in the 1930s/40s than that to the millions of migrants seeking new lives today.

Both then and now, there have been xenophobic forces at work in the form of political movements with popular followings, as well as mainstream parties (right, left, and centre) hoping to appease their allegedly hostile electorates. Such tendencies have been reinforced by a largely negative mass media. Yet there have also been counter movements, organised and individual, which have worked against the dehumanising processes in the creation of the 'illegal immigrant' – Agamben's 'Homo Sacer'. In the Nazi era it was not only the wider Jewish world that sought to protect Jewish

---

12 Aristide Zolberg, 'Matters of State: Theorizing Immigration Policy', in Charles Hirschman, Philip Kasinitz and Josh DeWind (eds), *The Handbook of International Migration* (New York: Russell Sage Foundation, 1999), p. 73.

refugees. Many ordinary people were appalled by Nazi persecution and were involved in rescue work and refugee advocacy in print and in wider cultural interventions. It was a form of counter-performativity to those who saw no common cause with the oppressed and viewed them purely as matter out of place, as 'a disquieting element in the order of the modern nation-state'.[13] Some came into contact with Jewish refugees more accidentally through their everyday life but were still moved to help those, in the words of Auschwitz survivor and asylum campaigner Hugo Gryn, 'to whom [they owed] nothing'.[14]

Alongside international humanitarian organisations, including the UNHCR, there are many more people involved with helping and working alongside refugees today. While millions of desperate migrants are hidden from view in camps and detention centres across the world, the scale and global nature of such movements means that many are confronted with their presence, often in the most incongruous circumstances. As illustrated, the Mediterranean is not only a space of migrant movement but also a place and centre of European tourism, in which these two worlds have recently collided. While some holidaymakers have resented the unsettling presence of 'boat people', others have been moved to help and support them. Most prominent has been the Migrant Offshore Aid Station (MOAS), started by Chris and Regina Catrambone after they came across clothing in the sea as they sailed in their yacht away from Lampedusa. Rather than ignore evidence of another migrant death, Chris (an American entrepreneur) and Regina (his Italian wife) decided to devote themselves to saving lives: 'Look at me out here cruising on my boat, at the same time people are out there dying. So our heaven is their hell, right? Our paradise is their hell.'[15] Of Italian immigrant origin, 'Catrambone saw the migrants as either desperate, entrepreneurial, or both – not too different from his own great-grandfather.' To him, the moral imperative to help was unambiguous: 'If you are against saving lives at sea then you are a bigot and you don't even belong in our community. If you allow your neighbour to die in your backyard, then you are responsible for that death.'[16] Catrambone purchased a yacht, the *Phoenix*, sailed across the Atlantic and in ten weeks from August 2014 rescued over 1400 people in the Mediterranean. As with those in Britain and elsewhere during the Nazi era, rather than wait for their governments and international organisations to act, Chris and Regina Catrambone have shown that individuals can make a critical difference themselves.

13 Giorgio Agamber, *Homo Sacer: Sovereign Power and Bare Life* (Stanford: Stanford University Press, 1998), p. 131.

14 Hugo Gryn, *A Moral and Spiritual Index* (London: Refugee Council, 1996).

15 Giles Tremlett, "'If you are against saving lives at sea then you are a bigot'", *Guardian*, 8 July 2015.

16 Ibid.

Ultimately, however, it is the nation state and bodies such as the European Union that have real power and which pressure from grassroots organisations and individual initiatives can only modify. Angela Merkel's intervention with a Palestinian refugee in July 2015 has already been commented on. A month later, faced with a much larger movement of refugees, mainly from Syria, Merkel presented a different face to the world, stating that even if the figure was to reach a million or more, Germany was obliged to take them in: 'Wir schaffen das' ['We can do it']. The memory of Germany's troubled past (and perhaps the forced migration origins of many of its citizens) and the ethical imperative to do the right thing, to put *WillkommensKultur* into practice, were clearly in her thoughts. In August alone some 160,000 were allowed entry to Germany.[17] Shortly after, with the revulsion following the drowning of Alan Kurdi, it appeared that Europe as a whole had rediscovered its commitment to granting asylum. The numbers involved, however, and a wave of anti-refugee feeling following the terrorist atrocities in Paris in November 2015 and in Brussels in March 2016, have seen a return to a world of borders, fences, and restrictive paperwork. In Britain, even at the time of greatest public outrage over Alan Kurdi's death and the refusal of Cameron's government to allow entry to any Syrian refugees, pressure from below led to the admittance of only 20,000 in over a five-year period. Even Abdullah Kurdi, father of Alan, was not immune to this backlash, with allegations thrown at him of profiteering and people-smuggling. Against all evidence, he is accused of not being a genuine refugee.[18] Closing this study late in 2016, the world with its hastily assembled fences and increasing paper walls seems a very different and less tolerant place from that of just a year earlier, at the time of the three-year-old's tragic death.

As with the Jewish refugees of the first half of the twentieth century, modern migrants have become bifurgated into the categories of desirable and undesirable, genuine refugees as against the opportunistic. The focus of sympathy, where articulated, has been on Syrian refugees, while black Africans undertaking far more dangerous journeys to Italy have been largely ignored in 2015. Whether Europe would retreat behind hastily assembled walls or follow the moral impetus provided by Merkel was unclear in the second half of 2015; the balance has subsequently swung towards control and attempts to return the migrants daring to have reached Europe. That numbers of forced migrants from across the globe will increase, however, is not in doubt. The claim of the president of the European Council, Donald Tusk, in March 2016 that 'the days of irregular migration to Europe are over' will lead to policies that will increase the misery of those turned back or

17 *Observer*, 13 September 2015.
18 Abdullah Kurdi in conversation with Adnan Khan, *The Guardian*, 23 December 2015.

detained.[19] Flows may be (partly) diverted, but stopping this movement as a whole is as likely to be successful as that illustrated by Canute and the sea to show his powerlessness against the natural forces of the world. Indeed, the desperation and exploitation of the three (intersecting) categories of contemporary migrants dealt with in this study – domestic workers, children, and boat people – in the late twentieth and early twenty-first centuries paints an extremely bleak picture of the future.

Human history, *Journeys from the Abyss* insists, is a history of migration. Humans have moved out of sheer curiosity to find out what is beyond the horizon, wandering out of an unquenchable desire for wonder, benefiting from 'the pleasure of voyaging and the pleasure of learning new places, new people and new ideas'.[20] Less romantically, they have also moved out of sheer necessity to find food, safety, and shelter for themselves and their families. Booker Prize winner Richard Flanagan, when visiting Syrian refugees in Lebanese, Serbian, and Greek camps, and on the move at the Croatian border, concludes 'It felt like history and I suppose it was history and is history, and you realise why anyone who has experienced history hates it so.'[21] Such journeys have often been framed in religious discourse, whether that of paradise/heaven or hell/purgatory, with especial reference to the Exodus story from slavery to freedom in the Promised Land; Flanagan calls those of 2015 'Old Testament in its stories, epic in scale'.[22] Yet even the goal of reaching Canaan is doubted as sincere: 'illegal' migrants, according to one articulation of all too common hate speech, have 'nothing to lose as long as Britain is still seen as the land of milk and honey'.[23] The reality is more complex and ambiguous for migrants past and present, certainly so in terms of their reasons for leaving, the journeys undertaken, the reception they have received, and their subsequent lives.

From its challenging examples, it should be clear that this study acts as a warning against the temptation towards any simplistic redemptive readings of refugeedom. Yet for the migrant the hope, however illusory and shattered, contained within the Exodus narrative remains essential. Returning to Warsan Shire's *Home*:

> no one burns their palms
> under trains
> beneath carriages ...

---

19 Quoted by Sky News, 8 March 2016.
20 Patrick Manning, *Migration in World History* (Abingdon: Routledge, 2013 [2nd ed.]), p. 8.
21 Richard Flanagan, 'Old Testament in its stories, epic in its scale: this is the great exodus of our age', *Guardian*, 5 March 2016.
22 Ibid.
23 *The Sun*, 24 July 2015.

unless the miles travelled
means something more than journey.[24]

The late modern forces attempting to stop such unstoppable human movements have to resort to forms of hate speech and hate action to justify, in some perverse performance of morality, restrictionism. For the most part, the example of the Holocaust is regarded as beyond comparison or irrelevant, as humanity faces ecological disaster and scarcity of resources that will only intensify as the twenty-first century progresses. Many politicians and commentators argue that those escaping Nazi persecution were genuine refugees who had no choice but to leave.

Alternatively, it is argued here that these Jewish journeys from the abyss do connect to wider crises and to a world that has the choice to either fragment further into exclusivity and short-sighted selfishness or embrace 'planetary humanism' and face the huge challenges ahead with common purpose.[25] Richard Flanagan admonishes:

> Refugees are not like you and me. They are you and me. That terrible river of the wretched and the damned flowing through Europe is my family. And there is no time in the future in which they might be helped. The only time we have is now.[26]

The last words will be left to the migrants themselves, exercising their political agency through the Charter of Lampedusa, which demands 'global freedom of movement for all'. There must be 'No Illegalisation of people'. Migration, they insist, 'is not a crime'.[27]

24 Shire, 'Home', p. xi.
25 The phrase is from Paul Gilroy, *Between Camps: Nations, Cultures and the Allure of Race* (London: Allen Lane, 2000), chapter 9.
26 Flanagan, 'Old Testament in its stories'.
27 The Charter of Lampedusa, 2014, in http://www.bildung-fuer-alle.ch/political-program-charter-lampedusa, accessed 22 June 2015.

Bibliography

Primary Sources

Archives in Public Collections

Association of Jewish Refugees
Refugee Voices video interview collection

BBC Written Archives
Script of Wynyard Browne's 'Dark Summer', 1948
Broadcasts on Palestine, September 1947

British Library
'Living Memory of the Jewish Community' oral history project

Hull History Centre
Jewish Association for the Protection of Girls and Women, Southampton Branch

Imperial War Museum
Britain and the Refugee Crisis oral history interviews
Theodora Bernstein, 'Warning to My Beloved England' (1940)

The Keep, Sussex
Mass-Observation Archive:
    Summer 2000 Directive 'Coming to Britain'
    Spring 2009 Directive 'Second World War'
    Summer 2010 Directive 'Belonging'
    Autumn 2012 Directive 'Human rights, immigration & the legal system'
File Reports
Second World War diaries

London Jewish Museum
Hilde Gerrard, 'We Were Lucky'

Landshoff papers
Oral history interview collection

London Library
Claude Montefiore pamphlet collection

Manchester Jewish Museum
Frances Goldberg, 'Memoirs'
Harris House diary
Oral history interview collection

Manchester Central Reference Library
Barash Papers

National Archives, Kew
Admiralty series, ADM 1, 239
Cabinet series, CAB 128
Colonial Office series, CO 537, 733
Foreign and Colonial Office series, FCO 141
Foreign Office series, FO 371, 921, 945, 1032
Home Office series, HO 45, 144, 213, 352, 367, 372, 382
Metropolitan Police series, MEPO 2
Ministry of Education series, ED 12, 91
Ministry of Health series, MH 8, 102
Ministry of Labour series, LAB 8,
Security Service series, KV 3, 4
Treasury series, T 1

SSEES Library, London
Seton-Watson papers

University of Birmingham Archives
Save the Children Fund records

University of Cape Town Archives
Cyril Orolowitz papers

University of Southampton Special Collections (Printed)
Peter Absolon, 'Exodus Hamburg 1947', 1997
Southampton City Council, Minutes of Proceedings
Leonard Montefiore, 'Address given to the Cambridge University Jewish Society', 18
    October 1946

University of Southampton Archives
Barclay papers
Central British Fund Archives (microfilms)
Jewish Association for the Protection of Women and Children papers

University of Warwick Archives
TUC archives

Archives in Private Collections
Another Space/Lake District Holocaust Project
    Correspondence
    Oral history interviews
    Press releases and plans

Esther Saraga
    Correspondence between her parents and Hilde Gerrard

Interviews with the Author
Trevor Avery, 8 July 2010, 12 July 2011, Windermere (both with Dr Aimee Bunting)
Nir Maor, 18 December 2016, Haifa
Rina Offenbach, 16 December 2016, Haifa

Autobiographical Material in the Author's Collection
Anna Bansci, 'The Life of Mr J.A. Hyman' (no date)
Lucy Long, 'Unpublished memoirs'
Inge Nord (Ader) correspondence
Philip Osment, email correspondence
Sea City Museum, autobiographical material from Rosalind Winton
Perec Zylberberg, 'Recollections'

Printed Primary Materials

Autobiographical
Mary Antin, *The Promised Land* (Princeton: Princeton University Press, 1969)
Hannah Arendt, 'We Refugees', in J. Kohn (ed.), *The Jewish Writings. Hannah Arendt* (New York: Schocken Books, 2007)
Edith Argy, *The Childhood and Teens of a Jewish Girl in Inter-War Austria and Subsequent Adventures* (Charleston: BookSurge, 2005)
Myra Baram, *The Girl With Two Suitcases* (Lewes: The Book Guild, 1988)
Lady Battersea, *Reminiscences* (London: Macmillan, 1922)
Ervin Birnbaum, 'On the "Exodus 1947"', *Jewish Frontier* vol. 24 no. 5 (May 1957)
Elaine Blond with Barry Turner, *Marks of Distinction* (London: Vallentine Mitchell, 1988)
Erika Bourguignon and Barbara Hill Rigney (eds), *Exile: A Memoir. Bronka Schneider* (Columbus: Ohio University Press, 1998)
Leslie Brent, *Sunday's Child* (New Romney: Bank House Books, 2009)
Richard Broad and Suzie Fleming (eds), *Nella Last's War: A Mother's Diary 1939–45* (Bristol: Falling Wall Press, 1981)
Child Survivors' Association, *Zachor: Child Survivors Speak* (London: Elliot & Thompson, 2005)
Sydney Clark, 'A Faversham Chameleon House', *Bygone Kent* vol. 23 no. 2 (2002)
G.D.H. and Margaret Cole (eds), *William Cobbett: Rural Rides* (London: Peter Davies, 1930)
Captain S.B. de Courcy-Ireland, *A Naval Life* (Poulton: England Publishing, 1990)

Sidney Finkel, *Sevek and the Holocaust: The Boy Who Refused to Die* (Matteson: Sidney Finkel, 2006)

Ronald Fraser, *In Search of a Past* (London: Verso, 2010)

Karen Gershon (ed.), *We Came as Children: A Collective Autobiography* (London: Gollancz, 1966)

Karen Gershon, 'Perturbed Adolescence', *AJR Information* vol. 29 no. 10 (October 1974)

Robert Graves, *Goodbye to All That* (London: Penguin, 1960)

Hugo Gryn with Naomi Gryn, *Chasing Shadows* (London: Penguin Books, 2001)

Arlette Guez, *La passagère de L'Exodus* (Paris: Editions Robert Laffont, 1978)

Roman Halter, *Roman's Journey* (London: Portobello Books, 2007)

Charles Hannam, *A Boy in Your Situation* (London: Andre Deutsch, 1977)

Mark Harris and Deborah Oppenheimer (eds), *Into the Arms of Strangers: Stories of the Kindertransport* (London: Bloomsbury, 2000)

Jack Hecht, 'Revisiting Wintershill Hall', *Journal of the '45 Aid Society* no. 30 (2006)

Arek Hersh, *A Detail of History* (Laxton: Beth Shalom, 1998)

Stanley Hyman, *Is Anything Alright? My Titanics Story* (Bowdon: Stellar Books, 2014)

Jewish Women in London Group, *Generations of Memories: Voices of Jewish Women* (London: Women's Press, 1989)

Yoram Kaniuk, *Commander of the Exodus* (New York: Grove Press, 1999)

William Knight (ed.), *Journals of Dorothy Wordsworth* (London: Macmillan, 1930)

Livia Laurent, *A Tale of Internment* (London: George Allen & Unwin, 1942)

Bertha Leverton and Shmuel Lowensohn (eds), *I Came Alone: The Stories of the Kindertransports* (Lewes: The Book Guild, 2000)

Primo Levi, *If This is a Man* (London: Abacus, 1987)

Primo Levi, *The Drowned and the Saved* (London: Michael Joseph, 1988)

Alfred Lom, *'Never Mind Mr Lom'* (London: Macmillan, 1941)

Martha Long, *Austrian Cockney* (London: Centerprise, 1980)

Vesna Maric, *Bluebird: A Memoir* (London: Granta, 2010)

Paul Oppenheimer, *From Belsen to Buckingham Palace* (Laxton: Beth Shalom, 1996)

Lilli Palmer, *Change Lobsters – and Dance: An Autobiography* (London: W.H. Allen, 1976)

Alfred Perles, *Alien Corn* (London: George Allen & Unwin, 1944)

Michael Perlmutter, 'The Bonds of Windermere', *Journal of the '45 Aid Society* no. 18 (December 1994)

Anne Powell (ed.), *Women in the War Zone: Hospital Service in the First World War* (Stroud: History Press, 2013)

Margaret Powell, *Below Stairs* (London: Peter Davies, 1975)

James Roose-Evans (ed.), *Joyce Grenfell. Darling Ma: Letters to Her Mother 1932–1944* (London: Hodder & Stoughton, 1988)

Imrich Rosenberg and Corey Goldman, *A Jew in Deed* (Manotick, Ontario: Penumbra Press, 2004)

Milena Roth, *Lifesaving Letters: A Child's Flight from the Holocaust* (Seattle: University of Washington Press, 2004)

David Rousset, *L'univers concentraire* (Paris: Editions du Pavois, 1946)

Lore Segal, 'Other People's Houses: A Liberal Education', *New Yorker*, 4 March 1961

Lore Segal, 'Other People's Houses: Santiago', *New Yorker*, 13 June 1964

Lore Segal, 'Other People's Houses: New York', *New Yorker*, 25 July 1964

Lore Segal, *Other People's Houses* (London: Gollancz, 1965)

Lore Segal, 'Memory: The Problems of Imagining the Past', in Berel Lang (ed.), *Writing and the Holocaust* (New York: Holmes & Meier, 1988)

Lore Segal, 'The Bough Breaks', in David Rosenberg (ed.), *Testimony: Contemporary Writers Make the Holocaust Personal* (New York: Times Books, 1989)

Lore Segal, *Other People's Houses: A Novel* (New York: New Press, 1994)

Raja Shehadeh, *Strangers in the House: Coming of Age in Occupied Palestine* (London: Profile Books, 2002)

Gary Shteyngart, *Little Failure: A Memoir* (London: Hamish Hamilton, 2014)

Hanna Spencer, *Hanna's Diary, 1938–1941. Czechoslavakia to Canada* (Montreal: McGill-Queen's University Press, 2002)

Randall Stewart (ed.), *The English Notebooks by Nathaniel Hawthorne* (New York: Oxford University Press, 1941)

I.F. Stone, *Underground to Palestine* (London: Hutchinson, 1979)

M.I. Tatham, 'The Great Retreat in Serbia', in C. Purdom (ed.), *Everyman at War* (London: J.M. Dent, 1930)

Elie Wiesel, *From the Kingdom of Memory: Reminiscences* (New York: Schocken, 1990)

Francesca Wilson, *In the Margins of Chaos: Recollections of Relief Work in and between Three Wars* (London: John Murray, 1944)

Dagmawi Yimer, 'Our Journey', in Alessandro Triulti and Robert McKenzie (eds), *Long Journey: African Migrants on the Road* (Leiden: Brill, 2013)

Reports and Other Contemporary Documents

A. Abrahams, 'On the subject of hell-ships', *Jewish Standard*, 1 August 1947

Bridget Anderson, *Britain's Secret Slaves: An Investigation into the Plight of Overseas Domestic Workers* (London: Anti-Slavery International/Kalayaan, 1993)

Bridget Anderson and Annie Phizacklea, 'Migrant Domestic Workers: A European Perspective' (unpublished report to the Equal Opportunities Unit, Commissioner of the European Communities, 1997)

Anon, *Britain's New Citizens: The Story of the Refugees from Germany and Austria* (London: AJR, 1951)

Anon, *George Heriot's School of Honour 1914–1919* (Edinburgh: War Memorial Committee, 1921)

Trevor Avery, *From Auschwitz to Ambleside* (Sedbergh: Another Space, 2008)

Tara Brian and Frank Laczko (eds), *Fatal Journeys: Tracking Lives Lost during Migration* (Geneva: International Organization for Migration, 2014)

Erskine B. Childers, 'The Other Exodus', *The Spectator*, 12 May 1961

J. Dow and M. Brown, *Evacuation to Westmorland from Home and Europe 1939–1945* (Kendal: Westmorland Gazette, 1946)

English Heritage, 'England's Heritage – your heritage' (unpublished, English Heritage, 2003)

Philippe Fargues, '2015: The year we mistook refugees for invaders', *Migration Policy Centre: Policy Brief* no. 12 (December 2015)

Alice Farmer, 'The impact of immigration detention on children', *FMR* no. 44 (September 2013)

Violet Firth, *The Psychology of the Servant Problem* (London: C.W. Daniel, 1925)

Richard Flanagan, 'Old Testament in its stories, epic in its scale: this is the great exodus of our age', *Guardian*, 5 March 2016

Giles Fraser, 'A church in the wild', *The Guardian*, 5 August 2015

Celia Fremlin, *The Seven Chars of Chelsea* (London: Methuen, 1940)

Anna Freud, 'An Experiment in Group Upbringing', *Psychoanalytical Study of the Child* vol. 6 (1951)

Lisa Frydman et al., *A Treacherous Journey: Child Migrants Navigating the US System* (San Franscisco: Center for Gender & Refugee Studies/Kids in Need of Defense, 2014)

William Evans Gordon, *The Alien Immigrant* (London: Heinemann, 1903)

Ruth Gruber, *Destination Palestine: The Story of the Haganah Ship Exodus 1947* (New York: Current Books, 1948)

Ruth Gruber, *Exodus 1947: The Ship that Launched A Nation* (New York: Union Square Press, 2007)

Hugo Gryn, *A Moral and Spiritual Index* (London: Refugee Council, 1996)

Philip Hoare, 'Sea of despair', *Guardian*, 22 April 2015

'J', 'The Refugee Housekeeper: First Year', *Manchester Guardian*, 13 July 1938

T. de Jastrzebski, 'The Register of Belgian Refugees', *Journal of the Royal Stastical Society* vol. 79 (March 1916)

Elizabeth Kennedy, 'No Childhood Here: Why Central American Children are Fleeing Their Homes' (unpublished report, American Immigration Council Perspectives, July 2014)

Katharine Knox, *Credit to the Nation: A Study of Refugees in the United Kingdom* (London: Refugee Council, 1997)

Tom Kuntz (ed.), *The Titanic Disaster Hearings: The Official Transcripts of the 1912 Senate Investigation* (New York: Pocket Books, 1998)

Hanif Kureishi, 'The migrant has no face, status or story', *Guardian Review*, 31 May 2014

Francois Lafitte, *The Internment of Aliens* (Harmondsworth: Penguin, 1940)

Dara Lind, '14 facts that help explain America's child-migrant crisis', http://www.vox.com/2014/16/5813406/explain-child-migrant-crisis-central-america-unaccompanied-children-immigrants-daca, accessed 6 February 2015

Leonard Montefiore, 'Our Children', *Jewish Monthly* vol. 1 no. 1 (April 1947)

Caroline Moorehead, *Human Cargo: A Journey Among Refugees* (London: Chatto & Windus, 2005)

Caroline Moorehead, 'Missing in the Mediterranean', *Intelligent Life Magazine*, May/June 2014

Lisa Nandy, *Going It Alone: Children in the Asylum Process* (London: Children's Society, 2007)

Zed Nelson, 'A long way home', *The Guardian*, 22 March 2014

Official Report of the Jewish International Conference (London: Jewish Association, 1910)

Mollie Panter-Downes, 'A Quiet Life in Hampshire', *New Yorker*, 2 March 1946

Janice Raymond et al., 'A Comparative Study of Women Trafficked in the Migration Process' (unpublished report, Coalition Against Trafficking in Women, 2002)

Brian Resnick, 'Why 90,000 Children Flooding Our Border is Not an Immigration Story', *National Journal* 16 June 2014, http://www.nationaljournal.com/domestic policy/why-90-000-children-flooding-our-borders-is-not-an-immigration-story, accessed 10 February 2015.

Save the Children Fund, *Annual Report 1938* (London: SCF, 1938)

Serbian Relief Fund, *For Serbia* (London: Serbian Relief Fund, 1916?)

John Hope Simpson, *The Refugee Problem: Report of a Survey* (London: Oxford University Press, 1939)

William Smith, *A Letter to William Wilberforce* (London: Richard Taylor, 1807)

Arieh Tartakower and Kurt Grossman, *The Jewish Refugee* (New York: Institute of Jewish Affairs, 1944)

Giles Tremlett, '"If you are against saving lives at sea then you are a bigot"', *Guardian*, 8 July 2015

UNHCR, 'Guidelines on Policies and Procedures in Dealing with Unaccompanied Children Seeking Asylum' (unpublished report, UNHCR, February 1997)

UNHCR, *Children on the Run: Unaccompanied Children Leaving Central America and Mexico and the Need for International Protection* (Washington, DC: UNHCR, 2014)

Chaim Weizmann, *The Jewish People and Palestine: Statement Made before the Palestine Royal Commission* (Jerusalem: Zionist Organisation, 1936)

Chaim Weizmann, *The Right to Survive: Testimony before the Anglo-American Committee of Enquiry on Palestine* (London: Jewish Agency for Palestine, 1946)

Denise Winterman, 'World War One: How 250,000 Belgian Refugees didn't leave a trace', *BBC News Magazine*, 15 September 2014, http://www.bbc.co.uk/news/magazine-28857769, accessed 15 September 2014

Vanina Wittenberg, *The New Bonded Labour?* (London: Oxfam/Kalayaan, 2008)

Literature, Drama, Poetry, Art, Film and Television

Helen Ashton, *Tadpole Hall* (London: Collins, 1941)

Agatha Christie, *A Murder is Announced* (London: HarperCollins, 2002)

Maureen Duffy, *Change* (London: Methuen, 1987)

Nathan Englander, *The Ministry of Special Cases* (London: Faber and Faber, 2007)

Europe's Immigration Disaster, Channel 4, 24 June 2014

Ruth Feiner, *Fires in May* (London: Harrap, 1935)

Fire at Sea (Gianfranco Rosi/Sternal Entertainment, 2015)

Daniel Fischin and Mark Fortier (eds), *Adaptations of Shakespeare* (London: Routledge, 2000)

Sue Frumin, 'The Housetrample', in Jill Davis (ed.), *Lesbian Plays: Two* (London: Methuen, 1989)

Louis Golding, *To the Quayside* (London: Hutchinson, 1954)

Linda Grant, *When I Lived in Modern Times* (London: Granta, 2000)

Naomi Gryn, *Chasing Shadows* (1989)

The Guernica Children (Steve Bowles, 2005, 2007)

Kazuo Ishiguro, *The Remains of the Day* (London: Faber and Faber, 1989)

Kazuo Ishiguro, 'On writing *The Remains of the Day*', *Guardian*, 6 December 2014

Anders Lustgarten, *Lampedusa* (London: Bloomsbury, 2015)

'No Country for Lost Kids', *PBS Newshour*, 20 June 2014

The Orphans Who Survived the Concentration Camps, BBC 1, 5 April 2010

Philip Osment (ed.), *Gay Sweatshop: Four Plays and a Company* (London: Methuen, 1989)

Julia Pascal, *The Holocaust Trilogy* (London: Oberon Books, 2000)

People of the Exodus, BBC 1, 15 May 1973

Clara Phillips, 'New Things to Discuss', Tate Britain, December 2014

The Promise, Channel 4, February 2011

The Remains of the Day (Columbia Films, Merchant Ivory Production, 1993)

Ripper Street, BBC 1, 24 February 2013

Bernice Rubens, *The Sergeants' Tale* (London: Little, Brown, 2003)

Servants, BBC 2, 21 November 2012

E. de Selincourt (ed.), *The Poetical Works of William Wordsworth* (Oxford: Clarendon Press, 1952)

Natasha Solomons, *The Novel in the Viola* (London: AudioGO, 2012)

Irene Stratenwerth, *Der Gelbe Schen: Madchenhandel 1860 bis 1930* (Bremerhaven: DAH, 2012)

Terraferma (Cattleya, 2012)

To Whom It May Concern (Archivio Memorie Migranti, 2012)

Upstairs, Downstairs, BBC 1, 2010 series

Leon Uris, *Exodus* (London: Corgi, 1961)

Travelogues and Guide Books

Trevor Avery and Rosemary Smith (eds), *The Lost Village of Calgarth* (Sedbergh: Another Space, 2009)

Alex Black and Hazel Gatford, *Wordsworth's Lake District: The Landscape and Its Writers* (Sevenoaks: Salmon, 2001)

Melvyn Bragg, *Land of the Lakes* (London: Secker & Warburg, 1983)

W.G. Collingwood, *The Lake Counties* (London: Frederick Warne, 1932)

Hunter Davies, *A Walk Around the Lakes: A Visit to Britain's Lake District* (London: Frances Lincoln, 2009)

Andrew and Suzanne Edwards, *Sicily: A Literary Guide for Travellers* (London: I.B. Tauris, 2014)

S.P.B. Mais, *The English Scene Today* (London: Rockliff, 1948)

Mordechai Naor (ed.), *The Atlit Camp* (Tel Aviv: Yehuda Dekel Library, 2010)

Peter Nock, *Tales and Legends of Windermere* (Windermere: Orinoco Press, 1989)

Hilda Stowell, *Wintershill Hall Hampshire from the Period of Roman Occupation to 1972* (Chichester: Chichester Press, 1972)

John Page White, *Lays and Legends of the English Lake District* (London: John Russell Smith, 1873)

William Wordsworth, *Guide to the Lakes* (Frances Lincoln, 2004)

Newspapers and Journals

AJR Information
Commentary
Daily Express
Daily Mail
Evening Standard
The Gates of Zion
The Guardian
Haaretz
The Herioter
Housewife
Independent
Jewish Chronicle
Jewish Standard
Journal of the '45 Aid Society
Listener
Manchester Guardian
The Metro
New Republic

News Chronicle
New Statesman
New York Times
Observer
Oxford Chronicle
People's Journal
Picture Post
Polish Fortnightly Bulletin
Primrose Leaves
Slate
Southampton Times
Southern Daily Echo
Spectator
The Standard
The Sun
Sunday Times
Taunton's School Journal
The Times
Times Literary Review
Westmorland Gazette

Official Publications
The 1919 Aliens Restriction (Amendment) Act
Aliens Act, 1905
The British Imperial Calendar and Civil Service List
First Report of the Departmental Committee Appointed by the President of the Local Government Board to Consider and Report on Questions Arising in Connection with the Reception and Employment of the Belgian Refugees in this Country (London: HMSO, 1914)
Hansard, House of Commons debates
Palestine: Statement of Policy by His Majesty's Government in the United Kingdom (London: HMSO, 1937)
Palestine: Statement of Policy (London: HMSO, 1939)
'The Prime Minister's Holocaust Commission: Terms of Reference' (Cabinet Office, 2014)

Museum and Site Visits
Atlit Immigration Detention Camp Visitor Centre, 16 December 2016
Calgarth, Lake Windermere, 18 August 2009
Clandestine Immigration and Naval Museum, Haifa, 18 December 2016
Deutsches Auswanderer Haus, Bremerhaven, 15 December 2014
'From Auschwitz to Ambleside', Windermere Library, July 2011
Golders Green crematoria, 17 October 2013
Imperial War Museum, 1 April 2010
'The Jews of District Six', Cape Town Jewish Museum, 2 April 2013
Kendal Railway Station, 8 July 2010
Lampedusa Island, 4–7 August 2015
Liverpool Street Station, 15 September 2007
London Jewish Museum, 4 December 2014

Websites and Blogs
Another Space
Archviomemoriemigranti
BBC News
Bildung-fueralle
Charter of Lampedusa
Adam Curtis
Daily Kos
Four Winds 10
Free Movement
Grough Magazine
IDISHLAND
International Organization for Migration
Italia
Jewish Tribal Review
JWIRE
Kent and Medway History Timeline
National Journal
Segretaria
Tourist Haifa
UNHCR
Vox
Westpoint
Wordsworth Country

Secondary Sources

Giorgio Agamben, *Homo Sacer: Sovereign Power and Bare Life* (Stanford: Stanford University Press, 1998)

Kathleen Alaimo, 'Historical Roots of Children's Rights in Europe and the United States', in Kathleen Alaimo and Brian Klug (eds), *Children as Equals: Exploring the Rights of the Child* (Lanham: University Press of America, 2002)

Gur Alroey, *Bread to Eat & Clothes to Wear: Letters from Jewish Migrants in the Early Twentieth Century* (Detroit: Wayne State University Press, 2011)

Bridget Anderson, 'Overseas Domestic Workers in the European Union', in Janet Momsen (ed.), *Gender, Migration and Domestic Service* (London: Routledge, 1999)

Bridget Anderson, *Doing the Dirty Work? The Global Politics of Domestic Labour* (London: Zed Books, 2000)

Bridget Anderson, 'A very private business: migration and domestic work', *Working Paper*, Centre on Migration, Policy and Society no. 28 (2006)

Bridget Anderson, 'Mobilizing migrants, making citizens: migrant domestic workers as political agents', *Ethnic and Racial Studies* vol. 33 no. 1 (2010)

Kay Anderson, '"The beast within": race, humanity, and animality', *Environment and Planning D* vol. 18 no. 12 (2000)

Kay Andrews, 'The British Government and the *Kindertransport*: Moving Away from the Redemptive Story', *Prism* vol. 5 (2013)

Hannah Arendt, *The Origins of Totalitarianism* (New York: Harcourt, 1951)

Elizabeth Baer and Myrna Goldenberg (eds), *Experience and Expression: Women, the Nazis and the Holocaust* (Detroit: Wayne State University Press, 2003)

Julia Baker, 'From *Other People's Houses* into *Shakespeare's Kitchen*', *The Yearbook of the Research Centre for German and Austrian Exile Studies* vol. 13 (2012)

Kenneth Ballhatchet, *Race, Class and Sex under the Raj* (London: Weidenfeld & Nicolson, 1980)

Frances Bartkowski, *Travelers, Immigrants, Inmates: Essays in Estrangement* (Minneapolis: University of Minnesota Press, 1995)

Bashir Bashir and Amos Goldberg, 'Deliberating the Holocaust and the Nakba: disruptive empathy and binationalism in Israel/Palestine', *Journal of Genocide Research* vol. 16 no. 1 (2014)

Yehuda Bauer, *The Holocaust in Historical Perspective* (London: Sheldon Press, 1978)

Yehuda Bauer, *A History of the Holocaust* (New York: Franklin Watts, 1982)

Rainer Baum, 'Holocaust: Moral Indifference as the Form of Modern Evil', in Alan Rosenberg and Gerald Myers (eds), *Echoes from the Holocaust: Philosophical Reflections on a Dark Time* (Philadelphia: Temple University Press, 1988)

Zygmunt Bauman, *Modernity and the Holocaust* (Ithaca: Cornell University Press, 1989)

Judith Taylor Baumel, *Double Jeopardy: Gender and the Holocaust* (London: Vallentine Mitchell, 1998)

Marietta Bearman et al., *Out of Austria: The Austrian Centre in London in World War II* (London: Tauris, 2008)

Gal Beckerman, *When They Come For Us We'll Be Gone: The Epic Struggle to Save Soviet Jewry* (New York: Houghton Mifflin Harcourt, 2010)

Adrian Bell, *Only For Three Months: The Basque Children in Exile* (Norwich: Mousehold Press, 1996)

Gadi Benezer and Roger Zetter, 'Searching for Directions: Conceptual and Methodological Challenges in Researching Refugee Journeys', *Journal of Refugee Studies* vol. 28 no. 3 (2015)

Norman Bentwich, *They Found Refuge: An account of British Jewry's work for victims of Nazi oppression* (London: Cresset Press, 1956)

Marion Berghahn, *Continental Britons: German–Jewish Refugees from Nazi Germany* (Oxford: Berg, 1988)

Daniel Bertaux and Isabelle Bertaux-Wiame, 'Life Stories in the Bakers' Trade', in Daniel Bertaux (ed.), *Biography and Society: The Life History Approach in the Social Sciences* (Beverly Hills: Sage, 1981)

Donald Bloxham, *The Final Solution: A Genocide* (Oxford: Oxford University Press, 2009)

Traude Bollauf, *Dienstmaden-Emigration Die Flucht jüdischer Frauen aus Österreich und Deutschland nach England 1938/39* (Vienna: Lit Verlag, 2011)

Richard Breitman and Alan Kraut, *American Refugee Policy and European Jewry, 1933–1945* (Bloomington: Indiana University Press, 1987)

Edward Bristow, *Prostitution and Prejudice: The Jewish Fight Against White Slavery 1870–1939* (Oxford: Oxford University Press, 1982)

Tom Buchanan, *Britain and the Spanish Civil War* (Cambridge: Cambridge University Press, 1997)

Alan Bullock, *Ernest Bevin: Foreign Secretary* (London: Heinemann, 1984)

Madeleine Bunting, *The Model Occupation: The Channel Islands under German Rule, 1940–1945* (London: HarperCollins, 1995)

Judith Butler, *Excitable Speech: A Politics of the Performative* (New York: Routledge, 1997)

Frank Caestecker and Bob Moore (eds), *Refugees from Nazi Germany and the Liberal Democracies* (New York: Berghahn, 2014)

Peter Cahalan, *Belgian Refugee Relief in England during the Great War* (New York: Garland, 1982)

Angus Calder, *Myth of the Blitz* (London: Jonathan Cape, 1991)

Stephen Castles, 'Towards a Sociology of Forced Migration and Social Transformation', *Sociology* vol. 37 no. 1 (2003)

Philip Cavanaugh, 'The Present is a Foreign Country: Lore Segal's Fiction', *Contemporary Literature* vol. 3 no. 3 (1993)

David Cesarani, 'The Myth of Origin: ethnic memory and the experience of migration', in Aubrey Newman and Stephen Massil (eds), *Patterns of Migration 1850–1914* (London: Jewish Historical Society of England, 1996)

David Cesarani, *Major Farran's Hat: Murder, Scandal and Britain's War Against Jewish Terrorism 1945–1948* (London: Heinemann, 2009)

David Cesarani and Suzanne Bardgett (eds), *Belsen 1945: New Historical Perspectives* (London: Vallentine Mitchell, 2006)

Mary Chamberlain and Paul Thompson, 'Genre and Narrative in Life Stories', in idem (eds), *Narrative and Genre* (London: Routledge, 1998)

Roland Chambers, *The Last Englishman: The Double Life of Arthur Ransome* (London: Faber and Faber, 2009)

A. Chapman and R. Knight, *Wages and Salaries in the United Kingdom 1920–1938* (Cambridge: Cambridge University Press, 1953)

David Charters, *The British Army and Jewish Insurgency in Palestine, 1945–47* (Basingstoke: Macmillan, 1989)

Bryan Cheyette, *Constructions of 'The Jew' in English Literature and Society: Racial Representations, 1875–1945* (Cambridge: Cambridge University Press, 1993)

B.S. Chimni, 'The Geopolitics of Refugee Studies: A View from the South', *Journal of Refugee Studies* vol. 11 no. 4 (1998)

B.S. Chimni, 'The Birth of a "Discipline": From Refugee to Forced Migration Studies', *Journal of Refugee Studies* vol. 22 no. 1 (2009)

Luca Ciabarri, 'Dynamics and Representation of Migration Corridors: the rise and fall of the Libya–Lampedusa route and forms of mobility from the Horn of Africa (2000–2009)', *ACME* vol. 13 no. 2 (2013)

James Clifford, *Travel and Translation in the Late Twentieth Century* (Cambridge, MA: Harvard University Press, 1997)

Cynthia Cohen, 'United Nations Convention on the Rights of the Child', in Kathleen Alaimo and Brian Klug (eds), *Children as Equals: Exploring the Rights of the Child* (Lanham: University Press of America, 2002)

Frederick Cohen, *The Jews in the Channel Islands during the Occupation 1940–1945* (Jersey: Jersey Heritage Trust, 2000)

Stanley Cohen, *Folk Devils and Moral Panics* (London: Routledge, 2002)

Steve Cohen, *Deportation is Freedom! The Orwellian World of Immigration Controls* (London: Jessica Kingsley, 2006)

Tim Cole, *Traces of the Holocaust: Journeying in and out of the Ghetto* (London: Continuum, 2011)

Paul Connerton, *How Societies Remember* (Cambridge: Cambridge University Press, 1989)

Rosie Cox, *The Servant Problem: Domestic Employment in a Global Economy* (London: I.B. Tauris, 2006)

Rosie Cox (ed.), *Au Pairs' Lives in Global Context* (Basingstoke: Palgrave Macmillan, 2015)

Jennifer Craig-Norton, 'From Dependence to Autonomy: *Kinder*, Refugee Organizations and the Struggle for Agency', *Prism* vol. 5 (Spring 2015)

Julia Creet and Andreas Kitzmann (eds), *Memory and Migration: Multidirectional Approaches to Memory Studies* (Toronto: University of Toronto Press, 2011)

Barbara Crossley, *The Triumph of Kurt Schwitters* (Ambleside: Armitt Trust, 2005)

Paolo Cuttitta, '"Borderizing the Island. Setting and Narratives of the Lampedusa "Border Play"', *ACME* no. 13 no. 2 (2014)

W. Darby, *Landscape and Identity: Geographies of Nation and Class in England* (Oxford: Berg, 2000)

Leonore Davidoff, 'Mastered for Life: Servant and Wife in Victorian and Edwardian England', *Journal of Social History* vol. 7 (Summer 1974)

Hunter Davies, *William Wordsworth: A Biography* (London: Weidenfeld and Nicolson, 1980)

Robert Davis, Maria Pia Di Bella, John Eade and Gerry Marvin, 'Introduction', *Journeys* vol. 1 no. 1 (2000)

Russell Davis and Liz Ottoway, *Vicky* (London: Secker & Warburg, 1987)

Lucy Delap, *Knowing Their Place: Domestic Service in Twentieth-Century Britain* (Oxford: Oxford University Press, 2011)

Nick Dines, Nicola Montagna and Vincenzo Ruggiero, 'Thinking Lampedusa: border construction, the spectacle of bare life and the productivity of migrants', *Ethnic and Racial Studies* vol. 43 no. 3 (2015)

Jo Doezema, 'Loose Women or Lost Women? The re-emergence of the myth of "white slavery" in contemporary discourses of "trafficking in women"', *Gender Issues* vol. 18 no. 1 (2000)

Mary Douglas, *Purity and Danger: An Analysis of the Concepts of Pollution and Taboo* (London: Routledge, 1996)

Margaret Drabble, 'Foreword', in *The Romantic Poets: William Wordsworth* (London: Guardian, 2009)

Seymour Drescher, 'The Atlantic Slave Trade and the Holocaust: A Comparative Analysis', in Alan Rosenbaum (ed.), *Is the Holocaust Unique? Perspectives on Comparitive Genocide* (Philadelphia: Westview Press, 2009)

Deborah Dwork, *Children With a Star: Jewish Youth in Nazi Europe* (New Haven: Yale University Press, 1991)

Deborah Dwork and Robert Jan Van Pelt, *Flight from the Reich: Refugee Jews, 1933–1946* (New York: Norton, 2009)

Abba Eban, *My People: The Story of the Jews* (New York: Random House, 1968)

Gillian Elinor, 'Stolen or Given: An Issue in Oral History', *Oral History* vol. 20 no. 1 (1992)

Todd Endelman, *The Jews of Britain 1656 to 2000* (Berkeley: University of California Press, 2002)

David Farrier, *Postcolonial Asylum: Seeking Sanctuary Before the Law* (Liverpool: Liverpool University Press, 2011)

Vera Fast, *Children's Exodus: A History of the Kindertransport* (London: I.B. Tauris, 2011)

Cherly Finley, 'Touring the African Diaspora', *Journeys* vol. 13 no. 2 (2012)

Carole Bell Ford, *After the Girls Club: How Teenaged Holocaust Survivors Built New Lives in America* (Lanham: Lexington Books, 2010)

Michel Foucault, 'Different Spaces', in James Foubion (ed.), *Essential Works of Michel Foucault* vol. 2 *Aesthetics, Method, and Epistomology* (London: Allen Lane, 1998)

David Fraser, *The Jews of the Channel Islands and the Rule of Law, 1940–1945* (Brighton: Sussex University Press, 2000)

Saul Friedlander, *Nazi Germany & The Jews: The Years of Persecution 1933–1939* (London: Weidenfeld & Nicolson, 1997)

Heidrun Friese, 'Border Economies: A Nascent Migration Industry Around Lampedusa', in Lisa Anteby-Yemini et al. (eds), *Borders, Mobilities and Migrations: Perspectives from the Mediterranean 19–21st Century* (Brussels: Peter Lang, 2014)

Joseph Gaer, *The Legend of the Wandering Jew* (New York: Mentor Books, 1961)

Lloyd Gartner, 'Anglo-Jewry and the Jewish international traffic in prostitution 1885–1914', *American Jewish Studies Review* vols 7–8 (1982–3)

Peter Gatrell, *Free World? The Campaign to Save the World's Refugees, 1956–1963* (Cambridge: Cambridge University Press, 2011)

Peter Gatrell, *The Making of the Modern Refugee* (Oxford: Oxford University Press, 2013)

Nicholas De Genova, 'Migrant "Illegality" and Deportability in Everyday Life', *Annual Review of Anthropology* vol. 31 (2002)

Matthew Gibney, 'Beyond the bounds of responsibility: western states and measures to prevent the arrival of refugees', *Global Migration Perspectives* no. 22 (January 2005)

Simone Gigliotti, *The Train Journey: Transit, Captivity, and Witnessing in the Holocaust* (New York: Berghahn Books, 2009)

Martin Gilbert, *The Boys: Triumph over Adversity* (London: Weidenfeld & Nicolson, 1996)

Anton Gill, *The Journey Back from Hell: Conversations with Concentration Camp Survivors* (London: Grafton, 1988)

Peter and Leni Gillman, *'Collar the Lot': How Britain Interned and Expelled Its Wartime Refugees* (London: Quartet Books, 1980)

Paul Gilroy, *Between Camps: Nations, Cultures and the Allure of Race* (London: Allen Lane, 2000)

Nora Glickman, *The Jewish White Slave Trade and the Untold Story of Raquel Liberman* (New York: Garland, 2000)

Corey Goldman, 'A Portrait of Imre Yitzhak Rosenberg', in Imrich Yitzhak Rosenberg and Corey Goldman, *A Jew in Deed* (Manotick, Ontario: Penumbra Press, 2004)

Nancy Green, 'The Comparative Method and Poststructural Structuralism – New Perspectives for Migration Studies', *Journal of American Ethnic History* vol. 13 (1994)

Shirley Green, *Rachman* (London: Michael Joseph, 1979)

Anthony Grenville, 'Underpaid, underfed and overworked', *AJR Information* vol. 8 no. 12 (December 2008)

Anthony Grenville, *Jewish Refugees from Germany and Austria in Britain, 1933–1970: Their Image in the Association of Jewish Refugees Information* (London: Vallentine Mitchell, 2010)

John Grenville, 'The Kindertransports: An Introduction', in Andrea Hammel and Bea Lewkowicz (eds), *The Kindertransports to Britain 1938/39: New Perspectives* (Amsterdam: Rodolphi, 2012)

Andrew Gross, 'Holocaust Tourism in Berlin: Global Memory, Trauma and the "Negation of the Sublime"', *Journeys* vol. 7 no. 2 (2006)

Bracha Habas, *The Gate Breakers* (New York: Herzl Press, 1963)

Ze'ev Venia Hadari and Ze'ev Tsahor, *Voyage to Freedom: an episode in the illegal immigration to Palestine* (London: Vallentine Mitchell, 1985)

Aviva Halamish, *The Exodus Affair: Holocaust Survivors and the Struggle for Palestine* (London: Vallentine Mitchell, 1998)

Aviva Halamish, 'Palestine as a Destination for Jewish Immigrants and Refugees from Nazi Germany', in Frank Caestecker and Bob Moore (eds), *Refugees from Nazi Germany and the Liberal Democracies* (New York: Berghahn, 2014)

Stuart Hall, 'Whose Heritage? The Impact of Cultural Diversity on Britain's Living Heritage', in Jo Littler and Roshi Naidoo (eds), *The Politics of Heritage: The Legacies of 'Race'* (London: Routledge, 2005)

Andrea Hammel and Bea Lewkowicz (eds), 'The Kindertransport to Britain 1938/39', *The Yearbook of the Research Centre for German and Austrian Exile Studies* vol. 13 (2012)

Harry Hanak, *Great Britain and Austria-Hungary during the First World War* (London: Oxford University Press, 1962)

Galit Hasan-Rokem and Alan Dundes (eds), *The Wandering Jew: Essays in the Interpretation of a Christian Legend* (Bloomington: Indiana University Press, 1986)

James Hathaway, 'Forced Migration Studies: Could We Agree Just to "Date"?', *Journal of Refugee Studies* vol. 20 no. 3 (2007)

John Higham, *Strangers in the Land: Patterns of American Nativism 1860–1925* (New York: Atheneum, 1978)

Raul Hilberg, *The Destruction of European Jews* vol. 3 (New York: Holmes & Meier, 1985)

Raul Hilberg, 'German Railroads/Jewish Souls', *Society* vol. 35 no. 2 (January/February 1998)

Gerhard Hirschfeld (ed.), *Exile in Great Britain: Refugees from Hitler's Germany* (Leamington: Berg, 1984)

Philip Hoare, *The Sea Inside* (London: Fourth Estate, 2013)

David Holly, *Exodus 1947* (Boston: Little, Brown, 1969)

Colin Holmes, *John Bull's Island: Immigration & British Society, 1871–1971* (Basingstoke: Macmillan, 1988)

bell hooks, 'Representing Whiteness', in Lawrence Grossberg, Cary Nelson and Paula Reichler (eds), *Cultural Studies* (New York: Routledge, 1992)

Pamela Horn, *Life Below Stairs in the 20th Century* (Stroud: Sutton, 2001)

Margaret Humphreys, *Empty Cradles* (London: Doubleday, 1994)

Clarissa Hyman, *The Jewish Kitchen: Recipes and Stories from Around the World* (London: Conran Octopus, 2003)

Michael Jackson, 'In the Footsteps of Walter Benjamin', *Journeys* vol. 13 no. 2 (2012)

Keith Jeffery, 'British secret service blew up Jewish ships taking war refugees to Palestine', *The Times*, 18 September 2010

Keith Jeffery, *MI6: The History of the Secret Intelligence Service, 1909–1949* (London: Bloomsbury, 2010)

Zoe Josephs, *Survivors: Jewish Refugees in Birmingham 1933–1945* (Oldbury: Meridian Books, 1988)

Steven Kagle, 'The Diary as Art: A New Assessment', *Genre* vol. 6 (1973)

Amy Kaplan, 'Zionism as Anticolonialism: The Case of *Exodus*', *American Literary History* vol. 25 no. 4 (2013)

David Katzman, *Seven Days a Week: Women and Domestic Service in Industrializing America* (New York: Oxford University Press, 1978)

Margaret Kertesz, 'To Speak for Themselves? Mass-Observation's Women's Wartime Diaries', *Feminist Praxis* nos 37–8 (1993)

Naseem Khan, 'Taking Root in Britain: the process of shaping heritage', in Jo Littler and Roshi Naidoo (eds), *The Politics of Heritage: The Legacies of 'Race'* (London: Routledge, 2005)

Jon and David Kimche, *The Secret Roads: The 'Illegal' Migration of a People 1938–1948* (London: Secker and Warburg, 1954)

Allan King, *Wings on Windermere: The history of the Lake District's forgotten flying boat factory* (Sandomierz: Stratus, 2008)

Phil Kinsman, 'Landscape, race and national identity: the photography of Ingrid Pollard', *Area* vol. 27 no. 4 (1995)

Brian Klug, *Being Jewish and Doing Justice: Bringing Argument to Life* (London: Vallentine Mitchell, 2010)

Paul Knepper, '"Jewish Trafficking" and London Jews in the Age of Migration', *Journal of Modern Jewish Studies* vol. 6 no. 3 (2007)

Anne Kelly Knowles, Tim Cole and Alberto Giordano (eds), *Geographies of the Holocaust* (Bloomington: Indiana University Press, 2014)

Arieh Kochavi, *Post-Holocaust Politics: Britain, the United States & Jewish Refugees* (Chapel Hill: University of North Carolina Press, 2001)

Arthur Koestler, *Promise and Fulfillment: Palestine 1917–1949* (London: Macmillan, 1949)

Thomas Kuhner, 'Colonialism and the Holocaust: Continuities, Causations and Complexities', *Journal of Genocide Research* vol. 15 no. 3 (2013)

Tony Kushner, *The Persistence of Prejudice: Antisemitism in British Society during the Second World War* (Manchester: Manchester University Press, 1989)

Tony Kushner, *The Holocaust and the Liberal Imagination: A Social and Cultural History* (Oxford: Blackwell, 1994)

Tony Kushner, 'Anti-Semitism and austerity: the August 1947 riots in Britain', in Panikos Panayi (ed.), *Racial Violence in Britain in the Nineteenth and Twentieth Centuries* (London: Leicester University Press, 1996)

Tony Kushner, 'The Holocaust and the Museum World in Britain: A Study of Ethnography', in Sue Vice (ed.), *Representing the Holocaust* (London: Vallentine Mitchell, 2003)

Tony Kushner, *Remembering Refugees: Then and Now* (Manchester: Manchester University Press, 2005)

Tony Kushner, 'Cowards or Heroes? Jewish Journeys, Jewish Families and the *Titanic*', in James Jordan, Tony Kushner and Sarah Pearce (eds), *Jewish Journeys from Philo to Hip Hop* (London: Vallentine Mitchell, 2010)

Tony Kushner, *The Battle of Britishness: Migrant Journeys 1685 to the Present* (Manchester: Manchester University Press, 2012)

Tony Kushner and Katharine Knox, *Refugees in an Age of Genocide: Global, National and Local Perspectives during the Twentieth Century* (London: Frank Cass, 1999)

Pieter Lagrou, 'Victims of Genocide and National Memory: Belgium, France and the Netherlands, 1945–1965', *Past & Present* no. 154 (February 1997)

Lawrence Langer, *Versions of Survival: The Holocaust and the Human Spirit* (Albany: State University of New York Press, 1982)

Daniel Langton, *Claude Montefiore: His Life and Thought* (London: Vallentine Mitchell, 2002)

Phyliss Lassner, *Anglo-Jewish Women Writing the Holocaust: Displaced Witnesses* (Basingstoke: Palgrave Macmillan, 2008)

Jeremy Leigh, *Jewish Journeys* (London: Haus Publishing, 2006)

Lucy Lethbridge, *Servants* (London: Bloomsbury, 2013)

Mark Levene, *Genocide in the Age of the Nation State* (London: I.B. Tauris, 2005)

Mark Levene, *The Crisis of Genocide* vol. 1 *Devastation: The European Rimlands, 1912–1938* (Oxford: Oxford University Press, 2014)

Naomi Lewis, 'Introduction', in Lore Segal, *Other People's Houses: A Refugee in England 1938–48* (London: Bodley Head, 1974)

Fritz Liebreich, *Britain's Naval and Political Reaction to the Illegal Immigration of the Jews to Palestine, 1945–1948* (London: Routledge, 2005)

Angela Lloyd, 'Regulating Consent: Protecting Undocumented Immigrant Children from Their (Evil) Step-Uncle Sam, Or How to Ameliorate the Impact of the 1997 Amendments to the SIJ Law', *Public Interest Law Journal* vol. 15 (Spring 2006)

Louise London, *Whitehall and the Jews 1933–1948: British Immigration Policy and the Holocaust* (Cambridge: Cambridge University Press, 2000)

Robert McKenzie and Alessandro Triulzi (eds), *Long Journey: African Migrants on the Road* (Leiden: Brill, 2013)

Liisa Malkki, 'National Geographic: The Rooting of Peoples and the Territorization of National Identity among Scholars and Refugees', *Cultural Anthropology* vol. 7 no. 1 (1992)

Liisa Malkki, 'Speechless Emissaries: Refugees, Humanitarianism and Dehistoricization', *Cultural Anthropology* vol. 11 no. 3 (1996)

Patrick Manning, *Migration in World History* (Abingdon: Routledge, 2013)

Harold Marcuse, *Legacies of Dachau: The Uses and Abuses of a Concentration Camp, 1933–2001* (Cambridge: Cambridge University Press, 2001)

Lara Marks, 'Jewish women and prostitution in the East End of London', *Jewish Quarterly* vol. 34 no. 2 (1987)

Michael Marrus, *The Unwanted: European Refugees in the Twentieth Century* (Oxford: Oxford University Press, 1985)

Michael Marrus, *The Holocaust in History* (London: Weidenfeld & Nicolson, 1988)

Doreen Massey, 'Double Articulation: A Place in the World', in A. Bammer (ed.), *Displacements: Cultural Identities in Question* (Bloomington: Indiana University Press, 1994)

Doreen Massey, 'Places and Their Pasts', *History Workshop Journal* no. 39 (Spring 1995)

Jean Medawar and David Pyke, *Hitler's Gift: Scientists Who Fled Nazi Germany* (London: Richard Cohen Books, 2000)

Andrej Mitrovic, *Serbia's Great War* (London: Hurst, 2007)

Stephen Morton, *Gayatri Chakrovorty Spivak* (London: Routledge, 2003)

A. Dirk Moses, 'Conceptual blockages and definitional dilemmas in the "racial century": genocides of indigenous peoples and the Holocaust', *Patterns of Prejudice* vol. 36 no. 4 (2002)

Sarah Moskovitz, *Love Despite Hate: Child Survivors of the Holocaust and their Adult Lives* (New York: Schocken Books, 1983)

Alison Mountz, *Seeking Asylum: Human Smuggling and Bureaucracy at the Border* (Minneapolis: University of Minnesota Press, 2010)

Kevin Myers, 'The hidden history of refugee schooling in Britain: the case of the Belgians, 1914–18', *History of Education* vol. 30 no. 2 (2001)

Amisan Nachman, *Great Power Discord in Palestine: The Anglo-American Committee of Inquiry into the Problems of European Jewry and Palestine 1945–46* (London: Frank Cass, 1987)

Mordechai Naor, *Hapala: Clandestine Immigration 1931–1948* (Tel Aviv: Ministry of Defence Publishing House, 1987)

Liza Navarro, 'An Analysis of Treatment of Unaccompanied Immigrant and Refugee Children in INS Detention and Other Forms of Institutionalized Custody', *Chicano-Latino Law Review* vol. 19 (1998)

Paul Nugat, 'From Magnolia Street to the Quayside', *Jewish Quarterly* vol. 1 no. 4 (spring 1954)

Felicity Nussbaum, 'Towards Conceptualizing the Diary', in James Olney (ed.), *Studies in Autobiography* (New York: Oxford University Press, 1988)

Dalia Ofer, *Escaping the Holocaust: Illegal Immigration to the Land of Israel, 1939-44* (New York: Oxford University Press, 1990)

Dalia Ofer and Lenore Weitzmann (eds), *Women and the Holocaust* (New Haven: Yale University Press, 1998)

Charles van Onselen, *The Fox and the Flies: The World of Joseph Silver, Racketeer and Psychopath* (London: Jonathan Cape, 2007)

Cynthia Ozick, 'A Contraband Life', *Commentary* vol. 39 (March 1965)

Judith Page, *Imperfect Sympathies: Jews and Judaism in British Romantic Literature and Culture* (New York: Palgrave Macmillan, 2004)

Ingrid Palmary, Erica Burman, Khatija Chantler and Peace Kiguwa (eds), *Gender and Migration: Feminist Interventions* (London: Zed Books, 2010)

Andrew Parker and Eve Kosofsky Sedgwick (eds), *Performativity and Performance* (New York: Routledge, 1995)

Rhacel Parrenas, *Servants of Globalization: Women, Migration and Domestic Work* (Stanford: Stanford University Press, 2001)

Artur Patek, *Jews on Route to Palestine 1934-1944: Sketches from the History of Aliyah Bet - Clandestine Jewish Immigration* (Krakow: Jagiellonian University Press, 2012)

Gunnar Paulsson, *Secret City: The Hidden Jews of Warsaw 1940-1945* (New Haven: Yale University Press, 2002)

Jill Pellew, 'The Home Office and the Aliens Act, 1905', *Historical Journal* vol. 32 no. 2 (1989)

Derek Penslar, *Jews and the Military: A History* (Princeton: Princeton University Press, 2013)

Greg Philo, Emma Briant and Pauline Donald, *Bad News for Refugees* (London: Pluto Press, 2013)

Harold Pollins, *Economic History of the Jews in England* (East Brunswick: Associated University Presses, 1982)

Alicia Pozo-Gutierrez and Padmini Broomfield, *'Here, Look After Him': Voices of Basque Evacuee Children of the Spanish Civil War* (Southampton: University of Southampton Press, 2012)

Nicholas Pronay, 'Defeated Germany in British Newsreels: 1944-45', in K.R.M. Short and Stephan Dolezel (eds), *Hitler's Fall: The Newsreel Witness* (London: Croom Helm, 1988)

Malcolm Proudfoot, *European Refugees: 1939-52. A Study in Forced Population Movement* (London: Faber and Faber, 1957)

Nigel Rapport, 'Walking Auschwitz, Walking Without Arriving', *Journeys* vol. 9 no. 2 (2008)

Timothy Raeymaekers, 'Introduction: Europe's Bleeding Border and the Mediterranean as a Relational Space', *ACME* vol. 13 no. 2 (2014)

Marcus Rediker, *The Slave Ship: A Human History* (New York: Penguin, 2007)

Laurence Rees, *Auschwitz: The Nazis and the 'Final Solution'* (London: BBC Books, 2005)

Joanne Reilly, *Belsen: The Liberation of a Concentration Camp* (London: Routledge, 1998)

Joanne Reilly et al. (eds), *Belsen in History and Memory* (London: Frank Cass, 1997)

Liz Rice (ed.), *Flying Boats and Fellow Travellers* (Sedbergh: Another Space, 2008)

Alan Rosenbaum (ed.), *Is the Holocaust Unique? Perspectives on Comparitive Genocide* (Philadelphia: Westview Press, 2009)

Pnina Rosenberg, 'Footsteps of Memory: Frank Meisler's *Kindertransport* Memorials', *Prism* vol. 5 (Spring 2013)

Pnina Rosenberg, 'When Private Became Public: The *Fur das Kind* Memorial', *Prism* vol. 5 (Spring 2013)

Regine Rosenthal, 'Inventing the Other: Ambivalent Constructions of the Wandering Jew/ess in Nineteenth Century American Literature', in Leonard Greenspoon and Bryan Le Beau (eds), *Representations of Jews Through the Ages* (Omaha: Creighton University Press, 1996)

Michael Rothberg, 'In the Nazi Cinema: Race, Visuality and Identification in Fanon and Kluger', *Wasafari* vol. 24 no. 1 (2009)

Michael Rothberg, *Multidirectional Memory: Remembering the Holocaust in the Age of Decolonization* (Stanford: Stanford University Press, 2009)

Maurice Roumani, *The Jews of Libya: Coexistence, Persecution, Resettlement* (Brighton: University of Sussex Press, 2009)

Emily Roxworthy, *The Spectacle of Japanese American Trauma: Racial Performativity and World War II* (Honolulu: University of Hawaii Press, 2008)

William Rubinstein, *The Myth of Rescue: Why the Democracies could not have Saved more Jews from the Nazis* (London: Routledge, 1997)

Dave Russell, *Looking North: Northern England and the National Imagination* (Manchester: Manchester University Press, 2004)

Raphael Samuel and Paul Thompson (eds), *The Myths We Live By* (London: Routledge, 1990)

Elsie Sandell, *Southampton Through the Ages: A Short History* (Southampton: G.F. Wilson, 1960)

Paul Sanders, *The British Channel Islands under German Occupation 1940–1945* (Jersey: Jersey Heritage Trust, 2005)

Raffaella Sarti, 'The Globalisation of Domestic Service – An Historical Perspective', in Helma Lutz (ed.), *Migration and Domestic Work: A European Perspective on a Global Theme* (Abingdon: Oxford, 2008)

Per Kristian Sebak, *Titanic's Predecessor: The SS Norge Disaster of 1904* (Laksevag: Seaward Publishing, 2004)

Gitta Sereny, *Into that Darkness: From Mercy Killing to Mass Murder* (London: Andre Deutsch, 1974)

Hugh and Christopher Seton-Watson, *The Making of a New Europe* (London: Methuen, 1981)

Nicholas Shakespeare, *Priscilla: the Hidden Life of an Englishwoman in Wartime France* (London: Harvill Secker, 2013)

A.J. Sherman, *Island Refuge: Britain and Refugees from the Third Reich* (Berkeley: University of California Press, 1973)

A.J. Sherman, *Mandate Days: British Lives in Palestine 1918–1948* (London: Thames and Hudson, 1997)

K.R.M. Short, 'Hollywood Fights Anti-Semitism, 1940–1945', in idem (ed.), *Film and Radio Propaganda in World War II* (London: Croom Helm, 1983)

M.M. Silver, *Our Exodus: Leon Uris and the Americanization of Israel's Founding Story* (Detroit: Wayne State University Press, 2010)

Georgina Sinclair and Chris Williams, '"Home and Away": The Cross-Fertilisation between "Colonial" and "British" Policing, 1921–85', *Journal of Imperial and Commonwealth History* vol. 35 no. 2 (2007)

Claudia Skran, *Refugees in Inter-War Europe: The Emergence of a Regime* (Oxford: Clarendon Press, 1995)

Lyn Smith, *Heroes of the Holocaust: Ordinary Britons Who Risked Their Lives to Make a Difference* (London: Ebury Press, 2013)

Michael Smith, *Foley: The Spy Who Saved 10,000 Jews* (London: Hodder & Stoughton, 1999)

Daniel Snowman, *The Hitler Emigres: The Cultural Impact on Britain of Refugees from Nazism* (London: Pimlico, 2003)

Sheila Spector (ed.), *British Romanticism and the Jews: History, Culture, Literature* (New York: Palgrave, 2002)

Gayatri Chakravorty Spivak, 'The Rani of Sirmur: An Essay in Reading the Archives', *History and Theory* vol. 24 no. 3 (1985)

Gayatri Chakravorty Spivak, 'Can the subaltern speak?', in G. Nelson (ed.), *Marxism and the Intepretation of Culture* (Basingstoke: Macmillan, 1988)

Gayatri Chakravorty Spivak, *A Critique of Postcolonial Reason: Toward A History of the Vanishing Present* (Cambridge, MA: Harvard University Press, 1999)

H. Spooner, *A History of Taunton's School 1760–1967* (Southampton: Taunton's School, 1968)

Axel Stahler, 'Metonymies of Jewish Postcoloniality: The British Mandate for Palestine and Israel in Contemporary British Jewish Fiction', *Journal for the Study of British Cultures* vol. 16 no. 1 (2009)

Carolyn Steedman, *Labours Lost. Domestic Service and the Making of Modern England* (Cambridge: Cambridge University Press, 2009)

Leonard Stein, 'Memoir', in Leonard Stein and C.C. Aronsfeld (eds), *Leonard Montefiore 1889–1961: In Memorium* (London: Vallentine Mitchell, 1964)

Leonard Stein and C.C. Aronsfeld (eds), *Leonard Montefiore 1889–1961: In Memorium* (London: Vallentine Mitchell, 1964)

Ninian Stewart, *The Royal Navy and the Palestine Patrol* (London: Frank Cass, 2002)

Katherine Storr, 'Belgian Children's Education in Britain in the Great War: the case of the Belgians, 1914–18', *History of Education Researcher* no. 72 (November 2003)

Katherine Storr, *Excluded from the Record: Women, Refugees and Relief 1914–1929* (Bern: Peter Lang, 2010)

Herbert Strauss, 'Jewish Emigration from Germany: Nazi Policies and Jewish Responses (I)', *Leo Baeck Institute Year Book* vol. 25 (1980)

Mary Tabor, 'A Conversation with Lore Segal', *Missouri Review* vol. 30 no. 4 (2007)

Susan Tananbaum, *Jewish Immigrants in London, 1880–1939* (London: Pickering & Chatto, 2014)

John Taylor, *A Dream of England: Landscape, Photography and the Tourist's Imagination* (Manchester: Manchester University Press, 1994)

Gabriele Tergit, 'How They Resettled', in Anon, *Britain's New Citizens: The Story of the Refugees from Germany and Austria* (London: AJR, 1951)

Gordon Thomas, *Operation Exodus* (London: JR Books, 2010)

Paul Thompson, *Oral History: The Voice of the Past* (Oxford: Oxford University Press, 1988)

Selina Todd, 'Domestic Service and Class Relations in Britain 1900–1950', *Past and Present* vol. 203 (2009)

Elizabeth Tonkin, *Narrating Our Pasts: The Social Construction of Oral History* (Cambridge: Cambridge University Press, 1992)

Barry Turner, ... *And the Policeman Smiled. 10,000 Children Escape from Nazi Europe* (London: Bloomsbury, 1990)

Robert Verkaik, 'The Voyage of the Exodus', *Independent*, 5 May 2008

Jacques Vernant, *The Refugees in the Post-War World* (London: George Allen & Unwin, 1953)

Isabel Vincent, *Bodies and Souls: The Tragic Plight of Three Jewish Women Forced into Prostitution in the Americas* (New York: Harper Perennial, 2006)

Steven Wagner, 'British Intelligence and the "Fifth" Occupying Power: The Secret Struggle to Prevent Jewish Illegal Immigration to Palestine', *Intelligence and National Security* vol. 29 no. 5 (2014)

Judith Walkowitz, *Prostitution and Victorian Society: Women, Class and the State* (Cambridge: Cambridge University Press, 1980)

Bernard Wasserstein, *Britain and the Jews of Europe 1939–1945* (Oxford: Clarendon Press, 1979)

Rachel Weissbrod, '*Exodus* as a Zionist Melodrama', *Israel Studies* vol. 4 no. 1 (1999)

Hayden White, 'Figural Realism in Witness Literature', *Parallax* vol. 10 no. 1 (2004)

Francesca Wilson, *They Came as Strangers: The Story of Refugees to Great Britain* (London: Hamish Hamilton, 1959)

Maria Lin Wong, *Chinese Liverpudlians: A History of the Chinese Population in Liverpool* (Birkenhead: Liver Press, 1989)

Jonathan Wordsworth, *William and Dorothy Wordsworth: The Dove Cottage Years* (Grasmere: Wordsworth Trust, 2008)

James Young, *Writing and Rewriting the Holocaust: Narrative and the Consequence of Interpretation* (Bloomington: Indiana University Press, 1988)

James Young, *The Texture of Memory: Holocaust Memorials and Meaning* (New Haven: Yale University Press, 1993)

Alexandra Zavos, 'Gender, migration and anti-racist politics in the continued project of the nation', in Ingrid Palmary, Erica Burman, Khatija Chantler and Peace Kiguwa (eds), *Gender and Migration: Feminist Interventions* (London: Zed Books, 2010)

Roger Zetter, 'More Labels, Fewer Refugees: Remaking the Refugee Label in an Era of Globalization', *Journal of Refugee Studies* vol. 20 no. 2 (2007)

Aristide Zolberg, 'Matters of State: Theorizing Immigration Policy', in Charles Hirschman, Philip Kasinitz and Josh DeWind (eds), *The Handbook of International Migration* (New York: Russell Sage Foundation, 1999)

Aaron Zwergbaum, 'Exile in Mauritius', *Yad Washem Studies* vol. 4 (1960)

Unpublished

Jennifer Craig-Norton, 'Contesting Memory: New Perspectives on the Kindertransport' (unpublished PhD thesis, University of Southampton, 2014)

Tereza Ward, 'Erasure of Memory: Children Who Survived the Holocaust and their Struggle for Identity' (MA dissertation, University of Manchester, 2013)

Index

and exclusion of ethnic minorities
206–207
idealised 86, 88
entry, restricting 224, 228–229, 235, 239,
241, 268, 273
Equality Commission 207
Eritrea 291–292, 296–297, 303
Estefanos, Meron 297
Ethiopia 295, 308
ethnic cleansing 172, 220, 308
European asylum procedures 297
European Council 312
European Union 301
responses 296
Evans-Gordon, William 303
Evening Standard 200, 224
*Excitable Speech: A Politics of the
Performative* 223
Exodus (Leon Uris) 252–254, 257–258,
274
Exodus 1947 35, 248–251, 253–254,
258–272, 276–283, 285–286, 294,
301–302
Exodus story (Biblical) 231, 263, 302,
313

family
desire to help 85
dispersal of 111
*Fatal Journeys: Tracking Lives Lost
during Migration* 295–296
Faversham 221
Feiertag, Hans 88–91
Feiner, Ruth 97–98
'Final Solution' 25–26, 233, 244, 269
Finkel, Isaac 189
Finkel, Lola 189
Finkel, Sidney (Sevek Finkelstein) 189,
199
Finkler, Hansi 134
Fire at Sea 300, 302
Flanagan, Richard 313–314
Foley, Frank 47–48, 50
Foreign Office 275, 277
Foreign Office Passport Control 48
'Fortress Europe' 273
Fortunoff Video Archive 119
Foucault, Michel 92, 225–226
Fraser, Giles 302

Fraser, Ronald 125–126, 154
Freiman, Solomon 189, 200, 203, 211
Freud, Anna 199
Friedlander, Saul 4–5
Friedmann, Fridolin 185–186
Friedmann, Oscar 203
Fremlin, Celia 94
Frumin, Sue 132–134, 142

Galina 264
gangs 308
The Gates of Zion 277
Gatrell, Peter 8, 11–13, 169
Gaza 286
aid ships attacked 284
Geller 240, 244
see also Marsalla
gender 34, 44, 48, 50–51, 53–54, 69, 76,
143, 204, 216–217, 308–309
Gerrard, Gerhard and Hilde 112–115
Gershon, Karen 118, 125
Gestapo 246–247
Gibney, Matthew 225
Gigliotti, Simone 24, 27
Gilbert, Martin 194, 198
Gippo 239
Goldberg, Amos 286
Goldberg, Frances 146–147, 149
Goldberg, Rose 146–147
Golden, Lewis 174
Golding, Louis 253, 283
Gordon, Hortese 54–55
gothic 179, 183–184
Glickman, Nora 63–65, 68
Grant, Linda 276, 285
gratitude, sense of 117, 122, 137, 139, 151,
198, 200
Graves, Robert 110
Greece 293
Gregson, Lieutenant Colonel 262
Grenfell, Joyce 54
Grenville, Anthony 138
Grossman, Kurt 8
Gruber, Ruth 250, 252–254, 258
Grunfeld, Marianne 159–60, 183
Gryn, Hugo 192, 197, 205, 210–211, 220,
311
Gryn, Naomi 197
Guez, Arlette 267–268